Eco-Economy

OTHER NORTON BOOKS
BY LESTER R. BROWN

Earth Policy Institute® is dedicated to providing a vision of an eco-economy and a roadmap on how to get from here to there. It is media-oriented, seeking to reach decisionmakers at all levels, ranging from the Secretary General of the United Nations to individual consumers. Its three primary products are *Eco-Economy: Building an Economy for the Earth*, a series of four-page Earth Policy Alerts, and similarly brief Eco-Economy Updates that identify major milestones or setbacks in building an eco-economy. All of these can be downloaded at no charge from the EPI Web site.

Web site: <www.earth-policy.org>

ECO-ECONOMY

Building an Economy for the Earth

Lester R. Brown

EARTH POLICY INSTITUTE®

W · W · NORTON & COMPANY
NEW YORK   LONDON

First Edition

The text of this book is composed in Sabon. Composition by
Maggie Powell; manufacturing by the Haddon Craftsmen, Inc.

ISBN 0-393-32193-2

W. W. Norton & Company, Inc., 500 Fifth Avenue, New York, N.Y. 10110
www.wwnorton.com

W. W. Norton & Company Ltd., Castle House, 75/76 Wells Street, London
W1T 3QT

1 2 3 4 5 6 7 8 9 0

 This book is printed on recycled paper.

To Roger and Vicki Sant,
who share the vision

Acknowledgments

Anyone who writes a book is indebted to a great number of people—for research assistance, ideas, reviews, editing, and publishing. On the publishing front, my debt to W.W. Norton & Company is longstanding. When compiling the list for the page of "Other Norton Books by Lester R. Brown" that appears in the front, I realized that Norton has published 38 books of which I am either the senior author or author, including 18 *State of the World* reports, 9 editions of *Vital Signs*, and 11 other titles.

At a time when authors' horror stories about working with publishers are common, this marriage with Norton must have been made in heaven. This delightful relationship, stretching over 28 years, began when George Brockway was president and served as our contact, and then shifted to Iva Ashner and now Amy Cherry. Working on this book, we have also benefited from working with Lucinda Bartley in the editorial department and the production team led by Andrew Marasia, who put *Eco-Economy* on the fast track. All have been a pleasure to work with.

Writing *Eco-Economy* and launching the Earth Policy Institute during the same year would have been impossible without the help of my assistant of 15 years, Reah Janise Kauffman. As Vice President of the Earth Policy Institute, she took care of endless details in creating the organization—from designing and furnishing the office space to working with Web site designers. With her assuming responsibility for all these matters, I was free to concentrate on the book.

In addition to her unflagging enthusiasm for this book from the beginning, Reah Janise transcribed the entire manuscript from tapes I dictated. As she did, she sometimes edited. She also read the full manuscript in three successive drafts, providing useful suggestions at each stage and helping to shape it.

Janet Larsen, who graduated from Stanford University's Earth

Systems program a year ago, helped with the research from the beginning. She also critiqued the manuscript as it evolved, helping me to think through many of the issues discussed here. In addition to her diligence and competence, she brought a maturity in judgment that I have come to rely on.

Shane Ratterman became a member of the Earth Policy team just in time to help supervise the installation of the computer system. He joined the book project in midstream, helping with both research and reviewing the manuscript as we came down the homestretch.

This book is built on some new associations, as with Janet and Shane, and several longstanding relationships. The list of my books that independent editor Linda Starke has edited over the last 20 years includes all but a few of those on the Norton list. She brought her usual efficiency and discipline to the editing of *Eco-Economy*. Apart from her editing skills, Linda's cumulative knowledge of environmental issues proved invaluable.

We are indebted to Maggie Powell not only for a great job with the layout and design of the book, but also for her willingness to work on a very tight timeline. We benefited from her years of design experience.

Many individuals provided information on a wide assortment of topics. My thanks go to Earle Amey, U.S. Geological Survey; Donald Bleiwas, U.S. Geological Survey; Eileen Claussen, Pew Center on Global Climate Change; Richard Dirks, National Center for Atmospheric Research; Daniel Edelstein, U.S. Geological Survey; Robert Engleman, Population Action International; Ned Habich, U.S. Department of the Interior; William Heenan, Steel Recycling Institute; Jeffrey Kenworthy, Murdoch University, Australia; Rattan Lal, Ohio State University; Bill Liefert, U.S. Department of Agriculture; Paul Maycock, PV Energy Systems; Iris Perticone, International Geothermal Association; Patricia Plunkert, U.S. Geological Survey; Brian Reaves, U.S. Department of Justice; Karyn Sawyer, National Center for Atmospheric Research; Robert Sohlberg, University of Maryland; Karen Stanecki, U.S. Bureau of the Census; Randall Swisher, American Wind Energy Association; Kenneth Visser, U.S. Department of the Interior; and Hania Zlotnik, United Nations Population Division. Many of my Worldwatch colleagues also provided useful information at various times along the way, including Lori Brown, Seth Dunn, Christopher Flavin, Gary Gardner, Brian Halweil, Anne Platt McGinn, Lisa Mastny,

Ashley Mattoon, Danielle Nierenberg, Michael Renner, and Molly O'Meara Sheehan.

Indeed, for information and insight I am grateful to my colleagues at Worldwatch Institute, whose work has been of great value. The frequency with which they are quoted and cited in this book provides some indication of the quality and range of Worldwatch research over the years. And needless to say, I have drawn heavily on my own many years of work at Worldwatch in writing this book.

Because of its scope, *Eco-Economy* was helped more by reviewers than most books. William Mansfield of our Board brought his many years of experience at the U.N. Environment Programme to bear on the manuscript as he read it at three different stages, helping to shape it along the way. Another EPI Board member, Judy Gradwohl, brought her perspective as a biologist and curator at the Smithsonian Institution to bear on the manuscript as we came down the homestretch. Scott McVay, president of the Chautauqua Institution and also an EPI Board member and enthusiastic supporter of the book, commented on an intermediate draft.

Toby Clark drew on his years of experience in environmental policy at the U.S. Environmental Protection Agency and the Council on Environmental Quality to provide several pages of detailed comments on a late draft of the manuscript. His comments dealing with the interface between economics and ecology were particularly useful.

Maureen Kuwano Hinkle, who worked for 18 years as the Audubon Society's agricultural lobbyist, both read intermediate and final drafts and provided encouragement along the way.

My colleague Dianne Saenz, our Director of Communications, offered useful comments on several chapters. Liz Abbett, an environmental science major at Cornell, joined us for the summer and provided many useful comments on two separate drafts of the manuscript, including some helpful structural suggestions. Both Liz and Millicent Johnson, our librarian and Manager of Publications Sales, assisted in gathering information for the book.

Among those who read parts of the manuscript and offered comments are Carl Haub, Population Reference Bureau; Ashley Mattoon, Worldwatch Institute; Sandra Postel, Global Water Policy Project; Mohan Wali, Ohio State University; and John Young, materials policy consultant. To all who reviewed the manuscript, I am grateful. And it goes without saying that I alone am responsible for the final product.

Finally, I am indebted to Roger and Vicki Sant, who provided a generous startup grant for the Earth Policy Institute, thus allowing me to concentrate my energy on this book during the Institute's early months.

Lester R. Brown

Contents

II. THE NEW ECONOMY

Foreword

The idea for this book came to me just over a year ago, shortly after I moved from President to Chairman of the Board of the Worldwatch Institute, an organization I founded in 1974. In this new role and with more time to think, three things became more apparent to me. One, we are losing the war to save the planet. Two, we need a vision of what an environmentally sustainable economy—an eco-economy—would look like. And three, we need a new kind of research organization—one that offers not only a vision of an eco-economy, but also frequent assessments of progress in realizing that vision.

When Worldwatch started 27 years ago, we were worried about shrinking forests, expanding deserts, eroding soils, deteriorating rangelands, and disappearing species. We were just beginning to worry about collapsing fisheries. Now the list of concerns is far longer, including rising carbon dioxide levels, falling water tables, rising temperatures, rivers running dry, stratospheric ozone depletion, more destructive storms, melting glaciers, rising sea level, and dying coral reefs.

Over this last quarter-century or so, many battles have been won, but the gap between what we need to do to arrest the environmental deterioration of the planet and what we are doing continues to widen. Somehow we have to turn the tide.

At present there is no shared vision even within the environmental community, much less in society at large. Unless we have such a vision of where we want to go, we are not likely to get there. The purpose of this book is to outline the vision of an eco-economy.

The good news is that when we started Worldwatch, we knew that an environmentally sustainable economy was possible, but we only had an abstract sense of what it would look like. Today we can actually describe with some confidence not only what it will look like but how it will work. Twenty-seven years ago, the modern wind power industry had not yet been born. Now, worldwide, we have behind us a phenomenal decade of 24 percent annual growth.

Thanks to the U.S. Department of Energy's National Wind Resources Inventory, we now know that North Dakota, Kansas, and Texas have enough harnessable wind energy to satisfy national electricity needs. In the United States, wind electric generation is projected to grow by more than 60 percent in 2001. With the low-cost electricity that comes from wind turbines, we have the option of electrolyzing water to produce hydrogen, the fuel of choice for the fuel cell engines that every major automobile manufacturer is now working on.

Wind turbines are replacing coal mines in Europe. Denmark, which has banned the construction of coal-fired power plants, now gets 15 percent of its electricity from wind. In some communities in northern Germany, 75 percent of the electricity needs are satisfied by wind power.

A generation ago we knew that silicon cells could convert sunlight into electricity, but the solar roofing material developed in Japan that enables rooftops to become the power plants of buildings was still in the future. Today more than 1 million homes worldwide get their electricity from solar cells.

Today major corporations are committed to comprehensive recycling, to closing the loop in the materials economy. STMicroelectronics in Italy and Interface in the United States, a leading manufacturer of industrial carpet, are both striving for zero carbon emissions. Shell Hydrogen and DaimlerChrysler are working with Iceland to make it the world's first hydrogen-powered economy.

What became apparent to me in my reflections a year ago was that to achieve these goals, we need a new kind of research institute. Thus in May of this year, with fellow incorporators Reah Janise Kauffman and Janet Larsen, I launched the Earth Policy Institute. *Eco-Economy: Building an Economy for the Earth* is our first book. We have also begun issuing Earth Policy Alerts, four-page pieces dealing with topics such as worldwide wind power development and the dust bowl that is forming in northwest China. These pieces highlight trends that affect our movement toward an eco-economy.

No one I know is qualified to write a book of this scope. Certainly I am not, but someone has to give it a try. Every chapter could have been a book in its own right. Indeed, individual sections of chapters have been the subject of books. Beyond the range of issues covered, an analysis that integrates across fields of knowledge is not easy, particularly when it embraces ecology and economics—two disciplines that start with contrasting premises.

People appear hungry for a vision, for a sense of how we can reverse the environmental deterioration of the earth. More and more people want to get involved. When I give talks on the state of the world in various countries, the question I am asked most frequently is, What can I do? People recognize the need for action and they want to do something. My response is always that we need to make personal changes, involving everything from using bicycles more and cars less to recycling our daily newspapers. But that in itself will not be enough. We have to change the system. And to do that, we need to restructure the tax system, reducing income taxes and increasing taxes on environmentally destructive activities so that prices reflect the ecological truth. Anyone who wants to reverse the deterioration of the earth will have to work to restructure taxes.

This book is not the final word. It is a work in progress. We will continue to unfold the issues, update the data, and refine the analysis. If you are interested in receiving the four-page Earth Policy Alerts, please visit our Web site at <www.earth-policy.org>, where you can sign up to receive them as they are released.

Our goal is to publish this book in all the world's major languages. In addition to the North American edition, there will also be a U.K./Commonwealth edition designed to reach most of the rest of the English-speaking world. In East Asia, arrangements are already being made for Chinese, Japanese, and Korean editions. We are also working on Italian and Portuguese editions. And we know that EPI Board member Hamid Taravaty from Iran is planning a Persian edition.

This book can be downloaded without charge from our Web site. Permission for reprinting or excerpting portions of the manuscript can be obtained from Reah Janise Kauffman at <rjkauffman@earth-policy.org> or by fax or mail.

We welcome your input in analyzing these issues. If you have any thoughts or recent papers or articles that you would like to share with us, we would be delighted to receive them.

Lester R. Brown

phone: 202.496.9290   Earth Policy Institute
fax: 202.496.9325   1350 Connecticut Ave., NW
e-mail: epi@earth-policy.org   Suite 403
Web site: www.earth-policy.org   Washington, DC0 20036

August 2001

Eco-Economy

1

The Economy and the Earth

In 1543, Polish astronomer Nicolaus Copernicus published "On the Revolutions of the Celestial Spheres," in which he challenged the view that the Sun revolved around the earth, arguing instead that the earth revolved around the Sun. With his new model of the solar system, he began a wide-ranging debate among scientists, theologians, and others. His alternative to the earlier Ptolemaic model, which had the earth at the center of the universe, led to a revolution in thinking, to a new worldview.[1]

Today we need a similar shift in our worldview, in how we think about the relationship between the earth and the economy. The issue now is not which celestial sphere revolves around the other but whether the environment is part of the economy or the economy is part of the environment. Economists see the environment as a subset of the economy. Ecologists, on the other hand, see the economy as a subset of the environment.

Like Ptolemy's view of the solar system, the economists' view is confusing efforts to understand our modern world. It has created an economy that is out of sync with the ecosystem on which it depends.

Economic theory and economic indicators do not explain how

the economy is disrupting and destroying the earth's natural systems. Economic theory does not explain why Arctic Sea ice is melting. It does not explain why grasslands are turning into desert in northwestern China, why coral reefs are dying in the South Pacific, or why the Newfoundland cod fishery collapsed. Nor does it explain why we are in the early stages of the greatest extinction of plants and animals since the dinosaurs disappeared 65 million years ago. Yet economics is essential to measuring the cost to society of these excesses.

Evidence that the economy is in conflict with the earth's natural systems can be seen in the daily news reports of collapsing fisheries, shrinking forests, eroding soils, deteriorating rangelands, expanding deserts, rising carbon dioxide (CO_2) levels, falling water tables, rising temperatures, more destructive storms, melting glaciers, rising sea level, dying coral reefs, and disappearing species. These trends, which mark an increasingly stressed relationship between the economy and the earth's ecosystem, are taking a growing economic toll. At some point, this could overwhelm the worldwide forces of progress, leading to economic decline. The challenge for our generation is to reverse these trends before environmental deterioration leads to long-term economic decline, as it did for so many earlier civilizations.

These increasingly visible trends indicate that if the operation of the subsystem, the economy, is not compatible with the behavior of the larger system—the earth's ecosystem—both will eventually suffer. The larger the economy becomes relative to the ecosystem, and the more it presses against the earth's natural limits, the more destructive this incompatibility will be.

An environmentally sustainable economy—an eco-economy—requires that the principles of ecology establish the framework for the formulation of economic policy and that economists and ecologists work together to fashion the new economy. Ecologists understand that all economic activity, indeed all life, depends on the earth's ecosystem—the complex of individual species living together, interacting with each other and their physical habitat. These millions of species exist in an intricate balance, woven together by food chains, nutrient cycles, the hydrological cycle, and the climate system. Economists know how to translate goals into policy. Economists and ecologists working together can design and build an eco-economy, one that can sustain progress.

Just as recognition that the earth was not the center of the solar system set the stage for advances in astronomy, physics, and related sciences, so will recognition that the economy is not the center of our world create the conditions to sustain economic progress and improve the human condition. After Copernicus outlined his revolutionary theory, there were two very different worldviews. Those who retained the Ptolemaic view of the world saw one world, and those who accepted the Copernican view saw a quite different one. The same is true today of the disparate worldviews of economists and ecologists.

These differences between ecology and economics are fundamental. For example, ecologists worry about limits, while economists tend not to recognize any such constraints. Ecologists, taking their cue from nature, think in terms of cycles, while economists are more likely to think linearly, or curvilinearly. Economists have a great faith in the market, while ecologists often fail to appreciate the market adequately.

The gap between economists and ecologists in their perception of the world as the new century begins could not be wider. Economists look at the unprecedented growth of the global economy and of international trade and investment and see a promising future with more of the same. They note with justifiable pride that the global economy has expanded sevenfold since 1950, raising output from $6 trillion of goods and services to $43 trillion in 2000, boosting living standards to levels not dreamed of before. Ecologists look at this same growth and realize that it is the product of burning vast quantities of artificially cheap fossil fuels, a process that is destabilizing the climate. They look ahead and see more intense heat waves, more destructive storms, melting ice caps, and a rising sea level that will shrink the land area even as population continues to grow. While economists see booming economic indicators, ecologists see an economy that is altering the climate with consequences that no one can foresee.[2]

As the new century gets under way, economists look at grain markets and see the lowest grain prices in two decades—a sure sign that production capacity is outrunning effective demand, that supply constraints are not likely to be an issue for the foreseeable future. Ecologists, meanwhile, see water tables falling in key food-producing countries, and know that 480 million of the world's 6.1 billion people are being fed with grain produced by overpumping aquifers. They are worried about the effect of eventual aquifer depletion on food production.[3]

Economists rely on the market to guide their decisionmaking. They respect the market because it can allocate resources with an efficiency that a central planner can never match (as the Soviets learned at great expense). Ecologists view the market with less reverence because they see a market that is not telling the truth. For example, when buying a gallon of gasoline, customers in effect pay to get the oil out of the ground, refine it into gasoline, and deliver it to the local service station. But they do not pay the health care costs of treating respiratory illness from air pollution or the costs of climate disruption.

Ecologists see the record economic growth of recent decades, but they also see an economy that is increasingly in conflict with its support systems, one that is fast depleting the earth's natural capital, moving the global economy onto an environmental path that will inevitably lead to economic decline. They see the need for a wholesale restructuring of the economy so that it meshes with the ecosystem. They know that a stable relationship between the economy and the earth's ecosystem is essential if economic progress is to be sustained.

We have created an economy that cannot sustain economic progress, an economy that cannot take us where we want to go. Just as Copernicus had to formulate a new astronomical worldview after several decades of celestial observations and mathematical calculations, we too must formulate a new economic worldview based on several decades of environmental observations and analyses.

Although the idea that economics must be integrated into ecology may seem radical to many, evidence is mounting that it is the only approach that reflects reality. When observations no longer support theory, it is time to change the theory—what science historian Thomas Kuhn calls a paradigm shift. If the economy is a subset of the earth's ecosystem, as this book contends, the only formulation of economic policy that will succeed is one that respects the principles of ecology.[4]

The good news is that economists are becoming more ecologically aware, recognizing the inherent dependence of the economy on the earth's ecosystem. For example, some 2,500 economists—including eight Nobel laureates—have endorsed the introduction of a carbon tax to stabilize climate. More and more economists are looking for ways to get the market to tell the ecological truth. This spreading awareness is evident in the rapid growth of the International Society of Ecological Economics, which has 1,200 members and chapters in Australia/New Zealand, Brazil, Canada, India, Russia, China, and throughout Europe. Its goal is to integrate the thinking of ecologists and economists into a transdiscipline aimed at building a sustainable world.[5]

Economy Self-Destructing

The economic indicators for the last half-century show remarkable progress. As noted earlier, the economy expanded sevenfold between 1950 and 2000. International trade grew even more rapidly. The Dow Jones Index, a widely used indicator of the value of stocks traded on the New York Stock Exchange, climbed from 3,000 in 1990 to 11,000 in 2000. It was difficult not to be bullish about the long-term economic prospect as the new century began.[6]

Difficult, that is, unless you look at the ecological indicators. Here, virtually every global indicator was headed in the wrong direction. The economic policies that have yielded the extraordinary growth in the world economy are the same ones that are destroying its support systems. By any conceivable ecological yardstick, these are failed policies. Mismanagement is destroying forests, rangelands, fisheries, and croplands—the four ecosystems that supply our food and, except for minerals, all our raw materials as well. Although many of us live in a high-tech urbanized society, we are as dependent on the earth's natural systems as our hunter-gatherer forebears were.

To put ecosystems in economic terms, a natural system, such as a fishery, functions like an endowment. The interest income from an endowment will continue in perpetuity as long as the endowment is maintained. If the endowment is drawn down, income declines. If the endowment is eventually depleted, the interest income disappears. And so it is with natural systems. If the sustainable yield of a fishery is exceeded, fish stocks begin to shrink. Eventually stocks are depleted and the fishery collapses. The cash flow from this endowment disappears as well.

As we begin the twenty-first century, our economy is slowly destroying its support systems, consuming its endowment of natural capital. Demands of the expanding economy, *as now structured,* are surpassing the sustainable yield of ecosystems. Easily a third of the world's cropland is losing topsoil at a rate that is undermining its long-term productivity. Fully 50 percent of the world's rangeland is overgrazed and deteriorating into desert. The world's forests have shrunk by about half since the dawn of agriculture and are still shrinking. Two thirds of oceanic fisheries are now being fished at or beyond their capacity; overfishing is now the rule, not the exception. And overpumping of underground water is common in key food-producing regions.[7]

Over large areas of the world, the loss of topsoil from wind and water erosion now exceeds the natural formation of new soil, gradually draining the land of its fertility. In an effort to curb this, the United States is retiring highly erodible cropland that was earlier plowed in overly enthusiastic efforts to expand food production. This process began in 1985 with the Conservation Reserve Program that paid farmers to retire 15 million hectares, roughly one tenth of U.S. cropland, converting it back to grassland or forest before it became wasteland.[8]

In countries that lack such programs, farmers are being forced to abandon highly erodible land that has lost much of its topsoil. Nigeria is losing over 500 square kilometers of productive land to desert each year. In Kazakhstan, site of the 1950s Soviet Virgin Lands project, half the cropland has been abandoned since 1980 as soil erosion lowered its productivity. This has dropped Kazakhstan's wheat harvest from roughly 13 million tons in 1980 to 8 million tons in 2000—an economic loss of $900 million per year.[9]

The rangelands that supply much of the world's animal protein are also under excessive pressure. As human populations grow, so do livestock numbers. With 180 million people worldwide now trying to make a living raising 3.3 billion cattle, sheep, and goats, grasslands are simply collapsing under the demand. As a result of overstocking, grasslands are now deteriorating in much of Africa, the Middle East, Central Asia, the northern part of the Indian subcontinent, and much of northwestern China. Overgrazing is now the principal cause of desertification, the conversion of productive land into desert. In Africa, the annual loss of livestock production from the cumulative degradation of rangeland is estimated at $7 billion, a sum almost equal to the gross domestic product of Ethiopia.[10]

In China, the combination of overplowing and overgrazing to satisfy rapidly expanding food needs is creating a dust bowl reminiscent of the U.S. Dust Bowl of the 1930s—but much larger. In a desperate effort to maintain grain self-sufficiency, China has plowed large areas of the northwest, much of it land that is highly erodible and should never have been plowed.[11]

As the country's demand for livestock products—meat, leather, and wool—has climbed, so have the numbers of livestock, far exceeding those of the United States, a country with comparable grazing capacity. In addition to the direct damage from overplowing and overgrazing, the northern half of China is literally drying out as aquifers are depleted by overpumping.[12]

These trends are converging to form some of the largest dust storms ever recorded. The huge dust plumes, traveling eastward, affect the cities of northeast China—blotting out the sun and reducing visibility. Eastward-moving winds also carry soil from China's northwest to the Korean Peninsula and Japan, where people regularly complain about the dust clouds that filter out the sunlight and blanket everything with dust. Unless China can reverse the overplowing and overgrazing trends that are creating the dust bowl, these trends could spur massive migration into the already crowded cities of the northeast and undermine the country's economic future.[13]

The world is also running up a water deficit. The overpumping of aquifers, now commonplace on every continent, has led to falling water tables as pumping exceeds aquifer recharge from precipitation. Irrigation problems are as old as irrigation itself, but this is a new threat, one that has evolved over the last half-century with the advent of diesel pumps and powerful electrically driven pumps.

Water tables are falling under large expanses of the three leading food-producing countries—China, India, and the United States. Under the North China Plain, which accounts for 25 percent of China's grain harvest, the water table is falling by roughly 1.5 meters (5 feet) per year. The same thing is happening under much of India, particularly the Punjab, the country's breadbasket. In the United States, water tables are falling under the grain-growing states of the southern Great Plains, shrinking the irrigated area.[14]

The diversion of water to provide supplies for irrigation and for cities is also excessive, leaving little or no water in some rivers. The Colorado, the major river in the southwestern United States, now rarely makes it to the sea. China's Yellow River, the cradle of Chinese civilization, runs dry for part of each year, depriving farmers in its lower reaches of irrigation water. The Indus and the Ganges barely reach the sea during the dry season. Little water from the Nile reaches the Mediterranean at any time. Draining rivers dry disrupts the symbiotic relationship between the oceans and the continents. The oceans water the continents as moisture-laden air masses move inland, and the continents nourish the oceans as the returning water carries nutrients with it.[15]

Economic demands on forests are also excessive. Trees are being cut or burned faster than they can regenerate or be planted. Overharvesting is common in many regions, including Southeast Asia, West Africa, and the Brazilian Amazon. Worldwide, forests are shrinking by over 9 million hectares per year, an area equal to Portugal.[16]

In addition to being overharvested, some rainforests are now being destroyed by fire. Healthy rainforests do not burn, but logging and the settlements that occur along logging roads have fragmented and dried out tropical rainforests to the point where they often will burn easily, ignited by a lightning strike or set afire by opportunistic plantation owners, farmers, and ranchers desiring more land.

In the late summer of 1997, during an El Niño–induced drought, tropical rainforests in Borneo and Sumatra burned out of control. This conflagration made the news because the smoke drifting over hundreds of kilometers affected people not only in Indonesia but also in Malaysia, Singapore, Viet Nam, Thailand, and the Philippines. A reported 1,100 airline flights in the region were canceled due to the smoke. Motorists drove with their headlights on during the day, trying to make their way through the thick haze. Millions of people became physically sick. [17]

Deforestation can be costly. Record flooding in the Yangtze River basin during the summer of 1998 drove 120 million people from their homes. Although initially referred to as a "natural disaster," the removal of 85 percent of the original tree cover in the basin had left little vegetative cover to hold the heavy rainfall.[18]

Deforestation also diminishes the recycling of water inland, thus reducing rainfall in the interior of continents. When rain falls on a healthy stand of dense forest, roughly one fourth runs off, returning to the sea, while three fourths evaporates, either directly or through transpiration. When land is cleared for farming or grazing or is clearcut by loggers, this ratio is reversed—three fourths of the water returns to the sea and one fourth evaporates to be carried further inland. As deforestation progresses, nature's mechanism for watering the interior of large continents such as Africa and Asia is weakening.[19]

Evidence of excessive human demands can also be seen in the oceans. As the human demand for animal protein has climbed over the last several decades, it has begun to exceed the sustainable yield of oceanic fisheries. As a result, two thirds of oceanic fisheries are now being fished at their sustainable yield or beyond. Many are collapsing. In 1992, the rich Newfoundland cod fishery that had been supplying fish for several centuries collapsed abruptly, costing 40,000 Canadians their jobs. Despite a subsequent ban on fishing, nearly a decade later the fishery has yet to recover.[20]

Farther to the south, the U.S. Chesapeake Bay has experienced a similar decline. A century ago, this extraordinarily productive estuary produced over 100 million pounds of oysters a year. In 1999, it produced barely 3 million pounds. The Gulf of Thailand fishery has suffered a similarly dramatic decline: depleted by overfishing, the catch has dropped by over 80 percent since 1963, prompting the Thai Fisheries Department to ban fishing in large areas.[21]

The world is also losing its biological diversity as plant and animal species are destroyed faster than new species evolve. This biological impoverishment of the earth is the result of habitat destruction, pollution, climate alteration, and hunting. With each update of its *Red List of Threatened Species*, the World Conservation Union–IUCN shows us moving further into a period of mass extinction. In the latest assessment, released in 2000, IUCN reports that one out of eight of the world's 9,946 bird species is in danger of extinction, as is one in four of the 4,763 mammal species and nearly one third of all 25,000 fish species.[22]

Some countries have already suffered extensive losses. Australia, for example, has lost 16 of 140 mammal species over the last two centuries. In the Colorado River system of the southwestern United States, 29 of 50 native species of fish have disappeared partly because their river habitats were drained dry. Species lost cannot be regained. As a popular bumper sticker aptly points out, "Extinction is forever."[23]

The economic benefits of the earth's diverse array of life are countless. They include not only the role of each species in maintaining the particular ecosystem of which it is a part, but economic roles as well, such as providing drugs and germplasm. As diversity diminishes, nature's pharmacy shrinks, depriving future generations of new discoveries.

Even as expanding economic activity has been creating biological deficits, it has been upsetting some of nature's basic balances in other areas. With the huge growth in burning of fossil fuels since 1950, carbon emissions have overwhelmed the capacity of the earth's ecosystem to fix carbon dioxide. The resulting rise in atmospheric CO_2 levels is widely believed by atmospheric scientists to be responsible for the earth's rising temperature. The 14 warmest years since recordkeeping began in 1866 have all occurred since 1980.[24]

One consequence of higher temperatures is more energy driving storm systems. Three powerful winter storms in France in December 1999 destroyed millions of trees, some of which had been standing for centuries. Thousands of buildings were demolished. These storms, the most violent on record in France, wreaked more than $10 billion worth of damage—$170 for each French citizen. Nature was levying a tax of its own on fossil fuel burning.[25]

In October 1998, Hurricane Mitch—one of the most powerful storms ever to come out of the Atlantic—moved through the Caribbean and stalled for several days on the coast of Central America. While there, it acted as a huge pump pulling water from the ocean and dropping it over the land. Parts of Honduras received 2 meters of rainfall within a few days. So powerful was this storm and so vast the amount of water it dropped on Central America that it altered the topography, converting mountains and hills into vast mud flows that simply inundated whole villages, claiming an estimated 10,000 lives. Four fifths of the crops were destroyed. The huge flow of rushing water removed all the topsoil in many areas, ensuring that this land will not be farmed again during our lifetimes.[26]

The overall economic effect of the storm was devastating. The wholesale destruction of roads, bridges, buildings, and other infrastructure set back the development of Honduras and Nicaragua by decades. The estimated $8.5 billion worth of damage in the region approached the gross domestic product of both countries combined.[27]

Natural disasters are on the increase. Munich Re, one of the world's largest re-insurance companies, reported that three times as many great natural catastrophes occurred during the 1990s as during the 1960s. Economic losses increased eightfold. Insured losses multiplied 15-fold. Although Munich Re's classification does not distinguish between natural and human-induced catastrophes, much of the increase appears to be due to catastrophes, including storms, droughts, and wild fires that are either exacerbated or caused by human activities.[28]

Insurers are keenly aware that even modest changes in climate can lead to quantum jumps in damage. For example, a 10-percent increase in a storm's wind speed can double the damage it inflicts. The cost of dealing with rising sea level from a modest temperature rise could easily overwhelm the economies of many countries.[29]

Andrew Dlugolecki, a senior officer at the CGMU Insurance Group—Britain's largest insurance group—reports that property damage worldwide is rising roughly 10 percent a year. He believes that we are only beginning to see the economic fallout from climate change. At this rate of growth, by 2065 the amount of damage would exceed the projected gross world product. Well before then, Dlugolecki notes, the world would face bankruptcy.[30]

Perhaps the most disturbing consequence of rising temperature is ice melting. Over the last 35 years, the ice covering the Arctic Sea has thinned by 42 percent. A study by two Norwegian scientists projects that within 50 years there will be no summer ice left in the Arctic Sea. The discovery of open water at the North Pole by an ice breaker cruise ship in mid-August 2000 stunned many in the scientific community.[31]

This particular thawing does not affect sea level because the ice that is melting is already in the ocean. But the Greenland ice sheet is also starting to melt. Greenland is three times the size of Texas and the ice sheet is up to 2 kilometers (1.2 miles) thick in some areas. An article in *Science* notes that if the entire ice sheet were to melt, it would raise sea level by some 7 meters (23 feet), inundating the world's coastal cities and Asia's rice-growing river floodplains. Even a 1-meter rise would cover half of Bangladesh's riceland, dropping food production below the survival level for millions of people.[32]

As the twenty-first century begins, humanity is being squeezed between deserts expanding outward and rising seas encroaching

inward. Civilization is being forced to retreat by forces it has created. Even as population continues to grow, the habitable portion
of the planet is shrinking.

Aside from climate change, the economic effects of environmental
destruction and disruption have been mostly local—collapsing fisheries, abandoned cropland, and shrinking forests. But if local damage keeps accumulating, it will eventually affect global economic
trends. In an increasingly integrated global economy, local ecosystem collapse can have global economic consequences.

Lessons from the Past

In *The Collapse of Complex Civilizations*, Joseph Tainter describes
the decline of early civilizations and speculates about the causes.
Was it because of the degradation of their environment, climate
change, civil conflict, foreign invaders? Or, he asks, "is there some
mysterious internal dynamic to the rise and fall of civilizations?"[33]

As he ponders the contrast between civilizations that once flourished and the desolation of the sites they occupied, he quotes ar-
cheologist Robert McC. Adams, who described the site of the ancient Sumerian civilization located on the central floodplain of the
Euphrates River, an empty, desolate area now outside the frontiers
of cultivation. Adams described how the "tangled dunes, long dis-
used canal levees, and the rubble-strewn mounds of former settlement contribute only low, featureless relief. Vegetation is sparse,
and in many areas it is almost wholly absent....Yet at one time,
here lay the core, the heartland, the oldest urban, literate civilization in the world."[34]

The early Sumerian civilization of the fourth millennium BC
was remarkable, advancing far beyond any that had existed before. Its irrigation system, based on sophisticated engineering concepts, created a highly productive agriculture, one that enabled farmers to produce a surplus of food that supported the formation of
the first cities. Managing the irrigation system required a complex
social organization, one that may have been more sophisticated
than any that had gone before. The Sumerians had the first cities
and the first written language, the cuneiform script. They were probably as excited about it as we are today about the Internet.[35]

It was an extraordinary civilization, but there was an environmental flaw in the design of the irrigation system, one that would
eventually undermine its agricultural economy. Water from behind

dams was diverted onto the land, raising crop yields. Some of the water was used by the crops, some evaporated into the atmosphere, and some percolated downward. Over time, this percolation slowly raised the water table until eventually it approached the surface of the land. When it reached a few feet from the surface it began to restrict the growth of deep-rooted crops. Somewhat later, as the water climbed to within inches of the surface, it began to evaporate into the atmosphere. As this happened, the salt in the water was left behind. Over time, the accumulation of salt reduced the productivity of the land. The environmental flaw was that there was no provision for draining the water that percolated downward.[36]

The initial response of the Sumerians to declining wheat yields was to shift to barley, a more salt-tolerant plant. But eventually the yields of barley also declined. The resultant shrinkage of the food supply undermined the economic foundation of this great civilization.[37]

The New World counterpart to Sumer is the Mayan civilization that developed in the lowlands of what is now Guatemala. It flourished from AD 250 until its collapse around AD 900. Like the Sumerians, the Mayans had developed a sophisticated, highly productive agriculture, one that relied on raised plots of earth surrounded by canals that supplied water.[38]

As with Sumer, the Mayan demise was apparently linked to a failing food supply. For this New World civilization, it was deforestation and soil erosion that undermined agriculture. Food scarcity may then have triggered civil conflict among the various Mayan cities as they competed for food.[39]

During the later centuries of the Mayan civilization, a new society was evolving on Easter Island, some 166 square kilometers of land in the South Pacific roughly 3,200 kilometers west of South America and 2,200 kilometers from Pitcairn Island, the nearest habitation. Settled around AD 400, this civilization flourished on a volcanic island with rich soils and lush vegetation, including trees that grew 25 meters tall with trunks 2 meters in diameter. Archeological records indicate that the islanders ate mainly seafood, principally dolphins—a mammal that could only be caught by harpoon from large sea-going canoes since it was not locally available in large numbers.[40]

The Easter Island society flourished for several centuries, reaching an estimated population of 20,000. As its human numbers gradually increased, tree cutting exceeded the sustainable yield of forests. Eventually the large trees needed to build the sturdy, ocean-going canoes disappeared, depriving islanders of access to the dolphins, thus dramatically shrinking the island's seafood supply. The archeological record shows that at some point human bones became intermingled with the dolphin bones, suggesting a desperate society that had resorted to cannibalism. Today the island is occupied by some 2,000 people.[41]

These are just three of the early civilizations that declined apparently because at some point they moved onto an economic path that was environmentally unsustainable. We, too, are on such a path. Any one of several trends of environmental degradation could undermine civilization as we know it. Just as the irrigation system that defined the early Sumerian economy had a flaw, so too does the fossil fuel energy system that defines our modern economy. It is raising CO_2 levels in the atmosphere and thus altering the earth's climate.

Whether it was from the salting of the land in Sumer, the soil erosion of the Mayans, or the loss of the distant-water fishing capacity of the Easter Islanders, collapse of the early civilizations appears to have been associated with a decline in food supply. Today the addition of 80 million people a year to world population at a time when water tables are falling suggests that food supplies again may be the vulnerable link between the environment and the economy.[42]

The Sumerians did not know that the New World even existed, much less that it would one day support flourishing civilizations, such as the Mayans. The Mayans had no idea that Easter Island existed. Each of these civilizations collapsed in isolation, with no effect on the others. But today, in an integrated global economy, a collapse in one country or region will affect all of us. Even a currency devaluation in a developing country, such as Indonesia, can send shock waves through Wall Street half a world away.

One unanswerable question about these earlier civilizations was whether they knew what was causing their decline. Did the Sumerians understand that rising salt content in the soil was reducing their wheat yields? If they knew, were they simply unable to muster the political support needed to lower water tables, just as we today are struggling unsuccessfully to lower carbon emissions?

Learning from China

The flow of startling information from China helps us understand why our economy cannot take us where we want to go. Not only is China the world's most populous country, with nearly 1.3 billion people, but since 1980 it has been the world's fastest-growing economy—expanding more than fourfold. In effect, China is telescoping history, demonstrating what happens when large numbers of poor people rapidly become more affluent.[43]

As incomes have climbed in China, so has consumption. The Chinese have already caught up with Americans in pork consumption per person and they are now concentrating their energies on increasing beef production. Raising per capita beef consumption in China to that of the average American would take 49 million additional tons of beef. If all this were to come from putting cattle in feedlots, American-style, it would require 343 million tons of grain a year, an amount equal to the entire U.S. grain harvest.[44]

In Japan, as population pressures on the land mounted during a comparable stage of its economic development, the Japanese turned to the sea for their animal protein. Last year, Japan consumed nearly 10 million tons of seafood. If China, with 10 times as many people as Japan, were to try to move down this same path, it would need 100 million tons of seafood—the entire world fish catch.[45]

In 1994, the Chinese government decided that the country would develop an automobile-centered transportation system and that the automobile industry would be one of the engines of future economic growth. Beijing invited major automobile manufacturers, such as Volkswagen, General Motors, and Toyota, to invest in China. But if Beijing's goal of an auto-centered transportation system were to materialize and the Chinese were to have one or two cars in every garage and were to consume oil at the U.S. rate, China would need over 80 million barrels of oil a day—slightly more than the 74 million barrels per day the world now produces. To provide the required roads and parking lots, it would also need to pave some 16 million hectares of land, an area equal to half the size of the 31 million hectares of land currently used to produce the country's 132-million-ton annual harvest of rice, its leading food staple.[46]

Similarly, consider paper. As China modernizes, its paper consumption is rising. If annual paper use in China of 35 kilograms per person were to climb to the U.S. level of 342 kilograms, China would need more paper than the world currently produces. There go the world's forests.[47]

We are learning that the western industrial development model is not viable for China, simply because there are not enough resources for it to work. Global land and water resources are not sufficient to satisfy the growing grain needs in China if it continues along the current economic development path. Nor will the existing fossil-fuel-based energy economy supply the needed energy, simply because world oil production is not projected to rise much above current levels in the years ahead. Apart from the availability of oil, if carbon emissions per person in China ever reach the U.S. level, this alone would roughly double global emissions, accelerating the rise in the atmospheric CO_2 level.[48]

China faces a formidable challenge in fashioning a development strategy simply because of the density of its population. Although it has almost exactly the same amount of land as the United States, most of China's 1.3 billion people live in a 1,500-kilometer strip on the eastern and southern coasts. Reaching the equivalent population density in the United States would require squeezing the entire U.S. population into the area east of the Mississippi and then multiplying it by four.[49]

Interestingly, the adoption of the western economic model for China is being challenged from within. A group of prominent scientists, including many in the Chinese Academy of Sciences, wrote a white paper questioning the government's decision to develop an automobile-centered transportation system. They pointed out that China does not have enough land both to feed its people and to provide the roads, highways, and parking lots needed to accommodate the automobile. They also noted the heavy dependence on imported oil that would be required and the potential air pollution and traffic congestion that would result if they followed the U.S. path.[50]

If the fossil-fuel-based, automobile-centered, throwaway economy will not work for China, then it will not work for India with its 1 billion people, or for the other 2 billion people in the developing world. In a world with a shared ecosystem and an increasingly integrated global economy, it will ultimately not work for the industrial economies either.

China is showing that the world cannot remain for long on the current economic path. It is underlining the urgency of restructuring the global economy, of building a new economy—an economy designed for the earth.

The Acceleration of History

The pace of change is reaching an extraordinary rate, driven in part by technological innovation. Bill Joy, cofounder and chief scientist of Sun Microsystems, warned in an early 2000 article in *Wired* magazine that rapid advances in robotics, genomics, and nanotechnology could yield potentially unmanageable problems. He is particularly concerned that our growing dependence on ever more intelligent computers could one day enable them to dominate us.[51]

Rapidly advancing technology is accelerating history, making it difficult for social institutions to manage it effectively. This is also true for unprecedented world population growth, even faster economic growth, and the increasingly frequent collisions between the expanding economy and the limits of the earth's natural systems. The current rate of change has no precedent.

Until recently, population growth was so slow that it aroused little concern. But since 1950 we have added more people to world population than during the preceding 4 million years since our early ancestors first stood upright. Economic expansion in earlier times was similarly slow. To illustrate, growth in the world economy during the year 2000 exceeded that during the entire nineteenth century.[52]

Throughout most of human history, the growth of population, the rise in income, and the development of new technologies were so slow as to be imperceptible during an individual life span. For example, the climb in grainland productivity from 1.1 tons per hectare in 1950 to 2.8 tons per hectare in 2000 exceeds that during the 11,000 years from the beginning of agriculture until 1950.[53]

The population growth of today has no precedent. Throughout most of our existence as a species, our numbers were measured in the thousands. Today, they measure in the billions. Our evolution has prepared us to deal with many threats, but perhaps not with the threat we pose to ourselves with the uncontrolled growth in our own numbers.

The world economy is growing even faster. The sevenfold growth in global output of goods and services since 1950 dwarfs anything in history. In the earlier stages of the Industrial Revolution, economic expansion rarely exceeded 1 or 2 percent a year. Developing countries that are industrializing now are doing so much faster than their predecessors simply because they do not have to invent the technologies needed by a modern industrial society, such as power plants, automobiles, and refrigerators. They can simply draw on the experiences and technology of those that preceded them.[54]

More sophisticated financial institutions enable societies to mobilize the capital needed for investment today more easily than in the past. As a result, the countries that were successfully industrializing in the late twentieth century did so at a record rate. Economic growth in the developing countries of East Asia, for instance, has averaged almost 7 percent annually since 1990—far higher than growth rates in industrial countries at any time in their history.[55]

In another example of rapid change, since 1974 some 28 new infectious diseases have been identified—ranging from HIV, which has claimed 22 million lives, to new variant Creutzfeldt-Jakob disease, the human form of bovine spongiform encephalopathy ("mad cow disease"), with nearly 100 known cases. Some disease agents are new; others that were located in remote regions are simply being linked to the rest of the world by modern transport systems.[56]

The pace of history is also accelerating as soaring human demands collide with the earth's natural limits. National political leaders are spending more time dealing with the consequences of the collisions described earlier—collapsing fisheries, falling water tables, food shortages, and increasingly destructive storms—along with a steadily swelling international flow of environmental refugees and the many other effects of overshooting natural limits. As change has accelerated, the situation has evolved from one where individuals and societies change only rarely to one where they change continuously. They are changing not only in response to growth itself, but also to the consequences of growth.

The central question is whether the accelerating change that is an integral part of the modern landscape is beginning to exceed the capacity of our social institutions to cope with change. Change is particularly difficult for institutions dealing with international or global issues that require a concerted, cooperative effort by many countries with contrasting cultures if they are to succeed. For example, sustaining the existing oceanic fish catch may be possible only if numerous agreements are reached among countries on the limits to fishing in individual oceanic fisheries. And can governments, working together at the global level, move fast enough to stabilize climate before it disrupts economic progress?

The issue is not whether we know what needs to be done or whether we have the technologies to do it. The issue is whether our social institutions are capable of bringing about the change in the time available. As H.G. Wells wrote in *The Outline of History*, "Human history becomes more and more a race between education and catastrophe."[57]

The Option: Restructure or Decline

Whether we study the environmental undermining of earlier civilizations or look at how adoption of the western industrial model by China would affect the earth's ecosystem, it is evident that the existing industrial economic model cannot sustain economic progress. In our shortsighted efforts to sustain the global economy, as currently structured, we are depleting the earth's natural capital. We spend a lot of time worrying about our economic deficits, but it is the ecological deficits that threaten our long-term economic future. Economic deficits are what we borrow from each other; ecological deficits are what we take from future generations.[58]

Herman Daly, the intellectual pioneer of the fast-growing field of ecological economics, notes that the world "has passed from an era in which manmade capital represented the limiting factor in economic development (an 'empty' world) to an era in which increasingly scarce natural capital has taken its place (a 'full' world)." When our numbers were small relative to the size of the planet, it was humanmade capital that was scarce. Natural capital was abundant. Now that has changed. As the human enterprise continues to expand, the products and services provided by the earth's ecosystem are increasingly scarce, and natural capital is fast becoming the limiting factor while humanmade capital is increasingly abundant.[59]

Transforming our environmentally destructive economy into one that can sustain progress depends on a Copernican shift in our economic mindset, a recognition that the economy is part of the earth's ecosystem and can sustain progress only if it is restructured so that it is compatible with it. The preeminent challenge for our generation is to design an eco-economy, one that respects the principles of ecology. A redesigned economy can be integrated into the ecosystem in a way that will stabilize the relationship between the two, enabling economic progress to continue.

Unfortunately, present-day economics does not provide the conceptual framework needed to build such an economy. It will have to be designed with an understanding of basic ecological concepts such as sustainable yield, carrying capacity, nutrient cycles, the hydrological cycle, and the climate system. Designers must also know that natural systems provide not only goods, but also services—services that are often more valuable than the goods.

We know the kind of restructuring that is needed. In simplest terms, our fossil-fuel-based, automobile-centered, throwaway economy is not a viable model for the world. The alternative is a solar/hydrogen energy economy, an urban transport system that is centered on advanced-design public rail systems and that relies more on the bicycle and less on the automobile, and a comprehensive reuse/recycle economy. And we need to stabilize population as soon as possible.

How do we achieve this economic transformation when all economic decisionmakers—whether political leaders, corporate planners, investment bankers, or individual consumers—are guided by market signals, not the principles of ecological sustainability? How do we integrate ecological awareness into economic decisionmaking? Is it possible for all of us who are making economic decisions to "think like ecologists," to understand the ecological consequences of our decisions? The answer is probably not. It simply may not be possible.

But there may be another approach, a simpler way of achieving our goal. Everyone making economic decisions relies on market signals for guidance. The problem is that the market often fails to tell the ecological truth. It regularly underprices products and services by failing to incorporate the environmental costs of providing them.

Compare, for example, the cost of wind-generated electricity with that from a coal-fired power plant. The cost of the wind-generated electricity reflects the costs of manufacturing the turbine, installing it, maintaining it, and delivering the electricity to consumers. The cost of the coal-fired electricity includes building the power plant, mining the coal, transporting it to the power plant, and distributing the electricity to consumers. What it does not include is the cost of climate disruption caused by carbon emissions from coal burning—whether it be more destructive storms, melting ice caps, rising sea level, or record heat waves. Nor does it include the damage to freshwater lakes and forests from acid rain, or the health care costs of treating respiratory illnesses caused by air pollution. Thus the market price of coal-fired electricity greatly understates its cost to society.

One way to remedy this situation would be to have environmental scientists and economists work together to calculate the cost of climate disruption, acid rain, and air pollution. This figure could then be incorporated as a tax on coal-fired electricity that, when added to the current price, would give the full cost of coal use. This procedure, followed across the board, would mean that all economic decisionmakers—governments and individual consumers—would have the information needed to make more intelligent, ecologically responsible decisions.

We can now see how to restructure the global economy so as to restore stability between the economy and the ecosystem on which it rests. When I helped to pioneer the concept of environmentally sustainable economic development some 27 years ago, at the newly formed Worldwatch Institute, I had a broad sense of what the new economy would look like. Now we can see much more of the detail. We can build an eco-economy with existing technologies. It is economically feasible if we can get the market to tell us the full cost of the products and services that we buy.

The question is not how much will it cost to make this transformation but how much it will cost if we fail to do it. Øystein Dahle, retired Vice President of Esso for Norway and the North Sea, observes, "Socialism collapsed because it did not allow prices to tell the economic truth. Capitalism may collapse because it does not allow prices to tell the ecological truth."[60]

This book has three purposes. The first is to make the case that we have no alternative to restructuring the economy if we want economic progress to continue in the decades ahead. The second is to describe not only the broad structure of the eco-economy, but some of its details. And the third is to outline a strategy for getting from here to there in the time available.

Building an eco-economy is exciting and satisfying. It means we can live in a world where energy comes from wind turbines instead of coal mines, where recycling industries replace mining industries, and where cities are designed for people, not for cars. And perhaps most important of all, we will have the satisfaction of building an economy that will support, not undermine, future generations.

I

A STRESSED RELATIONSHIP

2

Signs of Stress: Climate and Water

On August 19, 2000, the *New York Times* reported that an ice-breaker cruise ship had reached the North Pole only to discover this famous frozen site was now open water. For a generation that grew up reading the harrowing accounts of explorers such as American Richard Byrd trying to reach the North Pole as they battled bitter cold, ice, and snow, this new view taxed the imagination.[1]

In its many earlier trips to the North Pole, the cruise ship had allowed passengers to disembark in order to be photographed standing on the ice. This time, the ship had to move several miles away to find ice thick enough for the photo session. If the explorers of a century or so ago had been trekking to the North Pole in the summer of 2000, they would have had to swim the last few miles.

Media reports of melting ice typically focus on individual glaciers or ice caps, but the ice is melting almost everywhere. Given that the 14 warmest years since recordkeeping began in 1866 have all occurred since 1980, this does not come as a surprise.[2]

Water shortages are also in the news. Some of the world's major rivers are being drained dry, failing to reach the sea. Among them is the Colorado, the major river in the southwestern United States. In China, the Yellow River, the northernmost of the country's two major rivers, no longer reaches the sea for part of each year. In Central Asia, the Amu Darya sometimes fails to reach the Aral Sea because it has been drained dry by upstream irrigation.[3]

Wells are going dry on every continent. As population expands and incomes rise, the demand for water is simply outrunning the supply in many countries. Those with money drill deeper wells, chasing the water table downward. Those unable to deepen their wells are left in a difficult position.

The situation promises to become far more precarious, since the 3.2 billion people being added to world population by 2050 will be born in countries already facing water scarcity. With 40 percent of the world food supply coming from irrigated land, water scarcity directly affects food security. If we are facing a future of water scarcity, we are also facing a future of food scarcity.[4]

Temperature Rising

Since agriculture began, the earth's climate has been remarkably stable. Now the earth's temperature is rising, apparently due to the greenhouse effect—the warming that results from the rising concentration of heat-trapping gases, principally carbon dioxide (CO_2), in the atmosphere.

This rise in CO_2 concentration comes from two sources: the burning of fossil fuels and deforestation. Each year, more than 6 billion tons of carbon are released into the atmosphere as fossil fuels are burned. Estimates of the net release of carbon from deforestation vary widely, but they center on 1.5 billion tons per year.[5]

The release of CO_2 from these two sources is simply overwhelming nature's capacity to fix carbon dioxide. When the Industrial Revolution began in 1760, carbon emissions from the burning of fossil fuels were negligible. But by 1950, they had reached 1.6 billion tons per year, a quantity that was already boosting the atmospheric CO_2 level. In 2000, they totaled 6.3 billion tons. (See Figure 2–1.) This fourfold increase since 1950 is at the heart of the greenhouse effect that is warming the earth.[6]

The carbon emissions of individual fossil fuels vary. Coal burning releases more carbon per unit of energy produced than oil does, and oil more than natural gas. The global fleet of 532 million gasoline-burning automobiles, combined with thousands of coal-fired power plants, are literally the engines driving climate change.[7]

In addition, in recent years the world has been losing 9 million

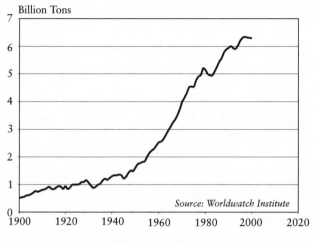

Figure 2–1. *World Carbon Emissions from
Fossil Fuel Burning, 1900–2000*

hectares of forest per year. Forests store easily 20 times as much
carbon per hectare as does land in crops. If the net loss of forests
can be eliminated, this source of carbon emissions will disappear.
In the northern hemisphere, the forested area is actually increasing
by 3.6 million hectares a year. The big challenge is to arrest and
reverse the deforestation in developing countries.[8]

At the start of the Industrial Revolution in 1760, the atmospheric
CO_2 concentration was estimated at 280 parts per million (ppm).
By 2000, it had reached 370 ppm, a rise of 32 percent from pre-
industrial levels. (See Figure 2–2.) The buildup of atmospheric CO_2
from 1960 to 2000 of 54 ppm far exceeded the 36 ppm rise from
1760 to 1960.[9]

Atmospheric CO_2 levels have risen each year since annual mea-
surements began in 1959, making this one of the most predictable
of all environmental trends. Physics textbooks point out that as
atmospheric CO_2 levels rise, so will the earth's temperature, and
this is exactly what is happening. As noted earlier, the 14 warmest
years since recordkeeping began have all come since 1980. Over
the last three decades, global average temperature has risen from
13.99 degrees Celsius in 1969–71 to 14.43 degrees in 1998–2000,
a gain of 0.44 degrees Celsius (0.8 degrees Fahrenheit).[10]

The dramatic rise in the earth's temperature since 1980 can be
clearly seen in Figure 2–3. Not only is it rising rapidly, but it is

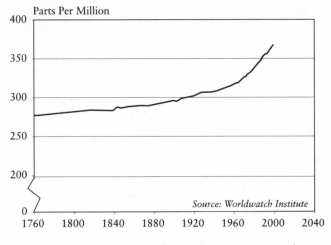

Figure 2–2. *Atmospheric Concentrations of
Carbon Dioxide, 1760–2000*

projected to rise even faster in the next century. If CO$_2$ concentrations in the atmosphere double pre-industrial levels by the end of this century, reaching 560 ppm, the temperature is projected to rise by 1.4–5.8 degrees Celsius. Rising temperatures lead to more extreme climatic events—record heat waves, the melting of ice, rising sea level, and more destructive storms.[11]

Projected temperature rises will not be distributed evenly over the earth's surface, but will be greater over land areas than over the oceans and also greater in the higher latitudes than in the equatorial regions. Inland regions in northern latitudes can expect some of the biggest temperature jumps. A taste of what is to come can be seen in the July 1995 heat wave in Chicago, when temperatures reached 38–41 degrees Celsius (100–106 degrees Fahrenheit) on five consecutive days. Although Chicago is a modern industrial city with extensive air conditioning, this heat wave claimed more than 500 lives. And because Chicago is in the center of the U.S. Corn Belt, the intense heat also helped shrink the 1995 U.S. corn harvest by some 15 percent or $3 billion.[12]

The Ice Is Melting

Ice melting is one of the most visible manifestation of global warming. Sometimes the evidence that mountain glaciers are melting takes novel forms. In late 1991, hikers in the southwestern Alps on the

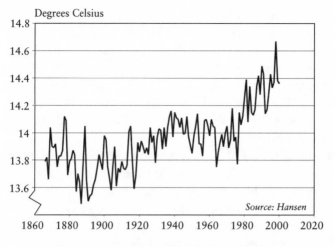

Figure 2–3. *Average Temperature at the Earth's Surface, 1866–2000*

Austrian-Italian border discovered an intact male human body protruding from a glacier. Apparently trapped in a storm more than 5,000 years ago and quickly covered with snow and ice, his body was remarkably well preserved. In 1999, another body was found in a melting glacier in the Yukon Territory of western Canada. As I noted at the time, our ancestors are emerging from the ice with a message for us: the earth is getting warmer.[13]

In the Arctic Ocean, sea ice is melting fast. As recently as 1960, the Arctic sea ice was nearly 2 meters thick. In 2001, it averaged scarcely a meter. Over the last four decades, the ice sheet has thinned by 42 percent and it has shrunk in area by 6 percent. Together, this thinning and shrinkage have reduced the Arctic Ocean ice mass by nearly half. This rapid melting is expected to continue. A recent study by two Norwegian scientists projects that within 50 years the Arctic Ocean could be ice-free during the summer.[14]

In 2000, four U.S. scientists published an article in *Science* reporting that the vast Greenland ice sheet is starting to melt. Lying largely within the Arctic Circle, Greenland is gaining some ice in higher elevations on its northern reaches, but it is losing much more at lower elevations, particularly along its southern and eastern coasts. This huge island of 2.2 million square kilometers (three times the size of Texas) is experiencing a net loss of 51 billion cubic meters of water each year, an amount approaching two thirds of the annual flow of the Nile River as it enters Egypt.[15]

The Antarctic peninsula is also losing ice. In contrast to the North Pole, which is covered by the Arctic Sea, the South Pole is covered by the continent of Antarctica, a land mass roughly the size of the United States. Its continent-sized ice sheet, which is on average 2.3 kilometers (1.5 miles) thick, is relatively stable. But the ice shelves, the portions of the ice sheet that extend into the surrounding seas, are fast disappearing.[16]

A team of U.S. and British scientists reported in 1999 that the ice shelves on either side of the Antarctic peninsula are in full retreat. From roughly mid-century through 1997, these areas lost 7,000 square kilometers as the ice sheet disintegrated. But then within scarcely one year they lost another 3,000 square kilometers. Delaware-sized icebergs that have broken off are a threat to ships in the area. The scientists attribute the accelerated ice melting to a regional temperature rise of 2.5 degrees Celsius (4.5 degrees Fahrenheit) since 1940.[17]

These are not the only examples of melting. Lisa Mastny of Worldwatch Institute, who reviewed some 30 studies on this topic, reports that mountain glaciers are melting worldwide—and at an accelerating rate. (See Table 2–1.) The snow/ice mass is shrinking in the world's major mountain ranges: the Rocky Mountains, the Andes, the Alps, and the Himalayas. In Glacier National Park in Montana, the number of glaciers has dwindled from 150 in 1850 to fewer than 50 today. The U.S. Geological Survey projects that the remaining glaciers could disappear within 30 years.[18]

In Europe's Alps, the shrinkage of the glacial volume by more than half since 1850 is expected to continue, with these ancient glaciers largely disappearing over the next half-century. Shrinkage of ice masses in the Himalayas has accelerated alarmingly. In eastern India, the Dokriani Bamak glacier, which retreated by 16.5 meters between 1992 and 1997, drew back by a further 20 meters in 1998 alone.[19]

A research report by Lonnie Thompson of Ohio State University indicates that the ice cap on Kilimanjaro could disappear within 15 years. This upset Tanzania's Minister of Tourism, Zokia Meghji, who told parliament that the projected melting was exaggerated, as he tried to allay fears about the effects on the country's lucrative tourism industry. In response, Thompson pointed out that his report was simply based on an extrapolation of the recent historical

Table 2–1. *Selected Examples of Ice Melt Around the World*

Name	Location	Measured Loss
Arctic Sea Ice	Arctic Ocean	Has shrunk by 6 percent since 1978, with a 14-percent loss of thicker, year-round ice. Has thinned by 40 percent in less than 30 years.
Greenland Ice Sheet	Greenland	Has thinned by more than a meter a year on its southern and eastern edges since 1993.
Glacier National Park	Rocky Mtns., United States	Since 1850, the number of glaciers has dropped from 150 to fewer than 50. Remaining glaciers could disappear completely in 30 years.
Larsen B Ice Shelf	Antarctic Peninsula	Calved a 300-square-kilometer iceberg in early 1998. Lost 1,714 square kilometers during the 1998–99 season, and 300 square kilometers during the 1999–2000 season.
Dokriani Bamak Glacier	Himalayas, India	Retreated by 20 meters in 1998, compared with 16.5 meters over the previous five years.
Tien Shan Mountains	Central Asia	Twenty-two percent of glacial ice volume has disappeared in the past 40 years.
Caucasus Mountains	Russia	Glacial volume has declined by 50 percent in the past century.
Alps	Western Europe	Glacial volume has shrunk by more than 50 percent since 1850. Glaciers could be reduced to only a small fraction of their present mass within decades.
Kilimanjaro	Tanzania	Ice cap shrunk by 33 percent from 1989 to 2000. Could disappear by 2015.
Quelccaya Glacier	Andes, Peru	Rate of retreat increased to 30 meters a year in the 1990s, up from only 3 meters a year; will likely disappear before 2020.

Source: Updated from Lisa Mastny, "Melting of Earth's Ice Cover Reaches New High," Worldwatch News Brief (Washington, DC: Worldwatch Institute: 6 March 2000).

trend.[20]

Researchers are discovering that a modest rise in temperature of 1–2 degrees Celsius in mountainous regions can dramatically alter the precipitation mix, increasing the share falling as rain while decreasing the share coming down as snow. The result is more flooding during the rainy season, a shrinking snow/ice mass, and less snowmelt to feed rivers during the dry season.[21]

These "reservoirs in the sky," where nature stores fresh water for use in the summer as the snow melts, have been there ever since irrigation began, supplying farmers with water for several thousand years. Now suddenly, in a matter of years, they are shrinking and some could disappear entirely, sharply reducing the water supply for irrigation and for cities.

If the massive snow/ice sheet in the Himalayas—which is the third largest in the world, after the Antarctic and Greenland ice sheets—continues to melt, it will affect the water supply of much of Asia. All of the region's major rivers—the Indus, Ganges, Mekong, Yangtze, and Yellow—originate in the Himalayas. Melting in this area could alter the hydrology of several Asian countries, including Pakistan, India, Bangladesh, Thailand, Viet Nam, and China. Less snowmelt in the summer dry season to feed rivers could worsen the hydrological poverty already afflicting so many in the region.[22]

We don't have to sit idly by as this scenario unfolds. There may still be time to stabilize atmospheric CO_2 levels before carbon emissions lead to unmanageable climate change. There is an abundance of wind, solar, and geothermal energy to harness for running the world economy. (See Chapter 5.) If we were to cut income taxes and offset this by incorporating a carbon tax that reflected the cost of climate disruption in the price of fossil fuels, investment would quickly shift from fossil fuels to these climate-stabilizing energy sources.

Sea Level Rising

Sea level is a sensitive indicator of global warming since it is affected by both thermal expansion and the melting of land-based glaciers. The respective contributions to sea level rise of thermal expansion and ice melting are estimated to be roughly the same.[23]

During the twentieth century, sea level rose by 10–20 centimeters (4–8 inches), more than half as much as it had risen during the preceding 2,000 years. If the earth's temperature continues to rise, further acceleration is in prospect. The model used in the Intergovernmental Panel on Climate Change 2001 Assessment projects that sea level could rise by as much as 1 meter during the twenty-first century.[24]

Rising sea level has numerous consequences. The most obvious is inundation as the oceans expand at the expense of continents. Another is saltwater intrusion. As sea level rises, salt water may invade coastal freshwater aquifers. This intrusion is exacerbated by the falling water tables that now plague coastal regions in many countries, including Israel, Pakistan, India, and China. A third effect is beach erosion: as waves break further inland, they erode the beach, compounding the effect of rising sea level.[25]

The most easily measured effect of rising sea level is the inundation of coastal areas. Donald F. Boesch, with the University of Maryland's Center for Environmental Sciences, estimates that for each millimeter rise in sea level, the shoreline retreats an average of 1.5 meters. Thus if sea level rises by 1 meter, the coastline will retreat by 1,500 meters, or nearly a mile.[26]

With a 1-meter rise in sea level, more than a third of Shanghai would be under water. For China as a whole, 70 million people would be vulnerable to a 100-year storm surge. The rice-growing river floodplains and deltas of Asia would be particularly vulnerable. A World Bank analysis shows that Bangladesh would be hardest hit, losing half of its rice production—the food staple of its 140 million people. (See Figure 2–4.) At current rice prices, this would cost Bangladesh $3.2 billion. Residents of the densely populated river valleys of Asia would be forced into already crowded interiors. Rising sea level could create millions of climate refugees in Bangladesh, China, India, Indonesia, the Philippines, and Viet Nam.[27]

Two thirds of the Marshall Islands and Kiribati would be under water. The United States would lose 36,000 square kilometers (14,000 square miles) of land, with the middle Atlantic and Mississippi Gulf states losing the most. And large portions of lower Manhattan and the Capitol Mall in Washington, D.C., would be flooded during a 50-year storm surge. A 1-meter rise in Japan would mean that 2,340 square kilometers of the country would be below high tide. Four million Japanese would be affected, many of them driven from their homes.[28]

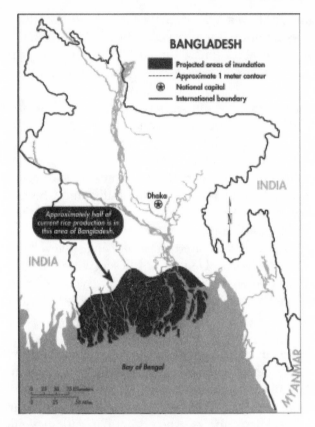

Figure 2–4. A 1-Meter Rise in Sea Level Would Cut
Bangladesh's Rice Production Approximately in Half

Coastal real estate prices are likely to be one of the first economic indicators to reflect the rise in sea level. People with heavy
investments in beachfront properties will suffer most. A half-meter
rise in sea level in the United States could bring losses ranging from
$20 billion to $150 billion. Beachfront properties, much like nuclear
power plants, are becoming uninsurable—as many homeowners
in Florida, for example, have discovered.[29]

Many developing countries already coping with population
growth and intense competition for living space and cropland are
now facing the prospect of rising sea level and substantial land
losses. Some of those most directly affected have contributed the
least to the buildup in atmospheric CO_2 that is causing this problem.

Rising sea level will pose difficult and costly choices. Consider, for example, the effort and cost involved in relocating a million Chinese from the area to be inundated by the Three Gorges Dam. This would be trivial compared with the tens of millions, and eventually hundreds of millions in Asia, who would have to be relocated as the ocean rises if we continue with business as usual. Climate refugees may come to dominate the international flow of migrants since they are losing not just land, but food supplies and livelihoods.[30]

More than 90 percent of the world's ice is in the Antarctic ice sheet, which, partly because of its size, is comparatively stable. The other 10 percent, however, is in the Greenland ice sheet and mountain glaciers, which are more vulnerable to climate change. Now that the Greenland ice sheet has started to melt, we must ask, What if this trend continues? Greenland's ice sheet is up to 2 kilometers (1.2 miles) thick in some areas. In an article in *Science*, NASA scientists calculate that if the Greenland ice sheet were to disappear entirely, sea level would rise by a staggering 7 meters (23 feet), markedly shrinking the earth's land area and engulfing many coastal cities.[31]

For the first time since civilization began, sea level has begun to rise at a measurable rate. It has become an indicator to watch, a trend that could force a human migration of almost unimaginable dimensions, and one that will shape the human prospect. It also raises questions of intergenerational responsibility that humanity has never before faced.

More Destructive Storms

Rising temperatures and the power of storms are directly related. As sea surface temperatures rise, particularly in the tropics and subtropics, the additional heat radiating into the atmosphere causes more destructive storms. Higher temperatures mean more evaporation. Water that goes up must come down. What is not clear is exactly where the additional water will fall.[32]

More extreme weather events are of particular concern to countries in the hurricane or typhoon belt. Among those most directly affected by increased storm intensity are China, Japan, and the Philippines in the western Pacific, India and Bangladesh in the Bay of Bengal, and the United States and the Central American and Caribbean countries in the western Atlantic.

Munich Re, which insures insurance companies, has maintained detailed, worldwide data on natural catastrophes—principally storms, floods, and earthquakes—over the last half-century. The company defines a great natural catastrophe as one that overwhelms the capacity of a region to help itself, forcing it to depend on international assistance. During the 1960s, economic losses from these large-scale catastrophes totaled $69 billion; during the 1990s, they totaled $536 billion, nearly an eightfold increase.[33]

Recent years have seen some extraordinarily destructive tropical storms. Among them was Hurricane Andrew, which cut a large swath across the state of Florida in 1992. Storm alerts held the loss of human life to 65, but Andrew destroyed 60,000 homes and other buildings, inflicting some $30 billion in damage. In addition to the buildings it destroyed, it also took down seven insurance companies, as mounting claims left them insolvent.[34]

Six years later, Hurricane Georges—a powerful storm with winds of close to 200 miles per hour—was stalled off the coast of Central America by a high-pressure system that blocked its normal path to the north. It claimed 4,000 lives and inflicted a staggering $10 billion worth of damage on El Salvador and Nicaragua. Damage on this scale, which approached the combined gross domestic products of the two countries, set economic development back by a generation. A storm that hit Venezuela in mid-December 1999 caused enormous flooding and landslides, claimed 20,000 lives, and registered economic losses of $15 billion—second only to Hurricane Andrew.[35]

In late September 1999, Typhoon Bart hit Japan's densely populated island of Kyushu. Its toll in human life was held to only 26, but it did $5 billion worth of damage. Countries such as Japan, China, and the Philippines are in a particularly vulnerable location, fully exposed to all the power that storms generated over the tropical Pacific can muster.[36]

Winter storms are also becoming more destructive in the northern hemisphere. S.J. Lambert, writing in the *Journal of Geophysical Research*, has analyzed the frequency of intense winter storms in this hemisphere over the last century. From 1920 until 1970, there were roughly 40 storms a year. But then as temperatures started to climb, so did the frequency of storms. Since 1985, the northern hemisphere has experienced close to 80 storms a year—a doubling in less than a generation. Over the past decade or so, Western Europe has been hit by numerous storms of record destructiveness. In 1987, the United Kingdom and France bore the brunt of a winter storm that claimed 17 lives and caused $3.7 billion worth of damage. In 1999, Western Europe was hit by three unusually powerful winter storms: Anatole, Martin, and Lothar. They claimed 150 lives and did $10.3 billion worth of damage. Lothar, which hit the continent during the holiday season on December 26, left $7.5 billion of damage in France, Germany, and Switzerland.[37]

Damage from storms is mounting both because of greater population density and because the investment per person in housing or other structures that are vulnerable to storm damage is greater than ever. There is also a disproportionately large gain in construction in coastal regions, which are much more vulnerable to storms and storm surges.

The bottom line is that storms are increasing both in number and in destructiveness. More powerful storms mean more damage. A doubling of the number of winter storms in the northern hemisphere within less than a generation, coupled with increasing severity, yields a dramatic rise in storm-related damage.

At this point, no one knows quite how this trend will unfold in the twenty-first century, but it seems likely that if we continue with business as usual and CO_2 levels continue to rise, the destructiveness in the future will dwarf that in the present—just as the destructiveness in the present is far greater than that of the recent past. The risk is that the cost of coping with these ever more destructive, human-induced catastrophes could overwhelm some societies, leading to their economic decline.

Rivers Drained Dry

We live in a water-challenged world, one that is becoming more so each year as 80 million additional people stake their claims to the earth's water resources. Even now, many people in developing countries lack enough water to satisfy basic needs for drinking, bathing, and producing food.

By 2050, India is projected to add 563 million people and China 187 million. Pakistan, one of the world's most arid countries, is projected to add over 200 million, going from 141 million today to 344 million. Egypt, Iran, and Mexico are slated to increase their populations by half or more by 2050. In these and other water-short countries, continuing population growth is sentencing hundreds of millions of people to hydrological poverty—a local form of impoverishment that is difficult to escape.[38]

One manifestation of emerging water scarcity is dry rivers. Several of the world's major rivers now either run dry part of the year, failing to reach the sea, or have little water left when they get there.[39]

As noted earlier, the Amu Darya in Central Asia, one of two rivers that feeds the Aral Sea, is now largely drained dry by Turkmen and Uzbek cotton farmers. With this river failing to reach the sea at times and the flow of the Syr Darya reduced to a shadow of its past flow, the Aral Sea is shrinking beneath the relentless sun in this semiarid region. Since 1960, the sea has dropped 12 meters (40 feet); its area has shrunk by 40 percent and its volume by 66 percent. Towns that were once coastal are now 50 kilometers from the water. If recent trends continue, the sea will largely disappear within another decade or two—existing only on old maps, a geographic memory.[40]

As the sea has shrunk, the salt concentrations in its water have increased to where fish can no longer survive. As a result, the fishery—which yielded 60,000 tons (130 million pounds) of fish per year as recently as 1960—is now dead.[41]

In 1990, the Soviet Academy of Sciences organized a conference in Nukus, a town near the Aral Sea, entitled "The Aral Sea: An Environmental Catastrophe." After attending the meeting, I joined other guests on an air tour over the sea and the former seabed. I later wrote in World Watch magazine, "From the air, the exposed floor of the Aral Sea looks like a moonscape. No plant or animal life is visible. From a few hundred feet above the ground, in an ancient canvas-winged, single-engine bi-plane, the signs of a dying ecosystem are evident. Fishing villages that once stood by the shoreline are abandoned and lie miles from the receding waters. Like ghost mining towns out of the American West, they reinforce the image of a dying ecosystem and a dying economy."[42]

When rivers go dry, the marine ecosystems within the rivers are destroyed. The estuaries as sometimes affected as well. For example, when the Colorado River was flowing into the Gulf of California, it supported a large fishery and several hundred Cocopa Indian families. Today this fishery is but a remnant of its former self.[43]

Upstream diversions for cities, industry, and irrigation from China's Yellow River are multiplying. After flowing uninterruptedly for thousands of years, this cradle of Chinese civilization ran dry in 1972, failing to reach the sea for some 15 days. In the following years, it ran dry intermittently until 1985. Since then, it has run dry for part of each year. In 1997, a drought year, the Yellow River did not connect with the sea for 226 days.[44]

In fact, during much of 1997, the river did not even make it to Shandong Province, the last of the eight provinces it flows through en route to the sea. Shandong, producing a fifth of China's corn and a seventh of its wheat, is more important agriculturally to China than Iowa and Kansas together are to the United States. Half of the province's irrigation water used to come from the Yellow River, but this supply is now shrinking. The other half comes from an aquifer whose water level is falling by 1.5 meters a year.[45]

As more and more water is diverted to industries and cities upstream, less is available downstream. Beijing is permitting the poverty-ridden upstream provinces to divert water for their development at the expense of agriculture in the lower reaches of the basin.

One of the hundreds of projects to divert water from the Yellow River in the upper reaches is a canal that will take water to Hohhot, the capital of Inner Mongolia, starting in 2003. This will help satisfy swelling residential needs as well as those of expanding industries, including the all-important wool textile industry that is supplied by the region's vast flocks of sheep. Another canal will divert water to Taiyuan, the capital of Shanxi Province, a city of 4 million that now rations water.[46]

The growing upstream claims on the Yellow River mean that one day it may no longer reach Shandong Province at all, cutting the province off from roughly half of its irrigation water. The resulting prospect of massive grain imports and growing dependence on U.S. grain, in particular, leads to sleepless nights for political leaders in Beijing.[47]

Another river that is leading to sleepless nights is the Nile, because its waters must be allocated not among provinces, as in China, but among countries. Ten countries share the Nile River basin, but just three—Egypt, Sudan, and Ethiopia—dominate. Eighty-five percent of the Nile's flow originates in Ethiopia, but the lion's share is used by Egypt. Most of the rest is used in Sudan. Once the claims of these two countries are satisfied, little water is left when it enters the Mediterranean.[48]

Egypt, where it almost never rains, is wholly dependent on the Nile. Without this lifeline, Egypt would not exist. Even if all the water in the Nile River were available to Egypt, it would still have to import some grain just to feed its current population. But it is already importing 40 percent of its grain, and its population, now 68 million, is projected to nearly double to 114 million by 2050. The population of Sudan, which is growing even faster, is projected to increase from 31 million today to 64 million by 2050, more than doubling its water needs.[49]

Ethiopia, where most of the precipitation falls that feeds the Nile, is growing faster still. With each family averaging nearly six children, its population is projected to triple from 63 million at the end of 2000 to 186 million by 2050. Thus far, Ethiopia has built only 200 very small dams that enable it to use 500 million cubic meters of the Nile's 84-billion-cubic-meter flow, or less than 1 percent. But the Ethiopian government is planning to use much more of the water to expand food production and provide electricity as it tries to lift its people out of poverty.[50]

The Nile, like the Yellow River, has wide disparities in income between the upper and lower reaches of the basin. It is difficult to argue that Ethiopia, with an annual income of scarcely $100 per person, should not use the upper Nile waters for its own development, even though it would be at the expense of Egypt, which has an annual income of over $1,000 per person. If the basin countries do not quickly stabilize their populations, they risk becoming trapped in hydrological poverty.[51]

Other river basins where competition for water is intensifying include the Jordan, the Ganges, and the Mekong. The competition over the river Jordan between Israel, Jordan, and the Palestinians is well known. The Jordan, which flows from Lebanon into Israel, where it joins the Sea of Galilee and eventually empties into the Dead Sea, is being overtaxed. As a result, the water level in the Sea of Galilee is gradually falling and the Dead Sea is shrinking.[52]

If India, which shares the Ganges with Bangladesh, were to use all the water that it wants, the Ganges might not even reach Bangladesh during the dry season. But fortunately a treaty has been signed that allocates an agreed-upon amount of water to Bangladesh. Competition in the Mekong River basin is also intensifying. As China builds dams on its upper reaches, less water is left for Cambodia, Laos, and Viet Nam—countries whose rice cultures depend on the Mekong water.[53]

Falling Water Tables

Even as major rivers are running dry, water tables are falling on every continent as the demand for water outruns the sustainable yield of aquifers. Overpumping is a new phenomenon, largely confined to the last half-century. Only since the development of powerful diesel and electric pumps have we had the capacity to pull water out of aquifers faster than it is replaced by precipitation.

Overpumping is now widespread in China, India, and the United States—three countries that together account for nearly half of the world grain harvest. Water tables are falling under the North China Plain, which produces 25 percent of China's grain harvest; under the Indian Punjab, the breadbasket of India; and under the southern Great Plains of the United States.[54]

Hydrologically, there are two Chinas—the humid south, which includes the Yangtze River basin and everything south of it, and the arid north, which includes the Yellow River basin and everything to the north. The south, with 700 million people, has one third of the nation's cropland and four fifths of its water. The north, with 550 million people, has two thirds of the cropland and one fifth of the water. The water per hectare of cropland in the north is one eighth that of the south.[55]

Northern China is drying out as the demand for water outruns the supply, depleting aquifers. In 1999 the water table under Beijing fell by 1.5 meters (5 feet). Since 1965, the shallow water table under the city has fallen by some 59 meters or nearly 200 feet. The deep aquifer that some wells draw from may have fallen even more. A 2001 World Bank report says, "Anecdotal evidence suggests that deep wells around Beijing now have to reach 1,000 meters (more than half a mile) to tap fresh water, adding dramatically to the cost of supply." Falling water tables under the capital remind China's leaders of the shortages that lie ahead as the country's aquifers are depleted.[56]

The North China Plain, a region that stretches from just north of Shanghai to well north of Beijing, embraces five provinces: Hebei, Henan, and Shandong, and the city provinces of Beijing and Tianjin. At the end of 1997, official data show that these five provinces had 2.6 million wells, the bulk of them for irrigation. During that year, 99,900 wells were abandoned, apparently because they ran dry as the water table fell. Some 221,900 new wells were drilled. In the two major cities, Beijing and Tianjin, the number of wells abandoned exceeded the number of new wells drilled. This wholesale abandonment of wells has no precedent. The drilling of so many new wells reflects the desperate quest for water as the water table falls.[57]

Although earlier data showed the water table dropping by an average of 1.5 meters (5 feet) a year under the North China Plain, these recent data on well abandonment and new well drilling suggest that it now could be falling much faster in some places. Overpumping is greatest in the Hai River basin, immediately to the north of the Yellow River basin. This area, which includes Beijing and Tianjin, both large industrial cities, is home to over 100 million people.[58]

Water use in the basin currently totals 55 billion cubic meters annually, while the sustainable supply totals only 34 billion cubic meters, leaving an annual deficit of 21 billion cubic meters to be satisfied by groundwater mining. When this aquifer is depleted, water pumping will necessarily drop to the sustainable yield, cutting the basin's water supply by nearly 40 percent. Given rapid urban and industrial growth in the area, and agriculture's relegation to third place in the line for water, irrigated agriculture in the basin could largely disappear by 2010—forcing a shift to less productive rain-fed agriculture. The 2001 World Bank report concluded that north China's fast deteriorating water situation could have "catastrophic consequences for future generations unless water use and supply could quickly be brought back into balance."[59]

In addition to losses of irrigation water from aquifer depletion, farmers are faced with a diversion of irrigation water to cities and industry. Between now and 2010, when China's population is projected to grow by 126 million, the World Bank projects that the nation's urban water demand will increase from 50 billion cubic meters to 80 billion, a growth of 60 percent. Industrial water demand, meanwhile, is projected to increase from 127 billion cubic meters to 206 billion, an expansion of 62 percent. In much of northern China, this growing demand for water is being satisfied either by investing in water efficiency or by taking irrigation water from agriculture.[60]

Under India's Punjab, where the double cropping of high-yielding winter wheat and summer rice produces a grain surplus for shipment to other states, the water table is falling. Dropping by an estimated 0.6 meters per year, it is forcing farmers with shallow wells to drill deeper.[61]

In the southern Great Plains of the United States, irrigated agriculture is based largely on water pumped from the Ogallala aquifer, which is essentially a fossil aquifer with little recharge. As the water table falls and the aquifer is depleted, farmers are forced to abandon irrigated agriculture, returning to dryland farming. In several states that dominate U.S. food production, including Colorado, Kansas, Oklahoma, and Texas, the irrigated area is slowly shrinking as the Ogallala is depleted.[62]

An economic analysis of the water situation in the high plains of Texas, where much of the state's irrigated cropland is located, concluded that crop production in the region will decline steadily as water supplies shrink. The big losers between 2000 and 2025 will be irrigated feedgrains, including both corn and sorghum. The area in wheat, a dryland crop, will expand slightly. Overall, grain production is projected to decline 17 percent. A similarly detailed analysis for nearby states, such as Oklahoma and Kansas, would likely also show production declines for the more water-dependent crops.[63]

In southern Texas, El Paso and its sister city across the border in Mexico, Juarez, both draw their water from the same aquifer. As population in the two fast-growing cities has climbed, demand has outstripped the sustainable yield of the aquifer. David Hurlbut, analyst with the Public Utility Commission of Texas, believes that because of their failure to address the water supply issue effectively, the two cities are moving toward hydrological bankruptcy.[64]

With continuing population growth, the world water situation can only get worse. Even with today's 6.1 billion people, the world has a huge water deficit. Using data on overpumping for China, India, Saudi Arabia, North Africa, and the United States, Sandra Postel, author of *Pillar of Sand*, calculates the annual overpumping of aquifers at 160 billion cubic meters or 160 billion tons. Using the rule of thumb that it takes 1,000 tons of water to produce 1 ton of grain, this 160-billion-ton water deficit is equal to 160 million tons of grain—or half the U.S. grain harvest.[65]

At average world grain consumption of just over 300 kilograms or one third of a ton per person a year, 160 million tons of grain would feed 480 million people. In other words, 480 million of the world's 6.1 billion people are being fed with grain produced with the unsustainable use of water. We are feeding ourselves with water that belongs to our children.[66]

Facing Water Scarcity

An estimated 70 percent of the water consumed worldwide, including that diverted from rivers and pumped from underground, is used for irrigation, while some 20 percent is used by industry and 10 percent for residential purposes. In the increasingly intense competition for water among these three sectors, the economics of water do not favor agriculture. In China, 1,000 tons of water can be used to produce 1 ton of wheat, worth perhaps $200, or to expand industrial output by $14,000—70 times as much. In a country that is desperately seeking economic growth and the jobs it generates, the gain in diverting water from agriculture to industry is obvious. The economics of water also helps explain the increasingly common sale of irrigation water rights by U.S. farmers in the West to cities.[67]

Urbanization, industrialization, and ecosystem maintenance also expand the demand for water. As developing-country villagers, traditionally reliant on the village well, move to urban high-rise apartment buildings with indoor plumbing, their residential water use can easily triple. Industrialization takes even more water than urbanization.

Rising affluence in itself generates additional demands for water. For example, as people move up the food chain, consuming more beef, pork, poultry, eggs, and dairy products, they use more grain. A U.S. diet rich in livestock products requires four times as much grain per person as a rice-based diet in a country like India. Using four times as much grain means using four times as much water.[68]

Once a localized phenomenon, water scarcity is now crossing national borders via the international grain trade. The world's fastest-growing grain import market is North Africa and the Middle East, an area that includes Morocco, Algeria, Tunisia, Libya, Egypt, and the countries eastward through Iran. Virtually every country in this region is simultaneously experiencing water shortages and rapid population growth.[69]

As the demand for water in the region's cities and industries rises, it is typically satisfied by diverting water from irrigation. The loss in food production capacity is then offset by importing grain from abroad. Since 1 ton of grain represents 1,000 tons of water, this is the most efficient way for water-deficit countries to import water.

In 2000, Iran imported 7 million tons of wheat, eclipsing Japan—for decades the world's leading wheat importer. In 2001, Egypt is also projected to move ahead of Japan. Iran and Egypt, each with nearly 70 million people and adding more than a million a year, are both facing acute water scarcity.[70]

The water required to produce the grain and other foodstuffs imported into North Africa and the Middle East in 2000 was roughly equal to the annual flow of the Nile River. Stated otherwise, the fast-growing water deficit of this region is equal to another Nile flowing into the region in the form of imported grain.[71]

It is now often said that future wars in the region will more likely be fought over water than oil. Perhaps, but given the difficulty in winning a water war, the competition for water seems more likely to take place in world grain markets. The countries that will "win" in this competition will be those that are financially strongest, not those that are militarily strongest.[72]

The world water deficit, as measured by the overpumping of aquifers, grows larger each year, making it progressively more difficult to manage. If countries everywhere decided this year to halt overpumping and to stabilize water tables, the world grain harvest would fall by some 160 million tons, or 8 percent, and grain prices would go off the top of the chart. The longer countries delay in facing this issue, the wider the water deficit becomes and the greater the eventual adjustment will be.

Unless governments in water-short countries act quickly to stabilize population and to raise water productivity, their water shortages may soon become food shortages. The risk is that the fast-growing ranks of water-short countries with rising grain import needs, including potentially the population giants China and India, will overwhelm the export capacity of the grain-surplus countries—the United States, France, Canada, and Australia. And this in turn will destabilize world grain markets.

The water situation is deteriorating rapidly in many countries, but it is the fast-growing water deficit in China that is likely to affect the entire world. The combination of 12 million additional people per year, urbanization, a projected economic growth rate of 7 percent, and the continuing movement of Chinese consumers up the food chain virtually ensures that the demand for water will continue to outstrip the supply for years to come. These trends also suggest that China's need for imported grain could soon start to climb, much as its imports of soybeans have in recent years. Between 1995 and 2000, China went from being self-sufficient in soybeans to being the world's largest buyer, importing over 40 percent of its supply.[73]

Water shortages can be ameliorated by raising water prices to reduce wastage and thus increase the efficiency of water use, but in China this is not always easy. An announcement in early 2001 that the government was planning to raise water prices in stages over the next five years was a welcome step in the right direction. But for Beijing, this option is fraught with political risks because the public response to increasing the price of water, which often has been free in the past, is akin to that when gasoline prices go up in the United States.[74]

Other recent announcements from Beijing indicate that the government has officially abandoned its long-standing policy of grain self-sufficiency. China has also announced that, in the intensifying competition for water, cities and industry will get priority—leaving agriculture as the residual claimant.[75]

As noted, China is not alone in facing water shortages. Other countries where water scarcity is raising grain imports or threatening to do so include India, Pakistan, Mexico, and dozens of smaller countries. But only China—with nearly 1.3 billion people and an $80 billion annual trade surplus with the United States—has the near-term potential to disrupt world grain markets. In short, falling water tables in China could soon mean rising food prices for the entire world.[76]

3

Signs of Stress:
The Biological Base

In April 2001, scientists at the National Oceanic and Atmospheric Administration laboratory in Boulder, Colorado, reported that a huge dust storm from northern China had reached the United States, "blanketing areas from Canada to Arizona with a layer of dust." People living in the foothills of the Rockies could not even see the mountains. Few Americans were aware that the dust on their cars and the haze hanging over the western United States was, in fact, soil from China.[1]

This Chinese dust storm, the most severe of a dozen in the spring of 2001, signals a widespread deterioration of the rangeland and cropland in that country's vast northwest. These huge dust plumes routinely travel hundreds of miles to populous cities in northeastern China, including Beijing—obscuring the sun, reducing visibility, slowing traffic, and closing airports. Reports of residents in eastern cities caulking windows with old rags to keep out the dust are reminiscent of the U.S. Dust Bowl of the 1930s.[2]

News reports in China typically attributed the dust storms to the drought of the last three years, but that has simply brought a fast-deteriorating situation into focus. Overgrazing and overplowing are widespread. For example, the United States, a country of comparable size and grazing capacity, has 98 million cattle and 9 million sheep and goats, whereas China now has 127 million cattle and 279 million sheep and goats. Feeding 1.3 billion people, a population nearly five times that of the United States, is not an easy matter. Millions of hectares of highly erodible land were plowed that should have stayed in grass.[3]

Evidence of the intensifying conflict between the economy and the ecosystem of which it is a part can be seen not only in the dust bowl emerging in China, but also in the burning rainforests in Indonesia, the collapsing cod fishery in the North Sea, falling crop yields in Africa, the expanding dead zone in the Gulf of Mexico, and falling water tables in India.

The ill-structured global economy's rising demands on ecosystems are diminishing the earth's biological productivity. The output of oceanic fisheries is reduced by overfishing, by oceanic pollutants, and by disruptions of the reproductive cycle of river-spawning fish as some rivers are dammed and others are drained dry. Overgrazing of rangelands is also taking a toll. Initially overgrazing reduces the productivity of rangelands, but eventually it destroys them—converting them into desert.

The productive capacity of the earth's forests is declining as they shrink by more than 9 million hectares per year. Lumbering, land clearing for crop production or ranching, and firewood gathering are responsible. Healthy rainforests do not burn, but fragmented tropical rainforests can be weakened to where they are easily ignited by lightning.[4]

An estimated 36 percent of the world's cropland is suffering a decline in inherent productivity from soil erosion. If this continues, eventually the cropland will become wasteland. In Africa, the failure to replace nutrients removed by crops is reducing crop yields in several countries. As local ecosystems deteriorate, the land's carrying capacity is reduced, setting in motion a self-reinforcing cycle of ecological degradation and deepening human poverty. With half the world's workforce dependent on croplands, fisheries, rangelands, and forests for their jobs and livelihood, any deterioration of these ecosystems can translate into a decline in living conditions.[5]

Fisheries Collapsing

Among the three ecosystems that supply our food—croplands, rangelands, and fisheries—the excessive demand on fisheries is perhaps most visible. After World War II, accelerating population growth and steadily rising incomes drove the demand for seafood upward at a record pace. At the same time, advances in fishing technologies, including refrigerated processing ships that enabled trawlers to exploit distant oceans, dramatically boosted fishing capacity.

In response, the oceanic fish catch climbed from 19 million tons in 1950 to its historic high of 93 million tons in 1997. This fivefold growth—more than double that of population during this period—raised seafood consumption per person worldwide from 8 kilograms in 1950 to a peak of 17 kilograms in 1988. Since then, it has fallen to scarcely 15 kilograms, a drop of one eighth.[6]

Oceanic fisheries were long a leading source of animal protein in the diet of island countries and those with long coastlines, such as Norway and Italy, but it was not until the second half of the twentieth century that fishing fleets began to systematically exploit the oceanic food potential. This, combined with improved inland transportation and refrigeration, made seafood a basic component of diets for most of humanity.

In the early 1990s, the U.N. Food and Agriculture Organization (FAO), which monitors oceanic fisheries, reported that all of the world's 17 major fisheries were being harvested at or beyond their sustainable capacity and that 9 were in a state of decline. Many countries were trying to protect their fisheries from overfishing and eventual collapse. In 1992, Canada, which had waited too long to restrict the catch in its 500-year-old cod fishery off the coast of Newfoundland, was forced to suspend fishing there entirely, putting some 40,000 fishers and fish processors out of work. Then in late 1993, Canada closed additional stretches of water to cod fishing, with the off-limits area creeping down toward the U.S. coast. The United States followed with restrictions designed to save its cod, haddock, and flounder fisheries off New England.[7]

On the West coast, conditions were no better. In April 1994, the Pacific Fishery Management Council banned salmon fishing off Washington State in an effort to protect the species from extinction. In Oregon and California, stringent salmon quotas were imposed. Actions by the United States and Canada, combined with

similar measures by governments elsewhere, implicitly acknowl-
edge that unrestricted harvesting could destroy fisheries, depriving
the world of a valuable food source.[8]

The inability of governments to cooperate in oceanic fishery
management means that instead of yielding maximum sustainable
catch indefinitely, many fisheries have been fished to the verge of
collapse. Atlantic stocks of the heavily fished bluefin tuna, a standby
in Tokyo's sushi restaurants, have been cut by a staggering 94 percent. It will take years for such long-lived species to recover, even if
fishing stops altogether.[9]

Inland fisheries are also suffering from environmental mismanagement—water diversion, acidification, and pollution. As noted
in Chapter 2, the Aral Sea fishery, which yielded 60,000 tons (close
to 130 million pounds) of fish per year as recently as 1960, is now
history. Rising salt content has left the sea biologically dead.[10]

A June 2001 report indicates that Russia's Azov Sea is also dying. Rising levels of salt, petroleum wastes, heavy metal pollution,
and radioactive materials are apparently involved. The commercial fish catch has dropped 97 percent over the last quarter-century. Many species are extinct. As one commentator noted, the Sea
of Azov has become "a body of water that cannot support either
life within it or the lives of the people who live around it."[11]

Acidification of lakes from acid rain, largely from coal burning,
is also still a problem. Canada alone now counts 14,000 dead lakes.
And pollution is taking a toll on freshwater lakes, either destroying the fish or rendering them unsafe for human consumption. In
the United States, fish in some 50,000 freshwater lakes, streams,
and ponds contain levels of mercury that make them unsafe for
human consumption. Mercury from the smokestacks of coal-fired
power plants is largely responsible. (See Chapter 6.)[12]

Overfishing and pollution are not the only threats to the world's
seafood supply. The spawning grounds and nurseries of many
aquatic creatures are disappearing as coastal wetlands, mangrove
forests, and coral reefs are destroyed. In addition, the damming of
rivers is depriving many species of their spawning grounds. Other
rivers are drained dry, with the same effect. Still others are simply
too polluted for fish to survive.

Some 90 percent of oceanic fish rely on coastal wetlands, mangrove swamps, or rivers as spawning areas. Well over half the original area of mangrove forests in tropical and subtropical countries

has been lost. The disappearance of coastal wetlands in industrial countries is even greater. In Italy, whose coastal wetlands are the nurseries for many Mediterranean fisheries, the loss is a staggering 95 percent.[13]

Damage to coral reefs, a breeding ground for fish in tropical and subtropical waters, is also taking a toll. Between 1992 and 2000, the share of severely damaged reefs worldwide expanded from 10 percent to 27 percent. As the reefs deteriorate, so do the fisheries that depend on them.[14]

Oceanic fisheries face numerous threats, but it is overfishing that most directly threatens their survival. Oceanic harvests expanded as new technologies evolved, ranging from sonar for tracking schools of fish to vast driftnets that are collectively long enough to circle the earth many times over. "With more powerful boats and fish finders, we basically have the capacity to wipe fish out, and we are," warns Douglas Foy of the Conservation Law Foundation in New England.[15]

Commercial fishing is now largely an economics of today versus tomorrow. Governments are seeking to protect tomorrow's catches by forcing fishers to keep their ships idle; fishing communities are torn between the need for income today versus the future. Ironically, one reason for excess fleet capacity is long-standing government subsidies that provide large loans and favorable terms for investing in new boats and fishing gear. By 2000, however, these loans had become unsupportable as catches dwindled. Catch quotas kept many fishing boats at anchor during what used to be peak fishing months.[16]

Fishing subsidies were based on an unfounded belief that past trends in oceanic harvests could be projected into the future—that past growth meant future growth. The long-standing advice of FAO marine biologists, who had warned that marine harvests would someday reach a limit, was largely ignored.[17]

As long as there were more fish in the oceans than we could hope to catch, managing oceanic fisheries was a simple matter. But with many fisheries already collapsing, and others facing imminent collapse, the management challenge of allocating the catch among competing nations and protein-hungry populations is infinitely more difficult. Merely sustaining the existing catch will require new levels of cooperation among national governments.

Even among countries accustomed to working together, such as those in the European Union (EU), the challenge of negotiating catch limits at sustainable levels can be difficult. In April 1997, after prolonged negotiations, agreement was reached in Brussels to reduce the fishing capacity of EU fleets by 30 percent for endangered species, such as cod, herring, and sole in the North Sea, and by 20 percent for overfished stocks, such as cod in the Baltic Sea, the bluefin tuna, and swordfish off the Iberian peninsula. The good news was that the EU finally reached agreement on reducing the catch. The bad news was that these cuts were not sufficient to arrest the decline of the region's fisheries.[18]

In January 2001, the EU went further, announcing a ban on fishing for cod, haddock, and whiting during the 12-week spring spawning period. With the annual cod catch falling from 300,000 tons during the mid-1980s to 50,000 tons in 2000, this most recent step was a desperate effort to save the fishery. EU officials are all too aware that Canada's once-vast Newfoundland cod fishery has not recovered since collapsing in 1992, despite the total ban on fishing imposed then.[19]

When some fisheries collapse, it puts more pressure on those that are left. With restrictions on the overfished EU fishery, the heavily subsidized EU fishing fleet has turned to the west coast of Africa, buying licenses to fish off the coasts of Senegal, Mauritania, Morocco, Guinea-Bissau, and Cape Verde. They are competing for space there with fleets from Japan, South Korea, Russia, and China. For impoverished countries like Mauritania and Guinea-Bissau, income from fishing licenses can account for up to half of government revenue. Unfortunately for the Africans, their fisheries too are collapsing. Most countries lack the ships and radar to ensure compliance with fishing agreements in the 200-mile exclusive economic zones off their coasts that were granted by the 1979 Law of the Sea Treaty.[20]

Fisheries everywhere are facing the same fate. On the west coast of India, the fishery off the coast of Goa has grown by leaps and bounds as the mechanized fishing fleet has jumped from 10 boats in 1964 to 2,200 in 1998. Meanwhile, the annual catch increased from 17,000 tons to 95,000 tons—well beyond the estimated maximum sustainable yield of 71,000 tons. Unless the Indian government can quickly reduce the catch here to the sustainable level, this fishery too will collapse, depriving India's coastal population of a sorely needed source of protein.[21]

If the oceans cannot sustain a catch of more than 95 million tons and if world population continues to grow as projected, the oceanic fish catch per person—which has already declined 9 percent since it peaked in 1988—is likely to drop to 10 kilograms per person in 2050. The generation that came of age during World War II saw the fish catch per person double during their lifetimes. Their grandchildren, the children of today, may witness a one-third reduction.[22]

The bottom line is that the growing worldwide demand for seafood can no longer be satisfied from oceanic fisheries. If it is to be satisfied, it will be by expanding fish farming, which will further intensify the pressure on land resources. Once fish are put in ponds or cages, they have to be fed. (See Chapter 7.)

Forests Shrinking

At the beginning of the twentieth century, the earth's forested area was estimated at 5 billion hectares. Since then it has shrunk to 2.9 billion hectares—an area roughly double the world's cropland area. The remaining forests are rather evenly divided between tropical and subtropical forests in developing countries and temperate/boreal forests in industrial countries.[23]

Deforestation is caused by the growing demand for forest products and the growing conversion of forested land to agricultural uses. This forest loss is concentrated in developing countries. From 1990 to 1995, the loss in these nations averaged 13 million hectares a year, an area roughly the size of Kansas. Overall, this means that the developing world is losing 6.5 percent of its forests per decade. The industrial world is actually gaining up to an estimated 3.6 million hectares of forestland each year, principally from abandoned cropland that is returning to forests on its own, as in Russia, and the spread of commercial forestry plantations.[24]

Unfortunately, even these official FAO data do not reflect the gravity of the situation. For example, tropical forests that are clearcut or burned off rarely recover. They simply become wasteland or at best scrub forest, but they are still included in the official forestry numbers if they are not included in another land use category such as cropland or building construction. The World Resources Institute's Forest Frontiers Initiative issued a report in 1997 on the status of the world's forests. They note that "hidden behind such familiar statistics is an equally sobering reality. Of the forests that do remain standing, the vast majority are no more than small or highly disturbed pieces of the fully functioning ecosystems they once were." The report notes that only 40 percent of the world's remaining forest cover can be classified as frontier forest, which they define as "large, intact, natural forest systems relatively undisturbed and big enough to maintain all of their biodiversity, including viable populations of the wide-ranging species associated with each type."[25]

Use of each of the principal forest products—firewood, paper, and lumber—is expanding. Of the 3.28 billion cubic meters of wood harvested worldwide in 1999, over half was used for fuel. In developing countries, the share was far higher, nearly four fifths of the total. In industrial countries, roughly 14 percent of the wood harvested was used for fuel, much of it the waste wood used by pulp and paper mills to generate electricity and to provide process heat. Using the bark and small branches for fuel, some paper mills are energy self-sufficient.[26]

Deforestation to satisfy fuelwood demand is extensive in the Sahelian zone of Africa and the Indian subcontinent. As urban firewood demand surpasses the sustainable yield of nearby forests, the woods slowly retreat from the city in an ever larger circle, a process clearly visible from satellite photographs taken over time. As the circles enlarge, the transport costs of firewood increase, triggering the development of an industry in charcoal, a more concentrated form of energy with lower transportation costs.[27]

Logging also takes a heavy toll, as is evident in countries in Africa, the Caribbean, and the Pacific. In almost all cases, logging is done by foreign corporations more interested in maximizing the harvest of forest products on a one-time basis than in managing forests to maximize sustainable yield in perpetuity. Once a country's forests are totally clearcut, companies typically move on, leaving only devastation behind.[28]

Another loss of forests comes from clearing land for agriculture and plantations, usually by burning, a loss that is concentrated in the Brazilian Amazon and more recently in Borneo and Sumatra in Indonesia. After losing 97 percent of the Atlantic rainforest, Brazil is now destroying its Amazon rainforest. This huge forest, roughly the size of Europe, was largely intact until 1970. Since then, 14 percent of Brazil's rainforest has been lost. In 1999 alone, 17,000 square kilometers were deforested.[29]

The progressive loss of forest cover has both economic and environmental consequences. Economically, the countries that have lost their exportable supplies of forest products, such as Nigeria and the Philippines, are now net importers of forest products. Also lost are the jobs and income that their forest industries once provided.[30]

The environmental effects of deforestation are becoming all too visible. Scores of countries are suffering from disastrous flooding as a result of deforestation. In 1998, the Yangtze River basin, which has lost 85 percent of its original tree cover, experienced some of the worst flooding in its history. In 2000, Mozambique was partially inundated as the Limpopo overflooded its banks, taking thousands of lives and destroying homes and crops on an unprecedented scale. The Limpopo river basin, which has lost 99 percent of its original tree cover, will likely face many more such floods.[31]

While deforestation accelerates the flow of water back to the ocean, it also reduces the airborne movement of water to the interior. The world's forests are in effect conduits or systems for transporting water inland. Eneas Salati and Peter Vose, two Brazilian scientists writing in *Science*, observed that as moisture-laden air from the Atlantic moves westward across the Amazon toward the Andes, it carries moisture inland. As the air cools and this moisture is converted into rainfall, it waters the rainforest below. In a healthy rainforest, roughly one fourth of the rainfall runs off into rivers and back to the Atlantic Ocean. The other three fourths evaporates and is carried further inland, where the process is again repeated. It is this water cycling capacity of rainforests that brings water inland to the Amazon's vast western reaches.[32]

If the rainforest is burned off and planted to grass for cattle raising, then the cycling of rainfall is dramatically altered—three fourths of the rainfall runs off and returns to the sea the first time it falls, leaving little to be carried inland. As more and more of the Amazon is cleared for cattle ranching or farming or is degraded by loggers, the capacity of the rainforest to carry water inland diminishes. As a result, the western part of the forest begins to dry out, changing it into a dryland forest or even a savanna.[33]

The burning and cutting of the Amazonian rainforest could also affect agriculture in regions to the south. As the air masses moving inland from the Atlantic reach the Andes, they turn southward, carrying moisture with them. It is this moisture that provides part of the rainfall in the agricultural regions of southwestern Brazil, Paraguay, and northern Argentina. As the deforestation of the Amazon progresses, the flow of moisture to these farming areas will likely diminish. Efforts to boost farm output by clearing land in the eastern Amazon basin could reduce farm output in southwestern Brazil.[34]

A similar situation may be developing in Africa, where deforestation and land clearing are proceeding rapidly as the demand on firewood mounts and as logging firms clear large tracts of virgin forests. As the forest area shrinks, the amount of rainfall reaching the interior of Africa is diminishing. A comparable trend is unfolding in China. Wang Hongchang, a Fellow of the Chinese Academy of Social Sciences, cites deforestation in the southern and eastern provinces of China as a key reason for the rainfall decline in the country's northwest, the area where the dust bowl is forming.[35]

A number of countries now have total or partial bans on logging in primary forests, including Cambodia, China, India, New Zealand, the Philippines, Sri Lanka, Thailand, and Viet Nam. Additionally, about 3 million square kilometers, accounting for roughly 9 percent of the earth's remaining forest area, are set aside as parks or nature preserves or for other conservation reasons. In some cases, the forests that are set aside are carefully protected, but all too often these "paper parks" exist only in theory and in the meaningless laws that set them up.[36]

Rangelands Deteriorating

One tenth of the earth's land surface is cropland, but an area twice this size is rangeland—land that is too dry, too steeply sloping, or too infertile to sustain crop production. This area—one fifth of the earth's land surface, most of it semiarid—supports the world's 3.3 billion cattle, sheep, and goats. (See Table 3–1.) These livestock are ruminants, animals with complex digestive systems that enable them to convert roughage into beef, mutton, and milk.[37]

An estimated 180 million people worldwide make their living as pastoralists tending cattle, sheep, and goats. Many countries in Africa depend heavily on their livestock economies for food and employment. The same is true for large populations in the Middle East, Central Asia (including Mongolia), northwest China, and much of India. India, which has the world's largest concentration of ruminants, depends on cattle and water buffalo not only for

Table 3–1. *Domesticated Ruminants by Country, 2000*

Country	Cattle and Buffalo	Sheep and Goats
	(million head)	
Argentina	55	17
Australia	26	117
Bangladesh	24	35
Brazil	169	31
China	127	279
Ethiopia	35	39
France	20	11
India	313	181
Mexico	30	16
Nigeria	20	45
Pakistan	45	72
Russia	28	16
United Kingdom	11	45
United States	98	9
Other	509	868
World	1,510	1,780

Source: FAO, *FAOSTAT Statistics* Database, <apps.fao.org>, updated 2 May 2001.

milk but also for draft power and fuel.[38]

In other parts of the world, rangelands are exploited by large-scale commercial ranching. Australia, whose land mass is dominated by rangeland, has one of the world's largest sheep flocks of 117 million sheep—6 for each Australian. Grass-based livestock economies also predominate in Argentina, Brazil, Mexico, and Uruguay. And in the Great Plains of North America, lands that are not suited to growing wheat are devoted to grazing cattle.[39]

Although public attention often focuses on the role of feedlots in beef production, the world's beef and mutton are produced largely on rangeland. The share of the world's cattle, sheep, and goats in feedlots at any time is a tiny fraction of the vast numbers feeding on grass. Even in the United States, which has most of the world's feedlots, the typical steer is in a feedlot for only a matter of months. If rangelands deteriorate, so too will this forage-based segment of the world's livestock economy.

Beef and mutton tend to dominate meat consumption where grazing land is abundant relative to population size. Among the countries with high beef consumption per person are Argentina, with 69 kilograms per year (152 pounds); the United States, with 45 kilograms; Brazil, 39 kilograms; and Australia, 36 kilograms. In some countries with extensive grazing land, mutton looms large in the diet, as in New Zealand with 25 kilograms, Australia 14 kilograms, and Kazakhstan 7 kilograms.[40]

These same ruminants that are uniquely efficient at converting roughage into meat and milk for human consumption are also a source of leather and wool. The world's leather goods and woolen industries, the livelihood for millions, depend on rangelands for their raw materials.

Worldwide, almost half of all grasslands are lightly to moderately degraded and 5 percent are severely degraded. The excessive pressure on grasslands, not unlike that on oceanic fisheries, afflicts industrial and developing countries alike. A survey of the U.S. public grazing lands managed by the Bureau of Land Management in 2000, for example, showed that only 36 percent of native public rangelands have forage that is in good or excellent condition, with most of the remainder of fair or poor quality.[41]

Although the data for grassland degradation are sparse, the problem is highly visible throughout Africa, where livestock numbers have tracked the growth in human numbers. In 1950, 238 million Africans relied on 273 million livestock. By 2000, there were 794 million people and 680 million livestock.[42]

In this continent where grain is scarce, 230 million cattle, 241 million sheep, and 209 million goats are supported almost entirely by grazing and browsing. The number of livestock, a cornerstone of the economy everywhere except in the tsetse-fly belt (roughly the western Congo Basin), often exceeds grassland carrying capacity by half or more. A study that charted the mounting pressures on grasslands in nine southern African countries found that the capacity to sustain livestock is diminishing.[43]

Iran—one of the most populous countries in the Middle East, with 70 million people—illustrates the pressures facing that region. With more than 8 million cattle and 81 million sheep and goats— the source of wool for its fabled rug-making industry—Iran is faced with the deterioration of its rangelands because of overstocking. In a country where the sheep and goats outnumber humans, mutton consumption looms large in the diet. However, with rangelands now being pushed to their limits and beyond, the current livestock population may not be sustainable.[44]

China faces similarly difficult challenges. In northwestern China, the buildup in livestock since the economic reforms in 1978 is destroying vast areas of grassland. Since then, livestock numbers have increased dramatically. In Gonge County, for example, in eastern Qinghai Province, the number of sheep that the local grasslands can support is estimated at 3.7 million, but by the end of 1998, the region's flock had reached 5.5 million—far beyond its carrying capacity. The result is fast-deteriorating grassland, desertification, and in some locations the creation of sand dunes. Erik Eckholm, writing in the *New York Times*, reports that "the rising sands are part of a new desert forming here on the eastern edge of the Qinghai-Tibet Plateau, a legendary stretch once known for grasses reaching as high as a horse's belly and home for centuries to ethnic Tibetan herders."[45]

Fodder needs of livestock in nearly all developing countries now exceed the sustainable yield of rangelands and other forage resources. In India, the demand for fodder in 2000 was estimated at 700 million tons, while the sustainable supply totaled just 540 million tons. The National Land Use and Wastelands Development Council there reports that in states with the most serious land degradation, such as Rajasthan and Karnataka, fodder supplies satisfy only 50–80 percent of needs, leaving large numbers of emaciated, unproductive cattle. [46]

After mid-century, world beef and mutton production expanded much faster than population, climbing from 9 kilograms per person in 1950 to 13 kilograms in 1972. (See Figure 3–1.) Since then, however, the growth in world beef and mutton production has fallen behind that of population, dropping the per capita supply to 11 kilograms, a decline of about one fifth.[47]

Land degradation from overgrazing is taking a heavy economic toll in the form of lost livestock productivity. In the early stages of overgrazing, the costs show up as lower land productivity. But if the process continues, it destroys vegetation, leading to the erosion of soil and the eventual creation of wasteland. A U.N. assessment of the earth's dryland regions showed that livestock production lost from rangeland degradation exceeded $23 billion in 1990. (See Table 3–2.)[48]

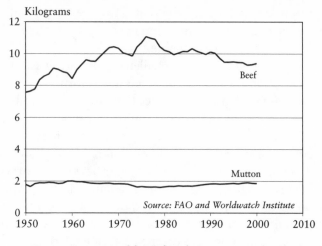

Figure 3–1. *World Beef and Mutton Production
Per Person, 1950–2000*

In Africa, the annual loss of rangeland productivity is estimated at $7 billion, more than the gross domestic product of Ethiopia. In Asia, livestock losses from rangeland degradation total over $8 billion. Together, Africa and Asia account for two thirds of the global loss.[49]

With most rangeland now being grazed at capacity or beyond, the prospect for substantial future gains in beef and mutton production from rangelands is not good. And given the inefficient conversion of grain to meat by cattle, substantial further gains in beef and mutton production may be possible only by feeding more crop residues. (See Chapter 7.)

Soils Eroding

After the earth was created, soil formed slowly over time from the weathering of rocks. It was this soil that supported early plant life on land. As plant life spread, the plants protected the soil from wind and water erosion, permitting it to accumulate and to support even more plant life. This symbiotic relationship facilitated an accumulation of topsoil until it could support a rich diversity not only of plants, but also of the animal life that depends on plants.

The thin mantle of topsoil, measured in inches over most of the earth, is the foundation of civilization. When earlier civilizations lost their productive topsoil from mismanagement and erosion, they

Table 3–2. *Livestock Production Loss from Land*
Degradation in Dryland Regions, 1990

Continent	Production Loss (billion dollars)
Africa	7.0
Asia	8.3
Australia	2.5
Europe	0.6
North America	2.9
South America	2.1
Total[1]	23.2

[1] Column does not add up to total due to rounding.
Source: See endnote 48.

crumbled as their food supply shrank. With an estimated 36 percent of the world's cropland now losing topsoil at a rate that is undermining its productivity, our food security is also at risk if this trend continues.[50]

As pressures to expand food production have climbed, farmers have been forced into marginal areas, plowing land that is too dry or too steeply sloping to sustain cultivation. At some point probably within the last century, the long-term accumulation of topsoil was reversed as erosion losses surpassed new soil formation, leading to a gradual depletion of this basic natural capital.

The United States, the world's breadbasket, has undergone two periods of extensive overplowing, each of which led to heavy losses of topsoil. The first occurred in the early 1930s when a severe multiyear drought led to extensive wind erosion in the southern Great Plains. The resulting environmental devastation not only gave the era its name, the Dust Bowl, but it triggered one of the largest internal migrations in U.S. history as droves of people left the southern Great Plains and headed west for California.[51]

After new agricultural practices were adopted in response to the Dust Bowl, such as planting windbreaks and strip-cropping land, with alternate-year fallowing, the soil was stabilized. But as demand for food began to climb rapidly after mid-century, and as grain prices reached record highs during the 1970s, farmers again began plowing from "fencerow to fencerow"—planting everything

in sight. By 1982, the United States was losing annually an estimated total of 3.08 billion tons of topsoil from its cropland.[52]

In contrast to the Dust Bowl, when wind erosion in the Great
Plains was the problem, this time it was mostly water erosion in
the Corn Belt. In states such as Iowa, with its rolling farmland,
farmers were losing almost 20 tons of topsoil per hectare each year
from water erosion. A dozen U.S. studies analyzing the effect of
erosion on land productivity found that losing an inch of topsoil
reduced corn and wheat yields an average of 6 percent. With nature needing centuries to form an inch of topsoil, current losses are
irreversible if time horizons are measured on a human time-scale.[53]

One consequence of overplowing is that countries eventually
have to pull back and reduce the harvested area. Some have done
this through carefully designed programs to convert highly erodible cropland back into grassland or forests. For example, the U.S.
Conservation Reserve Program (CRP) launched in 1985 was designed to simultaneously control surplus production and conserve
soil by retiring the most erodible land. Initiated and supported by
environmental groups, the program encouraged farmers to take
their highly erodible land out of production by providing government payments under 10-year contracts to plant the land in grass
or trees.[54]

Within five years, U.S. farmers had converted nearly 15 million
hectares of cropland, roughly 10 percent of the national total, to
grassland. This reduced excessive soil erosion nationwide by some
40 percent, helping to enhance food security for the entire world.
The nonmarket benefits from soil erosion reduction and the provision of habitat by the CRP between 1985 and 2000 are estimated
to exceed $1.4 billion.[55]

The Soviet Union overexpanded its plowing with the Virgin
Lands Project between 1954 and 1960. In an effort to boost farm
output and become an agricultural superpower, the Soviets plowed
up vast areas of grassland in Central Asia, an effort centered in
Kazakhstan. During this period, the increase in wheat area in
Kazakhstan was equal to the entire wheat area of Canada and
Australia combined.[56]

Unfortunately, not all of this land could sustain cultivation. Much
of the wheatland of Kazakhstan, a semiarid country, has eroded to
the point where it can no longer support cropping. After the grain
area reached 25 million hectares by 1960, it held there until 1984

or so, when it started shrinking as productivity fell and the less productive land was abandoned. By 2001, it had dropped to 12 million hectares. (See Figure 3–2.) Although this loss may have surprised the political leaders in Moscow who engineered the expansion in the 1950s, it did not surprise the soil scientists at the Institute of Soil Management in Alma Alta, who pointed out in 1994 that grain cultivation could be sustained on only half the area originally plowed. Even those estimates may prove to be overly optimistic.[57]

Whether topsoil loss, declining yields, and the abandonment of cropland in Kazakhstan can be arrested remains to be seen. Even the grainland still being farmed yields less than 1 ton of wheat per hectare—a fraction of the 7 tons per hectare in France, the leading wheat producer in Western Europe.[58]

If soil erosion proceeds too far, it can convert land to desert, becoming wasteland. At an intermediate stage of degradation, it can be returned to grassland, as in Kazakhstan, retaining some productive value. If the intervention comes early enough in the decline cycle, the land can be saved by managing it responsibly, as was the case during the Dust Bowl period. Or the land can be systematically retired and converted to grassland or woodland. Yet for many developing countries, where populations have doubled or even tripled over the last half-century, this is not always an option.

In the majority of developing countries, the growing demand

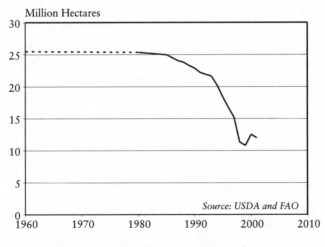

Figure 3–2. *Total Grain Harvested Area*
for Kazakhstan, 1960–2001

for food has forced agriculture onto marginal lands. In China, for instance, a doubling of population since 1950 combined with record rises in income since 1980 have nearly tripled the demand for grain.[59]

China's loss of cropland to the construction of factories, roads, and expanding cities, particularly in the prosperous coastal provinces, led to mounting concern in Beijing about the country's shrinking cropland area. The result was an attempt to offset these losses by plowing more land in the semiarid northwest. But the newly plowed land, much less productive, was highly vulnerable to wind erosion.[60]

As described at the beginning of this chapter, in recent years dust storms in China have become more frequent and more intense, often covering cities in the northeast with layers of dust. In May 2000, the *China Daily* reported, "Disastrous sand storms that hit several major cities recently in North China have alarmed the nation about the devastating consequences of the development strategy that turned a blind eye on the environment." The desertification now under way in northwest China aroused public concern as "dust-laden blasts began to bury villages, blow into cities, and suffocate residents."[61]

These new reports, coupled with scientific studies, indicate that a dust bowl is forming in northern China. The April 2001 dust storm mentioned earlier was one of the largest ever recorded. U.S. scientists in Colorado measured the dust in this storm above them in Boulder at altitudes up to 10,700 meters (35,000 feet). China is losing millions of tons of topsoil, a depletion of its natural capital that it can ill afford.[62]

In Africa, population growth and the degradation of cropland are also on a collision course. Rattan Lal, an internationally noted agronomist at Ohio State University's School of Natural Resources, has made the first estimate of yield losses due to soil erosion for the continent. Lal concluded that soil erosion and other forms of land degradation have reduced Africa's grain harvest by 8 million tons, or roughly 8 percent. Further, he expects the loss to climb to 16 million tons by 2020 if soil erosion continues unabated.[63]

Among the countries experiencing unusually heavy soil losses are Nigeria, Rwanda, and Zimbabwe. Nigeria, Africa's most populous nation, is suffering from extreme gully erosion. Lal reports gullies 5–10 meters deep and 10–100 meters wide. In January 2001, Alhaji Sanni Daura, Nigeria's Minister of Environment, announced that the country was losing some 500 square kilometers of crop-land to desertification each year. Daura is concerned that unless this desert encroachment can be reversed, Nigeria may soon face severe food shortages.[64]

On the northern edge of the Sahara, Algeria is also faced with the desertification of cropland. In December 2000, the agriculture ministry announced a four-year plan to halt the advancing desertification that they fear will soon threaten the fertile northern areas of the country. The plan is to convert the southernmost 20 percent of its grainland into tree crops, including fruit and olive orchards and vineyards. The government hopes that this barrier of permanent vegetation will halt the northward march of the Sahara. Out of desperation, Algeria, a country already dependent on imports for 40 percent of its grain, is willing to convert one fifth of its grain-producing land to tree crops in an attempt to protect the remaining four fifths.[65]

In East Africa, governments are facing a similar situation. Countries such as Ethiopia, Kenya, and Somalia are experiencing land degradation and cropland abandonment. Kenya's 1950 population of 6 million has increased to 31 million, putting unsustainable pressure on local forests, rangelands, and croplands. During the severe drought of 2000, the Masai, in an act of desperation, drove their cattle into Nairobi to feed on the grass in well-watered parks and residential lawns.[66]

The failure of Africa's governments to address the soil erosion threat effectively is depleting Africa's most essential natural capital—its soil. The next generation of farmers in Africa must try to feed not the 800 million people of today, but the projected 2 billion in the year 2025—and with far less topsoil.[67]

In Mexico, many of the 900,000 migrants who leave rural communities in arid and semiarid regions of the country each year are doing so because of desertification. Some of these environmental refugees end up in Mexican cities, others cross the northern border into the United States. U.S. analysts estimate that Mexico is forced to abandon 1,036 square kilometers (400 square miles) of farmland to desertification each year.[68]

The World Bank, citing studies for Costa Rica, Malawi, Mali, and Mexico, concludes that the gradual losses of agricultural productivity from soil erosion now translate into annual losses in farm output equal to 0.5–1.5 percent of these countries' gross domestic products. The toll of soil erosion on the earth's productivity can be seen in the abandoned villages in Ethiopia, where there is not enough soil left to support even subsistence-level agriculture. And in the former Soviet Union, land degradation, mostly from erosion, helped convert some 20 percent of the land in grain in 1977 either to soil-conserving forage crops, to alternate-year fallowing, or, where there was no effort to save the soil, to forest or wasteland by 1993.[69]

Unfortunately, many countries have not taken the initiative to reduce soil erosion and are paying a high price. For example, lost productivity on Africa's rain-fed cropland, virtually all from soil erosion, has reduced the annual harvest by an estimated $1.9 billion.[70]

The challenge is to arrest the excessive loss of topsoil on all land everywhere, reducing it to or below the level of new soil formation. The world cannot afford this loss of natural capital. If we cannot preserve the foundation of civilization, we cannot preserve civilization itself.

Species Disappearing

The archeological record shows five great extinctions since life began, each representing an evolutionary setback, a wholesale impoverishment of life on the earth. The last of these mass extinctions occurred some 65 million years ago, most likely when an asteroid collided with the earth, spewing vast amounts of dust and debris into the atmosphere. The resultant abrupt cooling obliterated the dinosaurs and at least one fifth of all other extant life forms.[71]

We are now in the early stage of the sixth great extinction. Unlike previous ones, which were caused by natural phenomena, this one is of human origin. For the first time in the earth's long history, one species has reached the point where it can eradicate much of life.

As various life forms disappear, they alter the earth's ecosystem, diminishing the services provided by nature, such as pollination, seed dispersal, insect control, and nutrient cycling. This loss of species is weakening the web of life, and if it continues it could tear huge gaps in its fabric, leading to irreversible and potentially unpredictable changes in the earth's ecosystem.

Species of all kinds are threatened by habitat destruction, principally through the loss of tropical rainforests. As we burn off the

Amazon rainforest, we are burning one of the great genetic store-houses, in effect one of the great libraries of genetic information. Our descendents may one day view the wholesale burning of this repository of genetic information much as we view the burning of the library in Alexandria in 48 BC.

Habitat alteration from rising temperatures, chemical pollution, or the introduction of exotic species can also decimate both plant and animal species. As human population grows, the number of species with which we share the planet shrinks. We cannot sepa-rate our fate from that of all life on the earth. If the rich diversity of life that we inherited is continually impoverished, eventually we will be as well.[72]

The share of birds, mammals, and fish that are vulnerable or in immediate danger of extinction is now measured in double digits: 12 percent of the world's nearly 10,000 bird species; 24 percent of the world's 4,763 mammal species; and an estimated 30 percent of all 25,000 fish species.[73]

When the World Conservation Union–IUCN released its new-est *Red List of Threatened Species* in 2000, it showed an increase in the "critically endangered" in all categories. For example, the number of critically endangered primates rose from 13 in 1996 to 19 in 2000. The number of freshwater species of turtles in this category, many of them in strong demand in Asia for food and for medicinal uses, increased from 10 to 24. For birds overall, the num-ber in the critically endangered category went from 168 in 1996 to 182 in 2000. Like many other trends of environmental decline, this one, too, is accelerating.[74]

Among mammals, the 600 known species of primates other than humans are most at risk. IUCN reports that nearly half of these species are threatened with extinction. Some 79 of the world's pri-mate species live in Brazil, where habitat destruction poses a par-ticular threat. Hunting, too, endangers many primate species. It is a threat principally in West and Central Africa, where the deterio-rating food situation is creating a lively market for "bushmeat."[75]

The bonobos of West Africa, a smaller version of the chimpan-zees of East Africa, may be our closest living relative both geneti-cally and in terms of social behavior. But this is not saving them from the bushmeat trade or the destruction of their habitat by log-gers. Concentrated in the dense forest of the Democratic Republic of the Congo, their numbers fell from an estimated 100,000 in

1980 to fewer than 10,000 by 1990. Today there are only 3,000 left. In less than one generation, 97 percent of the bonobos have disappeared.[76]

Birds, because of their visibility, are a useful indicator of the diversity of life. Of the 9,946 known bird species, roughly 70 percent are declining in number. Of these, an estimated 1,183 species are in imminent danger of extinction. Habitat loss and degradation affect 85 percent of all threatened bird species. For example, 61 bird species have become locally extinct with the extensive loss of lowland rainforest in Singapore. Some once-abundant species may have already dwindled to the point of no return. The great bustard, once widespread in Pakistan and surrounding countries, is being hunted to extinction. Ten of the world's 17 species of penguins are threatened or endangered, potential victims of global warming.[77]

The threat to fish may be the greatest of all, with nearly one third of all species—freshwater and saltwater—now facing possible extinction. Worldwide, the principal causes of this loss are habitat degradation in the form of pollution and the excessive extraction of water from rivers and other freshwater ecosystems. An estimated 37 percent of the fish species that inhabit the lakes and streams of North America are either extinct or in jeopardy. Ten North American freshwater fish species have disappeared during the last decade. In semiarid regions of Mexico, 68 percent of native and endemic fish species have disappeared. The situation may be even worse in Europe, where some 80 species of freshwater fish out of a total of 193 are threatened, endangered, or of special concern. Two thirds of the 94 fish species in South Africa need special protection to avoid extinction.[78]

Threatened species include both little known ones and those that are well known and highly valued. The harvest of the Caspian Sea sturgeon, for example, source of the world's most prized caviar, has fallen from 22,000 tons per year in the late 1970s to 1,100 tons in the late 1990s. Overfishing, much of it illegal, is responsible.[79]

Another indicator of the earth's environmental deterioration is the decline in various types of amphibians—frogs, toads, and salamanders. Widespread evidence that amphibian populations were disappearing initially surfaced at the first World Congress of Herpetology in Canterbury, England, in 1989. It was at this conference that scientists first realized that the seemingly isolated disappearances of amphibian populations were actually a worldwide phenomenon. Among the apparent contributing factors are the clearcutting of forests, the loss of wetlands, the introduction of alien species, changes in climate, increased ultraviolet radiation, acid rain, and pollution from both agriculture and industry. Spending their lives in both aquatic and terrestrial environments, amphibians are affected by changes in each, making them an unusually sensitive barometer of the earth's changing physical condition.[80]

The leatherback turtle, one of the most ancient animal species, and one that can reach a weight of 360 kilograms (800 pounds), is fast disappearing. Its numbers have dropped from 115,000 in 1982 to 34,500 in 1996. At the Playa Grande nesting colony on Costa Rica's west coast, the number of nesting females dropped from 1,367 in 1989 to 117 in 1999. James Spotila and colleagues, writing in *Nature*, warn that "if these turtles are to be saved, immediate action is needed to minimize mortality through fishing and to maximize hatchling production."[81]

One of the newer threats to species, and one that is commonly underestimated, is the introduction of alien species, which can alter local habitats and communities, driving native species to extinction. For example, non-native species are a key reason why 30 percent of the threatened bird species are on the IUCN *Red List*. For plants, alien species are implicated in 15 percent of all the listings. One consequence of globalization with its expanding international travel and commerce is that more and more species are being accidentally or intentionally brought into new areas where they have no natural predators.[82]

Efforts to save wildlife traditionally have centered on the creation of parks or wildlife reserves. Unfortunately, this approach may now be of limited value because of the nature of the principal threats to biological diversity. If we cannot stabilize population and climate, there is not an ecosystem on earth that we can save. To optimize resource use, this would argue for shifting some of the relatively abundant funds for parkland acquisition into efforts to stabilize population and climate.

The current species extinction rate is at least 1,000 times higher than the background rate, yet no one knows how many plant and animal species there are today, much less how many there were a half-century ago, when the explosion in human economic activity began. Current estimates range from 6 million species up to 20 million, with the best working estimates falling between 13 million and 14 million. We can measure losses where we have a complete inventory of species, as with birds, but with insects, where the species number in the millions, only a fraction of the species have been identified, described, and cataloged.[83]

Synergies and Surprises

One concern of environmental scientists is that some trends of environmental degradation will reinforce each other, accelerating the process. Chris Bright of Worldwatch Institute has analyzed several of these synergistic relationships among environmental trends, both local and global. One such concern is with ice melting. When land is covered with ice and snow, much of the sunlight reaching the earth's surface is simply bounced back into space by the high reflectivity of the surface. Once the snow and ice melts, the soil or the water beneath absorbs much of the energy in the sunlight, raising temperatures. The higher temperature leads to more melting, and the process begins to feed on itself in what scientists call a positive feedback loop.[84]

This is of particular concern in the Arctic Sea, where ice is melting, shrinking the reflective area. (See Chapter 2.) The synergistic relationship between rising temperatures and reduced reflectivity may now have reached the point of no return in the Arctic, suggesting a future when Arctic sea ice may disappear entirely during the summer months. This rise in temperature in the polar region may also help explain why the Greenland ice sheet is beginning to melt.[85]

Another set of synergies is threatening the earth's forests by fire. Intact, healthy rainforests do not burn, but forests weakened by logging or slash-and-burn farming become vulnerable to fire. The more they burn, the more vulnerable they become. The process, which feeds on itself, reinforces the global warming trend. As higher temperatures due to climate change lead to the drying out of forests and more burning, more carbon is emitted into the atmosphere. Rising atmospheric carbon dioxide levels accelerate the process of global warming. The trends of rising temperatures and burning forests begin to reinforce each other.[86]

One consequence of many interacting changes is that they can lead to developments that surprise even the scientific community.

One such event came in August 2000, as described in Chapter 2, when the icebreaker cruise ship discovered open water at the North Pole. Yet another recent surprise is the dieoff of coral reefs. Again, the reasons for the coral dieoff are complex, but a rise in surface water temperature may be responsible. What is surprising is that a temperature rise in sea surface water of less than 1 degree Celsius can lead to reef deaths. If the reefs continue to die, oceanic ecosystems will be altered, directly affecting the fisheries that depend on the coral reefs as nursery grounds.[87]

These are but a few of the surprises and synergies that have been encountered in recent years. No one knows how many the new century will bring. And unfortunately, synergistic trends such as those just described are often irreversible. As Chris Bright observes, "Nature has no reset buttons."[88]

II

THE NEW ECONOMY

4

The Shape of the Eco-Economy

In March 2000, at a briefing on *State of the World 2000* for World Bank staff, I noted that proposed projects should help build an economy that is environmentally sustainable, not one that self-destructs. In response, someone said that the Bank always does an environmental assessment of its projects. But that's the problem, I replied. Environmental scientists are assessing the effects of projects *after* economists have decided which investments to make. At best, the scientists can suggest steps to ameliorate the environmental damage from the projects selected by economists.

What are the odds that an economist not trained in ecology will independently design projects that collectively will build an economy that is environmentally sustainable? Not very high. The same could be said of all leading economic decisionmakers—corporate planners, government policymakers, and investment bankers.

As noted in Chapter 1, an economy is sustainable only if it respects the principles of ecology. These principles are as real as those of aerodynamics. If an aircraft is to fly, it has to satisfy certain principles of thrust and lift. So, too, if an economy is to sustain progress, it must satisfy the basic principles of ecology. If it does not, it will decline and eventually collapse. There is no middle ground. An economy is either sustainable or it is not.

Today's global economy has been shaped by market forces, not by the principles of ecology. Unfortunately, by failing to reflect the full costs of goods and services, the market provides misleading information to economic decisionmakers at all levels. This has created a distorted economy that is out of sync with the earth's ecosystem—an economy that is destroying its natural support systems.

The market does not recognize basic ecological concepts of sustainable yield nor does it respect the balances of nature. For example, it pays no attention to the growing imbalance between carbon emissions and nature's capacity to fix carbon, much less to the role of burning fossil fuels in creating the imbalance. For most economists, a rise in carbon dioxide (CO_2) levels is of little concern. For an ecologist, such a rise—driven by the use of fossil fuels—is a signal to shift to other energy sources in order to avoid rising temperatures, melting ice, and rising sea level.

An eco-economy is one that satisfies our needs without jeopardizing the prospects of future generations to meet their needs, as the Brundtland Commission pointed out nearly 15 years ago. The purpose of this chapter is to provide a sense of what an eco-economy will look like. It also offers some sense of the scope of this change. It is not a trivial undertaking.[1]

Ecology Over Economics

Ecologists understand the ecological processes that support life on earth. They understand the fundamental role of photosynthesis, the concept of sustainable yield, the role of nutrient cycles, the hydrological cycle, the sensitive role of climate, and the intricate relationship between the plant and animal kingdom. They know that the earth's ecosystems supply services as well as goods and that the former are often more valuable than the latter.

A sustainable economy respects the sustainable yield of the ecosystems on which it depends: fisheries, forests, rangelands, and croplands. A particular fishery can sustain a catch of a certain size, but if the demands on the fishery exceed the sustainable yield by even the smallest amount—say, 2 percent a year—the fish stocks will begin to shrink and will eventually disappear. As long as the harvest does not exceed the sustainable yield, it can be sustained in perpetuity. The same is true for forests and rangelands.

Nature also relies on balances. These include balances between soil erosion and new soil formation, between carbon emissions and carbon fixation, and between trees dying and trees regenerating.

Nature depends on cycles to maintain life. In nature, there are no linear flow-throughs, no situations where raw materials go in one end and garbage comes out the other. In nature, one organism's waste is another's sustenance. Nutrients are continuously cycled. This system works. Our challenge is to emulate it in the design of the economy.

Ecologists appreciate the role of photosynthesis, the process by which plants convert solar energy into the biochemical energy that supports life on the earth. Anything that reduces the photosynthetic product, such as desertification, the paving of productive land, or the acidification of lakes by acid rain, reduces the productivity of the earth in the most fundamental sense.

Despite this long-standing body of ecological knowledge, national governments have expanded economic activity with little regard for sustainable yields or the fragile balances in nature. Over the last half-century, the sevenfold expansion of the global economy has pushed the demand on local ecosystems beyond the sustainable yield in country after country. The fivefold growth in the world fish catch since 1950 has pushed the demand of most oceanic fisheries past their ability to produce fish sustainably. The sixfold growth in the worldwide demand for paper is shrinking the world's forests. The doubling of the world's herds of cattle and flocks of sheep and goats since 1950 is damaging rangelands, converting them to desert.[2]

An ecologist not only recognizes that the services provided by ecosystems may sometimes be worth more than the goods, but that the value of services needs to be calculated and incorporated into market signals if they are to be protected. Although calculating services is not a simple matter, any reasonable estimate is far better than assuming that the costs are zero, as is now the case. For example, a forest in the upper reaches of a watershed may provide services such as flood control and the recycling of rainfall inland that are several times more valuable than its timber yield. Unfortunately, market signals do not reflect this, because the loggers who are cutting the trees do not bear the costs of the reduction in services. National economic policies and corporate strategies are based largely on market signals. The clearcutting of a forest may be profitable for a logging firm, but it is economically costly to society.

Another major failure of the market to provide reliable information comes when governments subsidize the depletion of resources or environmentally destructive activities. (See also Chapter 11.) For example, over several decades the U.S. Forest Service used taxpayer money to build roads into national forests so that logging companies could clearcut forests. This not only artificially lowered the costs of lumber and paper, it led to flooding, soil erosion, and the silting of streams and rivers. In the Pacific Northwest, it destroyed highly productive salmon fisheries. And all this destruction was underwritten by taxpayers.[3]

In a world where the demands of the economy are pressing against the limits of natural systems, relying on distorted market signals to guide investment decisions is a recipe for disaster. Historically, for example, when the supply of fish was inadequate, the price would rise, encouraging investment in additional fishing trawlers. When there were more fish in the sea than we could ever hope to catch, the market worked well. Today, with the fish catch often exceeding the sustainable yield, investing in more trawlers in response to higher prices will simply accelerate the collapse of these fisheries.

A similar situation exists with other natural systems, such as aquifers, forests, and rangelands. Once the climbing demand for water surpasses the sustainable yield of aquifers, the water tables begin to fall and wells go dry. The market says drill deeper wells. Farmers engage in a competitive orgy of well drilling, chasing the water table downward. On the North China Plain, where 25 percent of the country's grain is produced, this process is under way. In Hebei Province, data for 1999 show 36,000 wells, mostly shallower ones, being abandoned during the year as 55,000 new, much deeper wells were drilled. In Shandong Province, 31,000 were abandoned and 68,000 new wells were drilled.[4]

In an eco-economy, by definition one that respects the principles of ecology, drilling additional wells would be banned once a water table showed signs of falling. Instead of spending money to dig deeper wells, investments would be channeled into measures to boost water efficiency and to stabilize population in order to bring water use into balance with the sustainable supply.

Evidence is accumulating that our global economy is slowly undermining itself on several fronts. If we want economic progress to continue, we have little choice but to systematically restructure the global economy in order to make it environmentally sustainable.

A Monumental Undertaking

Converting our economy into an eco-economy is a monumental undertaking. There is no precedent for transforming an economy shaped largely by market forces into one shaped by the principles of ecology.

The scale of projected economic growth outlines the dimensions of the challenge. The growth in world output of goods and services from $6 trillion in 1950 to $43 trillion in 2000 has caused environmental devastation on a scale that we could not easily have imagined a half-century ago. If the world economy continued to expand at 3 percent annually, the output of goods and services would increase fourfold over the next half-century, reaching $172 trillion.[5]

Building an eco-economy in the time available requires rapid systemic change. We will not succeed with a project here and a project there. We are winning occasional battles now, but we are losing the war because we do not have a strategy for the systemic economic change that will put the world on a development path that is environmentally sustainable.

Although the concept of environmentally sustainable development evolved a quarter-century ago, not one country has a strategy to build an eco-economy—to restore carbon balances, to stabilize population and water tables, and to conserve its forests, soils, and diversity of plant and animal life. We can find individual countries that are succeeding with one or more elements of the restructuring, but not one that is progressing satisfactorily on all fronts.

Nevertheless, glimpses of the eco-economy are clearly visible in some countries. For example, 31 countries in Europe, plus Japan, have stabilized their population size, satisfying one of the most basic conditions of an eco-economy. Europe has stabilized its population within its food-producing capacity, leaving it with an exportable surplus of grain to help fill the deficits in developing countries. Furthermore, China—the world's most populous country—now has lower fertility than the United States and is moving toward population stability.[6]

Among countries, Denmark is the eco-economy leader. It has stabilized its population, banned the construction of coal-fired power plants, banned the use of nonrefillable beverage containers, and is now getting 15 percent of its electricity from wind. In addition, it has restructured its urban transport network; now 32 percent of all trips in Copenhagen are on bicycle. Denmark is still not close to balancing carbon emissions and fixation, but it is moving in that direction.[7]

Other countries have also achieved specific goals. A reforestation program in South Korea, begun more than a generation ago, has blanketed the country's hills and mountains with trees. Costa Rica has a plan to shift entirely to renewable energy by 2025. Iceland, working with a consortium of corporations led by Shell and DaimlerChrysler, plans to be the world's first hydrogen-powered economy.[8]

So we can see pieces of the eco-economy emerging, but systemic change requires a fundamental shift in market signals, signals that respect the principles of ecological sustainability. Unless we are prepared to shift taxes from income to environmentally destructive activities, such as carbon emissions and the wasteful use of water, we will not succeed in building an eco-economy. (See Chapter 11.)

Restoring the balances of nature is a huge undertaking. For energy, it depends on shifting from a carbon-based economy to a hydrogen-based one. Even the most progressive oil companies, such as BP and Royal Dutch Shell, that are talking extensively about building a solar/hydrogen energy economy are still investing overwhelmingly in oil, with funds going into climate-benign sources accounting for a minute share of their investment.[9]

Reducing soil erosion to the level of new soil formation will require changes in farming practices. In some situations, it will mean shifting from intense tillage to minimum tillage or no tillage. Agroforestry will loom large in an eco-economy.

Restoring forests that recycle rainfall inland and control flooding is itself a huge undertaking. It means reversing decades of tree cutting and land clearing with forest restoration, an activity that will require millions of people planting billions of trees.

Building an eco-economy will affect every facet of our lives. It will alter how we light our homes, what we eat, where we live, how we use our leisure time, and how many children we have. It will give us a world where we are a part of nature, instead of estranged from it.

Restructuring the Economy

An economy that is in sync with the earth's ecosystem will contrast profoundly with the polluting, disruptive, and ultimately self-destructing economy of today—the fossil-fuel-based, automobile-centered, throwaway economy. One of the attractions of the western economic model is that it has raised living standards for one fifth of humanity to a level that our ancestors could not have dreamed of, providing a remarkably diverse diet, unprecedented levels of material consumption, and unimagined physical mobility. But unfortunately it will not work over the long term even for the affluent one fifth, much less for the entire world.

Among the key economic sectors—energy, materials, and food—the most profound changes will be in energy and materials. It is difficult to imagine a more fundamental sectoral restructuring than that in the energy sector as it shifts from oil, coal, and natural gas to wind, solar cells, and geothermal energy.

With materials, the change is not so much in the materials used as in the structure of the sector itself as it shifts from the linear economic model, where materials go from the mine or forest to the landfill, to the reuse/recycle model. In this closed loop system, which emulates nature, recycling industries will largely replace extraction industries.

In the food sector, the big changes are not in structure, but in the way the sector is managed. The challenge here is to better manage natural capital, to stabilize aquifers by increasing water productivity, and to conserve topsoil by altering agricultural practices. And above all else, it means sustaining the rise in land productivity in order to avoid clearing more forests for food production.

We can now see what an eco-economy looks like. Instead of being run on fossil fuels, it will be powered by sources of energy that derive from the Sun, such as wind and sunlight, and by geothermal energy from within the earth. (See Chapter 5.) It will be hydrogen-based instead of carbon-based. Cars and buses will run on fuel-cell engines powered by electricity produced with an electrochemical process using hydrogen as the fuel instead of internal combustion engines. With fuel cells powered by hydrogen, there is no climate-disrupting CO_2 or noxious health-damaging pollutants; only water is emitted.

In the new economy, atmospheric CO_2 levels will be stable. In contrast to today's energy economy, where the world's reserves of oil and coal are concentrated in a handful of countries, energy sources in the eco-economy will be widely dispersed—as widely distributed as sunlight and wind. The heavy dependence of the entire world on one geographic region—the Middle East—for much of its energy will likely decline as the new climate-benign energy sources and fuel-cell engines take over.

The energy economy will be essentially a solar/hydrogen economy with various energy sources deriving from the Sun used either directly for heating and cooling or indirectly to produce electricity. Wind-generated electricity, which is likely to be the lowest-cost source of energy, will be used to electrolyze water, producing hydrogen. This provides a means of both storing and transporting wind energy. Initially, existing natural gas pipelines will be used to distribute hydrogen. But over the longer term, both natural gas and oil pipeline networks can be adapted to carry hydrogen as the world shifts from a carbon-based to a hydrogen-based economy.

The transport systems of cities will change—indeed, they already are. Instead of the noisy, congested, polluting, auto-centered transport systems of today, cities will have rail-centered transport systems and they will be bicycle- and pedestrian-friendly, offering more mobility, more exercise, cleaner air, and less frustration. (See Chapter 9.) Historians looking back on the current system will likely see it as a dark age in urban evolution.

Urban transport systems will have the same components as they do today: automobile, rail, bus, and bicycle. The difference will be in the mix. As more and more city planners recognize the inherent conflict between the automobile and the city, new, cleaner, more efficient transport systems will develop. Urban personal mobility will increase as automobile use and traffic congestion decline.

The materials sector of the eco-economy will look far different too. (See Chapter 6.) Mature industrial economies with stable populations can operate largely by recycling the materials already in use. The materials loop will be closed, yielding no waste and nothing for the landfills.

One of the keys to reversing the deforestation of the earth is paper recycling; the potential here has been only partly realized. A second key is developing alternative energy sources that will reduce the amount of wood used as fuel. In addition, boosting the efficiency of wood burning can measurably lighten the load on forests.

Another promising option is the use of carefully designed, ecologically managed, and highly productive tree plantations. A small area devoted to plantations may be essential to protecting forests at the global level. Plantations can yield several times as much wood per hectare as can a natural forest.

In the economy of the future, the use of water will be in balance with supply. Water tables will be stable, not falling. The economic restructuring will be designed to raise water productivity in every facet of economic activity.

In this environmentally sustainable economy, harvests from oceanic fisheries, a major source of animal protein in the human diet, will be reduced to the sustainable yield. Additional demand will be satisfied by fish farming. This is, in effect, an aquatic version of the same shift that occurred during the transition from hunting and gathering to farming. The freshwater, herbivorous carp polyculture on which the Chinese rely heavily for their vast production of farmed fish offers an ecological model for the rest of the world.[10]

A somewhat similar situation exists for rangelands. One of the keys to alleviating the excessive pressure on rangelands is to feed livestock the crop residues that are otherwise being burned for fuel or for disposal. This trend, already well under way in India and China, may hold the key to stabilizing the world's rangelands. (See Chapter 7.)[11]

And finally, the new economy will have a stable population. Over the longer term, the only sustainable society is one in which couples have an average of two children.

New Industries, New Jobs

Describing the eco-economy is obviously a somewhat speculative undertaking. In the end, however, it is not as open-ended as it might seem because the eco-economy's broad outlines are defined by the principles of ecology.

The purpose of describing the restructuring of the overall economy before turning to chapters on the key sectors is to give a sense of the dynamics at work. The specific trends and shifts described are not projections of what will happen, though the term "will" is often used here for the sake of efficiency. No one knows if these shifts "will" in fact occur, but we do know that something like this is needed if we are to build an eco-economy.

What is not so clear is how ecological principles will translate into economic design since, for example, each country has a unique combination of renewable energy sources that will power its economy. Some countries may draw broadly on all their renewable energy sources, while others may concentrate heavily on one that is particularly abundant, say wind or solar energy. A country with a wealth of geothermal energy may choose to structure its energy economy around this subterranean energy source.

Building a new economy involves phasing out old industries, restructuring existing ones, and creating new ones. World coal use is already being phased out, dropping 7 percent since peaking in 1996. It is being replaced by efficiency gains in some countries; by natural gas in others, such as the United Kingdom and China; and by wind power in others such as Denmark.[12]

The automobile industry faces a major restructuring as it changes power sources, shifting from the gasoline-powered internal combustion engine to the hydrogen-powered fuel cell engine. This shift from the explosive energy that derives from igniting gasoline vapor to a chemical reaction that generates electricity will require both a retooling of engine plants and the retraining of automotive engineers and automobile mechanics.

The new economy will also bring major new industries, ones that either do not yet exist or that are just beginning. Wind electricity generation is one such industry. (See Table 4–1.) Now in its embryonic stage, it promises to become the foundation of the new energy economy. Millions of turbines soon will be converting wind into electricity, becoming part of the global landscape. In many countries, wind will supply both electricity and, through the electrolysis of water, hydrogen. Together, electricity and hydrogen can meet all the energy needs of a modern society.

In effect, there will be three new subsidiary industries associated with wind power: turbine manufacturing, installation, and maintenance. Manufacturing facilities will be found in scores of countries, industrial and developing. Installation, which is basically a construction industry, will be more local in nature. Maintenance, since it is a day-to-day activity, will be a source of ongoing local employment.

The robustness of the wind turbine industry was evident in 2000 and 2001 when high tech stocks were in a free fall worldwide. While high tech firms as a group were performing poorly, sales of wind turbines were climbing, pushing the earnings of turbine manu-

Table 4–1. *Examples of Eco-Economy Industries*

Industry	Description
Fish farming	Although growth will slow from the double-digit rate of the last decade, rapid expansion is likely to continue.
Bicycle manufacturing	Because bicycles are nonpolluting, quiet, require little parking space, and provide much-needed exercise in exercise-deprived societies, they will become increasingly common.
Wind farm construction	Wind electric generation, including off-shore wind farms, will grow rapidly over the next few decades, until wind is supplying most of the world's electricity.
Wind turbine manufacturing	Today the number of utility-scale wind turbines is measured in the thousands, but soon it will be measured in the millions, creating an enormous manufacturing opportunity.
Hydrogen generation	As the transition from a carbon-based to a hydrogen-based energy economy progresses, hydrogen generation will become a huge industry as hydrogen replaces coal and oil.
Fuel cell manufacturing	As fuel cells replace internal combustion engines in automobiles and begin generating power in buildings, a huge market will evolve.
Solar cell manufacturing	For many of the 2 billion people living in rural Third World communities who lack electricity, solar cells will be the best bet for electrification.
Light rail construction	As people tire of the traffic congestion and pollution associated with the automobile, cities in industrial and developing countries alike will be turning to light rail to provide mobility.
Tree planting	As efforts to reforest the earth gain momentum and as tree plantations expand, tree planting will emerge as a leading economic activity.

facturers to the top of the charts. Continuing growth of this sector is expected for the next few decades.

As wind power emerges as a low-cost source of electricity and a mainstream energy source, it will spawn another industry—hydrogen production. Once wind turbines are in wide use, there will be a large, unused capacity during the night when electricity use drops. With this essentially free electricity, turbine owners can turn on the hydrogen generators, converting the wind power into hydrogen, ideal for fuel cell engines. Hydrogen generators will start to replace oil refineries. The wind turbine will replace both the coal mine and the oil well. (See Table 4–2.) Both wind turbines and hydrogen generators will be widely dispersed as countries take advantage of local wind resources.

Changes in the world food economy will also be substantial. (See Chapter 7.) Some of these, such as the shift to fish farming, are already under way. The fastest growing subsector of the world food economy during the 1990s was aquaculture, expanding at more than 11 percent a year. Fish farming is likely to continue to expand simply because of its efficiency in converting grain into animal protein.[13]

Even allowing for slower future growth in aquaculture, fish farm output will likely overtake beef production during this decade. Perhaps more surprising, fish farming could eventually exceed the oceanic fish catch. Indeed, for China—the world's leading consumer of seafood—fish farming already supplies two thirds of the seafood while the oceanic catch accounts for the other third.[14]

With this development comes the need for a mixed-feed industry, one analogous to that which provides the nutritionally balanced rations used by the poultry industry today. There will also be a need for aquatic ecologists, fish nutritionists, and marine veterinarians.

Another growth industry of the future is bicycle manufacturing and servicing. Because the bicycle is nonpolluting, frugal in its use of land, and provides the exercise much needed in sedentary societies, future reliance on it is expected to grow. As recently as 1965, the production of cars and bikes was essentially the same, but today more than twice as many bikes as cars are manufactured each year. Among industrial countries, the urban transport model being pioneered in the Netherlands and Denmark, where bikes are featured prominently, gives a sense of the bicycle's future role worldwide.[15]

Table 4–2. *Examples of Eco-Economy Sunset Industries*

Industry	Description
Coal mining	The 7 percent decline in world coal burning since it peaked in 1996 will continue in the years ahead.
Oil pumping	Projections based on shrinking oil reserves indicate production will peak and start declining in the next 5–20 years. Concern about global warming could bring the decline closer.
Nuclear power generation	Although public concern focuses on safety issues, it is the high cost that is ensuring the industry's decline.
Clearcut logging	The rapid spread in eco-labeling of forest products will likely force logging firms to change to sustainable harvesting or be driven out of business.
Manufacture of throwaway products	As efforts to close the materials cycle intensify, many throwaway products will be either banned or taxed out of existence.
Automobile manufacturing	As world population urbanizes, the conflict between the automobile and the city will intensify, reducing dependence on automobiles.

As bicycle use expands, interest in electrically assisted bikes is also growing. Similar to existing bicycles, except for a tiny battery-powered electric motor that can either power the bicycle entirely or assist elderly riders or those living in hilly terrain, its soaring sales are expected to continue climbing in the years ahead.

Yet another growth industry is raising water productivity. Just as the last half-century has been devoted to raising land productivity, the next half-century will be focused on raising water productivity. Virtually all societies will be turning to the management of water at the watershed level in order to manage available supply most efficiently. Irrigation technologies will become more efficient. Urban waste water recycling will become common. At present, water tends to flow into and out of cities, carrying waste with it. In the future, water will be used over and over, never discharged. Since water does not wear out, there is no limit to how long it can be used, as long as it is purified before reuse.

Another industry that will play a prominent role in the new economy, one that will reduce energy use, is teleconferencing. Increasingly for environmental reasons and to save time, individuals will be "attending" conferences electronically with both audio and visual connections. This industry involves developing the electronic global infrastructure, as well as the services, to make this possible. One day there will likely be literally thousands of firms organizing electronic conferences.

Restructuring the global economy will create not only new industries, but also new jobs—indeed, whole new professions and new specialties within professions. (See Table 4–3.) For example, as wind becomes an increasingly prominent energy source, there will be a need for thousands of wind meteorologists to analyze potential wind sites, monitor wind speeds, and select the best sites for wind farms. The better the data on wind resources, the more efficient the industry will become.

Closely related to this new profession will be the wind engineers who design the wind turbines. Again, the appropriate turbine size and design can vary widely according to site. It will be the job of wind engineers to tailor designs to specific wind regimes in order to maximize electricity generation.

Environmental architecture is another fast-growing profession. Among the signposts of an environmentally sustainable economy are buildings that are in harmony with the environment. Environmental architects design buildings that are energy- and materials-efficient and that maximize natural heating, cooling, and lighting.

In a future of water scarcity, watershed hydrologists will be in demand. It will be their responsibility to understand the hydrological cycle, including the movement of underground water, and to know the depth of aquifers and determine their sustainable yield. They will be at the center of watershed management regimes.

As the world shifts from a throwaway economy, engineers will be needed to design products that can be recycled—from cars to computers. Once products are designed to be disassembled quickly and easily into component parts and materials, comprehensive recycling is relatively easy.

Technologies used in recycling are sometimes quite different from

Table 4–3. *Expanding Professions in an Eco-Economy*

Profession	Description
Wind meteorologists	Wind meteorologists will play a role in the new energy economy comparable to that of petroleum geologists in the old one.
Family planning midwives	If world population is to stabilize soon, literally millions of family planning midwives will be needed.
Foresters	Reforesting the earth will require professional guidance on what species to plant where and in what combination.
Hydrologists	As water scarcity spreads, the demand for hydrologists to advise on watershed management, water sources, and water efficiency will increase.
Recycling engineers	Designing consumer appliances so they can be easily disassembled and completely recycled will become an engineering specialty.
Aquacultural veterinarians	Until now, veterinarians have typically specialized in either large animals or small animals, but with fish farming likely to overtake beef production before the end of this decade, marine veterinarians will be in demand.
Ecological economists	As it becomes clear that the basic principles of ecology must be incorporated into economic planning and policymaking, the demand for economists able to think like ecologists will grow.
Geothermal geologists	With the likelihood that large areas of the world will turn to geothermal energy both for electricity and for heating, the demands for geothermal geologists will climb.
Environmental architects	Architects are learning the principles of ecology so they can incorporate them into the buildings in which we live and work.
Bicycle mechanics	As the world turns to the bicycle for transportation and exercise, bicycle mechanics will be needed to keep the fleet running.
Wind turbine engineers	With millions of wind turbines likely to be installed in the decades ahead, there will be strong worldwide demand for wind turbine engineers.

those used in producing from virgin raw materials. Within the U.S. steel industry, for example, where nearly 60 percent of all steel is produced from scrap, the technologies used differ depending on the feedstock. Steel manufactured in electric arc furnaces from scrap uses far less energy than traditional open-hearth furnaces using pig iron. It will be the responsibility of the recycling engineers to close the materials loop, converting the linear flow-through economy into a comprehensive recycling economy.[16]

In countries with a wealth of geothermal energy, it will be up to geothermal geologists to locate the best sites either for power plants or for tapping directly to heat buildings. Retraining petroleum geologists to master geothermal technologies is one way of satisfying the likely surge in demand for geothermal geologists.

If the world is to stabilize population sooner rather than later, it will need far more family planning midwives in Third World communities. This growth sector will be concentrated largely in developing countries, where millions of women lack access to family planning. The same family planning counselors who advise on reproductive health and contraceptive use can also play a central role in controlling the spread of HIV.

Another pressing need, particularly in developing countries, is for sanitary engineers who can design sewage systems not dependent on water, a trend that is already under way in some water-scarce countries. As it becomes clear that using water to wash waste away is a reckless use of a scarce resource, a new breed of sanitary engineers will be in wide demand. Washing waste away is even less acceptable today as marine ecosystems are overwhelmed by nutrient flows. Apart from the ecological disruption of a water-based disposal method, there are also much higher priorities in the use of water, such as drinking, bathing, and irrigation.

Yet another new specialty that is likely to expand rapidly in agriculture as productive farmland becomes scarce is agronomists who specialize in multiple cropping and intercropping. This requires an expertise both in the selection of crops that can fit together well in a tight rotation in various locales and in agricultural practices that facilitate multiple cropping.

History's Greatest Investment Opportunity

Restructuring the global economy so that economic progress can be sustained represents the greatest investment opportunity in history. As noted in Chapter 1, the conceptual shift is comparable to that of the Copernican Revolution in the sixteenth century. In scale, the Environmental Revolution is comparable to the Agricultural and Industrial Revolutions that preceded it.

The Agricultural Revolution involved restructuring the food economy, shifting from a nomadic life-style based on hunting and gathering to a settled life-style based on tilling the soil. Although agriculture started as a supplement to hunting and gathering, it eventually replaced it almost entirely. The Agricultural Revolution entailed clearing one tenth of the earth's land surface of either grass or trees so it could be plowed. Unlike the hunter-gatherer culture that had little effect on the earth, this new farming culture literally transformed the surface of the earth.[17]

The Industrial Revolution has been under way for two centuries, although in some countries it is still in its early stages. At its foundation was a shift in sources of energy from wood to fossil fuels, a shift that set the stage for a massive expansion in economic activity. Indeed, its distinguishing feature is the harnessing of vast amounts of fossil energy for economic purposes. While the Agricultural Revolution transformed the earth's surface, the Industrial Revolution is transforming the earth's atmosphere.

The additional productivity that the Industrial Revolution made possible unleashed enormous creative energies. It also gave birth to new life-styles and to the most environmentally destructive era in human history, setting the world firmly on a course of eventual economic decline.

The Environmental Revolution resembles the Industrial Revolution in that each is dependent on the shift to a new energy source. And like both earlier revolutions, the Environmental Revolution will affect the entire world.

There are differences in scale, timing, and origin among the three revolutions. Unlike the other two, the Environmental Revolution must be compressed into a matter of decades. The other revolutions were driven by new discoveries, by advances in technology, whereas this revolution is being driven more by our instinct for survival.

As noted earlier, there has not been an investment situation like this before. The amount that the world spends now each year on oil, the leading source of energy, provides some insight into how much it could spend on energy in the eco-economy. In 2000, the world used nearly 28 billion barrels of oil, some 76 million barrels per day. At $27 a barrel, this comes to $756 billion per year. How many wind turbines will it take to produce this much energy? How many solar rooftops? How many geothermal wells?[18]

One big difference between the investments in fossil fuels and those in wind power, solar cells, and geothermal energy is that the latter will supply energy in perpetuity. These "wells" will not run dry. If the money spent on oil in one year were invested in wind turbines, the electricity generated would be enough to meet one fifth of the world's needs.[19]

Investments in the infrastructure for the new energy economy, which would eventually have to be made as fossil fuels are depleted, will obviously be huge. These include the transmission lines that connect wind farms with electricity consumers, and the pipelines that link hydrogen supply sources with end-users. To a substantial degree, the infrastructure for the existing energy economy—the transmission lines for electricity and the pipelines for natural gas—can be used in the new energy economy as well. The local pipeline distribution network in various cities for natural gas can easily be converted to hydrogen.

For developing countries, the new energy sources promise to reduce dependence on imported oil, freeing up capital for investment in domestic energy sources. Although few countries have their own oil fields, all have wind and solar energy. In terms of economic expansion and job generation, these new energy technologies are a godsend.

Investments in energy efficiency are also likely to grow rapidly simply because they are so profitable. In virtually all countries, industrial and developing, saved energy is the cheapest source of new energy. Replacing inefficient incandescent light bulbs with highly efficient compact fluorescent lamps offers a rate of return that stock markets are unlikely to match.

There are also abundant investment opportunities in the food economy. It is likely that the world demand for seafood, for example, will increase at least by half over the next 50 years, and perhaps much more. If so, fish farming output—now 31 million tons a year—will roughly need to triple, as will investments in fish farming. Although aquaculture's growth is likely to slow from the 11 percent a year of the last decade, it is nonetheless likely to be robust, presenting a promising opportunity for future investment.[20]

A similar situation exists for tree plantations. At present, tree plantations cover some 113 million hectares. An expansion of these by at least half, along with a continuing rise in productivity, is likely to be needed both to satisfy future demand and to eliminate one of the pressures that are shrinking forests. This, too, presents a huge opportunity for investment.[21]

No sector of the global economy will be untouched by the Environmental Revolution. In this new economy, some companies will be winners and some will be losers. Those who anticipate the emerging eco-economy and plan for it will be the winners. Those who cling to the past risk becoming part of it.

5

Building the Solar/Hydrogen Economy

In May of 2001, the Bush White House released with great fanfare a 20-year plan for the U.S. energy economy. It disappointed many people because it largely overlooked the enormous potential for raising energy efficiency. It also overlooked the huge potential of wind power, which is likely to add more to U.S. generating capacity over the next 20 years than coal does. The plan was indicative of the problems some governments are having in fashioning an energy economy that is compatible with the earth's ecosystem.[1]

Prepared under the direction of Vice President Dick Cheney, the administration's plan centered on expanding production of fossil fuels, something more appropriate for the early twentieth century than the early twenty-first. It emphasized the role of coal, but the authors were apparently unaware that world coal use peaked in 1996 and has declined some 7 percent since then as other countries have turned away from this fuel. Even China, which rivals the United States as a coal-burning country, has reduced its coal use by an estimated 14 percent since 1996.[2]

The energy future that I see is very different from the one outlined in the Bush energy plan. For example, the plan noted that the 2 percent of U.S. electricity generation that today comes from renewable sources, excluding hydropower, would increase to 2.8 percent in 2020. But months before the Bush energy plan was released, the American Wind Energy Association (AWEA) was projecting a staggering 60-percent growth in U.S. wind-generating capacity in 2001. Worldwide, use of wind power alone has multiplied nearly fourfold over the last five years, a growth rate matched only by the computer industry.[3]

Although the Bush energy plan does not reflect it, the world energy economy is on the edge of a major transformation. Historically, the twentieth century was the century of fossil fuels. Coal, already well established as a major fuel source in 1900, was joined by oil when the automobile came on the scene. It was not until 1967, however, that oil finally replaced coal as the workhorse of the world energy economy. Natural gas gained in popularity during the closing decades of the century as concern about urban air pollution and global climate change escalated, moving ahead of coal in 1999.[4]

As the new century begins, the Sun is setting on the fossil fuel era. The last several decades have shown a steady shift from coal, the most polluting and climate-disrupting fossil fuel, to oil, which is somewhat less environmentally disruptive, and then to natural gas, the cleanest and least climate-disrupting of the three. It is this desire for clean, climate-benign fuels—not the depletion of fossil fuels—that is driving the global transition to the solar/hydrogen age.[5]

In addition to world coal use peaking in 1996, oil production is expected to peak either in this decade or the next. Natural gas use will keep expanding somewhat longer because of its generous reserves and its popularity as a clean-burning, carbon-efficient fuel. Because it is a gas, it is also the ideal fuel for the transition from a carbon-based energy economy to one based on hydrogen. If it keeps expanding at 2 percent or so a year, as it has for the last decade, natural gas use will require the continued construction of pipelines and storage facilities—an infrastructure that can one day easily be adapted for hydrogen.[6]

Even the oil companies are now beginning to recognize that the time has come for an energy transition. After years of denying any link between fossil fuel burning and climate change, John Browne, the chief executive officer of British Petroleum (BP) announced his new position in a historic speech at Stanford University in May

1997. "My colleagues and I now take the threat of global warming seriously," said Browne. "The time to consider the policy dimensions of climate change is not when the link between greenhouse gases and climate change is conclusively proven, but when the possibility cannot be discounted and is taken seriously by the society of which we are a part. We in BP have reached that point." In February 1999, ARCO chief executive Michael Bowlin said at an energy conference in Houston, Texas, that the beginning of the end of the age of oil was in sight. He went on to discuss the need to shift from a carbon-based energy economy to a hydrogen-based one.[7]

Seth Dunn writes in *World Watch* magazine that a consortium of corporations led by Shell Hydrogen and DaimlerChrysler reached an agreement in 1999 with the government of Iceland to make that country the world's first hydrogen-powered economy. Shell is interested because it wants to begin developing its hydrogen production and distribution capacity, and DaimlerChrysler expects to have the first fuel cell–powered automobile on the market. Shell plans to open its first chain of hydrogen stations in Iceland.[8]

The signs of restructuring the global energy economy are unmistakable. Events are moving far faster than would have been expected even a few years ago, driven in part by the mounting evidence that the earth is indeed warming up and that the burning of fossil fuels is responsible.[9]

The Energy Efficiency Base

When the new Bush energy plan was announced, many were surprised at the near-exclusive emphasis on expanding production, with little attention given initially to the potential for using energy more efficiently. In response, the Washington-based Alliance to Save Energy issued a counterproposal, one that would eliminate the need to build most of the 1,300 proposed power plants. It would also be far less costly and less polluting.[10]

Bill Prindle, Director of the Alliance's building and utility programs, pointed out that adopting the household appliance efficiency standards agreed to by both the Clinton and the Bush administrations would eliminate the need for 127 power plants by 2020. If the more stringent residential air conditioner efficiency standard that was approved by the Clinton administration were adopted, this would do away with the need for another 43 power plants.

Stronger standards for commercial air conditioning would take care of needing 50 plants. Increasing the energy efficiency of new buildings over the next 20 years using tax credits and energy codes would save another 170 plants. And improving the energy efficiency of existing buildings, including air conditioners, commercial lighting, and commercial cooling, would save 210 plants.[11]

Prindle's list goes on, but these five measures alone would eliminate the need for 600 power plants. The costs of the measures to avoid these plants would be far less than the cost of building them. All of these steps to save electricity are cost-effective, some of them offering 30 percent annual rates of return.[12]

Peter Coy, economics editor at *Business Week*, points out that time-of-day pricing of electricity, which would increase prices during the peak daytime hours and reduce them at night, would also greatly reduce the generating capacity needed. Although he did not calculate the number of plants that could be saved, it would undoubtedly eliminate the need for another large block.[13]

Amory Lovins of the Rocky Mountain Institute has gained a worldwide reputation selling the idea that it is cheaper to save energy than to buy it. In response to his persuasive presentations about the returns on investment in improved efficiency being often 30 percent or more a year, many companies have invested heavily in reducing their energy use. But even with the efficiency gains since the oil price hikes of the 1970s, Lovins believes that U.S. businesses could still cut their electric utility bills in half while making money doing so.[14]

Europe's example provides ample proof of the latent energy savings potential in the United States. Europeans routinely use 30 percent less energy per unit of gross national product than Americans do. The United States could easily meet its requirements for carbon reduction under the Kyoto Protocol by 2010 simply by moving to European efficiency levels, and these are far below the efficiency levels that are possible using state-of-the-art technologies.[15]

Although Europe is already well ahead of the United States in energy efficiency, individual countries are continuing to advance. In early August 2001, the British introduced a new tax scheme to encourage investment in energy-saving equipment. Expenditures on capital equipment can now be subtracted from taxable profits if the equipment meets established energy efficiency standards. Among the categories of equipment eligible for the tax break are cogeneration (combined heat and power), boilers, electric motors, lighting, and refrigeration. This plan was modeled on a similar system already operating successfully in the Netherlands.[16]

China is now setting the pace in increasing energy efficiency and reducing carbon emissions. Over the last four years, China has apparently reduced its carbon emissions, even while its economy grew 7 percent annually, using subsidy phaseouts for coal, market pricing for fuels, and new energy conservation initiatives. For example, China will soon start to produce a high-efficiency refrigerator that will use only half as much electricity as conventional models.[17]

Some of the worldwide potential for saving energy can be seen in the substitution of compact fluorescent lamps (CFLs) for traditional incandescent light bulbs. The compact fluorescent uses less than one fourth as much electricity, and though it costs more than an incandescent, it lasts 13 times as long. Over three years, using the light four hours a day, the electricity and bulb cost $19.06 for a compact fluorescent and $39.54 for an incandescent. Even excluding the labor costs of replacing the short-lived incandescent bulbs six times during the three years, the return on investing in a compact fluorescent lamp is still close to 30 percent a year.[18]

As I travel from country to country launching books and addressing conferences, I routinely check the light bulbs in hotel rooms. Some hotel chains use CFLs almost exclusively. Others use very few or none at all. The worldwide potential for investing in compact fluorescent lamps and closing power plants in the process is not only huge, it is also profitable.

Another area with enormous potential for efficiency improvements is automobile fuel. In the United States, which has one of the world's most inefficient vehicle fleets, the new 2001 models get an estimated 24.5 miles per gallon, down from the peak of 26.2 miles per gallon in 1987. Thus fuel efficiency dropped 6 percent when, given the advances in technology and growing concern about global warming, it should have been rising. Fortunately, at this writing, it appears that Congress may take the lead and establish new fuel efficiency standards for the next decade or so.[19]

The fuel efficiency among the 2001 models sold in the United States varies widely, ranging from the hybrid electric Honda Insight, which gets 68 miles per gallon on the highway and 61 in the city, to a Ferrari, with 13 miles per gallon on the highway and 8 in the city. Just above the Ferrari in the fuel ratings are several large sport utility vehicles. The more efficient cars on the market, such as the Honda Insight and the Toyota Prius, easily double the average fuel efficiency of the U.S. fleet, underlining the enormous potential for fuel savings.[20]

Regardless of the source of energy, it makes economic and environmental sense to make sure the energy is used efficiently. At a minimum, the world should be making all the investments in energy efficiency that are profitable with current prices. That alone would drop world energy use by a substantial amount.

Sometimes a simple measure can make a big difference. In Bangkok, the city government decided that at 9 p.m. on a given weekday evening, all major television stations would be co-opted in order to show a big dial with the city's current use of electricity. Once the dial appeared on the screen, everyone was asked to turn off unnecessary lights and appliances. As viewers watched, the dial dropped, reducing electricity use by 735 megawatts, enough to shut down two moderate-sized coal-fired power plants. For viewers, this visual experiment had a lasting effect, reminding them that individually they could make a difference and that collectively they could literally close power plants.[21]

The purpose of this section is simply to provide a sense of potential energy savings. A successful global effort in this direction would lower energy expenditures and help reduce air pollution and climate disruption while the new energy sources are coming online. Even as hydrogen-fueled engines are being developed, it would reduce vulnerability to oil price hikes—a matter of concern for many governments.

Harnessing the Wind

The modern wind industry was born in California in the early 1980s in the wake of the oil price hikes of 1973 and 1979. Under the leadership of Governor Jerry Brown, the state added its own tax incentive to an existing federal one to develop renewable energy resources, creating an investment climate that yielded enough wind-generating capacity statewide to satisfy the residential needs of San Francisco. But after a fast beginning in California, U.S. interest in wind energy lagged, almost disappearing for a decade.[22]

While interest in wind energy was sagging in the United States, it was continuing to advance in Europe, led initially by Denmark, which had built many of the wind turbines that were installed in

California. From 1995 to 2000, as noted earlier, wind energy world-wide expanded nearly fourfold, a computer industry growth rate. (See Figure 5–1.) And the United States got back into the race, with AWEA projecting 60 percent growth in U.S. wind generating capacity in 2001.[23]

Today Denmark gets 15 percent of its electricity from wind power. For Schleswig-Holstein, the northernmost state of Germany, the figure is 19 percent—with some parts of that state getting an impressive 75 percent. Spain's industrial state of Navarra, starting from scratch six years ago, now gets 22 percent of its electricity from wind. But in terms of absolute generating capacity, Germany has emerged as the world leader, with the United States in second place. (See Table 5–1.) Spain, Denmark, and India round out the top five.[24]

Advances in wind turbine technology, drawing heavily on the aerospace industry, have lowered the cost of wind power from 38¢ per kilowatt-hour in the early 1980s to less than 4¢ in prime wind sites in 2001. (See Figure 5–2.) In some locations, wind is already cheaper than oil or gas-fired power. With major corporations such as ABB, Royal Dutch Shell, and Enron plowing resources into this field, further cost cuts are in prospect.[25]

Wind is a vast, worldwide source of energy. The U.S. Great Plains are the Saudi Arabia of wind power. Three wind-rich states—North Dakota, Kansas, and Texas—have enough harnessable wind to meet

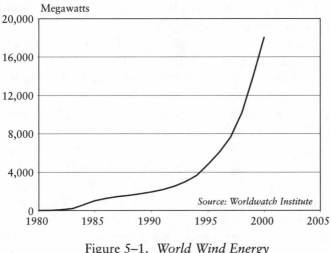

Figure 5–1. *World Wind Energy Generating Capacity, 1980–2000*

Table 5–1. *Wind Energy Generating Capacity*
in Selected Countries, 2000

Country	Capacity
	(megawatts)
Germany	6,113
United States	2,554
Spain	2,250
Denmark	2,140
India	1,167

Source: See endnote 24.

national electricity needs. China can double its existing generating capacity from wind alone. Densely populated Western Europe can meet all its electricity needs from offshore wind power out to an ocean depth of 30 meters.[26]

As wind generating costs fall and as concern about climate change escalates, more and more countries are climbing onto the wind energy bandwagon. Beginning in December 2000, the scale of world wind energy development climbed to a new level. Early in the month, France announced it will develop 5,000 megawatts of wind power by 2010. Later in the month, Argentina announced a plan to develop 3,000 megawatts of wind power in Patagonia by 2010. Then in April 2001, the United Kingdom accepted offshore bids for 1,500 megawatts of wind power. In May, a report from Beijing indicated that China plans to develop some 2,500 megawatts of wind power by 2005.[27]

The actual growth in wind power is consistently outrunning earlier estimates. The European Wind Energy Association, which in 1996 had set a target of 40,000 megawatts for Europe by 2010, recently upped its goal to 60,000 megawatts.[28]

In the United States, wind power was once confined to California, but during the last three years wind farms coming online in Colorado, Iowa, Minnesota, Oregon, Pennsylvania, Texas, and Wyoming have boosted U.S. capacity by half—from 1,680 megawatts to 2,550 megawatts. (One megawatt of wind generating capacity typically supplies 350 homes.) The 1,500 or more megawatts to be added in 2001 will be located in a dozen states. A 300-megawatt wind farm under construction on the Oregon/Washington border, currently the world's largest, can supply 105,000

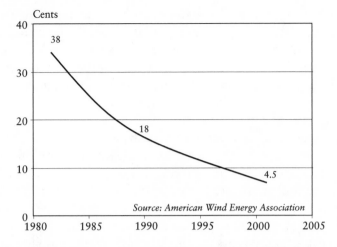

Figure 5–2. *Average Cost per Kilowatt-hour of Wind-powered Electricity in the United States, 1982, 1990, and 2001*

homes with electricity.[29]

But this is only the beginning. The Bonneville Power Administration (BPA), a U.S. federal agency power supplier, indicated in February that it wanted to buy 1,000 megawatts of wind-generating capacity and requested proposals. Much to its surprise, it received enough proposals to build 2,600 megawatts of capacity in five states, with the potential of expanding these sites to over 4,000 megawatts. BPA, which may accept most of these proposals, expects to have at least one site online by the end of 2001.[30]

A 3,000-megawatt wind farm in the early planning stages in east central South Dakota, near the Iowa border, is 10 times the size of the Oregon/Washington wind farm. Named Rolling Thunder, this proposed project—initiated by Dehlsen Associates and drawing on the leadership of Jim Dehlsen, a wind energy pioneer in California—is designed to feed power into the Midwest around Chicago. It is not only large by wind power standards, it is one of the largest energy projects of any kind in the world today.[31]

Income from wind-generated electricity tends to remain in the community, bolstering local economies by providing local income, jobs, and tax revenue. One large advanced-design wind turbine, occupying a quarter-acre of land, can easily yield a farmer or rancher $2,000 in royalties per year while providing the community with $100,000 of electricity.[32]

For farmers and ranchers, discovering the value of their wind resources is like striking oil—except that the wind is never depleted. One of wind's attractions is that the turbines scattered about a farm or ranch do not interfere with the use of the land for farming or cattle grazing. For ranchers with prime wind sites, income from wind can easily exceed that from cattle sales. The wind boom can rejuvenate rural communities throughout the world.

Once we get cheap electricity from wind, we can use it to electrolyze water, splitting the water molecule into its component elements of hydrogen and oxygen. Hydrogen is the simplest of fuels and, unlike coal or oil, is entirely carbon-free. It is the fuel of choice for the new, highly efficient fuel cell engine on which every major auto manufacturer is now working. DaimlerChrysler plans to market fuel cell–powered cars by 2003. Ford, Toyota, and Honda will probably not be far behind.[33]

Surplus wind power can be stored as hydrogen and used in fuel cells or gas turbines to generate electricity, leveling supply when winds are variable. Wind, once seen as a cornerstone of the new energy economy, is likely to become its foundation.

With the advancing technologies for harnessing wind and powering motor vehicles with hydrogen, we can now see a future in which U.S. farmers and ranchers supply not only much of the country's electricity, but much of the hydrogen for its fleet of automobiles as well. For the first time, the United States has the technology to divorce itself from Middle Eastern oil.

Within the United States, a new lobby is developing for wind power. In addition to the wind industry and environmentalists, U.S. farmers and ranchers are now also urging lawmakers to support development of this abundant alternative to fossil fuels.[34]

In manufacturing the turbines that convert wind into electricity, Denmark is the world leader. Sixty percent of all the turbines installed in 2000 were either manufactured by Danish companies or licensed by them. This illustrates how a country can translate foresight and a strong environmental commitment into a dominant position in the fast-emerging eco-economy. The United States, although now experiencing an extraordinary growth in wind energy development, is struggling to get back into the race in the manufacturing of wind energy turbines. The first utility-scale wind turbine manufacturing facility to be built in the United States outside of California has recently started operation in Champaign, Illinois, in the heart of the Corn Belt.[35]

The world is beginning to recognize wind for what it is—an energy source that is both vast and inexhaustible, an energy source that can supply both electricity and hydrogen for fuel. In the United States, farmers are learning that two harvests—crops and energy—are better than one. Political leaders are realizing that harnessing the wind can contribute to both energy security and climate stability. And consumers opting for green electricity are learning that they can help stabilize climate. This is a winning combination.

Turning Sunlight into Electricity

After wind power, the second fastest growing source of energy—solar cells—is a relatively new one. In 1952, three scientists at Bell Labs in Princeton, New Jersey, discovered that sunlight striking a silicon-based material produced electricity. The discovery of this photovoltaic or solar cell opened up a vast new potential for generating electricity.[36]

Initially very costly, solar cells could be used only for high-value purposes such as providing the electricity to operate satellites. Another early economical use was powering pocket calculators. Once run on batteries, pocket calculators now typically rely on a thin strip of silicon for power.

The next use to become economical was providing electricity in remote sites, such as summer mountain homes in industrial countries and villages in developing countries not yet linked to an electrical grid. In the more remote villages, it is already more economical to install solar cells than to build a power plant and connect the villages by grid. By the end of 2000, about a million homes worldwide were getting their electricity from solar cell installations. An estimated 700,000 of these were in Third World villages.[37]

As the cost of solar cells continues to decline, this energy source is becoming competitive with large, centralized power sources. For many of the 2 billion people in the world who do not have access to electricity, small solar cell arrays provide a shortcut, an affordable source of electricity. In villages in the Peruvian highlands, for example, village families spend roughly $4 a month on candles. For just a bit more, they can have much higher quality lighting from solar cells. In some Third World communities not serviced by a centralized power system, local entrepreneurs are investing in solar cell generating facilities and selling the energy to village families.[38]

Perhaps the most exciting technological advance has been the development of a photovoltaic roofing material in Japan. A joint effort involving the construction industry, the solar cell manufacturing industry, and the Japanese government plans to have 4,600 megawatts of electrical generating capacity in place by 2010, enough to satisfy all of the electricity needs of a country like Estonia.[39]

With photovoltaic roofing material, the roof of a building becomes the power plant. In some countries, including Germany and Japan, buildings now have a two-way meter—selling electricity to the local utility when they have an excess and buying it when they do not have enough.[40]

Newly constructed office buildings in the United States, Germany, and Switzerland have incorporated photovoltaic materials in their facades to generate electricity. Nothing in the appearance of these buildings would indicate to the casual observer that their glass walls and windows are in fact small power plants.

Growth in the sales of photovoltaic cells averaged 20 percent a year from 1990 to 2000. Then in 2000, sales jumped by 43 percent. Over the last decade, worldwide sales of photovoltaic cells have increased more than sixfold—from 46 megawatts of capacity in 1990 to 288 megawatts in 2000. (See Figure 5–3.)[41]

The big three in solar cell manufacturing are Japan, the United States, and the European Union. In 1999, production of solar cells in Japan alone jumped to 80 megawatts, pushing it into first place ahead of the United States. A large share of the solar cells produced

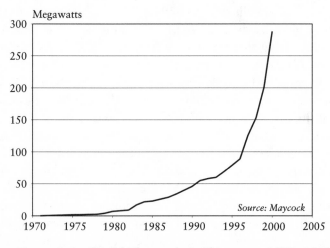

Figure 5–3. *World Photovoltaic Shipments, 1971–2000*

in the United States, which reached 60 megawatts in 1999, was exported to developing countries. Europe is currently in third place, with 40 megawatts of production in 1999, but its capacity expanded by more than half when Royal Dutch Shell and Pilkington Glass opened a 25-megawatt solar cell manufacturing facility in Germany.[42]

When BP merged with Amoco, it also acquired Solarex, the solar cell arm of Amoco, making BP overnight the world's third-ranking manufacturer of solar cells after Sharp and Kyocera, both of Japan. Siemens/Shell is in fourth place. The world solar cell market is marked by intense competition among companies and among countries. One reason leading industrial countries have ambitious solar roof programs is to help develop their solar cell manufacturing industries.[43]

Japan, Germany, and the United States all have strong programs to support this industry. The new Shell/Pilkington manufacturing facility in Germany was built in response to a vigorous German program to increase the use of solar energy, particularly on rooftops. In contrast to the Japanese, which rely on a cash subsidy to the buyers of solar roofing systems, the German government offers a bonus price for solar cell electricity and uses low-interest loans to encourage investment. Germany has a 100,000 Roofs program, with a goal of installing 300 megawatts of solar cells by 2005. The U.S. Million Solar Roofs program was launched in 1997. Although it is an impressive goal, government financial support is not nearly as strong as in Japan and Germany. Italy, too, has begun to move forward on the solar front, with a 10,000 Solar Roofs program.[44]

The potential in the solar arena is enormous. Aerial photographs show that even in the notoriously cloudy climate of the British Isles, putting solar cells on the country's existing roofs could generate 68,000 megawatts of power on a bright day, about half of Britain's peak power demand.[45]

The costs of solar cells has fallen from more than $70 per watt of production capacity in the 1970s to less than $3.50 per watt today. And it is expected to continue dropping, possibly falling to only $1 per watt as technologies advance and as manufacturing capacity expands by leaps and bounds. Research designed to improve photovoltaic technology is under way in literally hundreds of laboratories. Scarcely a month goes by without another advance in either photovoltaic cell design or manufacturing technology.[46]

Tapping the Earth's Heat

In contrast to other sources of renewable energy, such as wind power, solar cells, and hydropower, which rely directly or indirectly on sunlight, geothermal energy comes from within the earth itself. Produced radioactively within the earth and by the pressures of gravity, it is a vast resource, most of which is deep within the earth. Geothermal energy can be economically tapped when it is relatively close to the surface, as evidenced by hot springs, geysers, and volcanic activity.

This energy source is essentially inexhaustible. Hot baths, for example, have been used for millennia. It is possible to extract heat faster than it is generated at any local site, but this is a matter of adjusting the extraction of heat to the amount generated. In contrast to oil fields, which are eventually depleted, properly managed geothermal fields keep producing indefinitely.

Geothermal energy is much more abundant in some parts of the world than in others. The richest region is the vast Pacific Rim. In the East Pacific, geothermal resources are found along the coastal regions of Latin America, Central America, and North America all the way to Alaska. On the west side, they are widely distributed in Eastern Russia, Japan, the Korean Peninsula, China, and island countries such as the Philippines, Indonesia, New Guinea, Australia, and New Zealand.[47]

This buried energy source is used directly both to supply heat and to generate electricity. When used for heat, hot water or steam is typically pumped from underground, heat is extracted, and then the water is re-injected into the earth. Electricity can be generated from hot water pumped from beneath the earth's surface, from steam extracted directly, or from steam produced by circulating water into fissures in hot rock below the surface. Geothermal energy extracted directly can be used for space heating, as in Iceland, where it heats some 85 percent of buildings; for hot baths where springs bring geothermal energy to the surface, as in Japan; and for generating electricity, as in the United States.[48]

First harnessed for electricity generation in Italy in 1904, geothermal energy is now used in scores of countries, although in many cases it is used primarily to supply hot water to bath houses. During the first seven decades of the twentieth century, the growth in geothermal electrical generating capacity was modest, reaching only 1,100 megawatts in 1973. With the two oil price hikes in 1973 and 1979, however, use of geothermal energy began to grow. By 1998, it had expanded nearly eightfold, to 8,240 megawatts. (See Figure 5–4.)[49]

The United States, with more than 2,800 megawatts of capacity, is the world leader in tapping this energy source. But as a share of national electricity generation, other, smaller countries are far ahead. Whereas the United States gets only 1 percent of its electricity from geothermal energy, Nicaragua gets 28 percent and the Philippines, 26 percent.[50]

Most countries have barely begun to tap their wealth of geothermal energy. For countries rich in geothermal energy, such as those on the Pacific Rim, bordering the Mediterranean Sea, and along Africa's Great Rift, geothermal heat is potentially a huge source of energy—and one that does not disrupt the earth's climate. In Japan, an abundance of geothermal energy is close to the surface, as the thousands of hot spring spas throughout the country attest. It is estimated that the potential electrical generating capacity of geothermal energy in Japan could meet 30 percent of the country's needs. Some countries are so well endowed that they can run their economies entirely on geothermal energy.[51]

In a time of mounting concern about climate change, many governments are beginning to exploit the geothermal potential. The U.S. Department of Energy, for example, announced in 2000 that it was launching a program to develop the rich geothermal energy resources in the western United States. The goal is to have 10 per-

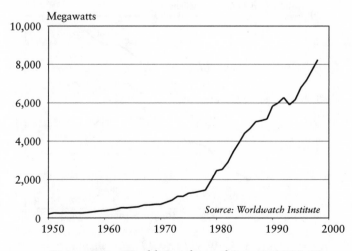

Figure 5–4. *World Geothermal Power, 1950–98*

cent of the electricity in the West coming from geothermal energy by 2020.[52]

Natural Gas: The Transition Fuel

Over the last half-century, the use of natural gas has increased 12-fold. Indeed, in 1999 natural gas eclipsed coal as a world source of energy, making it second only to oil. (See Figure 5–5.) This growth in natural gas use is fortuitous, because as this energy source grows, the storage and distribution system—whether long-distance pipelines or the detailed distribution networks within cities that supply natural gas to individual residences—is also expanding, setting the stage for the eventual switch to a hydrogen economy.[53]

Natural gas could overtake oil as the world's leading source of energy within the next 20 years, particularly if an anticipated downturn in oil production comes in this decade rather than the next. Natural gas has gained in popularity both because it is a clean-burning source of energy and because it is less carbon-intensive than either coal or oil. It emits scarcely half as much carbon as coal does for each unit of energy produced. In contrast to both coal and oil, which often emit sulfur dioxide and nitrous oxides when burned, gas burns cleanly.[54]

It is this clean-burning quality that has appealed to governments as a way of reducing air pollution. In China, for example, shifting from coal to natural gas for both industrial and residential uses is

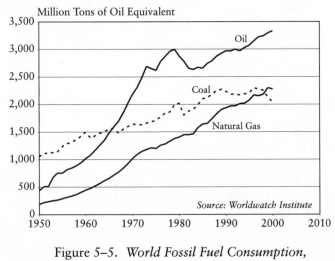

Figure 5–5. *World Fossil Fuel Consumption, 1950–2000*

reducing the urban air pollution that has claimed literally millions of lives in recent years. As part of its long-term planning, China is building a new pipeline from gas fields discovered in its far northwest to the city of Lanzhou in Gansu Province. The government has also approved the import of natural gas and is now planning to build a pipeline linking Russia's Siberian gas fields with Beijing and Tianjin, both leading industrial cities.[55]

Natural gas's potential to play a central role in the transition from the fossil fuel era to the solar/hydrogen era has not escaped the more progressive leaders in this industry. For example, Gasunie, the Netherlands natural gas utility, expects to be a major player in this transition. Although Gasunie now transports natural gas from the North Sea gas fields across the Netherlands to other countries in Europe, the firm plans eventually to use offshore wind power to generate electricity, converting it into hydrogen that will then be moved through the pipeline system now used for natural gas.[56]

In the United States, Enron, a Texas-based natural gas company that in recent years has become a global energy company, is also keenly aware of the part it can play in the transition to the new energy economy. In recent years, it has purchased two wind companies, which gives it the capacity to exploit the vast wind resources of Texas. This abundance of wind to generate cheap electricity and produce hydrogen gives Enron the option of one day feeding the hydrogen into the same distribution network of pipelines that it now uses to distribute natural gas in the Northeast and Midwest.[57]

A similar situation exists in China, where the development of natural gas fields in the northwest and the pipelines used to carry the gas eastward to industrial cities could one day be used to carry hydrogen produced with the region's wealth of wind resources. (The installation of wind turbines along with the more traditional windbreaks of trees in areas where soil is vulnerable to wind erosion could also help control erosion and the dust storms that blow across the country to Beijing and other cities.)

Natural gas companies are well positioned to be leaders in building the solar/hydrogen economy. They may someday invest in wind electric generation in remote regions that have a wealth of wind, and then use that electricity to electrolyze water and produce hydrogen. This could then be exported in liquid form, much as natural gas is now compressed into liquid form for shipping in tankers.

Getting to the Hydrogen Economy

The transition from fossil fuels to a solar/hydrogen energy economy can be seen in the widely differing growth rates among the various sources of energy. (See Table 5–2.) During the 1990s, wind power grew by a phenomenal 25 percent annually, expanding from 1,930 megawatts in 1990 to 18,449 megawatts in 2000. Sales of solar cells, meanwhile, grew at 20 percent a year, while geothermal energy grew by 4 percent annually. Hydropower, the fourth renewable energy source, grew at 2 percent a year.

Table 5–2. *Trends in Energy Use, by Source, 1990–2000*

Energy Source	Annual Rate of Growth
	(percent)
Wind power	25
Solar cells	20
Geothermal power	4
Hydroelectric power	2
Natural Gas	2
Oil	1
Nuclear Power	0.8
Coal	– 1

Source: Worldwatch Institute, *Vital Signs 2001* (New York: W.W. Norton & Company, 2001), pp. 40–47.

Among the fossil fuels, natural gas grew the fastest, at 2 percent annually, followed by oil at 1 percent. Coal use declined by 1 percent a year, with the actual decline coming after 1996. Nuclear power continued to grow, but just barely, averaging less than 1 percent a year during the decade.

The contrasting growth rates among the various energy sources were even greater in the year 2000 than during the 1990s. World wind generating capacity grew by 32 percent and sales of solar cells by 43 percent. The burning of coal, the fossil fuel that launched the industrial era, declined by 4 percent in 2000; natural gas increased by 2 percent; and oil increased by 1 percent. Nuclear power expanded by less than 1 percent. These data for the latest year—with the dramatic gains in wind and solar combined with the sharp decline for coal—indicate that the restructuring of the energy economy is gaining momentum.[58]

Coal is the first fossil fuel to peak and begin to decline. After reaching a historic high in 1996, production dropped 7 percent by 2000 and is expected to continue declining as the shift to natural gas and renewables gains momentum. Coal consumption is declining sharply in both the United Kingdom, the country where the Industrial Revolution began, and in China, the world's largest user.[59]

The shift in the fortunes of nuclear power could hardly be more dramatic. In the 1980s, world nuclear generating capacity expanded by 140 percent; during the 1990s, it expanded by 6 percent. Confronted with decommissioning costs of power plants that could rival the original construction costs, the energy source that was to be "too cheap to meter" is now too costly to use. Wherever electricity markets are opened to competition, nuclear power is in trouble. With a number of older plants scheduled to close, its worldwide use is likely to peak and start declining in a matter of years.[60]

Nuclear power plant closings are now under way or slated in the years immediately ahead in many countries, including Bulgaria, Germany, Kazakhstan, the Netherlands, Russia, the Slovak Republic, Sweden, and the United States. In three countries once solidly committed to this energy source—France, China, and Japan—nuclear power is losing its appeal. France has extended its moratorium on new plants. China has said it will not approve any additional plants for the next three years. Japan's once ambitious program is in trouble. A serious accident in September 1999 at a nuclear fuel fabrication plant north of Tokyo has reinforced rising public concerns about nuclear safety in Japan.[61]

Meanwhile, the use of wind and solar cells is growing by leaps and bounds. The spectacular growth in wind-generated electricity is driven by its falling cost. With the new advanced-design wind turbines, electricity is being generated at less than 4¢ per kilowatt-hour in prime wind sites—down from 18¢ a decade ago. Surpluses of wind-generated electricity on long-term contracts can guarantee the price, something those relying on oil or natural gas cannot do. With annual additions of wind capacity during the late 1990s exceeding those of nuclear power, the torch is passing to a new generation of energy technologies.[62]

In contrast to the old energy economy, in which a handful of countries control the supply, the new energy sources are widely dispersed. The economic opportunity for developing countries to develop their indigenous energy sources promises a strong boost to their overall development. New coalitions are evolving in support of the new energy sources, such as the one between U.S. environmental and agricultural groups in support of wind power development.

Satisfying the local demand for electricity from wind is not the end of the story. As noted earlier, cheap electricity produced from wind can be used to electrolyze water, producing hydrogen. At night, when electricity demand falls, electricity from wind farms can be used to power hydrogen generators to produce fuel for automobiles, trucks, and tractors.

With the first automobiles powered by fuel cell engines expected on the market in 2003 and with hydrogen as the fuel of choice for these new engines, a huge new market is opening up. As noted earlier, Royal Dutch Shell is already opening hydrogen stations in Europe. William Ford, the youthful chairman of the Ford Motor Company board, has said he expects to preside over the demise of the internal combustion engine.[63]

The economic benefits of developing local low-cost renewable sources of energy are obvious. In a community, for example, that gets its electricity from wind power, the money spent for electricity stays largely in the region. Developing wind resources thus promises to help rural communities in many countries, providing a welcome supplemental source of income and employment.

As the world energy economy is restructured, so, too, will the rest of the economy change. The geography of economic activity will be altered, in some cases dramatically. The traditional siting of heavy industry, such as steel production, in areas where coal and iron ore are found in close proximity will no longer be necessary. In the future, energy-intensive industries will be located in wind-rich regions rather than coal-rich regions. Countries that were once importers of energy may become self-sufficient, even exporting electricity or hydrogen.

One of the characteristics of the new energy economy is that it will rely much more on decentralized small-scale power sources rather than a few large, centralized systems. Small-scale energy systems designed to satisfy the needs of individual homes, factories, or office buildings will become much more common. Instead of a few highly concentrated energy sources, the world will be turning to vast numbers of small individual sources of energy. Fuel cells powered with hydrogen and the highly efficient combined-cycle gas turbines that are powered by either natural gas or hydrogen will become common. Fuel cells can be used to generate electricity for office buildings, factories, or individual homes or to power automobiles.

In the eco-economy, hydrogen will be the dominant fuel, replacing oil, much like oil replaced coal and coal replaced wood. Since hydrogen can be stored and used as needed, it provides perfect support for an energy economy with wind and solar power as the main pillars. If this pollution-free, carbon-free energy source can be developed sooner rather than later, many of our present energy-related problems can be solved. Electricity and hydrogen can together provide energy in all the forms needed to operate a modern economy, whether powering computers, fueling cars, or manufacturing steel.

On first reflection, such an energy system may seem a farfetched idea. But two decades ago, the idea of desktop or laptop computers and Internet communication seemed equally farfetched. As Seth Dunn of Worldwatch Institute notes, what is most inconceivable is that an information-age economy should be powered by a primitive, industrial-age energy system. As corporate and government decisionmakers begin to understand the need to restructure the energy economy, and just how economical and practical a zero-emissions, carbon-free energy system can be, then they may finally summon the sort of effort that supported the last great energy transition—the one from wood to fossil fuels a century ago.[64]

If the goal is to expand wind electric generation fast enough to accelerate the phaseout of coal, it would mean extraordinarily rapid growth in wind energy. Is such growth possible? Yes. The growth in the Internet provides a model. Between 1985 and 1995, the number of host computers on the Internet more than doubled each year. In 1985, there were 2,300 host computers on the Internet. By 1995, there were 14,352,000.[65]

A back-of-the-envelope calculation indicates what kind of growth would be needed for wind to become the foundation of the global energy economy, and how much it would cost. What would happen if wind electric generation doubled each year for the next 10 years, as adoption of the Internet did? Assume for the sake of calculation that in 2000 the world had 20,000 megawatts of wind-generating electricity online and that in 2001 this doubled to 40,000 megawatts, then in 2002 to 80,000 megawatts, and so forth. At this rate, by 2005, it would be 640,000 megawatts—nearly enough to meet all U.S. electricity demand. By 2010, it would reach 20.4 million megawatts of wind generating capacity, far beyond today's 3.2 million megawatts of world generating capacity or the projection of 4 million or so megawatts of capacity needed by 2010. This would not only satisfy world electricity needs, it could meet other energy needs as well—including those for transportation and heavy industry as well as residential uses.[66]

How much would this cost? Assuming generously that it would take $1 million of investment per megawatt of electricity, 10 million megawatts of wind power capacity would require an investment over the next 10 years of $10 trillion. This would amount to roughly $1 trillion a year—about double what the world spent for oil in 2000, or just 2.5 percent of the gross world product of $40 trillion. Another financial reference point, which is in some ways more relevant, is the $700 billion that the world's governments have been spending each year on environmentally destructive activities, such as coal mining, excess fishing capacity, and overpumping of aquifers. (See Chapter 11.) Shifting these subsidies into investment in wind development would accelerate the evolution of an eco-economy on several fronts simultaneously. This calculation simply illustrates that if the world wants to move quickly to eliminate excessive carbon emissions, it can do so.[67]

The transition from a fossil-fuel- or carbon-based economy to a high-efficiency, hydrogen-based economy will provide enormous investment and employment opportunities across the globe. The question is not whether there will be an energy revolution. It is already under way. The only questions are how rapidly it will unfold, whether it will move fast enough to prevent climate change from getting out of hand, and who will benefit most from the transition.

Realistically, how fast could wind generation expand during this decade? During the 1990s it expanded at 25 percent a year, with only a half-dozen countries accounting for most of the growth. If all countries with commercially viable wind sites began developing their wind, how fast could it expand? Could it double each year? That would be tough, requiring a mobilization akin to that during World War II. There might be a few annual doublings early in the decade while the base is still small, but then the rate of expansion would slow. How fast the world develops wind resources will depend in part on how fast climate changes and how alarmed we become by record heat waves, rapid ice melting, and more destructive storms. Although predicting the rate of future growth is not possible, it is clearly safe to assume that the world could be getting much of its electricity from wind by 2010 if it becomes important to do so.[68]

In his Worldwatch Paper *Hydrogen Futures*, Seth Dunn quotes President John F. Kennedy: "There are risks and costs to a program of action. But they are far less than the long-range risks and costs of comfortable inaction." Dunn then goes on to establish the parallel between Kennedy's cold war observation and the current energy transition. "There are risks and costs involved in rapidly building a hydrogen economy, but they are far less than the long-range risks and costs of remaining comfortably committed to the hydrocarbon economy."[69]

The key to accelerating the transition to a hydrogen economy is to get the market to incorporate ecological costs in the prices. *The Economist* argues that there is a need to level the playing field and then let the market take it from there: "That means, for example, dismantling the many subsidies that prop up coal and other fossil fuels. It also means introducing a carbon tax or similar mechanism to ensure that prices for fossil fuels reflect the harm they do to human health and to the environment." More and more analysts are reaching this same conclusion. A recent study by the Organisation for Economic Co-operation and Development also argues for restructuring taxes in order to reduce carbon emissions. Phasing in a carbon tax so that the burning of fossil fuels would reflect their full cost to society would accelerate the transition to wind energy, solar cells, and geothermal energy, expanding them far faster during this decade than during the last.[70]

6

Designing a New Materials Economy

In March 2001, the Fresh Kills landfill, the local destination for New York City's daily output of 12,000 tons of garbage, was permanently closed. Now the garbage is hauled to distant sites in New Jersey, Pennsylvania, and Virginia—some of them more than 480 kilometers (300 miles) away. Assuming a load of 20 tons of garbage for each of the tractor-trailers that are used for the long-distance hauling, some 600 rigs are needed to remove garbage from New York City each day. These tractor-trailers form a convoy nearly 15 kilometers (9 miles) long, impeding traffic, polluting the air, and raising carbon emissions. This daily convoy of trucks leaving the city led Deputy Mayor Joseph J. Lhota, who supervised the Fresh Kills shutdown, to say that getting rid of the city's trash is now "like a military-style operation on a daily basis."[1]

What is happening in New York will occur in other cities if they also fail to adopt comprehensive recycling programs. Instead of focusing efforts on reducing garbage as the Fresh Kills landfill was filling, the decision was made to simply haul the garbage to more remote sites. Even a simple measure like recycling all its paper could shorten the daily convoy leaving the city by 187 tractor-trailers or 4.5 kilometers (2.8 miles).[2]

Fiscally strapped local communities are willing to take the garbage if New York pays enough. Some see it as a bonanza. For the state governments, however, that have to deal with the traffic congestion, noise, increased air pollution, and complaints from nearby communities, this arrangement is not so attractive. The Governor of Virginia wrote to New York Mayor Rudy Giuliani complaining about the use of Virginia as a dumping ground. "I understand the problem New York faces," he noted. "But the home state of Washington, Jefferson and Madison has no intention of becoming New York's dumping ground." Whether New York can continue to dump its garbage in others states over the long term remains to be seen.[3]

Earlier periods in human history were marked by the material that distinguished the era—the Stone Age and the Bronze Age, for example. Our age is simply the Material Age, an age of excess whose distinguishing feature is not the use of any particular material, but the sheer volume of materials consumed.

Worldwide, we process or use 26 billion tons of materials each year, including 20 billion tons of stone, gravel, and sand used for road building and construction; over 1 billion tons of iron ore processed for steelmaking; and 700 million tons of gold ore for extracting gold. From forests, we take 1.7 billion tons of wood for fuel, roughly 1 billion tons for wood products, and just over 300 million tons for manufacturing paper. To obtain phosphorus and potassium to replace the nutrients that our crops remove from soils, we annually mine 139 million tons of phosphate rock and 26 million tons of potash.[4]

Each of the earth's 6.1 billion inhabitants uses on average 137 kilograms (300 pounds) of steel per year in automobiles, household appliances, buildings, and other products. This means that each of us consumes nearly double our body weight in steel each year. Producing that steel means processing more than 340 kilograms of iron ore per person.[5]

The scale of the materials economy is far larger than most of us ever imagine, simply because we come in contact with only the final product—we see, for example, the steel in our car or refrigerator, but not the tons of ore from which it was extracted, or we see the paper in our newspapers and stationery, but not the stack of logs from which it was processed.

The production of some seemingly innocuous items, such as

gold jewelry, can be incredibly destructive. For example, the gold rings exchanged by couples during weddings require the processing of tons of ore, most likely by cyanide leaching. Worldwatch researcher John Young calculated that to create a pair of gold wedding rings, the ore processed is the equivalent of a hole in the ground that is 10 feet long, 6 feet wide, and 6 feet deep. Fortunately for the newlyweds, this hole is in someone else's backyard. So, too, is the cyanide used to separate the gold from the ore.[6]

All the figures just cited are global averages, but the use of materials—like that of energy and food—varies widely among societies. For example, steel production per person in the United States totals 352 kilograms annually; in China, it is 98 kilograms, and in India, just 24 kilograms.[7]

The processing of vast quantities of ore to produce metals is polluting local air and water. The energy use, the physical disruption of the land, and the pollution associated with processing ever growing quantities of ore are becoming less and less acceptable.

The sheer size of the materials economy is not only physically disruptive, it also uses vast quantities of energy. In the United States, the steel industry alone uses as much electricity as the country's 90 million homes.[8]

Building an eco-economy depends on restructuring the materials economy because—like the energy economy—it is in conflict with the earth's ecosystem. Architect William McDonough and chemist Michael Braungart talk about doing this. They describe an economy that is regenerative rather than depletive, one whose products "work within cradle-to-cradle life cycles rather than cradle-to-grave ones." In effect, this redesign means replacing the current linear flow-through model with a circular model that emulates nature, one that closes the loop. It means replacing mining industries with recycling industries, a step that will allow a mature, industrial economy with a stable population to live largely on the materials already in use.[9]

Throwaway Products

Two concepts that emerged during the mid-twentieth century have shaped the evolution of the global economy—planned obsolescence and throwaway products. Both were seized on enthusiastically in the United States after World War II as a way of promoting economic growth and employment. The faster things wore out and the sooner they could be thrown away, the faster the economy would grow.

For numerous consumer products, year-to-year changes in design became a key to stimulating sales. For automobiles, models changed each year. The unveiling of the new models, a major event on the economic calendars in leading industrial countries, automatically reduced the value of the previous year's cars. Model changes were intended not so much to improve performance as to sell more cars.

A similar situation exists with clothing, especially for women. Annual fashion shows trot out the latest designs. The changes for women's wear may involve raising or lowering hemlines, or emphasizing particular colors or fabrics in any given year. For many people, self-worth depends on wearing clothes that are "in fashion."

The throwaway economy evolved during the last half of the twentieth century. Throwaway products, facilitated by the appeal to convenience and the artificially low cost of energy, account for much of the garbage we produce each day and an even larger share of the material that ends up in landfills.

It is easy to forget how many throwaway products there are until we actually begin making a list. We have substituted facial tissues for handkerchiefs, disposable paper towels and table napkins for cloth, and throwaway beverage containers for refillable ones. In perhaps the ultimate insult, the shopping bags that are used to carry home throwaway products are themselves designed to be discarded. (The question at the supermarket checkout counter, "Paper or plastic?" should be replaced by, "Do you have your canvas shopping bag with you?")

The U.S.-based GrassRoots Recycling Network has calculated the "wasting rates" of products—that is, the share that is thrown away versus that recycled or reused. (See Table 6–1.) Not surprisingly, products designed for disposal score the highest. By definition, the wasting rate of disposable diapers is 100 percent, as is that of disposable tissues, plates, and cups. Although Americans have markedly improved their record on newspaper recycling over the last decade or so, 45 percent of all newsprint is still discarded rather than recycled. Tossing newspapers is a way of converting forests into landfill.

The advent of disposable paper plates and cups, plus plastic

Table 6–1. *Wasting Rates and Quantities of Commonly Discarded Items in the United States, 1997*

Product	Wasting Rate (percent discarded)	Quantity (million tons)
Disposable diapers	100	3.1
Disposable tissues, plates, cups	100	4.9
Clothing, footwear	87	5.0
Tires	77	3.3
Magazines	77	1.7
Office paper	49	3.5
Appliances	48	2.1
Newsprint	45	6.1
Aluminum cans	42	0.7
Steel cans	40	1.1

Source: U.S. Environmental Protection Agency, "Characterization of Municipal Solid Waste in the United States: 1998 Update," as reported by GrassRoots Recycling Network (Athens, Georgia).

"silverware," coincided with the emergence of the fast-food industry. The extraordinary growth of this sector helped ensure growth in the use of throwaway plates, cups, and eating utensils. These and other throwaways are routinely hauled by garbage trucks to landfills on a one-way trip through the economy.

Even while wrestling with traditional throwaway products, the world is now facing a new disposal challenge in desktop computers. Although they are not obsolescent by plan, the pace of innovation in the industry quickly makes them obsolete, giving the average computer a life expectancy of less than two years. In contrast to refrigerators, which are relatively easy to recycle, computers contain a diverse array of materials, many of them toxic, including lead, mercury, and cadmium, that makes them difficult to recycle. This helps explain why only 11 percent of computers are recycled, compared with 70 percent of refrigerators.[10]

A study by the Silicon Valley Toxics Coalition estimated that between 1997 and 2004, some 315 million computers would become obsolete in the United States alone. With each computer containing nearly 4 pounds of lead, the United States is facing the need to deal with 1.2 billion pounds of lead. While the world has been quite successful in getting it out of paint and gasoline, lead is still widely used in computers. Once in landfills, the lead can leach into aquifers and contaminate drinking water supplies. These same computers contain some 400,000 pounds of mercury and 2 million pounds of cadmium.[11]

Materials and the Environment

The materials used in our modern economy fall into three categories. The first is metals, including steel, aluminum, copper, zinc, and lead. The second category is nonmetallic minerals, such as stone, sand, gravel, limestone, and clay—materials that are used directly in the building of highways, roads, and buildings or in manufacturing concrete. This group also includes three minerals—phosphate, potash, and lime—that are used in agriculture to raise soil fertility. (See Table 6–2.) The final group of raw materials includes those of organic origin, such as wood from the forest sector and cotton, wool, and leather from agriculture.[12]

Table 6–2. *World Production of Nonmetallic Minerals*

Mineral	Production (million tons)
Stone	11,000
Sand and gravel	9,000
Clays	500
Salt	210
Phosphate rock	139
Lime	117
Gypsum	110
Soda ash	31
Potash	26

Source: See endnote 12.

In the nonmetallic category, stone at 11 billion tons produced per year and sand and gravel at 9 billion tons a year totally dominate other minerals. But stone, sand, and gravel are usually available locally and do not involve long-distance transport. Used primarily for the construction of roads, parking lots, and buildings, these materials are chemically inert. Once stone or gravel is in place in a roadbed, it may last for generations or even centuries.[13]

This chapter concentrates on metals because their mining and processing are so environmentally destructive and energy-intensive. Their production uses seemingly endless quantities of energy to remove earth to reach the ore, extract it, transport it to a smelter, and then process it into a pure metal. What's more, much of this energy comes from coal, which itself must be mined. Over time, as high-grade ores have been depleted, miners have shifted to lower-grade ores, inflicting progressively more environmental damage with each ton of metal produced.[14]

Ever since the Industrial Age began, steel production has been a basic indicator of industrialization and economic modernization. In the late twentieth century, the Soviet Union was the international steel giant. In the early 1990s, however, the breakdown of Soviet steel output paralleled the breakdown of the Soviet regime. Currently, China leads the world in steel production, followed by the United States and Japan. In quantity, the 833 million tons of raw steel produced each year (see Figure 6–1) dwarfs the use of all other metals combined. It compares with 24 million tons of aluminum and 13 million tons of copper, the second and third ranking metals. While steel consists predominantly of iron, it is an alloy, and many of its attractive characteristics come from the addition of small quantities of other metals such as zinc, magnesium, and nickel.[15]

World steel production per person reached its historical high in 1979 and has since dropped by 20 percent. The decline reflects a

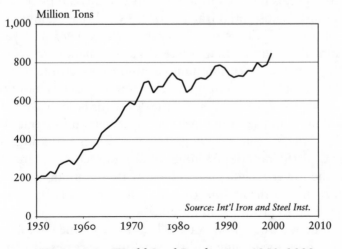

Figure 6–1. *World Steel Production, 1950–2000*

shift to smaller cars, the partial collapse of the former Soviet economy, and a shift in the growth of advanced industrial economies from heavy industry to services, especially information services.[16]

Every year, 1.4 billion tons of ore are mined worldwide to produce steel primarily for automobiles, household appliances, and construction. A comparable quantity of ore is mined to produce 13 million tons of copper. In an age when open pit mining has largely replaced underground mines, vast areas are physically disfigured. The mine tailings are then left behind—often disrupting the flow of nearby streams and contaminating water supplies. Anything that reduces the use of steel, particularly that produced from virgin ore, markedly lightens the human footprint on the earth.[17]

Although aluminum production is quite small compared with steel, the 24 million tons produced annually greatly understate aluminum's role because it is such a light, low-density metal. Australia produces one third of the world's aluminum-containing bauxite, with Guinea, Jamaica, and Brazil also contributing significantly to the world total.[18]

In the United States, well over half of all aluminum use is accounted for by the food packaging and transportation industries. For beverage containers, alternative materials such as glass can be used. However, aircraft, automobiles, and bicycles all currently rely heavily on aluminum.[19]

Much of the world's stock of aluminum, with its light weight and strength, is invested in the fleet of commercial planes. At any given time, a substantial fraction of the world's aluminum is actually airborne. With air travel expanding at 6 percent a year, the investment of aluminum in aircraft is also expanding.[20]

Although the use of aluminum in aircraft is well established, the substitution of aluminum for steel in automobiles is more recent, spurred by rising fuel prices and the desire for better gasoline mileage. Aluminum use in the average American automobile, for example, climbed from 87 kilograms in 1991 to 110 kilograms by the end of the decade. Although aluminum costs far more than steel, the lower weight of a vehicle with aluminum reduces fuel use, which over the lifetime of a car can more than offset the extra energy used to produce aluminum.[21]

Aluminum production exacts a heavy environmental toll as well, through both the mining and the smelting processes. Because aluminum typically occurs in thin layers of bauxite ore, extracting it by surface mining scars the landscape. For each ton of aluminum produced, a ton of "red mud"—a caustic brew of chemicals—is left after the bauxite is extracted. This red muck is left untreated in large, biologically lifeless ponds, eventually polluting both surface and underground water supplies.[22]

But most of the damage done by aluminum production comes from generating electricity to run the smelters. Worldwide, the aluminum industry uses as much electric power as the entire continent of Africa. In some cases, the electricity for aluminum smelting comes from coal-fired power plants, but often it comes from hydroelectricity. Scores of dams have been built, particularly in remote regions, to produce cheap electricity to manufacture aluminum. Governments eager to build indigenous industry in their countries compete with each other for aluminum smelters by subsidizing the cost of electricity. As a result, aluminum is one of the world's most heavily subsidized raw materials.[23]

Among the metals, gold is distinguished by two things—its minute production and vast environmental disruption. In 1991, producing a meager 2,445 tons of gold required the removal and processing of more than 741 million tons of ore—a mass equal to nearly two thirds of the iron ore used to produce 571 million tons of iron that year. (See Table 6–3.) The leading gold producer is South Africa. Other producers include Australia, Brazil, Russia, and the United States. Eighty-five percent of the gold mined goes into jewelry.[24]

Beginning in the nineteenth century, gold was used to guarantee the value of paper currencies. As a result, much of the world's gold is stored in the vaults of national banks. Once the United States moved off the gold standard in 1971, however, many countries followed suit, and some have since sold gold from their vaults, including Australia, the Bank of England, the Netherlands, and the Swiss National Bank. This means that gold is being transformed from the final barometer of the value of paper currency to just another commodity. *The Economist* observes that gold is "the spent fuel of an obsolete monetary system."[25]

In damage per ton of metal produced, nothing comes close to gold. Each ton of gold requires the processing of roughly 300,000 tons of ore—the equivalent of a small mountain. Over the last decade, a new technique of processing gold ore, called cyanide heap

Table 6–3. *Metal Production and Ore Mined for Each Metal, 1991*

Metal	Production	Ore Mined	Ore Mined Per Ton of Metal Produced
	(tons)		
Iron	571,000,000	1,428,000,000	3
Copper	12,900,000	1,418,000,000	110
Gold	2,445	741,000,000	303,000
Zinc	8,000,000	1,600,000,000	200
Lead	2,980,000	119,000,000	40
Aluminum	23,900,000	104,000,000	4
Manganese	7,450,000	25,000,000	3
Nickel	1,230,000	49,000,000	40
Tin	200,000	20,000,000	100
Tungsten	31,500	13,000,000	400

Source: U.S. Geological Survey; John E. Young, *Mining the Earth* (Washington, DC: Worldwatch Institute, July 1992); W.K. Fletcher, Department of Earth and Ocean Sciences, University of British Columbia

leaching, has come into widespread use. Cyanide solution is leached through a pile of crushed ore, picking up bits of gold as it passes through. This reduces the cost of gold mining, but it leaves behind toxic waste. Cyanide is so toxic that the ingestion of a teaspoon of 2 percent cyanide solution will lead to death within 40 seconds.[26]

In January 2000, a giant spill of 130 million liters of cyanide solution from a gold mine in Romania drained into the Tisza River, flowed through Hungary into Yugoslavia, merged with the Danube, and emptied into the Black Sea. The lethal solution from the Australian-operated mine left an estimated 1 million kilograms of dead fish in the Hungarian segment of the river alone. This cyanide spill, which left long stretches of river lifeless, has been called Europe's worst environmental disaster since Chernobyl.[27]

Cyanide spills have occurred in many countries. A similar incident in 1992 in the Alamosa River, a tributary of the Colorado River in the United States, killed everything in a 17-mile stretch and left the state of Colorado with a $170-million cleanup bill after the company responsible declared bankruptcy.[28]

Another common mining technology uses mercury to extract gold from ore. Mercury accumulates in the environment, concentrating as it moves up the food chain. It was discharges of mercury into Japan's Minamata Bay a generation ago that demonstrated the brain damage and birth defects this heavy metal can cause.[29]

In the Amazon, gold miners release 200,000 pounds of mercury each year into the ecosystem, reports John Young. Although mercury levels in fish in the Amazon often exceed the levels for safe human consumption, people in the area have no alternative protein source. One teaspoon of mercury in a 25-acre lake can render fish unsafe for human consumption. No one knows when the effects of mercury intake will begin to show up as brain damage and birth defects in the Amazon, but we do know that they first appeared in Japanese infants roughly a decade after fertilizer plants began releasing mercury into Minamata Bay.[30]

Aside from the discharge of highly toxic cyanide and mercury into the ecosystem, gold mining is also a physically dangerous activity. In South Africa, where most of the gold comes from underground, death in the mines is routine, claiming one life for each ton of gold produced.[31]

Gold is not the only metal that is damaging the planet. The extraction of other metals, such as copper, lead, and zinc, also disfigures the landscape and pollutes the environment. Reducing this destruction of the natural landscape and the pollution of air, water, and soil depends on designing a new materials economy, one where mining industries are largely replaced by recycling industries.

The Earth's Toxic Burden

No one knows exactly how many chemicals are manufactured today, but with the advent of synthetic chemicals, most of them organic in nature, the number of chemicals in use has climbed over 100,000. A random blood test of Americans will show measurable amounts of easily 200 chemicals that did not exist a century ago.[32]

A number of these chemicals are highly persistent and found in remote corners of the globe, far from their origin. Recent research at the Norwegian Polar Institute indicates that polar bears living within the Arctic Circle have high concentrations of persistent organic pollutants (POPs) in their fatty tissue. One apparent consequence of the buildup of POPs, some of which are endocrine disruptors, is that 1.5 percent of all female bears have deformed sexual organs.[33]

Most of these new chemicals have not been tested for toxicity. Those that are known to be toxic are included in a list of 644 chemicals whose discharge by industry into the environment must be reported to the U.S. Environmental Protection Agency (EPA). The annual publication of EPA's Toxic Release Inventory (TRI) makes public some of the more dangerous chemicals being put into the air or water or simply buried underground. Although these detailed data for the United States, compiled from reports submitted by industrial, mining, and electrical generating firms, are not readily available for most other countries, they do provide some sense of the global situation.[34]

In 1999, some 7.8 billion pounds of toxic chemicals—28 pounds for each person—were released into the U.S. environment. Metal mining accounted for 4 billion pounds and electrical generating facilities for 1.2 billion pounds. The primary metals industry, which refines metals and manufactures metal products ranging from steel plates to copper wire and aluminum cans, released 684 million pounds of toxic chemicals. Compounds containing copper, zinc, and arsenic accounted for nearly three fourths of all the toxic chemicals released from these industries. The chemical manufacturing industry was close behind, with 671 million pounds. Paper manufacturing was third, with 226 million pounds of toxics released.[35]

For the electric utility sector, hydrochloric acid and sulfuric acid were among the leading toxics released. This does not include the emissions of sulfur dioxide and various nitrous oxides that interact with moisture in the atmosphere to form the sulfuric and nitric acid that damage respiratory systems and produce acid rain. While gold miners release an estimated 200,000 pounds of mercury into the Amazon ecosystem each year, coal-burning power plants release over 100,000 pounds of mercury into the air in the United States. EPA reports that "mercury from power plants settles over waterways, polluting rivers and lakes and contaminating fish." The risks to human health, and particularly prenatal damage to nervous system development, have led to restrictions on fish consumption in an estimated 50,000 U.S. freshwater lakes, rivers, and ponds. The 35,000 pounds of mercury deposited in New England each year from coal-burning power plants led the region's six states to warn children and pregnant women to limit their consumption of freshwater fish. A report by the National Academy of Sciences for the United States as a whole indicates that 60,000 infants may face neurological damage from mercury exposure before birth.[36]

The Toxic Release Inventory, now accessible on the Internet, also provides information on a community-by-community basis, arming local groups with data needed to evaluate the potential threats to their health and that of the environment. Since the TRI was inaugurated in 1988, toxic chemical emissions have declined steadily.[37]

Unfortunately, few other countries have instituted such comprehensive reporting procedures. And the U.S. system still has some gaps, such as on pesticides, which are released into the environment by farmers, homeowners, and golf course managers.

Some chemicals that are used in large quantities are lethal even in small quantities. For example, swallowing one teaspoonful of arsenic leads to death in less than a minute. Exposure to varying levels of toxic chemicals and in various combinations can lead to birth defects, impaired immune systems, damage to the central nervous system (including mental retardation), respiratory illnesses, a disruption of endocrine systems and hormonal balances, and cancer of almost every kind.[38]

Pollutants also damage the environment. Acid rain from sulfur dioxide emissions, for example, has damaged forests in industrial regions, including Europe, North America, and China. A 2000 survey reports that one quarter of Europe's forests are damaged. A nickel smelter in Norilsk, Siberia, has killed all the trees in a 3,500-square-kilometer area. Thousands of lakes in the northern tier of industrial countries are now lifeless because of acidification from acid rain.[39]

In some countries, environmental pollutants have accumulated to the point where they are reducing life expectancy. In Russia, the combination of a breakdown in the health care system, a dramatic rise in poverty over the last decade, and some of the world's highest pollution levels has helped reduce male life expectancy to less than 60 years. Horror stories of the health effects of uncontrolled industrial pollution in Russia are commonplace. For example, in the industrial town of Karabash in the foothills of the Ural Mountains, children routinely suffer from lead, arsenic, and cadmium poisoning. This translates into congenital defects, neurological disorders, and cancer. Pollutants also disrupt metabolic systems and impair immune systems.[40]

Developing countries, too, are beginning to suffer from uncontrolled pollution. Payal Sampat of Worldwatch Institute writes that the largest city in the agricultural state of the Punjab in northern India, Ludiana, is now paying the price for industrial pollution. A

combination of industries, ranging from textiles to metal electro-
plating, has left the underground water supply contaminated with
cyanide, cadmium, and lead. The well water on which the city's
residents depend is no longer safe to drink. Other cities in India,
such as Jaipur, and in China, such as Shenyang, that once depended
on local groundwater supplies must now also seek water from elsewhere.[41]

Scientists analyzing underground water pollution quickly point
out that thus far we are seeing only the tip of the iceberg, because it
takes time for water-soluble toxic chemicals to percolate through
the soil and eventually pollute underground aquifers. The toxics in
underground aquifers today may be the product of industrial activities from a generation ago.[42]

The dispersal of some toxics is relatively new. This is the case in
Japan, for example, where the incineration of municipal waste is
discharging dioxins into the air. Dioxins—which are so toxic that
their presence is measured not in parts per million but in parts per
billion—are a product of burning plastic. Tokyo has become the
dioxin capital of the world. Although Japan's emissions of dioxin,
the highest of any country, total only 4 kilograms per year, they are
at a level that could cause cancer or other maladies.[43]

One of the big challenges the world now faces is how to detoxify
the earth. How do we make the air safe to breathe, the water safe
to drink, and the soil safe for producing food? One important step
was taken in December 2000 when delegates from 122 countries
meeting in Stockholm approved a landmark agreement banning
12 of the most toxic chemicals now in use. These 12 persistent
organic pollutants included pesticides, such as DDT, aldrin, en-
drin, chlordane, and dieldrin, as well as industrial chemicals like
hexachlorbenzene and PCBs. Once 50 countries ratify the treaty, a
process expected to take at least three years, then implementation
will begin. Swedish Prime Minister Goeran Persson observed, "Dangerous substances do not respect international or national borders.
They can only be fought with common strategies." Most countries
have already banned the use of lead in gasoline, a common source
of mental retardation in children.[44]

If we restructure the energy economy to stabilize climate (see
Chapter 5), then the burning of coal for electrical generation—the
source of the mercury that is making fish unsafe for human consumption, and the hydrochloric and sulfuric acids that are destroy-

ing forests and impairing respiratory systems—will largely disappear.

If recycling industries replace mining industries, the flow of pollutants will be greatly reduced. If countries ban the use of nonrefillable beverage containers, as Denmark and Finland have done, then both the amount of energy and the materials used in manufacturing beverage containers will be sharply reduced. In building an eco-economy, many of the goals are mutually reinforcing.[45]

The Role of Recycling

As the economy metabolizes more and more metals and other raw materials, the damage mounts. Although recycling is typically justified as an economically attractive alternative to rising landfill costs, it also greatly reduces ecosystem damage.

As noted earlier, steel, copper, gold, and aluminum mining and processing account for much of the carbon emissions, pollutants, and landscape devastation associated with the materials economy. For recycling, the three materials to focus on are steel, copper, and aluminum, since the high value of gold virtually ensures that it is not discarded.

In terms of recycling potential, steel—with world output of 833 million tons per year—leads the list. Long a measure of industrialization, steel use is dominated by a few manufacturing industries, importantly automobiles and household appliances, and by the construction industry. Among the various products using steel in the United States, the highest rate of recycling is for automobiles. Cars today are simply too valuable to be left to rust in out-of-the-way junkyards. In the United States, nearly all discarded automobiles are recycled.[46]

The recycling rate for household appliances is estimated at 77 percent. For the construction industry, the recycling of steel beams and plates is even higher, some 95 percent; the steel used in reinforcing rods embedded in concrete, however, is not so easily recycled. For these and other construction uses, the recycling rate is 45 percent, according to the Steel Recycling Institute. For steel cans, the U.S. recycling rate in 1999 of 58 percent can be traced in part to municipal recycling campaigns launched in the late 1980s.[47]

In the United States, roughly 58 percent of all steel produced in 1999 was from scrap, leaving 42 percent to be produced from virgin ore. (See Figure 6–2.) Steel recycling started climbing more than

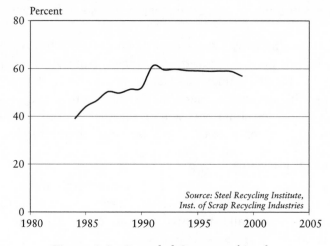

Figure 6–2. *Recycled Content of Steel*
in the United States, 1984–99

a generation ago with the advent of the electric arc furnace, a highly efficient method of producing steel from scrap. Steel produced from scrap uses only one third as much energy as that produced from virgin ore. And since it does not require any mining of ore, it completely eliminates one source of environmental disruption. In the United States, Italy, and Spain, electric arc furnaces now account for half or more of all steel production. Over the last two decades, the U.S. steel industry has shifted from using largely virgin ore to feeding primarily on scrap metal.[48]

It is easier for countries with mature industrial economies and stable populations to get most of their steel from recycled scrap than it is for developing countries, simply because the stock of steel embedded in the economy is essentially fixed. The number of household appliances, the fleet of automobiles, and the stock of buildings is increasing little or none. In countries in the early stages of industrialization, however, the creation of infrastructure—whether factories, bridges, high-rise buildings, or transportation, including automobiles, buses, and rail cars—leaves little steel for recycling.

As the U.S. steel industry has shifted to primary reliance on scrap, its geographic distribution has shifted. Once concentrated in western Pennsylvania, where there was an abundance of both iron ore and coal, the modern industry that uses electric arc minimills feeding on scrap is widely scattered across the country, in North Carolina, Nebraska, and Texas, for example. Minimills supply steel to local industries, enabling local communities to rely primarily on steel already in the system.[49]

The other metal with a pervasive environmental effect is aluminum. Some aluminum products are easily recycled. Others are not. For example, within the food industry, the aluminum foil used to package prepared frozen meals is not readily recycled. Aluminum beverage cans, by contrast, are much easier to take care of. In the United States, some 64 billion of the 102 billion aluminum cans used in 1998 were recycled. Yet this recycling rate of 63 percent is low compared with some other countries. In Japan, the current leader, 79 percent of aluminum beverage cans are recycled. Brazil is close behind, with 77 percent. In Japan, aluminum recycling is being driven by a scarcity of sites for garbage, whereas in many developing countries it is being driven by widespread unemployment.[50]

In Brazil, where unemployment is high, the recycling of aluminum beverage cans has become a major source of employment. An estimated 150,000 Brazilians make a living by collecting used beverage cans and taking them to recycling centers, earning $200 a month, compared with the minimum wage of $81 a month. Forty-five used cans can be traded for 1 kilogram of black beans, and 35 cans for a kilogram of rice. The system that has evolved in Brazil for recycling aluminum cans now employs more people than the automotive industry does.[51]

Despite the high recycling rate for cans, the overall aluminum recycling rate worldwide is not high. In the United States, the scrap share of aluminum production in 1998 was 33 percent. Roughly half of this was from scrap generated at the plants where various aluminum products are manufactured. Thus the amount recycled from consumer products containing aluminum was quite small. One reason for this is that investing aluminum in cars and airplanes is relatively recent, thus restricting the amount currently available for recycling. In contrast to worldwide steel use, which has increased little since 1973, aluminum production is still rising.[52]

The encouraging news is that the recycling of both steel and aluminum is increasing. The discouraging news is that neither is doing so fast enough. Far too much aluminum and steel end up in landfills.

As noted earlier, in the eco-economy societies will rely heavily on raw materials already in the system. For example, in the small, densely populated state of New Jersey, there are eight steel minimills that rely almost exclusively on scrap and 13 paper mills that use only waste paper. Collectively, these steel mills and paper plants market more than $1 billion worth of products each year, providing both local jobs and tax revenues. Ironically, these thriving steel and paper mills exist in a state that has no iron mines and little forested area.[53]

In an eco-economy, electric arc steel minimills that efficiently convert scrap steel into finished steel will largely replace iron mines. Advanced industrial economies will come to rely primarily on the stock of materials already in the economy rather than on virgin raw materials. For metals such as steel and aluminum, the losses through use will be minimal. With the appropriate policies, metal— once it is invested in the economy—can be used indefinitely.

Redesigning the Materials Economy

In nature, one-way linear flows do not long survive. Nor, by extension, can they long survive in the human economy that is a part of the earth's ecosystem. The challenge is to redesign the materials economy so that it is compatible with the ecosystem. This initiative has several components. It includes designing products so that they can be easily disassembled and recycled, redesigning industrial processes to eliminate waste generation, banning the use of throwaway beverage containers, using government purchases to expand the market for recycled materials, developing and using technologies that require less material, banning gold mining or at least its use of cyanide solution and mercury, adopting a landfill tax, and eliminating subsidies for environmentally destructive activities.

Some countries are adopting these measures. Germany and recently Japan have begun to require that products such as automobiles, household appliances, and office equipment be designed so that they can be easily disassembled and recycled. In May of 2001, the Japanese Diet enacted a tough appliance recycling law, one that prohibits discarding household appliances, such as washing machines, televisions, or air conditioners. With consumers bearing the cost of disassembling appliances in the form of a disposal fee to recycling firms, which can come to $60 for a refrigerator or $35 for a washing machine, the pressure to design appliances so they can be more easily and cheaply disassembled is strong.[54]

With computers becoming obsolete often within a couple of years as technology advances, the need to be able to quickly disassemble and recycle computers is a paramount challenge in building an eco-economy.

Another policy initiative that can greatly reduce materials use is the banning of one-way beverage containers, something that Denmark and Finland have both done. Denmark, for example, banned one-way soft drink containers in 1977 and beer containers in 1981. Canada's Prince Edward Island has adopted a similar ban on one-way containers. The result in all three cases has been dramatically reduced flows of garbage to landfills.[55]

The environmental costs of beverage containers vary widely. A refillable glass bottle requires less than one fifth as much energy as a recycled aluminum beverage container, assuming the bottle is refilled 15 times, which may be a conservative estimate.[56]

There are also large transport savings, since the containers are simply back-hauled to the original soft drink bottling plants or breweries. If nonrefillable containers are used, whether glass or aluminum, and they are recycled, then they must be transported to a factory where they can be melted down and refashioned into containers and transported back to the bottling plant or brewery.

Another area of potential reduction in materials use is the transportation sector. As cities redesign urban transport systems to better achieve social goals of increased individual mobility, clean air, less traffic congestion and frustration, and more opportunities for exercise, the use of cars will decline accordingly. (See Chapter 9.)

Even more fundamental than the design of products is the redesign of manufacturing processes to eliminate the discharge of pollutants entirely. Many of today's manufacturing processes evolved at a time when the economy was much smaller and when the volume of pollutants did not threaten to overwhelm the ecosystem. More and more companies are now realizing that this cannot continue and some, such as Dupont, have adopted zero emissions as a goal.[57]

Another way to reduce waste is to systematically cluster factories so that the waste from one process can be used as the raw material for another. NEC, the large Japanese electronics firm, is one of the first multinationals to adopt this approach for its various production facilities. In effect, industrial parks are being designed by corporations and by governments specifically to combine factories that have usable waste products. Now in industry, as in nature, one firm's waste becomes another's sustenance.[58]

Market incentives to recycle can be generated by government procurement policies. For example, when the Clinton administration issued an Executive Order in 1993 requiring that all paper purchased for government agencies contain 20 percent or more post-consumer waste by 1995 (increasing to 25 percent by 2000), it created a strong incentive for paper manufacturers to incorporate wastepaper in their manufacturing process. Since the U.S. government is the world's largest paper buyer, this provided a burgeoning market for recycled paper.[59]

A number of state governments achieved a similar goal by setting minimum recycled content standards for newsprint, reports John Young. He notes that the number of newsprint recycling plants in North America increased from 9 in 1988 to 29 in 1994. This created a market for recycled newspapers, converting them from an economic liability into an asset, something that could be sold.[60]

Dematerialization of the economy is facilitated by new technologies that are less material-dependent. Cellular phones, which rely on widely dispersed towers or on satellites for signal transmission, account for most of the growth in telephone use in developing countries. These nations will not need to invest in millions of miles of copper wires, as the industrial countries did. As recently as 1990, cellular phones were rare. But in 1996, cellular phone sales of 51 million overtook the 47 million new phones linked by wire. By 1999, cellular phone sales at 172 million nearly tripled the 63 million sales of fixed-line phones. There were 491 million cell phones in use by then, compared with 907 million traditional ones. By 2005, the number of cellular phones in use will probably exceed the number of telephones linked by wire.[61]

The new technology has arrived on the scene just in time for developing countries, such as China and India, which have few of the traditional linked telephones. Within just a few years, China has overtaken Japan in the number of cellular phone subscribers, trailing only the United States. We can now look forward to a world population linked by a phone network that does not require millions of tons of copper wire.[62]

Efforts to reduce materials use to date have been rather modest, consisting largely of recycling programs. In 1992, a group called the Factor 10 Institute was organized in France under the leadership of Friedrich Schmidt-Bleeck. Its goal is to increase resource productivity by a factor of 10, which they believe is well within the reach of existing technology and management, given the appropriate policy incentives. They recognize that increasing resource productivity by 10-fold—that is, reducing materials use by 90 percent—would "constitute a radical change from the traditional assumption that a healthy economy is one that uses increasing amounts of energy, materials, and resources to produce more goods, more jobs, and more income." Some reductions could be even greater; for example, replacing automobiles with bicycles to increase mobility in congested cities could lower materials use by more than 90 percent.[63]

Although relatively little attention is paid to the building construction industry, it is a leading user of material, including steel and cement. Simple measures like increasing the longevity of buildings can greatly reduce the use of these materials and of the energy used in their manufacture.

The brief review of gold mining in this chapter raises questions about whether the social benefits of gold mining exceed the ecological costs. Some 85 percent of all the gold mined each year is used to produce jewelry that is worn as a status symbol, often a way of displaying wealth by a tiny minority of the world's people.

Turkish environmentalist Birsel Lempke, a recipient of the Right Livelihood Award (often called the alternative Nobel), also questions the future of gold mining. As analyses provide more information on the ecological costs of goal mining, they raise serious doubts as to whether it is worth turning large areas into what Lempke calls "a lunar landscape." She indicates she is not against gold per se, but against the deadly chemicals, such as cyanide and mercury, that are released into the earth's ecosystem in processing the gold ore.[64]

If the costs to society of gold mining outweigh the benefits, then the question is how best to phase out gold mining. One way would be to put a tax on gold that would reflect the environmental costs to society, including the landscape disruption of processing over 700 million tons of ore annually, plus the cost to society of mercury and cyanide pollution. Such a tax would likely raise the price of gold several times. Another approach would be to simply negotiate an international ban on the use of cyanide and mercury in gold mining, much as the international community has recently banned use of a dozen toxic chemicals. Either policy approach could be used. Regardless of which one prevails, both current and future generations would be the beneficiaries.[65]

Another industry whose value to society is being questioned by the environmental community is the bottled water industry. The World Wide Fund for Nature (WWF), an organization with 5.2 million members, released a study in April 2001 urging consumers to forgo bottled water, observing that it was no safer or healthier than tap water, even though it can cost 1,000 times as much.[66]

WWF notes that in the United States and Europe there are more standards regulating tap water quality than that of bottled water. Although clever marketing in industrial countries has convinced many consumers that bottled water is healthier, the WWF study could not find any support for this claim. For those living where water is unsafe, as in some Third World cities, it is far cheaper to boil or filter water than to buy it in bottles.[67]

Phasing out the use of bottled water would eliminate the need for the fleets of trucks that haul the water and distribute it. This in turn would reduce the materials needed to manufacture the trucks as well as the traffic congestion, air pollution, and rising carbon dioxide levels associated with their operation.[68]

One of the most environmentally productive policy initiatives would be to eliminate subsidies that encourage the use of raw materials. Nowhere are these greater than in the electricity sector. In France, for example, the state-owned aluminum company gets electricity at the heavily subsidized rate of 1.5¢ per kilowatt-hour, while other industries pay 6¢ and residential users pay close to 12¢. In Canada, the government of Quebec also offers the aluminum industry electricity at 1.5¢ per kilowatt-hour. Without this huge subsidy, the industry probably could not profitably manufacture nonrefillable beverage containers. This subsidy to aluminum indirectly subsidizes transportation, including both airlines and automobiles, thus encouraging travel, an energy-intensive activity.[69]

The most pervasive policy initiative to dematerialize the economy is the proposed tax on the burning of fossil fuels, a tax that would reflect the full cost to society of mining coal and pumping oil, of the air pollution associated with their use, and of climate disruption. A carbon emissions tax will lead to a more realistic price for energy, one that will permeate the energy-intensive materials economy and reduce materials use.

The challenge in building an eco-economy materials sector is to ensure that the market is sending honest signals. In the words of Ernst von Weizsäcker, an environmentalist and leader in the German Bundestag, "The challenge is to get the market to tell the *ecological* truth." To help the market to tell the truth, for example, we need not only a carbon tax, but also a landfill tax so that those generating the garbage pay the full cost of getting rid of it and of managing the landfill and its potentially toxic waste flows in perpetuity.[70]

7

Feeding Everyone Well

In November 1965, U.S. Secretary of Agriculture Orville Freeman asked if I would draft a plan to get India's agriculture moving. The monsoon had failed that summer, leaving India to face a potential famine of historic proportions. India had been neglecting its agriculture in favor of industrial development and had no grain reserves. As one official in New Delhi put it, "Our reserves are in the grain elevators in Kansas."

President Lyndon Johnson was concerned, because he knew that the United States could not feed India's growing population over the long term. He wanted a plan for India to develop its agriculture and an agreement that India would implement the plan promptly in exchange for massive food relief. Since I was working as an Asian agricultural analyst in the U.S. Department of Agriculture and was familiar with India, having spent part of 1956 living in villages there, I was chosen to draft the plan.

The key steps for India to take were straightforward. The first was to shift from an urban-oriented policy of ceiling prices for

This chapter is adapted from "Eradicating Hunger: A Growing Challenge," in Lester R. Brown et al., *State of the World 2001* (New York: W.W. Norton & Company, 2001).

grain that discouraged investment in agriculture to a rural-oriented policy of support prices that would encourage farmers to invest in improving their land and other output-expanding measures. The second step was to move the fertilizer industry out of the government sector, where it took up to nine years to build a fertilizer plant, into the private sector, where plants could be built in two years. The third was to harness the abundant underground water resources for irrigation. The fourth was to disseminate quickly the high-yielding wheats that had already been tested and approved for use in India.

During the year following signature of the agreement, the United States shipped a fifth of its wheat crop to India to offset the poor harvest. Two ships left U.S. ports each day laden with grain for India—part of the largest movement of grain between two countries in history. Between 1965 and 1973, India doubled its wheat harvest, a record gain for a major country. The agricultural plan succeeded beyond our hopes as India became self-sufficient in grain.[1]

The plan I drafted in November 1965 was not difficult. Any number of people could have come up with such a scheme because the needed steps were so obvious. Today, however, with its population projected to grow by 563 million by 2050, India is facing a far more complex challenge. Achieving a humane balance between food and people may now depend more on the success of family planners in accelerating the shift to smaller families than on farmers. In India, as in the world as a whole, soil erosion, aquifer depletion, and climate change are the principal threats to the sustainability of agriculture, to building the food sector of an eco-economy.[2]

Expanding food production to feed the world's growing numbers will be far more difficult during this half-century than it was over the last. During the last half of the twentieth century, the world's farmers nearly tripled grain production, boosting it from 631 million tons in 1950 to 1,835 million tons in 2000. This half-century gain was nearly double that from the beginning of agriculture, some 11,000 years ago, until 1950.[3]

Impressive though this achievement was, most of the progress was cancelled by population growth. Today, 1.1 billion of the world's 6.1 billion people are still undernourished and underweight. Hunger and the fear of starvation quite literally shape their lives.[4]

Eradicating the hunger that exists today and feeding those to be added tomorrow is a worthy challenge, one made all the more difficult because two of the world's three food systems—rangelands and oceanic fisheries—are already being pushed to or even beyond their sustainable yields. The output of croplands has not yet reached its limit, but the rise in cropland productivity has slowed over the last decade.

In its most basic form, hunger is a productivity problem. Typically people are hungry because they do not produce enough food to meet their needs or because they do not earn enough money to buy it. The only lasting solution is to raise their productivity—a task complicated by the ongoing shrinkage in both the cropland area and irrigation water per person in developing countries.

A Status Report

As noted, 1.1 billion people are undernourished and underweight. The meshing of this number with a World Bank estimate of 1.3 billion living in poverty, defined as those living on $1 a day or less, comes as no surprise. Poverty and hunger go hand in hand.[5]

Gains in eradicating hunger in East Asia and Latin America leave most of those who are still hungry concentrated in the Indian subcontinent and sub-Saharan Africa. In these regions, most of the hungry live in the countryside. The World Bank reports that 72 percent of the world's 1.3 billion poor live in rural areas. Most of them are undernourished, sentenced to a short life. These rural poor usually live not on the productive irrigated plains but on the semiarid/arid fringes of agriculture or in the upper reaches of watersheds on highly erodible, steeply sloped land. Eradicating hunger depends on stabilizing these fragile ecosystems.[6]

Demographically, most of the world's poor live in countries with rapidly growing populations, where poverty and population growth are reinforcing each other. The Indian subcontinent, for example, is adding 21 million people a year, the equivalent of another Australia. By mid-century, the population of this region—already the hungriest on earth—is expected to include another 900 million people.[7]

No single factor bears so directly on the prospect of eradicating hunger in this region as population growth. In rural societies, when a farm passes from one generation to the next, it is typically subdivided among the children. With the second generation of rapid population growth and subsequent land fragmentation, farms are shrinking to the point where they can no longer support the people living on them.

Between 1970 and 1990, the number of farms in India with less than 2 hectares (5 acres) of land increased from 49 million to 82 million. Assuming that this trend has continued since then, India now has more than 90 million farms of less than 2 hectares. If each family has six members, then 540 million people—over half of India's population—are trapped in a precarious balance with the land.[8]

In Bangladesh, average farm size has already fallen below 1 hectare. According to one study, Bangladesh's "strong tradition of bequeathing land in fixed proportions to all male and female heirs has led to increasing landlessness and extreme fragmentation of agricultural holdings." In addition to the millions who are now landless, millions more have plots so small that they are effectively landless.[9]

Africa, with the world's fastest population growth, is facing a similar reduction in cropland per person. For example, as Nigeria's population goes from 114 million today to a projected 278 million in 2050, its per capita grainland—most of it semiarid and unirrigated—will shrink from 0.15 hectares to 0.06 hectares. Nigeria's food prospect, if it stays on this population trajectory, is not promising.[10]

Further complicating efforts to expand food production are water shortages. As noted earlier, almost all of the 3.2 billion people to be added to world population in the next 50 years will be born in countries already facing water shortages, such as India, Pakistan, and those in the Middle East and semiarid Africa. In India, water tables are already falling in large areas as demand exceeds the sustainable yield of aquifers. For many countries facing water scarcity, trying to eradicate hunger while population continues to grow rapidly is like trying to walk up a down escalator.[11]

Even as the world faces the prospect of adding 80 million people a year over the next two decades, expanding food production is becoming more difficult. In each of the three food systems—croplands, rangelands, and oceanic fisheries—output expanded dramatically during most of the twentieth century's last half. Now this is changing.

Between 1950 and 2000, as noted earlier, world production of grain nearly tripled. Production per person climbed nearly 40 percent as growth in the grain harvest outstripped that of population.

The rising tide of grain production improved nutrition for much of humanity, but after 1984 growth in production slowed, falling behind that of population. By 2000, production per person had dropped 11 percent from the peak. (See Table 7–1.) The decline is concentrated in Africa, where rapid population growth has simply outrun grain production, and in the former Soviet Union, where the economy has shrunk by half since 1990 and living standards have deteriorated.[12]

Table 7–1. *World Production Per Person of Grain, Beef and Mutton,*
and Seafood, 1950–2000

Food	Growth Period	Growth	Decline Period	Decline
		(percent)		(percent)
Grain	1950–84	+ 38	1984–2000	– 11
Beef and Mutton	1950–72	+ 44	1972–2000	– 15
Seafood	1950–88	+112	1988–98	– 17

Source: See endnote 12.

Roughly 1.2 billion tons of the world grain harvest are consumed directly as food, with most of the remaining 635 million tons (36 percent) consumed indirectly in livestock, poultry, and aquacultural products. The share of total grain used for feed varies widely among the "big three" food producers—ranging from a low of 4 percent in India to 25 percent in China and 65 percent in the United States.[13]

Over the last half-century, the soaring world demand for animal protein was satisfied largely by expanding the output of meat from rangelands and of seafood from oceanic fisheries. World production of beef and mutton increased from 24 million tons in 1950 to 65 million tons in 2000, a near tripling. Most of the growth, however, occurred from 1950 to 1972, when output went up 44 percent. Since 1972, beef and mutton production per person has fallen by 15 percent.[14]

An estimated four fifths of the beef and mutton produced worldwide in 2000, roughly 52 million tons, comes from animals that forage on rangelands. With the world's rangelands now being grazed at or beyond capacity, future gains in output will likely be limited.[15]

The growth in the oceanic fish catch exceeded even that of beef and mutton, climbing from 19 million tons in 1950 to 86 million tons in 1998, the last year for which data are available. This four-fold growth was also concentrated in 1950–88, a time during which the annual growth in the catch—at 3.8 percent—was easily double that of world population. As a result, the oceanic fish catch per person climbed from 8 kilograms in 1950 to 17 kilograms in 1988. Since then, it has fallen by some 17 percent. The new reality is that fishers and ranchers can no longer satisfy much of the growing demand for food. For the first time since civilization began, farmers must try to meet future food needs on their own.[16]

Raising Cropland Productivity

In a world where there is little new land to plow, raising the productivity of existing cropland is the key to feeding the 80 million people added each year. It is also essential for protecting the earth's ecosystem. If farmers had not been able to nearly triple land productivity since 1950, it would have been necessary to clear half of the world's remaining forestland for food production.

There are at least three ways of raising cropland productivity: raise the yield per crop, increase the number of crops per year through multiple cropping, and get more out of the existing harvest by "processing" crop residues through ruminants to produce meat and milk.

Raising world cropland productivity is becoming progressively more difficult. Over the last century or so, plant breeders dramatically boosted the genetic yield potential of wheat, rice, and corn—the leading grains. At the heart of this effort was an increase in the share of the plant's photosynthate, the product of photosynthesis, going to the seed. While the originally domesticated wheats did not use much more than 20 percent of their photosynthate to produce seed, today's highly productive varieties devote half or more to seed formation. The theoretical upper limit is estimated at 60 percent since the plant's roots, stem, and leaves also require photosynthate.[17]

Realizing the genetic potential of the new seeds depends on alleviating any nutrient or moisture constraints on yields. Fertilizers are designed to remove the limits imposed by nutrient deficiencies. As cities have grown over the past century, there has been a massive disruption of the nutrient cycle, making it more difficult to return the nutrients in human waste to the land, and leaving the world ever more dependent on fertilizer. In earlier times, when food was produced and consumed locally, nutrients were automatically recycled back onto the land in the form of livestock and human waste. But as cities developed, as the world shifted from a subsistence economy to a market economy, and as international trade expanded, farmers offset the growing loss of nutrients with fertilizer.

As world fertilizer use climbed from 14 million tons in 1950 to 141 million tons in 2000, in some countries it began to press against the physiological limits of plants to absorb nutrients. In response, fertilizer use has leveled off in the United States, Western Europe, Japan, and now possibly China. In these countries, applying additional nutrients has little effect on production. Some parts of the world, such as the Indian subcontinent and Latin America, can still profitably use additional fertilizer. But for the world as a whole, the rapid growth in fertilizer use—the engine that helped triple the world grain harvest since 1950—is now history.[18]

Where fertilizer use is excessive, nutrient runoff into rivers and oceans can lead to algal blooms that then use up all available oxygen in the water as the algae decompose, creating dead zones with no sea life. Food output on land is expanding in part at the expense of that from the oceans.[19]

The accumulation of nitrates in underground water supplies in Western Europe led to European Union regulations to restrict fertilizer use. In Denmark, farmers are required to compile an annual nitrogen balance for the application and crop use of nitrogen. If this balance, submitted to the government each year, shows excessive runoff, farmers can be fined. The state of Iowa, concerned about nitrogen in underground water, levied a tax on fertilizer to discourage its excessive use.[20]

Just as fertilizer removes nutrient constraints on production, irrigation can remove moisture constraints, enabling plants to realize their full genetic potential. In some cases, irrigation simply boosts land productivity, but in others it permits dry season cropping or an expansion of cropping onto arid land.

While the world as a whole has nearly tripled land productivity since 1950, some countries have done even better. Over the last half-century, China, France, the United Kingdom, and Mexico have quadrupled wheat yield per hectare. India has nearly done the same. And the United States has quadrupled its corn yield.[21]

For several decades scientists generated a steady flow of new technologies designed to raise land productivity, but this flow is now ebbing. In some countries, farmers are now literally looking over the shoulder of scientists at agricultural experiment stations. In countries where yields have already tripled or quadrupled, it is becoming difficult for farmers to continue raising yields. For example, wheat yields in the United States have increased little since 1983. Rice yields in Japan have risen little since 1984.[22]

Even some developing countries are now experiencing a plateauing of grain yields. Between 1961 and 1977, rice yields in South Korea increased nearly 60 percent, but during the quarter-century since they have risen by only 1 percent. Similarly, wheat yields in Mexico climbed from 0.9 tons per hectare in 1950 to 4.4 tons in 1982, a rise of nearly fivefold. Since then there has been little change. (See Figure 7–1.) As the rise in land productivity levels off in more and more countries, expanding global grain output will become progressively more difficult.[23]

Over the last half-century, the world's farmers nearly tripled land productivity, but now future gains in productivity are more difficult to come by. Farmers managed to double the 1950 grain yield of 1 ton per hectare by 1982, when they surpassed 2 tons. By 2000 they were at 2.8 tons, close to a tripling of the 1950 yield. But the rise in yields is slowing.[24]

Raising crop yields is primarily a biological challenge, not un-

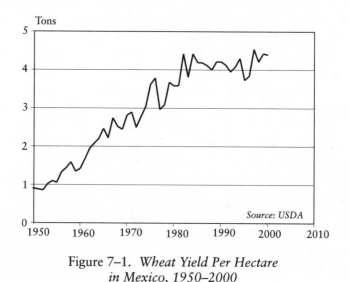

Figure 7–1. *Wheat Yield Per Hectare*
in Mexico, 1950–2000

like increasing athletic performances. Somewhere in antiquity, someone ran a mile in less than six minutes. Well before the first modern-day Olympics, held in 1896, runners were covering a mile in under five minutes. In 1954, Roger Bannister broke the four-minute barrier. A half-century has passed since then, but no one talks about running a three-minute mile. We have reached the point where cutting another minute from our mile time may be physiologically impossible.[25]

We are faced with a similar situation with grain yields. For the world's farmers, going from an average of 1 ton per hectare to 2 was easy. Getting from 2 tons to nearly 3, where we are now, was much more difficult. For the world to move from 3 to 4 tons per hectare may be almost as difficult as going from a four-minute to a three-minute mile. If so, family planners will be under a lot of pressure to slow population growth.

For the world as a whole, the rise in land productivity has slowed markedly since 1990. From 1950 until then, world grain yield per hectare rose 2.1 percent a year. Between 1990 and 2000, however, the annual gain was only 1.1 percent. (See Table 7–2.)

Biotechnology is often cited as a potential source of higher yields, but although biotechnologists have been engineering new plant varieties for two decades, they have yet to produce a single variety of wheat, rice, or corn that can dramatically raise yields. The reason is that conventional plant breeders had already done most of the things they could think of to raise grain yields. Biotechnology's contributions are more likely to come in developing crop varieties that reduce insecticide use, are more drought-tolerant, or are more salt-tolerant. If genetic engineers can breed salt-tolerant varieties, it would alleviate water shortages. Perhaps the largest question hang-

Table 7–2. *Gains in World Grain Yield Per Hectare, 1950–2000*

Year	Yield Per Hectare[1]	Annual Increase
(tons)	(percent)	
1950	1.06	
1990	2.47	2.1
2000	2.75	1.1

[1]Yield for 1990 is three-year average.
Source: USDA, *Production, Supply, and Distribution,* electronic database, Washington, DC, updated May 2001.

ing over the future of biotechnology is the possible long-term environmental and human health effects of using genetically modified crops.

Land productivity can also be raised by increasing the number of crops per year, where temperature and soil moisture permit. In China, for instance, double cropping winter wheat and corn is widespread, enabling farmers in the North China Plain to harvest two high-yielding grain crops each year. In northern India, the double cropping of winter wheat and summer rice is now commonplace, a key to sustaining India's population of 1 billion. Argentina and the United States both double crop winter wheat with a summer crop of soybeans.[26]

Although the United States occupies a latitude similar to that of China, double cropping is not nearly as common, partly because until recently farmers' eligibility for government support prices depended on restricting the area planted, which discouraged multiple cropping. While there was surplus land, there was little reason to seriously consider double cropping or to develop the technologies that would facilitate it.

At present, roughly 10 percent of the 30-million-hectare U.S. soybean crop is double-cropped with winter wheat. If world food supplies tighten, this area could be expanded substantially, providing a strategic assist in increasing the food supply.[27]

Raising cropland productivity is the key to saving the world's remaining forests. If the world's farmers cannot raise land productivity enough to satisfy the future growth in demand for food, then further clearing of forests for agriculture will be unavoidable.

Raising Water Productivity

Over the last half-century, world irrigated area tripled, climbing from 90 million hectares in 1950 to nearly 270 million in 2000. Most of the growth occurred from 1950 to 1978, when irrigation expanded faster than population and boosted irrigated land per person from 0.037 hectares to 0.047 hectares, an increase of one fourth. After 1978, however, the growth in irrigation slowed, falling behind that of population and shrinking the irrigated land per person 8 percent. (See Figure 7–2.)[28]

In the years immediately ahead, the combination of aquifer depletion and the diversion of irrigation water to nonfarm uses may end the historical growth in irrigated area. If so, it will be more difficult

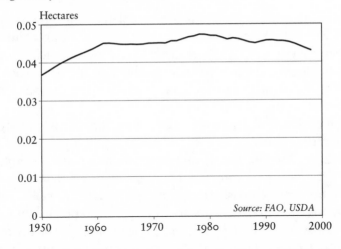

Figure 7–2. *World Irrigated Area Per Person, 1950–98*

to feed 3 billion more people.

In many countries, the competition for water between the countryside and cities is intensifying, underlining the value of raising water productivity. Although projections of the future diversion of irrigation water to residential and industrial uses do not exist for most countries, a World Bank forecast for South Korea—a relatively well watered country—gives some sense of what may lie ahead. Like many countries, Korea is now using virtually all available water. The Bank calculates that if the Korean economy grows 5.5 percent annually until 2025, growth in water withdrawals for residential and industrial use will reduce the yearly supply remaining for irrigation from 13 billion to 7 billion tons. Rising water prices and associated gains in water productivity will likely ameliorate the loss of water for irrigation, but this analysis nonetheless shows how difficult it may be for some countries even to maintain existing irrigated area.[29]

Farmers everywhere face an uphill battle in the competition for water since the economics of water use do not favor agriculture. Industry can often pay 50 to 100 times as much for water as farmers do. Wherever economic growth and the creation of jobs are a central preoccupation of political leaders, scarce water will likely go to industry.[30]

In addition, countries that are overpumping, including key food-producing ones such as China, India, and the United States, will lose irrigation water as aquifers are depleted. Once the rising demand for water surpasses the sustainable yield of an aquifer, the gap between demand and sustainable yield widens each year. As it does, the annual drop in the water table also increases each year, accelerating depletion of the aquifer and setting the stage for an abrupt fall in the food supply.[31]

The need for water in the Indian subcontinent is already outrunning the supply. Water tables are falling in much of India, including the Punjab, the country's breadbasket. (See Chapter 2.) The excessive use of water is encouraged by heavy electricity subsidies to farmers, who use electric pumps for irrigation.[32]

In sub-Saharan Africa, the potential for irrigation is limited simply because so much of the continent is arid or semiarid. The greater promise here may lie in water harvesting and systematically building soil organic matter so that soils can absorb and retain more of the low rainfall. The construction of earthen terraces supported by rocks retains water and reduces soil erosion. Leguminous trees planted as windbreaks reduce wind erosion and add nitrogen and organic matter to the soil.

The world water situation today is similar to that with cropland at the middle of the last century: the opportunities for developing new supplies are fast disappearing. By 1950, the frontiers of agricultural settlement had largely vanished, leaving little productive new land to plow. In response, governments launched a broadbased effort to raise land productivity, one that included price supports for farm commodities that encouraged farmers to invest in yield-raising inputs and land improvements, heavy public investment in agricultural research to raise crop yields, and the building of public institutions to support this effort—from agricultural extension services to farm credit banks. Societies mobilized a wide array of resources that doubled land productivity between 1950 and 1984.

The doubling of grainland productivity in little more than a generation is one of the remarkable scientific feats of the modern age. As the new century begins, a similar broad-based effort is needed to raise water productivity. There are several avenues to raising water productivity, but the key is pricing water at closer to market value, a step that leads to systemic advances in efficiency. China, facing acute water shortages, has recently announced a plan to raise water prices each year over the next five years. The attraction of market pricing is that it is systemic, promoting more-rational water use throughout the economy.

With 70 percent of the water that is diverted from rivers or pumped from underground being used for irrigation, any gains in irrigation water efficiency have benefits that extend far beyond agriculture. Indeed, getting enough water for cities and industry while maintaining food production may be possible only if irrigation productivity is systematically raised worldwide.[33]

The use of more water-efficient irrigation practices is the key. There are many ways to irrigate crops, including furrow, flood, overhead sprinkler, and drip irrigation. Furrow irrigation, probably the earliest form, is used with row crops, with a small trench being cut near each row of plants. Flood irrigation, traditionally used on rice, is now being reconsidered since recent research indicates that at least in some situations periodic flooding will produce the same yield as continuous flooding, but use much less water.[34]

Overhead sprinkler irrigation, which is widely used in the U.S. southern Great Plains, is often coupled with the use of underground water. The circles of green crops that can be seen when flying over this region during the summer are created with water from center-pivot overhead sprinklers that use well water to irrigate. (In this region, most of the water is drawn from the Ogallala aquifer—essentially a fossil aquifer since its recharge is limited.) Shifting from a high-pressure to a low-pressure overhead sprinkler system can boost irrigation efficiency from 65 percent to 80 percent. Shifting to a low-energy precision application sprinkler system can raise it to 90 percent or better.[35]

Drip irrigation technology, pioneered in Israel, is the most efficient of all irrigation systems. It typically uses a plastic hose with small holes or emitters, which either rests on the soil surface or is installed several inches below it. Sandra Postel and her colleagues report that studies in several countries show drip irrigation reducing water use by 30–70 percent. And because it provides a steady supply of water carefully geared to crop needs, it raises yields by 20–90 percent. The combination of reduced water use and higher yields can easily double water productivity, an attractive prospect.[36]

In the past, this high-cost, labor-intensive form of irrigation was used only on high-value crops such as fruits and vegetables. But this is now changing. New low-cost drip irrigation systems designed specifically for small farms, typically with a payback period of one year, are opening broad new horizons for expansion. Because they are more labor-intensive, these drip systems are well adapted to small holdings where labor is more plentiful. Postel reports that India has an estimated 10 million hectares that can profitably be irrigated with drip systems. There may be a similar potential in China.[37]

Another way to raise water productivity is to shift to more water-efficient crops. For example, wheat typically produces half again as much grain per unit of water as rice does. This is why Egypt restricts rice planting in favor of wheat.[38]

As a general matter, the higher the yield of a crop, the more productive the water use. For example, a rice crop that yields four tons per hectare uses little more water than one that yields two tons per hectare simply because so much of the water used to produce rice is lost through evaporation from the water surface. Simply put, raising land productivity also raises water productivity.

Restructuring the Protein Economy

The demand for meat—beef, pork, poultry, and mutton—typically rises with income, perhaps driven by the taste for meat acquired during our 4 million years as hunter-gatherers. This innate hunger for animal protein, which manifests itself in every society, has lifted the world demand for meat each year for 40 consecutive years. One of the most predictable trends in the global economy, world meat production climbed from 44 million tons in 1950 to 233 million tons in 2000, more than a fivefold increase. (See Figure 7–3.) This growth, roughly double that of population, raised meat intake per person worldwide from 17 kilograms to 38 kilograms.[39]

Once the limits of rangelands and fisheries are reached, then the growing demand for animal protein can be satisfied by feeding cattle in feedlots or fish in ponds; by expanding the production of pork, poultry, and eggs, all largely dependent on feed concentrates; or by producing more milk.

In this new situation, the varying efficiency with which grain is converted into protein—beef, pork, poultry, and fish—is shaping production trends. Cattle in feedlots require roughly 7 kilograms of feed concentrate per additional kilogram of live weight. For pigs, the ratio is nearly 4 to 1. Chickens are much more efficient, with a 2-to-1 ratio. Fish, including both herbivorous and omnivorous species, require less than 2 kilograms of grain concentrate per kilo-

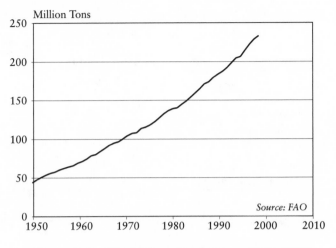

Figure 7–3. *World Meat Production, 1950–2000*

gram of gain.[40]

There are three ways to increase animal protein supply without consuming more grain: improve the efficiency of grain conversion into animal protein; shift from the less efficient forms of conversion, such as beef or pork, to the more efficient ones, such as poultry or farmed fish; and rely on ruminants to convert more roughage into either meat or milk.

Not surprisingly, the economics of the varying conversion rates is accelerating growth in output among the more efficient converters. The world's existing feedlots are being maintained, but there is little new investment in feedlots simply because of the higher cost of fed beef. From 1990 to 2000, world beef production increased only 0.5 percent a year compared with 2.5 percent for pork. The most rapidly growing source of meat during this period was poultry, expanding at 4.9 percent annually. (See Table 7–3.)[41]

The oceanic fish catch has not increased appreciably since 1990, thus falling far behind the soaring growth in demand for seafood. In response, aquacultural output expanded from 13 million tons of fish in 1990 to 31 million tons in 1998, growing by more than 11 percent a year. Even if aquacultural growth slows somewhat during the current decade, world aquacultural output is still on track to overtake the production of beef by 2010.[42]

China is the leading aquacultural producer, accounting for 21 million tons of the global output in 1998. Its output is rather evenly

Table 7–3. *World Growth in Animal Protein*
Production, by Source, 1990–2000

Source	Annual Rate of Growth
	(percent)
Aquaculture[1]	11.4
Poultry	4.9
Pork	2.5
Beef	0.5
Oceanic fish catch[1]	0.1

[1] 1990–98 only.
Source: See endnote 41.

divided between coastal and inland areas. Coastal output is dominated by shellfish—mostly oysters, clams, and mussels. It also includes small amounts of shrimp or prawns and some finfish. Coastal aquaculture is often environmentally damaging because it depends on converting wetlands into fish farms or because it concentrates waste, leading to damaging algal blooms.[43]

Except for shellfish, most of China's aquacultural output is produced inland in ponds, lakes, reservoirs, and rice paddies. Some 5 million hectares of land are devoted exclusively to fish farming, much of it to carp polyculture. In addition, 1.7 million hectares of riceland produce rice and fish together.[44]

Over time, China has evolved a fish polyculture using four types of carp that feed at different levels of the food chain, in effect emulating natural aquatic ecosystems. Silver carp and bighead carp are filter feeders, eating phytoplankton and zooplankton respectively. The grass carp, as its name implies, feeds largely on vegetation, while the common carp is a bottom feeder, living on detritus that settles to the bottom. Most of China's aquaculture is integrated with agriculture, enabling farmers to use agricultural wastes, such as pig manure, to fertilize ponds, thus stimulating the growth of plankton. Fish polyculture, which typically boosts pond productivity over that of monocultures by at least half, also dominates fish farming in India.[45]

As land and water become ever more scarce, China's fish farmers are feeding more grain concentrates in order to raise pond productivity. Between 1990 and 1996, China's farmers raised the annual pond yield per hectare from 2.4 tons of fish to 4.1 tons.[46]

In the United States, catfish, which require less than 2 kilograms of feed per kilogram of live weight, are the leading aquacultural product. U.S. catfish production of 270,000 tons (600 million pounds) is concentrated in four states: Mississippi, Louisiana, Alabama, and Arkansas. Mississippi, with some 45,000 hectares (174 square miles) of catfish ponds and easily 60 percent of U.S. output, is the catfish capital of the world.[47]

Public attention has focused on aquacultural operations that are environmentally disruptive, such as the farming of salmon, a carnivorous species, and shrimp. Yet these operations account for only 1.5 million tons of output. World aquaculture is dominated by herbivorous species, importantly carp in China and India, but also catfish in the United States and tilapia in several countries.[48]

Just as aquaculture is supplementing the fish catch, new practices are evolving to efficiently expand livestock output. Although rangelands are being grazed to capacity and beyond, there is a large unrealized potential for feeding agricultural residues—rice straw, wheat straw, and corn stalks—to ruminants, such as cattle, sheep, and goats. This can mean that a given grain crop yields a second harvest—the meat or the milk that is produced with the straw and corn stalks. Ruminants have a highly sophisticated digestive system, one that can convert straw and corn stalks into meat and milk without using the grain that can be consumed by humans. At present, most human food comes from the photosynthate going into the seed of cereals, but by feeding animals straw and corn stalks, the photosynthate that goes into stems and leaves also can be converted into food.[49]

In India, both water buffalo, which are particularly good at converting coarse roughage into milk, and cattle figure prominently in the dairy industry. India has been uniquely successful in converting crop residues into milk, expanding production from 20 million tons in 1961 to 79 million tons in 2000—a near fourfold increase. Following a path of steady growth, milk became India's leading farm product in value in 1994. In 1997, India overtook the United States to become the world's leading milk producer. (See Figure 7–4.) Remarkably, it did so almost entirely by using farm byproducts and crop residues, avoiding the diversion of grain from human consumption to cattle.[50]

Between 1961 and 2000, India's milk production per person

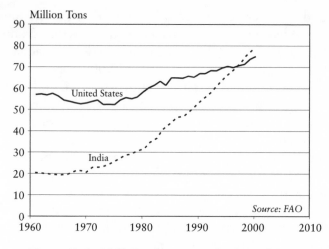

Figure 7–4. *Milk Production in the United States
and India, 1961–2000*

increased from 0.9 liters per week to 1.5 liters, or roughly a cup of milk per day. Although this is not a lot by western standards, it is a welcome expansion in a protein-hungry country.[51]

The dairy industry structure in India is unique in that the milk is produced almost entirely by small farmers, who have only one to three cows. Milk production is integrated with agriculture, involving an estimated 70 million farmers for whom it is a highly valued source of supplemental income. Dairying, even on a small scale, is a labor-intensive process, including gathering the roughage where cows are stall-fed, milking them, and transporting the milk to market. Ownership of a few cows or buffalo also means a supply of manure for cooking fuel and for fertilizer. If India can introduce new energy sources for cooking, it will free up more cow manure for fertilizer.[52]

China also has a large potential to feed corn stalks and wheat and rice straw to cattle or sheep. As the world's leading producer of both rice and wheat and the second ranked producer of corn, China annually harvests an estimated 500 million tons of straw, corn stalks, and other crop residues. At present, much of this either is burned, simply to dispose of it, or is used in villages as fuel. Fortunately, China has vast wind resources that can be harnessed to produce electricity for cooking, thus freeing up roughage for feeding additional cattle or sheep.[53]

The ammoniation of crop residues (that is, the incorporation of nitrogen) in the roughage helps the microbial flora in the rumen of the cattle and sheep to digest the roughage more completely. The use of this technology in the major crop-producing provinces of east central China—Hebei, Shandong, Henan, and Anhui—has created a "Beef Belt." Beef output in these four provinces now dwarfs that of the grazing provinces of Inner Mongolia, Qinghai, and Xinjiang.[54]

Ruminants also produce soil-enriching manure that not only returns nutrients to the soil, but also adds organic matter, which improves both soil aeration and water retention capacity, thus enhancing soil productivity. Roughage-based livestock systems are almost necessarily local in nature because roughage is too bulky to transport long distances.

Satisfying the demand for protein in a protein-hungry world where water scarcity is likely to translate into grain scarcity is a challenge to agricultural policymakers everywhere. If grain becomes scarce, as now seems likely, other countries, such as the United States, Canada, and France, may follow India's example of using ruminants to systematically convert more crop residues into food.

Eradicating Hunger: A Broad Strategy

This chapter began by noting that sustaining a sufficient growth in food output to eradicate hunger will now take a superhuman effort both within agriculture and in related activities outside that sector. Soil erosion, aquifer depletion, and climate change threaten future food production. Food security may depend as much on the efforts of family planners as on farmers and as much on the decisions made in ministries of energy that shape future climate trends as on decisions made in ministries of agriculture. The difficulty in eradicating hunger is matched only by the urgency of doing so.

In countries where farm size is shrinking fast, raising land productivity deserves even greater priority than in the past. And increasingly, raising water productivity is the key to further gains in land productivity. Governments running the risk of an abrupt drop in food production as a result of aquifer depletion may be able to avoid such a situation only by simultaneously slowing population growth and raising water productivity in order to stabilize water tables.

Stabilizing population is as essential as it is difficult. If rapid population growth continues, it will lead to further fragmentation of land holdings, as well as to hydrological poverty on a scale that is now difficult to imagine. Hundreds of millions of people will not have enough water to meet their most basic needs, including food production. Chapter 10 discusses further the urgent need to stabilize world population.

With the rise in land productivity slowing, continuing rapid population growth makes eradicating rural hunger much more difficult, if not impossible. Perhaps the single most important thing India, for example, can do to enhance its future food security is to accelerate the shift to smaller families. This would enable it to move to the low-level U.N. population projection instead of the medium-level one, thereby adding only 289 million people instead of 563 million in the next 50 years.[55]

As the backlog of unused agricultural technology shrinks, providing enough food will increasingly depend on strengthening international agricultural research assistance. Appropriations for agricultural research are lagging far behind needs. For some farmers, the technology pipeline is running dry. More locally oriented investment in agricultural research that will help expand multiple cropping and intercropping could pay large dividends.

Raising grain yield per hectare in the two regions where the world's hungry are concentrated will not be easy. India's wheat yield, for example, has already tripled since 1960. The rise in rice yield, which went from just under 1 ton per hectare in 1965 to 1.9 tons in 1993, has slowed. Lifting land productivity in India is constrained by the country's proximity to the equator. Day length during the summer is relatively short, and since rice is typically grown during the summer monsoon season, when cloud cover is heavy, solar intensity is low.[56]

Now that water scarcity is becoming a constraint on efforts to expand world food production, the time has come for an all-out effort to raise water productivity. Such a campaign could be patterned on the earlier effort to raise land productivity, involving a wide range of government initiatives—including research on raising productivity, water pricing that will reflect the value of water, government loans for farmers' attempts to raise water productivity, and the training of agricultural extension agents to help farmers in this effort.

As water scarcity translates into food scarcity, countries everywhere need to reexamine the potential for multiple cropping. This is particularly true for a country like the United States, where crop acreage limits have traditionally discouraged multiple cropping.

In India, the multiple-cropped area can be expanded by harvesting and storing water during the monsoon season so that more land can be cropped during the dry season. If agricultural extension workers are trained in water harvesting techniques, they can then work with local farmers to increase water storage. This will help raise yield per crop and also the crops produced per year.

With cropland becoming scarce, efforts to protect prime farmland are needed the world over. Here, Japan is the model. It has successfully protected rice paddies even within the boundaries of the city of Tokyo, thus enabling Japan to remain self-sufficient in its staple food—rice.

Similarly with soil conservation: with erosion now taking a measurable toll on food production in so many countries, the adoption of farming practices that reduce soil erosion will pay handsome dividends. The model is the United States, which has both converted highly erodible cropland back to grassland and adopted conservation practices to reduce erosion. The conversion of erodible cropland back to grassland or to trees, coupled with the adoption of conservation tillage on 37 percent of all cropped land, reduced soil erosion from 3.1 billion tons in 1982 to 1.9 billion tons in 1997.[57]

Another potential for expanding food production, one that has been neglected in many industrial countries, is the feeding of crop residues to ruminants, as described earlier. This can reduce pressure on rangelands, as it has done in India and China. This potential for a second harvest from a single crop deserves to be systematically exploited worldwide.

Recognizing that malnutrition is largely the result of rural poverty, the World Bank is replacing its long-standing, crop-centered agricultural development strategies with rural development strategies that use a much broader approach. Bank planners believe that a more systemic approach to eradicating rural poverty—one that embraces agriculture but that also integrates human capital development, the development of infrastructure, and social development into a strategy for rural development—is needed to shrink the number living in poverty. One advantage of encouraging investment in the countryside in both agribusiness and other industries is that it encourages breadwinners to stay in the countryside, keeping families and communities intact. In the absence of such a strategy, rural poverty simply feeds urban poverty.[58]

In countries such as India, where farm size is shrinking, it becomes more difficult to raise land productivity enough to provide adequate nutrition. The challenge in these areas is to mobilize capital both through domestic savings and by attracting investment from abroad to build the factories needed to provide employment and income in rural areas. This will help rural families and communities stay together. For this the model is China, which has achieved high savings rates and attracted record amounts of foreign capital.[59]

Another demand-side initiative, in addition to stabilizing population growth, is for the affluent to eat further down the food chain. The best nourished people in the world are not those living low on the food chain, such as Indians who consume roughly 200 kilograms of grain per year, or those living high on the food chain, such as Americans who consume some 800 kilograms of grain per year, mostly in the form of livestock products. It is people living at an intermediate level, such as Italians, who consume 400 kilograms of grain a year. Life expectancy in Italy—a country with the highly touted Mediterranean diet (rich in starches and fresh fruits and vegetables and only moderate amounts of livestock products)— exceeds that in both India and the United States. Even though the United States spends more on health care per person than Italy does, life expectancy in the latter is higher, apparently because of a lower consumption of livestock products. For those living high on the food chain, moving down to a more moderate level would enhance not only their health, but also the health of the planet.[60]

A half-century ago, no one was concerned about climate change. But if we cannot now accelerate the phaseout of fossil fuels, more extreme climate events may disrupt food production, threatening food security. Of particular concern is the rise in sea level that could inundate the river floodplains in Asia that produce much of the region's rice. The rise over the last century of 20 centimeters (8 inches) or more is already affecting some low-lying coastal regions. If sea level rises by 1 meter during this century, which is the upper level projected, it will take a heavy toll on food production, especially in Asia. Here the principal responsibility lies with the United States, a country whose carbon emissions are so great that it can single-handedly alter the earth's climate. If the United States does not assume a leadership role in phasing out fossil fuels, the global effort to stabilize climate is almost certain to fail.[61]

With the many countries that are facing acute land and water scarcity expecting to import growing quantities of grain, exporting countries will need to expand output to cover import needs. Over the last half-century, the growing ranks of grain-importing countries, now numbering over 100, have become dangerously dependent on the United States.[62]

This concentration of dependence applies to each of the big three grains—wheat, rice, and corn. Just five countries—the United States, Canada, France, Australia, and Argentina—account for 88 percent of the world's wheat exports. Thailand, Viet Nam, the United States, and China account for 68 percent of all rice exports. For corn, the concentration is even greater, with the United States alone accounting for 78 percent of exports and Argentina for 12 percent.[63]

With more extreme climate events in prospect, this dependence on a few exporting countries leaves importers vulnerable to climate change. If the United States were to experience a summer of severe heat and drought in its agricultural heartland like that of 1988, when grain production dropped below domestic consumption for the first time in history, chaos would reign in world grain markets simply because the near-record grain reserves that cushioned the huge U.S. crop shortfall that year no longer exist.[64]

One of the principal causes of hunger is the indifference of governments, an attitude that is often all too visible in their priorities. In some ways, India today is paying the price for its earlier indiscretions when, despite its impoverished state, it invested in a costly effort to produce nuclear weapons. After spending three times as much for military purposes as for health and family planning, India now has a nuclear arsenal capable of protecting the largest concentration of hungry people on the earth.[65]

Unless political leaders are willing to take the difficult steps to build an agricultural eco-economy, bland assertions that we must eradicate hunger are meaningless. If world leaders do not act decisively, the food situation could deteriorate rapidly in some developing countries. The risk for the low-income, grain-importing countries is that grain prices could rise dramatically, impoverishing more people in a shorter period of time than any event in history. Spreading food insecurity could lead to political instability on a scale that would disrupt global economic progress.

8

*Protecting Forest
Products and Services*

In the summer of 1998, the Yangtze River basin of China suffered some of the worst flooding in its history. An estimated 120 million people were driven from their homes by the floodwaters. A reported 3,656 people died. This near record flooding—with damages totaling $30 billion—came in a year when rainfall, though well above average, was not close to being a record. What was different from earlier years of comparable rainfall was the loss of forests. By 1998, the Yangtze River basin had lost fully 85 percent of its original forest cover, leaving little to hold the above-normal monsoon rainfall.[1]

Although it was too late to prevent massive deforestation, in August 1998 Chinese officials announced that they were imposing a total ban on tree cutting in the upper reaches of the Yangtze River basin. A senior official observed that trees standing were worth three times as much as trees cut. The state logging firms that had been cutting the trees were converted into tree planting organizations. As one employee noted, "It's now time to put down the ax and pick up the shovel."[2]

Because deforestation increases flooding, accelerates soil erosion, inhibits aquifer recharge, and decimates plant and animal life, it directly affects several other trends that are shaping our future. Although we do not rely as universally on forests for fuelwood as we once did, forests still provide material for building our homes and for manufacturing the paper that remains the principal medium for communicating information. In addition, 2 billion people depend on forests for fuel.[3]

Since the beginning of agriculture, the world has lost nearly half of its forests. Much of the loss occurred during the last century. Although some individual countries have reversed the tide of forest loss, the world's forested area continues to shrink. As this area diminishes, so does the human prospect.[4]

Fuel, Lumber, and Paper

As of 2000, the forested area of the earth covered some 3.9 billion hectares, or roughly 30 percent of the earth's land surface, but each year world tree cover is shrinking. Between 1990 and 2000, the U.N. Food and Agriculture Organization (FAO) reported a net loss of 94 million hectares. The developing countries lost 130 million hectares and the industrial countries gained 36 million hectares. The gains were largely from the conversion of abandoned agricultural land to forest.[5]

While farmland was returning to forests in industrial countries, forests in developing countries were being turned into farmland, grazing land, and wasteland. The 13 million hectares of forested area lost in developing countries each year is equal to 0.65 percent of their forested area. Stated otherwise, every three years, developing countries lose 2 percent of their forestland.[6]

These FAO estimates of forest loss are substantial, yet even they fall short of conveying the full extent of deforestation. The FAO definition of forest is tree crown cover of more than 10 percent of an area—a threshold that includes as forest land what is otherwise sometimes classified as tundra, savanna, scrubland, or even desert. Another shortcoming of the FAO data is that harvested areas count as forest until they have been permanently converted to another use. Thus it may appear that the global rate of deforestation is slowing, but recent satellite images and country reports reveal that the opposite is true.[7]

Historically, forests were managed by cutting selectively, removing only mature, highly valued trees. Under this system the forested area was remarkably stable, shrinking only when land was converted to agriculture or other nonforest uses. In recent decades, with new logging technologies and massive machines that can mow forests the way farmers mow hay, clearcutting has become much more economical as a harvesting technique, particularly when environmental costs are ignored.[8]

The world wood harvest in 1999 totaled 3.28 billion cubic meters, or just over 0.5 cubic meters for each person worldwide. Some 53 percent of this was used for fuel, supplying the 2 billion people who rely on wood for cooking. In developing countries, wood used for fuel accounted for 80 percent of all the wood harvested.[9]

Worldwide, wood accounts for 7 percent of the energy supply. In developing countries, it accounts for 15 percent of the total, compared with just 3 percent in industrial countries. Of the roughly 1.5 billion cubic meters of wood harvested that is not used for fuel, close to one third is used to make paper and paperboard. And over one fourth is sawed into lumber. Wood-based panels, often made with reconstituted wood, account for roughly a tenth of the non-fuelwood total.[10]

The paper sector of the world wood economy is the fastest growing of all. Between 1980 and 1999, world paper use climbed 86 percent, or 3.3 percent a year. At a total of nearly 317 million tons in 1999, this amounted to 52 kilograms, or more than 110 pounds, per person worldwide. (See Table 8–1.)[11]

Worldwatch researchers Janet Abramovitz and Ashley Mattoon note that nearly half of this paper was used for packaging. An estimated 30 percent was used for printing and writing paper, while 12 percent was used for newsprint. Paper towels and tissue account for most of the remainder.[12]

Looking ahead, the latest FAO projections show fuelwood consumption climbing to 2.35 billion cubic meters in 2015 and then leveling off as increased efficiency in wood burning offsets growth in fuelwood demand. For non-fuelwood use, FAO estimates that consumption will reach 2 billion cubic meters in 2015 and 2.4 billion cubic meters in 2030.[13]

In the decades ahead, the growing demand for wood products and the demand to convert forestland to both crop production and cattle ranching will continue to intensify pressures on the earth's forests. If recent deforestation trends continue, both the loss of forest productive capacity and, perhaps more important, the loss

Table 8–1. *World Paper Consumption by Country, 1999*

Country	Consumption (thousand tons)	Consumption Per Person (kilograms)
United States	95,829	338
China	44,677	35
Japan	30,482	240
Germany	17,592	214
United Kingdom	11,871	200
France	10,844	183
Italy	10,236	178
Canada	7,960	259
Brazil	7,044	41
South Korea	6,642	142
Top 10 Consumers	243,177	111
Others	73,499	19
World Total	316,676	52

Source: FAO, *FAOSTAT Statistics Database,* <apps.fao.org>, forest data updated 7 February 2001.

of key services that forests provide could disrupt local economies in some countries.

Forest Services

We are all familiar with the goods that forests supply, as just described. We are less familiar with the services they provide. Prominent among these are climate regulation, flood control, soil conservation, water cycling, nutrient storage and recycling, and recreation—all of which are a basic part of any economy's support systems.

In a landmark article in *Nature* in May 1997, Robert Costanza and 12 collaborators estimated that the earth's ecosystems provide $33 trillion worth of services per year—only slightly less than the $43 trillion worth of goods and services provided by the global economy. Of this total, Costanza and his coauthers estimated that the earth's forestland provides $4.7 trillion worth of services, or $969 of services per hectare per year. (See Table 8–2.) This can be compared with roughly $800 worth of corn produced per hectare

Table 8–2. *Principal Services Provided by Forests*

Service	Annual Value per Hectare
	(dollars)
Climate regulation	141
Erosion control	96
Nutrient storage and recycling	361
Recreation	66
Other	305
Total	969

Source: See endnote 14.

a year in the U.S. Corn Belt, one of the world's most productive farming regions.[14]

Impressive though the Costanza team's analysis is, it omits one of the most valuable services provided by forests—namely, their role in the recycling of rainfall inland that makes the interior of continents productive and habitable. If we continue to destroy coastal forests, the interior deserts of continents will continue expanding, squeezing humanity into an ever smaller area.

We often discover the services that forests provide when it is too late, after the trees have been cut. This is perhaps most true of flood control, as China, Thailand, and Mozambique have belatedly discovered.[15]

Forests also store nutrients. This is particularly important in the tropics, where almost all nutrients in forest ecosystems are stored in the vegetation itself. Many tropical soils have little organic matter and almost no nutrient storage capacity. If a forest is burned off to plant grass for cattle ranching or crops, whatever is planted can do relatively well in the first few years because of the nutrients remaining in the ashes. But once the ash washes away, as it soon does, the nutrients are gone. This is why much of the land cleared in the tropics quickly becomes wasteland and is abandoned.

Tropical rainforests are highly productive ecosystems, efficiently converting sunlight into plant material. But they can do this only as long as they are intact. Once they are destroyed, they can take centuries to regenerate. And some may never recover—simply because the conditions that existed at the time of their original formation may no longer exist.

Forests help control soil erosion by adding organic matter to the soil and by slowing the flow of water runoff. Leaf litter on the floor protects the soil from being loosened by raindrops, creating a tight link between the vegetation and the soils. The forest vegetation permits soil to accumulate and keeps it from washing away. The accumulated soil in turn provides a healthy medium for the forest to develop. In this symbiotic relationship, losing the forests sometimes means losing the soil, which may in turn prevent the return of the forest.

The ability of forests to slow rainfall runoff and let it percolate downward also means forests play a central role in the hydrological cycle. They recharge aquifers, the underground rivers that supply water for the wells downstream. The more water that runs off when it is raining, the less there is to recharge aquifers. Thus the loss of forest cover leads to a double loss—more damage from flooding and a reduced recharge of aquifers.

Forests can purify drinking water as well. Walt Reid, who works with the Millennium Ecosystem Assessment, notes that "within the United States more than 60 million people in 3,400 communities rely on National Forest lands for their drinking water, a service estimated to be worth $3.7 billion per year." He then notes that this single service, one among many provided by national forests, is worth more than the annual value of timber harvested from these lands.[16]

New York City, with its population of nearly 17 million, recently discovered just how valuable nature's services are. Faced with the residential and industrial development of the Catskill forest region, the basin that is the source of its water, the city was told it needed a water purification plant that would cost $8 billion to build and $300 million a year to operate. The bill for this would reach $11 billion over 10 years. After analyzing the situation, city officials realized that they could restore the watershed to its natural condition for only $2 billion, thus avoiding the need for the purification plant and saving taxpayers $9 billion.[17]

As mentioned in Chapter 3, forests also help carry water to the interior of continents. Reduced recycling of rainfall inland is already evident in China. Deforestation in southern and eastern parts of the country is reducing the moisture transported inland from the Bay of Bengal, the South China Sea, the East China Sea, and the Yellow Sea, notes Wang Hongchang, a Fellow at the Chinese Academy of Social Sciences. Rainfall in the northwestern interior is declining, contributing to the dust bowl conditions that are developing there. The Central Asian desert region extends from northwestern China north and west across Kazakhstan. The desert is expanding outward from the interior of the continent, moving northwest in Kazakhstan and southward and eastward in China. Indeed, Kazakhstan has lost the southern half of its croplands since 1980. [18]

A similar phenomenon is evident in Africa, as noted earlier. Both rangeland and cropland are turning to desert on the northern fringe of the Sahara Desert. Algeria is now working to convert the southernmost 20 percent of its grainland into orchards and vineyards in an effort to check the northward spread of desertification. And in Nigeria, the desert is moving southward, encroaching on the country's rangeland and cropland. [19]

A study as part of NASA's Earth Observing System reports that Lake Chad in Africa has shrunk from 25,000 square kilometers in 1963 to 1,350 square kilometers today. Declining rainfall in the central Sahelian region of Africa is primarily responsible for the shrinkage, although higher temperatures and the growth in irrigation, which diverts water from the rivers feeding the lake, are also contributing. As deforestation in Africa's high rainfall coastal regions and in the southern Sahel itself progresses, the capacity of the land to recycle water to the continent's interior is diminishing. [20]

Forests also have a stabilizing effect on local climate, modulating the more extreme day-to-night temperature fluctuations, such as those found in deserts. They store huge amounts of carbon that otherwise would be in the atmosphere in the form of carbon dioxide, contributing to climate change. When forests are cleared, this carbon storage capacity is lost not only in the vegetation above ground but also in the organic matter in the soil from roots and the leaf litter on the forest floor. [21]

Another service provided by forests is protection of streams and rivers from silting. In the U.S. Northwest, for example, the clearcutting of forests has destroyed nearby salmon fisheries because of increased muddy runoff. Mismanagement of one natural asset is decimating another. [22]

Silting also affects the productivity of dams, whether they are built for power generation or for irrigation. As they silt up, they lose their storage capacity and hence their ability to generate electricity and provide water for irrigation. In extreme cases, reservoirs fill with silt and the investment in the dam is lost.[23]

Sustainable Forestry

There are many definitions of sustainable forestry, most having to do with the sustainable yield of timber. A more appropriate definition, a broader and more relevant one, includes the capacity of the forest to supply both products and services sustainably. In many situations, the latter is now far more important than the former.

Despite the high value of intact forests, only about 290 million hectares of global forest area are legally protected from logging (See Table 8–3.) An additional 1.4 billion hectares are unavailable for harvesting because of economic deterrents. Of the remaining area available for exploitation, 665 million hectares are undisturbed by humans and nearly 900 million hectares are seminatural and not in plantations.[24]

One type of forest that is marginal in economic terms is that supporting only low-quality wood, with few, if any, commercial species. Protected from timber harvesting by their poor quality, such forests continue to provide services. In other forests, logging is precluded solely because of physical or infrastructure constraints.

Table 8–3. *Area of World Forestland Available and Unavailable for Wood Supply*

Classification	Area (million hectares)
Available for wood supply	1,563
Semi-natural	898
Undisturbed	665
Unavailable for wood supply	1,657
Legal restrictions	290
Economic restriction	
Physical reasons	256
Transport or infrastructure constraints	365
Other	746
Total forested area	3,221

Source: See endnote 24.

Unfortunately, these areas can quickly become accessible to the chainsaw if the forest products industry or a government invests in transportation or other infrastructure.[25]

A large share of the forests that are protected by national decree are safeguarded not so much to preserve the long-term wood supply capacity as to ensure that the forest can continue to provide services. Countries that take this step often have been heavily deforested. The Philippines, for example, has banned all logging in old-growth and virgin forests largely because the country has become so vulnerable to flooding, erosion, and landslides. Once covered by rich stands of tropical hardwood forests, the Philippines was a major exporter of forest products. But after years of massive clearcutting, the country became a net importer of forest products. It lost both the goods and the services provided by its forests.[26]

Although some nongovernmental organizations (NGOs) have been working for years to protect forests or restrict their exploitation, public institutions such as the World Bank have only recently begun to consider sustainable forestry systematically. The Bank's current goal is to have 200 million hectares of forestland in its client countries under sustainable management by 2005. It proposes to have 50 million hectares of natural forest that is high in biological diversity under protection by 2005.[27]

For many landowners in the tropics who lack access to timber markets, trees are seen simply as an obstacle to agriculture or ranching—something to be burned or cut down. They are not interested in either the goods or the services provided. These forests are difficult to protect.

Where forest products are exported, access to timber markets can often be used to ensure that forests are managed sustainably. NGOs and governments in many importing countries are requiring that all timber marketed, including both domestically produced and imported timber, be certified as coming from sustainably managed forests. (For further discussion of forest certification, see Chapter 11.)

There are several forest products certification programs, which have varying success in promoting sustainable forestry. These link environmentally conscious consumers with the management of the forest where the product originates. Some certification programs are national while others are international. Some of the latter originate with the importing countries and others with exporters.

The most rigorous international program that is certified by a number of NGOs worldwide is the Forest Stewardship Council (FSC). Some 24 million hectares of forests in 45 countries are certified by FSC-accredited bodies as responsibly managed. Among the leaders in certified forest area are Sweden, with 10 million hectares; the United States, with nearly 3 million hectares; Bolivia, with over 1 million hectares; and South Africa and Brazil with just under 1 million hectares each.[28]

On the export end of the sustainable forest products industry, Brazil has also developed a national certification program. It is called Cerflor, a System for the Certification of Origin of Forest Raw Materials. This initiative was economically motivated so that Brazilian pulp and paper products would have an ecolabel to ensure access to the European Union market. The label aimed to distinguish Brazilian forestry products from those of other countries that might not be managing their forests sustainably. In the case of Brazil, this was a relatively easy goal to reach simply because so much of its paper comes from plantations.[29]

Although the world is far from managing its forests well, the concept of sustainable forest management is taking root to some degree in many parts of the world. It at least holds out the hope that the annual forest loss of 13 million hectares in developing countries can be reduced and eventually eliminated as balance is restored between the production and harvesting of forestry products. Arresting the deforestation would also help protect the services that forests currently provide.[30]

Lightening the Load

There is enormous potential in all countries to lessen the demand pressure that is shrinking the earth's forest cover. In industrial nations the greatest opportunity lies in reducing the amount of wood used to manufacture paper. In developing countries it also depends on reducing that used as fuel.

An examination of paper recycling in the top 10 paper-producing countries shows a wide variation. (See Table 8–4.) On the low end are China, which recycles 27 percent of its paper, and Italy, at 31 percent. At the high end are Germany at 72 percent and South Korea at 66 percent. The rate in Germany is high because the government has consistently emphasized the recycling of paper in order to reduce the flow to landfills. If every country recycled as much

Table 8–4. *Paper Recycling Rates, 10 Leading Paper-Producing Countries and World, 1997*

Country	Recycling Rate
	(percent)
Germany	72
South Korea	66
Sweden	55
Japan	53
Canada	47
United States	46
France	41
Finland	35
Italy	31
China	27
World	43

Source: Janet N. Abramovitz, "Paper Recycling Remains Strong," in Lester R. Brown et al., *Vital Signs 2000* (New York: W.W. Norton & Company, 2000), pp. 132–33.

as Germany does, nearly one third less wood would be needed worldwide to produce paper.

The United States, the world's largest producer and consumer of paper, is far behind Germany but making progress. Twenty years ago, roughly one fourth of the paper used in the United States was recycled. By 1997, the figure had reached 46 percent. Contributing to this were the introduction of convenient curbside recycling, the banning of paper in many landfills, and mandates imposed by both the federal and state governments on recycled content in purchased paper, such as the one adopted by the Clinton administration in 1993.[31]

Some countries not among the top 10 producers are also making impressive progress. The Netherlands, for example, has set a goal of recycling 72 percent of all the paper used within its borders by 2001. This goal, which will put it on a par with Germany, seems likely to be reached.[32]

The use of paper, perhaps more than any other single product, still reflects the throwaway mentality that evolved during the second half of the last century. There are enormous possibilities for reducing paper use, including replacing facial tissues, paper napkins, disposable diapers, and paper shopping bags with cloth alternatives.

The Japanese have a special problem since their wooden chopsticks are often discarded after one use. As a result, some 25 billion chopsticks a year end up in the garbage in Japan. In attempts to solve a comparable problem, China is launching a program to reduce the use of throwaway chopsticks.[33]

In the electronic era, some uses of paper could be phased out almost entirely. Among these is the use of paper telephone directories, which can be replaced by online phone directories available on the Internet. Not all residences have access to the Internet, but it may now make sense to discontinue automatic distribution of phone directories and give them out only on request. This could save millions of tons of paper each year.

Newspapers devote most of their space to advertising. For example, a typical city newspaper in the United States will carry two pages of used car ads each day for 365 days a year. Although some people never buy a car, much less a used one, they nonetheless automatically get these pages with their daily newspaper. An online electronic directory of used cars in each city could largely dispense with this use of newsprint. Indeed, electronic directories for cars, apartment rentals, and various services such as home repair and plumbing will undoubtedly reduce newspaper ads and save paper.

The *International Herald Tribune*, published in Paris and printed at several different locations around the world, is a model of a paper-efficient newspaper. Owned jointly by the *New York Times* and the *Washington Post*, it carries material from both newspapers. It is trim and easy to read, with few ads. Within the United States, *USA Today* also has an unusually high rate of news to advertising. These newspapers are also available on the Internet.[34]

The largest single demand on our trees—the need for fuelwood—accounts for just over half of all wood removed from forests. One way of reducing the pressure of fuelwood demand is to use wood more efficiently. While attention in the industrial world focuses on increasing the fuel efficiency of automobiles, much less attention has been given to the efficiency of cook stoves, the leading use of energy in many developing countries. A number of international aid agencies, including the U.S. Agency for International Development, have begun to sponsor projects in this area, and with some success. One of its more promising projects undertaken in Kenya has involved the distribution of new cook stoves to 780,000 people. Investing public resources in replacing outmoded cook stoves could earn handsome dividends in forest protection and regeneration, including the restoration of forest services.[35]

Over the longer term, the key to reducing pressure on forests is to develop alternative sources of energy for cooking in the Third World. As the world shifts from an energy economy based on fossil fuels to one based on wind, solar, or geothermal energy (see Chapter 5), it will be much easier for developing countries without fossil fuels to develop indigenous sources of renewable energy. Although we do not know exactly what form the substitution will take as the world moves toward a hydrogen-based economy, we do know there is an abundance of locally available renewable energy in the developing world.

As the energy transition accelerates, the potential for replacing fuelwood with other local energy sources will become more evident. Whether countries replace firewood with electric hotplates fed by wind-generated electricity, solar thermal cookers, or some other source of energy, it will lighten the load on forests.

The Role of Plantations

As of 2000, the world had 113 million hectares in forest plantations, less than 3 percent of the total 3.9 billion hectares in forest. By comparison, this area is roughly one sixth of the 700 million hectares planted in grain each year worldwide.[36]

These plantations produce mostly wood either for pulp mills to make paper or for mills to reconstitute wood. Increasingly, reconstituted wood is substituting for natural wood in the world lumber market as industry adapts to a shrinking supply of large logs from natural forests.[37]

Production of wood on plantations is estimated at 331 million cubic meters, or 10 percent of world wood production. Stated otherwise, nine tenths of the world timber harvest came from natural forest stands, while one tenth came from plantations.[38]

Five countries account for two thirds of the 113 million hectares of plantations. (See Table 8–5.) China, which has little original forest remaining, is the largest, and Russia and the United States follow. U.S. plantations are concentrated in the southeastern part of the country. India and Japan are fourth and fifth. Brazil is further back, but expanding fast.[39]

Table 8–5. *Forest Plantations in Key Countries, 2000*

Country	Area
	(million hectares)
China	39.9
Russia	17.3
United States	16.2
India	12.4
Japan	10.7
All other	16.3
World Total	112.8

Source: See endnote 39.

The average productivity of existing plantations worldwide is estimated at 6.6 cubic meters per hectare a year. This figure could easily go to 10 cubic meters with more sophisticated management and the use of fast-growing tree species. New Zealand, for example, harvests 18 or more cubic meters per hectare a year. Brazil was averaging 14 cubic meters per hectare in 1990 and could go to 33 cubic meters with advanced management, according to FAO.[40]

As the industry expands, it is also undergoing a geographic shift, with more and more of the new plantations located in the moist tropical or subtropical regions. In contrast to grain yields, which tend to rise with distance from the equator and the longer growing days of summer, tree plantation yields rise with proximity to the equator and the year-round growing conditions. For example, in the southeastern United States, it takes 15 years for fast-growing pines to reach harvestable size. Brazilian plantation managers can have eucalyptus trees ready for harvest in 7 years—less than half the time.[41]

In eastern Canada, the average hectare of forest plantation produces 4 cubic meters per year. In the southeastern United States, it is 10 cubic meters. But in Indonesia, it is 25 cubic meters, and in Brazil, newer plantations may be close to 30 cubic meters. While corn yields in the United States average almost 9 tons per hectare, Brazil's are less than 3 tons. So while the ratio of corn yields between the United States and Brazil is nearly 3 to 1, timber yields favor Brazil by nearly 3 to 1. To satisfy a given demand for wood, Brazil requires only one third as much land as the United States.

This tree-growing advantage of tropical countries helps explain why growth in pulp capacity from 1995 to 2000 was estimated at 1.5 percent for the United States, 3.5 percent for Canada, 166 percent for Thailand, and 123 percent for Indonesia.[42]

In addition to warm, year-round temperatures and abundant moisture in the tropics, land and labor are cheaper in developing countries. As a result, for example, Chile's exports of forest products, largely from plantations, increased from $334 million in 1985 to $2 billion in 1995, expanding employment and boosting export earnings.[43]

Many northern firms are investing in countries in the South. Japanese firms are investing in the Western Pacific, and U.S. firms are investing in the western hemisphere, especially Brazil. Some U.S. firms are buying into forest plantations in Brazil to supply wood chips for their pulp mills in the southern United States. Brazil, now with 5 million hectares of forest plantations, gets 60 percent of its industrial wood from plantations.[44]

Projections of future growth show that plantations are constrained by land scarcity. An increase in land in plantations can come on deforested land, but it is more likely to come at the expense of existing natural stands of forests. There is also competition with agriculture, since land that is suitable for growing trees is often suitable for crop production too. Water scarcity is yet another constraint. Fast-growing plantations require an abundance of moisture.

Nonetheless, FAO projects that the current 113 million hectares of plantations could easily increase to 145 million hectares in 2030. Meanwhile, as yields rise, the harvest could more than double, climbing from 331 million cubic meters to 766 million. This assumes that this growth will be concentrated in the tropics and subtropics, where the yields are high.[45]

It is entirely conceivable that plantations could one day satisfy most of the world's demand for industrial wood. While part of the modest projected growth in plantation area will undoubtedly come at the expense of existing forests, the area of forests that would be protected is several times greater.

Reclaiming the Earth

Reforestation is essential to restoring the earth's health, a cornerstone of the eco-economy. Reducing flooding and soil erosion, recycling rainfall inland, and restoring aquifer recharge depend not merely on slowing deforestation or arresting it, but on reforesting the earth. Planting trees helps to reduce topsoil loss caused by erosion to or below the level of new soil formation.

Historically, some highly erodible agricultural lands have been reforested by natural regrowth. New England, a geographically rugged region of the United States, was reforested beginning a century or so ago. Settled early by Europeans, this mountainous region was having difficulty sustaining cropland productivity because soils were thin and vulnerable to erosion. As highly productive farmland opened up in the Midwest and the Great Plains during the nineteenth century, pressures on New England farmland lessened, permitting much of the land that was cropped to return to forest. Although the share of New England covered by forest has increased from a low of roughly one third two centuries ago to perhaps over three fourths today, this reforested area still has not regained its original health and diversity.[46]

A somewhat similar situation exists now in the republics of the former Soviet Union and in several East European countries. After the economic reforms in the early 1990s, which replaced central planning with market-based agriculture, farmers on marginal land simply could not make ends meet and were forced to seek their livelihoods elsewhere. Precise figures are difficult to come by, but millions of hectares of farmland are now returning to forest, much as happened in New England.[47]

Perhaps the most successful national reforestation effort is the one undertaken in South Korea beginning more than a generation ago. By the end of the Korean War, South Korea was almost totally deforested by a combination of heavy logging and reliance on fuelwood during the Japanese occupation. Despite being one of the world's poorest countries, it launched a national reforestation program. Trees were planted on mountainsides throughout the country. While driving across South Korea in November 2000, I was thrilled to see the luxuriant stand of trees on mountains that a generation ago were bare. It made me even more confident that we can reforest the earth.

This model reforestation program helps explain why North Korea regularly has floods and droughts, while South Korea does not. South Korea benefits from the flood control services of reforested mountains, and with the forests' capacity to store water and recharge aquifers, the nation rarely faces serious drought. Environmental degradation is contributing to chronic famine in one country while environmental restoration helped set the stage for economic success in an adjacent nation.

In Turkey, a mountainous country largely deforested over the millennia, one leading environmental group, TEMA (Turkiye Erozyonia Mucadele, Agaclandima), has made reforestation its principal activity. Founded by two prominent Turkish businessmen, Hayrettin Karuca and Nihat Gokyiğit, TEMA has launched a 10-billion-acorn campaign to restore tree cover and reduce runoff and soil erosion. In 1998, it mobilized forestry ministry staff, army units, and volunteers to plant 45 million acorns, 15 million of which were expected to emerge as seedlings. Aside from the planting of acorns, this program is raising national awareness of the services that forests provide.[48]

China also is engaging in a reforestation effort. In addition to planting trees in the recently deforested upper reaches of the Yangtze River basin to control flooding, China is planting a belt of trees across its northwest to protect land from the expanding Gobi Desert. This green wall, a modern version of the Great Wall, is some 4,480 kilometers (2,800 miles) long. An ambitious, long-term plan, it is projected to take 70 years. One local village leader said, "We'll plant trees every day for five years. And if that doesn't work, we'll plant for five more. That's what they tell us." Residents in this region are no longer permitted to burn wood for heating or cooking. The raising of animals, other than for household use, is also banned.[49]

But this green wall treats the symptoms of declining rainfall and desertification in the northwest, not the need to restore rainfall in the region by restoring the forests in the southern and eastern provinces that help recycle rainfall inland. An official within the Ministry of Agriculture's ecology section worries that Beijing lacks a cohesive, comprehensive plan. He sees tree planting as a positive step, but thinks grasses need to be planted first to stabilize the soil. He says, "But everything is going fast now and there is no master plan."[50]

In response to water shortages in the north, China is now planning to construct two major south-north water diversions, each of which will cost tens of billions of dollars. If completed, they will bring water from the south to the north, but they will not restore the rainfall that is desperately needed in the northwest if the vegetation and ecological health of the region is to be restored.[51]

Wang Honchang of the Chinese Academy of Social Sciences has proposed reforestation and tree planting wherever possible to recycle more water to the interior. This might well carry more water from south to north than the diversion canals that are being planned, and at a lower cost.[52]

Shifting subsidies from building logging roads to tree planting would increase tree cover worldwide. The World Bank has the administrative capacity to lead an international program that would emulate South Korea's success in blanketing mountains and hills with trees.

In addition, FAO and the bilateral aid agencies can work with individual farmers in national agroforestry programs to integrate trees wherever possible into agricultural operations. Aptly chosen and well-placed trees provide shade, serve as windbreaks to check soil erosion, and fix nitrogen, which reduces the need for fertilizer. The only forest policy that is environmentally acceptable is one that expands the earth's tree cover.

A successful effort to reclaim the earth calls for a global reforestation effort, coordinated country by country, integrated with population planning and improved efficiency of fuelwood burning. Reducing wood use by developing alternative energy sources as well as systematically recycling paper and using fewer forest products are integral components of the campaign to lighten pressure on the land. With such an integrated plan, humanity can arrest the spread of deserts that threatens agriculture and human settlements in so many countries.

9

Redesigning Cities for People

As I was being driven through Tel Aviv en route from my hotel to a conference center in November 2000, I could not help but note the overwhelming presence of cars and parking lots. Tel Aviv, expanding from a small settlement a half-century ago to a city of some 2 million today, has evolved during the automobile era. It occurred to me that the ratio of parks to parking lots may be the best single indicator of the livability of a city—an indication of whether the city is designed for people or for cars.

We live in an urbanizing world. Aside from the growth of population itself, urbanization is the dominant demographic trend of our time. The 150 million people living in cities in 1900 swelled to 2.9 billion people by 2000, a 19-fold increase. Meanwhile, the urban share of world population increased from 10 percent to 46 percent. If recent trends continue, by 2007 more than half of us will live in cities. For the first time, we will be an urban species.[1]

Urbanization on anything like the current scale is historically quite new. For most of our existence, we have lived in small bands of hunter-gatherers in a natural environment. As recently as 1800, only Peking (now Beijing) had a million people. Today 326 cities have at least that many inhabitants. And there are 19 megacities, with 10 million or more residents. Tokyo's population of 26 million approaches that of Canada. Mexico City's population of 18 million is nearly equal to that of Australia. Mumbai (formerly Bombay), São Paulo, New York, Lagos, Los Angeles, Calcutta, and Shanghai follow close behind.[2]

Cities are unnatural. They require a concentration of food, water, energy, and materials that nature cannot provide. These masses of materials must then be dispersed in the form of garbage, human waste, and air and water pollutants. Worldwatch researcher Molly O'Meara Sheehan reports that although cities cover less than 2 percent of the earth's surface and have less than half the world's people, they account for 78 percent of carbon emissions, 60 percent of residential water use, and 76 percent of the wood used for industrial purposes.[3]

Cities, particularly those centered on the automobile, deprive people of needed exercise, creating an imbalance between caloric intake and caloric expenditures. As a result, there is a rapid growth in obesity in both industrial and developing countries. Overweight populations in industrial countries, sometimes in the majority among adults, combined with the swelling ranks of overweight people in developing countries, have pushed the global overweight population to 1.1 billion. Epidemiologists now see this as a public health threat of historic proportions—a growing source of heart disease, high blood pressure, diabetes, and a higher incidence of several forms of cancer.

The process of urbanization is changing. Whereas migration to the early cities came largely from urban pull, it is now driven more by lack of opportunity in the countryside. In most developing countries, this flow from rural areas far exceeds the capacity of cities to provide jobs, housing, electricity, water, sewerage, and social services, thus resulting in squatter settlements where multitudes live in marginal, often subhuman conditions.

An Urbanizing Species

Agriculture set the stage for the formation of cities. Advances in agricultural productivity that came with the beginning of irrigation some 6,000 years ago in the fertile soils of the Euphrates Basin freed up people to create the first cities. Several thousand years later the Industrial Revolution gave cities another boost. The early factories required a concentration of workers not possible in rural communities. The evolution of cities is tied to advances in transport—initially ships and trains, then motor vehicles. It was the internal combustion engine, combined with cheap oil, that provided the mobility of people and of freight that fueled the phenomenal growth of cities during the twentieth century.

Although the first cities were formed several thousand years ago, the urbanization of world population has been concentrated in the last half-century. In 1950, an estimated 750 million people lived in cities. By 2000, this number had climbed to 2.9 billion, nearly a fourfold increase. The United Nations predicts that by 2050 more than two thirds of us will be living in cities.[4]

Cities have been at the center of the evolution of modern civilization. It is probably not a coincidence that the first written language apparently evolved in the earliest cities. At the beginning of the Christian era, there were already several great cities: Athens, Alexandria, and Rome. A list of the world's 10 most populous cities in selected years since then tells us much about history, the rise and decline of civilizations, the growth and disintegration of empires, industrialization, and, more recently, wide population growth variations among countries. (See Table 9–1.)

In the year 1000, the world's 10 largest cities were widely dispersed throughout the Old World. But by 1900, a century after the Industrial Revolution began, nearly all the large cities were in the

Table 9–1. *Population of World's 10 Largest Metropolitan Areas in 1000, 1900, and 2000*

City	1000 (million)	City	1900 (million)	City	2000 (million)
Cordova	0.45	London	6.5	Tokyo	26.4
Kaifeng	0.40	New York	4.2	Mexico City	18.1
Constantinople	0.30	Paris	3.3	Mumbai (Bombay)	18.1
Angkor	0.20	Berlin	2.7	São Paulo	17.8
Kyoto	0.18	Chicago	1.7	New York	16.6
Cairo	0.14	Vienna	1.7	Lagos	13.4
Bagdad	0.13	Tokyo	1.5	Los Angeles	13.1
Nishapur	0.13	St. Petersburg	1.4	Calcutta	12.9
Hasa	0.11	Manchester	1.4	Shanghai	12.9
Anhilvada	0.10	Philadelphia	1.4	Buenos Aires	12.6

Source: Molly O'Meara Sheehan, *Reinventing Cities for People and the Planet,* Worldwatch Paper 147 (Washington, DC: Worldwatch Institute, June 1999), pp. 14–15, with updates from United Nations, *World Urbanization Prospects: The 1999 Revision* (New York: 2000).

industrial west. In 2000, after a century of record population growth—most of it concentrated in the Third World—7 of the top 10 were in developing countries.

People living in cities impose a disproportionately heavy burden on the earth's ecosystems simply because so many resources must be concentrated in urban areas to satisfy residents' daily needs. Vast quantities of food and water must be moved into cities, and the resulting concentration of human waste must then be dispersed.

The industries that take advantage of the labor force in cities require raw materials. These, too, must be transported, often over long distances. Finished goods must then be shipped to markets within the country and, as globalization proceeds, other parts of the world.

The early cities relied heavily on food and water resources in the surrounding countryside. But today cities often depend on distant sources even for such basic amenities as food and water. Los Angeles, for example, draws much of its water supply from the Colorado River, some 970 kilometers (600 miles) away. Mexico City's burgeoning population, living at 3,000 meters, must now depend on the costly pumping of water from 150 kilometers away and a kilometer or more lower in altitude to augment its inadequate water supplies. Water-starved Beijing is contemplating drawing water from the Yangtze River basin nearly 1,500 kilometers away.[5]

Food comes from even greater distances, as is illustrated by Tokyo, whose population exceeds that of the world's 10 largest cities in 1900 combined. While Tokyo still depends for its rice on the highly productive farmers in Japan, with their land vigorously protected by government policy, its wheat comes largely from the Great Plains of the United States and Canada and from Australia. Its corn supply comes largely from the U.S. Midwest. Soybeans in Tokyo come from the U.S. Midwest and the Brazilian *cerrado*.[6]

Many cities today are linked more tightly to each other than to their own countryside. Air travel ties cities together, often making it easier to get to a city in another country than to the more remote rural regions within the same country. The trading of goods and services now occurs proportionately more among cities than between cities and the surrounding countryside.

It is widely assumed that urbanization will continue. But this is not necessarily so. If the world is facing water scarcity, the availability and cost of transporting water over long distances may itself begin to constrain urban growth. Beyond this, a future of water scarcity is almost certainly also a future of food scarcity, since 70 percent of all the water pumped from underground and diverted from rivers is used for irrigation. (See Chapter 7.)[7]

In a world of land and water scarcity, the value of both may increase substantially, shifting the terms of trade between the countryside and cities. Ever since the beginning of the Industrial Revolution, the terms of trade have favored cities because they control capital and technology, the scarce resources. But if land and water become the scarcest resources, then the people in rural areas who control them may have the upper hand. If so, the terms of trade could even reverse urbanization in some situations.

Beyond resource shortages, the evolution of the Internet, which is changing how we think about such basic parameters as distance and mobility, could also affect urbanization. The availability of e-mail and the potential for telecommuting may reduce the advantages of living in the city. Cultural amenities, such as museums, once found only in cities may now be toured over the Internet, further diminishing the draw to urban life. Internet commerce, offering more options than any shopping mall, may also lessen the role of urban centers as supply sources for a wide variety of goods and services.

Car-Centered Urban Sprawl

One of the less desirable dimensions of the extraordinary urban growth of the last half-century has been the sprawl of cities. In an article in *Scientific American* entitled "The Science of Smart Growth," Donald Chen writes about the phenomenal development of Atlanta, Georgia, during the 1990s. In a decade that began with preparations to host the Olympic Games, Atlanta led all other U.S. cities in population growth, home building, job openings, and highway construction. A part of the "new South," the city exploded in size. Today it has become a nightmare, one with worsening air pollution, congestion verging on gridlock, and an escalating sense of frustration among residents. Sprawling over an area the size of Delaware, it has the longest commute time of any city in the country—longer even than in Los Angeles or Houston.[8]

Atlanta is unique among American cities because its unusually fast development turned it into a disaster so abruptly and dramatically. With the rapidly spreading ownership of automobiles after World War II, a home in the suburbs—with access to the city but life in a low-density community with a yard and a driveway—appeared highly desirable. Zoning regulations requiring large lots for individual homes ensured that cities would be surrounded by low-density suburbs. Areas were often exclusively residential, with no mixing of shops or businesses among the residences.[9]

One analyst defined sprawl as "the degenerate urban form that is too congested to be efficient, too chaotic to be beautiful, and too dispersed to possess the diversity and vitality of a great city." In countries such as the United States and in many developing nations, where cities have developed largely after the arrival of the automobile and have ignored land-use planning, sprawl has become the dominant form of urban development.[10]

Among the consequences of this extensive low-density development are rising automobile dependency, rising real estate taxes, longer commute times, worsening air pollution, and, above all, frustration because the population density is too low to support a meaningful public transport system. The American dream became the American nightmare.

Once low-density suburbs surround a city, people living in these areas do not have many housing options. Donald Chen points out that they have "a very limited range of choices in the style and location of new housing—typically, single-family homes in automobile-oriented neighborhoods built on what was once forest or farmland."[11]

One consequence of the low-density development associated with one-acre building lots is high taxes to cover the sheer cost of providing water and sewerage services and maintaining roads. As the suburbs expand, they require new schools. Meanwhile, existing schools within the city close. It is not uncommon, even in states with declining populations, to be investing heavily in new school construction simply because of the concentration of young couples in the suburbs that are sprawling ever farther from the city itself. Other services, such as ambulance and fire fighting, also cost more in sprawling communities.[12]

Long and frustrating commutes are taking a toll on those living in the suburbs. Public concern about sprawl and whether it can be stopped or even reversed is on the rise. A poll taken in 2000 by the Pew Charitable Trust indicates that more Americans are concerned with traffic congestion and sprawl than with crime, jobs, or education, the traditional issues of primary concern.[13]

Increasing traffic delays are commonplace. A Texas Transportation Institute (TTI) study on mobility notes that in the larger U.S. urban communities, time spent sitting in traffic jams increased from 11 hours per person in 1982 to 36 hours in 1999. Los Angeles ranked number one in time wasted—56 hours a year, nearly half of the typical annual vacation time of three weeks. (See Table 9–2.) In Washington, D.C., the typical automobile commuter spends 46 hours sitting in traffic jams each year, reducing the time spent with family or exercising. The worse the traffic congestion, the more sedentary the life-style.[14]

TTI calculates the congestion bill for the 68 areas analyzed in 1999 at $78 billion a year—nearly $300 for every American. This includes the value of 4.5 billion hours wasted in traffic and nearly 7 billion gallons of excessive gasoline consumption. It does not, however, include any of the costs associated with the worsening air pollution from the millions of idling engines or the effect of addi-

Table 9–2. *Annual Costs of Traffic in Selected U.S. Cities*

Urban Areas	Annual Delay Per Person (hours)	Excess Fuel Consumed Per Person (gallons of gas)	Cost of Congestion Per Person[1] (dollars)
Los Angeles, CA	56	84	1,000
Seattle–Everett, WA	53	81	930
Atlanta, GA	53	84	915
Houston, TX	50	76	850
Washington, DC-MD-VA	46	69	780
Denver, CO	45	67	760
San Francisco– Oakland, CA	42	65	760
Boston, MA	42	63	715
Portland, OR– Vancouver, WA	34	53	610
New York, NY– Northeastern NJ	34	52	595

[1]Including delay and fuel cost.
Source: David Schrank and Tim Lomax, *The 2001 Urban Mobility Report* (Texas Transportation Institute and The Texas A&M University System, May 2001).

tional carbon emissions on the earth's climate.[15]

Many communities try to deal with traffic congestion by building more roads. But that has not worked. As Richard Moe, head of the National Trust for Historic Preservation, observes, "Building more roads to ease traffic is kind of like trying to cure obesity by loosening the belt."[16]

The automobile promised mobility, and in largely rural settings it delivered just that. But as societies have urbanized, the inherent conflict between the automobile and the city has become all too visible, with almost all the world's cities now plagued with traffic congestion, noise, and vehicular air pollution. The average speed of a car in London today is little different from that of a horse-drawn carriage a century ago. In Bangkok, which seems to suffer from perpetual gridlock, the average motorist in 1999 spent the equivalent of 44 working days sitting in an automobile going nowhere.[17]

Cities surrounded by low-density suburbs are facing a new challenge—how to attract or even keep investment in factories and offices. Increasingly, corporations use congestion pricing in deciding whether to locate in a particular city. If traffic congestion raises commute times for employees and the cost of moving raw materials and finished products, a company may well decide to move elsewhere. In Atlanta, Hewlett Packard has begun rethinking whether it wants to continue with expansion. Traffic congestion affects both the productivity and morale of employees.[18]

At the local level, some U.S. communities have taken steps to control urban sprawl. At the state level, the leader has been Oregon, which 20 years ago adopted boundaries to urban growth. State law required each community to project its growth needs for the next 20 years and then, based on the results, draw an outer boundary for the city that would accommodate that growth. Richard Moe observes, "This has worked in Oregon because it forced development back to the city. Lot sizes are smaller. There is more density, which is made possible by mass transit. There has been a doubling in the workforce in downtown Portland over the last 20 years without one new parking lot, without one new parking space."[19]

Arthur Nelson of the Lincoln Land Institute has analyzed growth patterns in U.S. cities using numerous economic and environmental indicators. The contrasting experience of Portland, which has engaged urban sprawl head on, and Atlanta, which ignored the issue, is revealing. Between the mid-1980s and mid-1990s, the growth in population, jobs, and income in the two cities were about the same, but that's where the similarity ends. (See Table 9–3.) Property taxes dropped 29 percent in Portland and rose 22 percent in Atlanta. Energy use, which actually declined in Portland, climbed in Atlanta. Air pollution (ozone) dropped 86 percent in Portland while climbing 5 percent in Atlanta. And finally, neighborhood quality, measured by an amalgam of indicators, improved by 19 percent in Portland while declining 11 percent in Atlanta.[20]

Table 9–3. *Changes in Portland and Atlanta Regions from Mid-1980s to Mid-1990s*

Indicator	Portland, OR	Atlanta, GA
	(percent change)	
Population growth	+ 26	+ 32
Job growth	+ 43	+ 37
Income	+ 72	+ 60
Property tax	– 29	+ 22
Vehicle miles traveled	+ 2	+ 17
Single occupant vehicle	– 13	+ 15
Commute time	– 9	+ 1
Air pollution (ozone)	– 86	+ 5
Energy consumption	– 8	+ 11
Neighborhood quality	+ 19	– 11

Source: See endnote 20.

There is another, more fundamental issue associated with car-centered transport systems. Will they be viable for land-scarce developing countries? Given the density of population and the crop-land shrinkage per person, countries like Bangladesh, China, Egypt, India, Indonesia, Iran, and Pakistan simply lack the land needed to accommodate an auto-centered transport system and to feed their people. Increasingly, they will have to choose between the automobile and food security.[21]

Urbanization and Obesity

Until recently, the principal link between urbanization and health was air pollution, but now this is changing as obesity spreads, eclipsing air pollution as a health threat. One consequence of urbanization, particularly when it is auto-centered, is the lack of opportunity for walking, cycling, and other forms of exercise. Exercise deprivation and dietary excesses together often translate into weight gain. As a result, obesity—which is concentrated in cities—is reaching epidemic proportions worldwide. No longer confined to the industrial world, obesity is emerging as a leading global public health issue. In both China and Indonesia, for instance, the incidence of obesity in cities is double that in the countryside. In the Congo, it is six times higher.[22]

Obesity is afflicting a growing number of people in industrial and developing countries alike. It is damaging human health—raising the incidence of heart disease, stroke, breast cancer, colon cancer, arthritis, and adult onset diabetes. In the United States, the Centers for Disease Control and Prevention estimates that 300,000 Americans now die prematurely each year from obesity-related illnesses.[23]

In recent years, efforts to reduce obesity have focused on lowering caloric intake to the level of caloric use by dieting, as the perpetual presence of diet books on bestseller lists in industrial countries indicates. Unfortunately, this can be physiologically difficult given the abnormally low calorie burning associated with sedentary life-styles. Ninety-five percent of Americans who attempt to achieve a healthy body weight by dieting alone fail, largely because exercise deprivation is also contributing to obesity. With metabolic systems shaped by millions of years of highly active hunting and gathering, many people may not be able to maintain a healthy body weight without regular exercise. [24]

For the first time in history, a majority of adults in some highly urbanized societies are overweight. In the United States, this applies to 61 percent of all adults. In Russia, the figure is 54 percent; in the United Kingdom, 51 percent; and in Germany, 50 percent. For Europe as a whole, more than half of the adults between 35 and 65 years of age are overweight. The numbers are rising in developing countries as well. In Brazil, for example, 36 percent of adults are overweight.[25]

Not only are more people overweight than ever before, but their ranks are expanding at a record rate. In the United States, obesity among adults increased by half between 1980 and 1994. Among Americans, 20 percent of men and 25 percent of women are more than 30 pounds (13.6 kilograms) overweight. Surveys in China showed that during the boom years of the early 1990s, the share of adults who were overweight jumped from 9 percent to 15 percent.[26]

Juvenile obesity is rising rapidly too. In the United States, where at least 1 out of 10 youngsters 6 to 17 years of age is overweight, the incidence of obesity among children has doubled over the last generation. Not only does juvenile obesity typically translate into adult obesity, but it also causes metabolic changes that make the disease difficult to treat in adulthood.[27]

In a Worldwatch Paper entitled *Underfed and Overfed,* Gary Gardner and Brian Halweil report that the number who are overnourished and overweight has climbed to 1.1 billion worldwide, rivaling the number who are undernourished and underweight. Peter Kopelman of the Royal London School of Medicine summarizes medical thinking: "Obesity should no longer be regarded simply as a cosmetic problem affecting certain individuals, but [as] an epidemic that threatens global well being."[28]

Damage to health from obesity takes many forms. In addition to the illnesses noted earlier, heavier body weight increases resistance to the heart's pumping of blood, elevating blood pressure. It also raises the stress on joints, often causing lower back pain. People who are obese are four times as likely to have diabetes as those who are not.[29]

As weight goes up, life expectancy goes down. In analyzing this relationship for Americans between the ages of 30 and 42, one broad-based study found that the risk of death within 26 years increased by 1 percent with each additional pound (0.45 kilograms) of excess weight.[30]

The estimated 300,000 Americans who die prematurely each year as a result of being overweight compares with the 400,000 who die prematurely from cigarette smoking. But there is one difference. The number of cigarettes smoked per person in the United States is on the decline, falling some 42 percent between 1980 and 2000, while obesity is on the rise. If recent trends continue, it is only a matter of time before deaths from obesity-related illnesses in the United States overtake those related to smoking.[31]

Gaining weight is a result of consuming more calories than are burned. With modernization, caloric intake has climbed. Over the last two decades, caloric intake in the United States has risen nearly

10 percent for men and 7 percent for women. Modern diets are rich in fat and sugar. In addition to sugars that occur naturally in food, the average American diet now includes a staggering 53 teaspoons of added sugar a day, much of it in soft drinks and prepared foods. Unfortunately, diets in developing countries, especially in urban areas, are moving in this same direction.[32]

While caloric intake has been rising, exercise has been declining. The latest U.S. survey shows that 57 percent of Americans exercise only occasionally or not at all, a number that corresponds closely with the share of the population that is overweight.[33]

Economic modernization has systematically eliminated exercise from our lives. Workers commute by car from home to work in an office or factory, driving quite literally from door to door. Automobiles have eliminated daily walking and cycling. Elevators and escalators have replaced stairs. Leisure time is spent watching television. In the United Kingdom, the two life-style variables that correlate most closely with obesity are television viewing and automobile ownership.[34]

Children who watch television five or more hours a day are five times as likely to be overweight as those who watch less than two hours a day. Time spent playing computer games and surfing the Internet in lieu of playing outside is also contributing to the surge in obesity.[35]

Another manifestation of diet failures is the extent to which people are turning to liposuction to remove body fat. Resorting to this surgical procedure, which vacuums out fat from under the skin, is a desperate last measure for those whose diets have failed. In 1998, there were some 400,000 liposuction procedures in the United States.[36]

For many of those who are overweight, achieving a healthy body weight depends on both reducing caloric intake and burning more calories through exercise. Metabolically, we are hunter-gatherers. Given our heritage, exercise may be a genetic imperative.

Restoring exercise in our daily lives will not be easy. Today's cities, designed for automobiles, are leading to a life-threatening level of exercise deprivation. Our health depends on creating neighborhoods that are conducive to walking, jogging, and bicycling.

The challenge is to redesign communities, making public transportation the centerpiece of urban transport, and augmenting it with sidewalks, jogging trails, and bikeways. This also means replacing parking lots with parks, playgrounds, and playing fields. Unless we can design a life-style that systematically restores exercise to our daily routines, the obesity epidemic—and the health deterioration associated with it—will continue to spread along with urbanization.

Urban Rail and Bicycle Systems

Urban transport systems based on a combination of rail, bicycles, and pedestrian walkways offer the best of all possible worlds in providing low-cost transportation and a healthy urban environment. Large cities invariably need rail systems to provide adequate mobility. Whether cities develop underground rail systems, light-rail surface systems, or both depends in part on size. Megacities almost certainly need underground rail systems to move a large volume of passengers in a timely fashion. For cities of intermediate size, light rail might provide a better base for efficient transport.

A rail system provides the foundation on which a city's transportation system can be developed. Trains are a fixed service, providing a permanent means of transportation that people can count on in a location-specific manner. Once in place, the nodes on such a system become the obvious places to concentrate office buildings, high-rise apartment buildings, factories, and shops.

The bicycle, a form of personal transportation, provides the versatility to complement the rail system. The bicycle's attractions are many. It alleviates congestion, lowers pollution, reduces obesity, increases physical fitness, does not emit climate-disrupting carbon dioxide, and is affordable for billions of people who cannot buy an automobile.

The bicycle can increase mobility while reducing congestion and the amount of land paved over. Six bicycles can typically fit into the road space used by one car. For parking, the advantage is even greater, with 20 bicycles occupying the space required to park one car.[37]

Few characteristics of car-centered cities are more annoying than persistent pollution, which affects both those who use the cars and those who do not. The bicycle is an ideal antidote to pollution, especially for short trips. Automobile engines burn least efficiently when they are first started. Once they are warmed up, they burn fuel more cleanly, but by that time short trips are over. Although global public attention focuses on the 885,000 auto-related fatalities each year, this figure is overshadowed by the estimated 3 million urban lives lost annually to air pollution.[38]

The bicycle is not only a flexible means of transportation, it is an ideal way of restoring a balance between caloric intake and expenditure. Exercise has value in its own right. Regular exercise of the sort provided by cycling to work reduces cardiovascular disease, osteoporosis, and arthritis and strengthens the immune system. Millions of people pay a monthly fee to use a fitness center (which they often drive to), where they ride stationary bikes, trying to achieve the same benefits.

Few methods of reducing carbon emissions are as effective as substituting the bicycle for the automobile on short trips. A bicycle, which typically weighs 13 kilograms (28 pounds), is from an engineering point of view a marvel of efficiency. An automobile, which requires 1–2 tons of material to transport often only one person, is extraordinarily inefficient in comparison. In addition to providing mobility and helping the rider to be physically fit, the bicycle also helps stabilize climate whenever it substitutes for a car.

The capacity of the bicycle to provide mobility for low-income populations has been dramatically demonstrated in China. In 1976, China was producing 6 million bicycles a year. After the reforms in 1978 that led to rapid economic growth, rising incomes, and a market economy in which people could exercise their preferences, annual bicycle production started climbing, eventually soaring over 40 million in 1988. After the market was largely saturated, production dropped somewhat and has remained between 20 million and 40 million a year since then. This vast surge to 540 million bicycle owners in China after the economic reforms in 1978 provided the greatest increase in human mobility in history. Bicycles took over city streets and rural roads.[39]

Cities in many parts of the world are turning back to bicycles for numerous uses. In the United States, more than 80 percent of police departments serving populations of 50,000 to 249,999 and 96 percent of those serving over 250,000 residents now have routine patrols by bicycle. Officers on bikes are more productive in cities partly because they are more mobile and can reach the scene of an accident or crime quicker. They typically make 50 percent more arrests per day than officers in squad cars. For fiscally sensitive officials, the cost of operating a bicycle is trivial compared with a car. Higher productivity at lower cost is a winning formula in the minds of many city managers. Better community relations for officers on bikes provides an additional bonus.[40]

Urban bicycle messenger services are common in the world's larger cities. Bicycles can usually deliver small parcels in cities much more quickly and efficiently than motor vehicles can and at a much lower cost. As the information economy unfolds and as e-commerce expands, the need for quick, reliable, urban delivery services is escalating. For many competitive Internet marketing firms, quick delivery wins customers. In a city like New York, this creates an enormous potential for the use of bicycle messengers. As of 2000, an estimated 300 bicycle messenger firms were operating in New York City, competing for $700 million worth of business each year. In large cities, the bicycle is becoming an integral part of the support system for e-commerce.[41]

The key to realizing the potential of the bicycle is to create a bicycle-friendly transport system. This means providing both bicycle trails and designated lanes on streets for bicycles. These should be designed to serve both commuters and people biking for recreation. In addition, bicycle use is enhanced by the provision of parking facilities and showers at workplaces. Among the industrial-country leaders in designing bicycle-friendly transport systems are the Dutch, the Danes, and the Germans.[42]

The Netherlands, the unquestioned leader among industrial countries, has incorporated a vision of the role of bicycles into a Bicycle Master Plan. In addition to creating bicycle lanes and trails in all its cities, the system also gives cyclists the advantage over motorists in right-of-ways and at traffic lights. Traffic signals permit cyclists to move out before cars.[43]

Roughly 30 percent of all urban trips in the Netherlands are on bicycle. This compares with 1 percent in the United States. Both the Netherlands and Japan have made a concerted effort to integrate bicycles and rail commuter services by providing for bicycle parking at each rail station, making it easier for cyclists to commute to the station. In Japan, the use of bicycles for commuting to rail transportation has reached the point where some stations invested in vertical parking garages for bicycles, much as is often done for automobiles.[44]

Spain, one of the latest countries to climb on the bicycle bandwagon, had opened 80 newly constructed bicycle trails by the end of 2000. It now has some 965 kilometers (about 600 miles) with new surface and signposts. Another 640 kilometers have been designated and can be used, but have not yet been surfaced.[45]

The combination of rail and bicycle, and particularly their integration into a single, overall transport system, makes cities eminently more livable than those centered around car transport systems. Noise, pollution, congestion, and frustration are all lessened. Both the people and the environment are healthier.

Planning Cities for People

As the new century begins, it is becoming increasingly evident to urban dwellers, whether in an industrial or a developing country, that there is an inherent conflict between the automobile and the city. The vehicle that promised mobility and delivered it in largely rural societies cannot provide mobility in cities. Indeed, after a certain point, as more and more people try to achieve mobility by driving in a city, they become progressively less mobile.

The automobile-centered urban transport system can lead to frustration with congestion, a frustration that sometimes becomes what is now known as "road rage." Urban air pollution, often largely from automobiles, claims millions of lives.

Congestion also takes a direct economic toll in the form of rising transportation inefficiency and greater costs in time and energy. As indicated, longer commuting times are now a source of daily frustration in a diverse array of cities, including Bangkok, Beijing, Houston, Rome, São Paulo, and Tel Aviv.

Another cost of cities devoted to cars is a psychological one, a deprivation of contact with the natural world—an asphalt complex. There is a growing body of evidence that there is an innate need for human contact with nature. Both ecologists and psychologists have been aware of this for some time. Ecologists, led by E.O. Wilson, have formulated the "biophilia hypothesis," which argues that those who are deprived of contact with nature suffer psychologically, and that this deprivation leads to a measurable decline in well-being.[46]

Meanwhile psychologists have coined their own term—ecopsychology—in which they make the same argument. Theodore Roszak, a leader in this field, cites a study that documents humans' dependence on nature by looking at the rate of recovery of patients in a hospital in Pennsylvania. Those who were in rooms overlooking the parking lot took longer to recover from illnesses than those whose rooms overlooked gardens with grass, trees, flowers, and birds.[47]

One of the arguments for community gardens is that in addition to providing food, they also provide greenery and a sense of community. Working with soil and watching things grow has a therapeutic effect, apparently harkening back to earlier times when everyone worked the soil.

The exciting news is that there are signs of change, daily indications of an interest in redesigning cities for people, not for cars. One encouraging trend comes from the United States. Rising public transit ridership of 5 percent a year since 1995 indicates that some people are abandoning their cars for buses, subways, and light rail. The country that led the world into the automobile age is starting to lead it away from such complete dependence on the car.[48]

Mayors and city planners the world over are beginning to rethink the role of the car in urban transportation systems. Some of the most fundamental challenges come from the developing world. As noted in Chapter 1, a group of eminent scientists in China challenged Beijing's decision to promote an automobile-centered transportation system. They point out a simple fact: China does not have enough land to accommodate the automobile and to feed its people. What is true for China is also true for India and dozens of other densely populated developing countries.[49]

Some cities in industrial and developing countries alike are dramatically increasing the mobility of their people by moving away from the car. The mayor of Curitiba, Brazil, has come up with an alternative transportation system, one that does not mimic those in the West but that is inexpensive and commuter-friendly. Since 1974 the transportation system has been totally restructured. As Molly O'Meara Sheehan points out, although one third of the people in Curitiba own cars, two thirds of all trips in the city are by bus. The population has doubled since 1974, but car traffic in the city has declined by 30 percent—a remarkable achievement.[50]

Some cities are far better at planning their growth than others. They plan transport systems that provide mobility, clean air, and exercise—a sharp contrast to cities that offer congestion, health-impairing air, and little opportunity for exercise. When 95 percent of a city's workers depend on the automobile for commuting, as happens in Atlanta, the city is in trouble. (See Table 9–4.) By con-

Table 9–4. *Commute to Work in Selected Cities, Early 1990s*

City	Population	Private Vehicle	Public Transit	Foot/Bicycle/ Other
	(million)	(percent)	(percent)	(percent)
Amsterdam	1.4	40	25	35
Atlanta, GA	2.5	95	5	0
Bangkok	6.5	60	30	10
Bogota	6.1	9	75	16
Cairo	9.7	10	58	31
Copenhagen	1.3	43	25	32
Curitiba	2.2	14	72	15
Lagos	10.3	18	54	22
Los Angeles, CA	13.1	87	6	6
New York, NY	16.6	61	30	9
Paris	9.5	49	36	15
Portland, OR	1.3	90	6	4
Singapore	3.3	22	56	22
Tokyo	27.0	29	49	22
Washington, DC	3.5	77	16	7

Source: See endnote 51.

trast, in Amsterdam only 40 percent of workers in the city commute by car; 35 percent commute by bike or walk, while 25 percent use public transit. Copenhagen's commuting patterns are almost identical to Amsterdam's. In Paris, just under half of commuters rely on cars. Even though these European cities are older, often with narrow streets, they have far less congestion than Atlanta.[51]

Not surprisingly, cities that are more car-dependent have more congestion and less mobility than those that offer more commuting options. The very vehicle whose great promise was mobility is in fact immobilizing entire urban populations, making it difficult for rich and poor alike to move about.

The design of transport systems, especially rail-based ones, shapes land use and the evolution of cities, but throughout the modern era, budget allocations for transportation have invariably been heavily biased toward the construction and maintenance of highways and streets. Creating more livable cities and the mobility that people desire depends on reallocating budgets to emphasize the development of rail- or bus-based public transport and facilities that support the bicycle. Existing long-term transportation strategies in many developing countries assume that everyone will one day be able to own a car. Unfortunately, given the constraints of land available to accommodate the automobile, not to mention those imposed by low incomes, this is simply not realistic. Given that reality, these countries will provide more mobility if they support public transportation and the bicycle.

If developing-country governments continue to invest most of the public resources available for transportation in support of the automobile, they will end up with a system built for the small fraction of their people who own cars—15 percent or so in many countries. Much of the remaining 85 percent will be deprived of mobility. Recognition now that most of the world's people are not likely to ever own automobiles can lead to a fundamental reorientation of transport system planning and investment.[52]

There are many ways to restructure the transportation system so that it satisfies the needs of all people, not just the affluent, so that it provides mobility, not immobility, and so that it improves health rather than damaging it. One way is to eliminate the subsidies that many employers provide for parking. For example, parking subsidies in the United States that are worth an estimated $31.5 billion a year obviously encourage people to drive to work.[53]

In 1992, California mandated that employers match parking subsidies with cash that can be used by the recipient either to pay public transport fares or to invest in bicycles. In firms where data were collected, this shift in policy reduced automobile use by some 17 percent. At the national level, a provision was incorporated into the 1998 Transportation Equity Act of the 21st Century to change the tax code so that those who used public transit or vanpools would enjoy the same tax-exempt subsidies as those who received free parking. What societies should be striving for is not parking subsidies, but parking taxes—taxes that begin to reflect the cost to the community of congestion associated with excessive numbers of automobiles.[54]

Some cities are reducing traffic congestion by charging cars to enter the city. Singapore, long a leader in urban transport innovation, has imposed a tax on all roads leading into the city. Electronic sensors identify each car as it enters, and then debit the owner's credit card. This has reduced the number of automobiles in Singapore, providing its residents with much more mobility than in most other cities. [55]

Singapore has been joined by Trondheim, Norway's third largest city. And now London too is planning to charge motorists driving in the city in order to alleviate the congestion that is strangling it. This obviously works best when it is coordinated with investment in improved public transportation and bicycle options. Other cities suffering from traffic gridlock seem likely to follow.[56]

More and more cities are declaring car-free areas. These have proved to be universally popular. Scores of cities have adopted this approach, including Stockholm, Vienna, Prague, and Rome. Paris experimented with a total ban on cars along stretches of the Seine River during the summer of 2001.[57]

Another social innovation that has substantially reduced parking congestion is car sharing. This approach, which emerged in Europe, is designed to provide access to cars for people who do not use them on a daily basis. The car sharing organization may be publicly sponsored, as in Amsterdam, or privately operated, as in Berlin. In the latter, Carsten and Marcus Petersen invested in a few cars and started taking reservations for those who wished to use them. For people who do not regularly use a car, an automobile represents a huge investment in materials and, for the community, in parking space. Crowding neighborhoods with parked automobiles is no longer necessary with car sharing.[58]

The success of this approach is evident in its growth. Car sharing groups in Europe now have 70,000 members in 300 towns and cities in eight countries from Ireland to Austria. Worldwatch researcher Gary Gardner reports that each shared vehicle eliminates four private cars, thus saving money and reducing material use and parking congestion in urban centers.[59]

Another initiative gaining attention is the idea of making subways attractive, even cultural centers. In Moscow, with works of art in the stations, the subway system is justifiably referred to as Russia's crown jewel. In Washington, D.C., Union Station, which links the city's subway system with intercity train lines, is an architectural delight. With its restoration completed in 1988 it has become a social gathering place with a rich array of restaurants, shops, and conference rooms.

One of the more interesting innovations designed to encourage the use of public transportation comes from State College, a small town in central Pennsylvania that is home to Pennsylvania State

University. In an effort to reduce traffic and parking congestion on campus, Penn State decided in 1999 that it would provide $1 million to the bus-based local transit system in exchange for unlimited free rides for its students, faculty, and staff. As a result, bus ridership in State College jumped by 240 percent in one year, requiring the transit company to invest heavily in new buses to accommodate the additional passengers. This initiative by the university has created a far more pleasant, attractive campus—an asset in recruiting both students and faculty.[60]

An innovation that is attracting attention in the United States is the provision of "location-efficient" mortgages. These are designed to reward home buyers or renovators who invest in housing near transportation hubs. By living near these, people can dispense with automobile ownership, or perhaps own just one car instead of two. This reduction in their cost of living is reflected in the larger loan they are able to obtain. This financial instrument, which was designed by the Natural Resources Defense Council, a leading U.S. environmental group, is available on a trial basis in Chicago, Los Angeles, and Seattle.[61]

Another public interest group initiative that is paying dividends has been undertaken by a group in India called the Public Affairs Center. It surveys residents of major cities about the quality of services that they receive. The group then publishes the results in the form of a report card for each Indian city on the adequacy of various services provided to their citizens. This is distributed to the media and widely circulated. Among its contributions was the discovery of widespread corruption in Bangalore, where one of every eight citizens surveyed indicated they had to pay a bribe to get city officials to respond to their needs.[62]

One of the most disturbing dimensions of the evolution of cities in developing countries is that this process is shaped by the nature of squatter settlements. As one study notes, the unnamed millions of squatters who are settling in cities are actually shaping the development of these areas. Curitiba, Brazil, again on the cutting edge of thinking, has designated tracts of land for squatter settlements. The alternative, which is to let squatters settle wherever they can—on steep slopes, on river floodplains, or on other high-risk areas—makes it difficult to provide basic services such as transport, water, and sewerage. By setting aside tracts of land for squatter settlements, the process can at least be structured in a way that is consistent with the official development plan of the city.[63]

As the new century begins, the world is being forced to reconsider the future role of the automobile in cities in one of the most fundamental shifts in transportation thinking over the last century. It is ironic that the very cars and trucks that made massive urbanization possible are now contributing to the deterioration of cities.

Some years ago, while attending a conference in Boston, I was making my way one morning on foot to the conference several blocks away. Between my hotel and the conference site, a thruway cut across the city. I had to wait some time for a break in the traffic so I could cross the congested thoroughfare. As I stood there, witnessing the effect of this thruway on the community, noting the noise, the pollution, and the congestion, I felt sorry for the people who lived in the neighborhood. And I felt sorry for us as a species. I don't think this represents the ultimate in human social evolution. We can do better.

III

GETTING FROM HERE TO THERE

10

Stabilizing Population by Reducing Fertility

World population has more than doubled since 1950. Those born before 1950 are members of the first generation in history to witness such a doubling during their lifetime. Stated otherwise, more people have been added to the world's population since 1950 than during the 4 million preceding years since we first stood upright.[1]

Throughout most of these 4 million years, we were few—numbering only in the thousands. When agriculture began, world population was estimated at 8 million—less than a third the size of Tokyo today. After farming got under way, population growth slowly gained momentum. With the Industrial Revolution, it accelerated further. After 1950, it soared.

We are struggling to understand the dimensions of population growth over the last half-century. We can relate to 100,000 people, the number filling a large stadium for an athletic event or a concert, but relating to an annual increase of 80 million is difficult. To grasp the dimensions of this growth, we can equate it to the combined population of the United Kingdom, Belgium, Denmark, and Sweden today. As someone who spends more time than I would like in planes and airports, it is easier for me to relate population growth to the passenger capacity of a jumbo jet. It takes the world's growing population less than 3 minutes to fill a jumbo jet with 400 passengers.

Despite the stresses associated with continuing population growth, the United Nations projects that our numbers will grow from 6.1 billion in 2000 to 9.3 billion in 2050. Of even more concern, all of the 3.2 billion additional people will be added in developing countries. Given the analysis in this book, there is reason to doubt that this will actually happen. What is unclear is whether the projections will not materialize because we accelerate the shift to smaller families in time or because we fail to do so and death rates begin to rise.

Many countries that have experienced rapid population growth for several decades are showing signs of demographic fatigue. Governments struggling with the simultaneous challenge of educating growing numbers of children, creating jobs for swelling ranks of young job seekers, and dealing with the environmental effects of population growth are stretched to the limit. Without a concerted effort by national governments and the international community to shift quickly to smaller families, land scarcity and water shortages could become unmanageable—leading to political instability, economic decline, and rising death rates.

In this situation, when a major new threat arises—such as the HIV epidemic or aquifer depletion—governments often cannot cope. Problems routinely managed in industrial societies are becoming full-scale humanitarian crises in many developing ones. As the HIV epidemic continues to spread, rising death rates in some African countries will likely bring their population growth to a halt. This rise in the death rate marks a tragic new development in world demography.

The issue is not whether population growth will slow, but how. In its 1998 update of long-range population projections, the United Nations reduced the predicted population for 2050 by some 500 million. Two thirds of this reduction was due to fertility falling faster than projected. But the other one third was the result of a projected rise in death rates, largely because of HIV in Africa. For the first time in nearly half a century of world population updates, projections were being reduced by rising mortality. The challenge is to slow population growth in all developing countries by lowering birth rates, because if we fail, it will be slowed by rising death rates.[2]

Breaking Out or Breaking Down

Today we find ourselves in a demographically divided world, one where national projections of population growth vary more widely than at any time in history. In most European countries and Japan, population has stabilized or is declining; but in others, such as Ethiopia, Pakistan, and Saudi Arabia, population is projected to double or even triple before stabilizing.

Demographers use a three-stage model to understand how population growth rates change over time as modernization proceeds. In the first stage, birth and death rates are both high, resulting in little or no population growth. In the second stage, death rates fall while birth rates remain high, leading to rapid growth. In the third stage, birth rates fall to a low level, balancing low death rates and again leading to population stability while offering greater possibilities for comfort and dignity than in stage one. It is assumed that countries will progress from stage one to stage three. [3]

Today there are no countries in stage one; all are either in stage two or stage three. However, instead of progressing steadily forward toward stage three as expected, some countries are falling back toward stage one as the historical fall in death rates is reversed, leading the world into a new demographic era. If countries do not break out of the middle stage of the demographic transition in a matter of decades, rapid population growth will eventually overwhelm natural systems, leading to economic decline and forcing societies back into stage one as mortality rises. Over the long term, there is no middle ground. Countries either break out or break down. Unfortunately, a number of countries, mostly in Africa, are showing signs of breaking down.

For the first time since China's great famine claimed 30 million lives in 1959–61, world population growth is being slowed by rising death rates. (See Figure 10–1.) Although rapid population growth continues in scores of countries, the world is beginning to divide into two parts: one where population growth is slowing as fertility falls, and another where population growth is slowing as mortality rises. One way or the other, population growth will slow. That rising death rates from AIDS have already reduced the projected population for 2050 by more than 150 million represents a failure of our political institutions unmatched since the outbreak of World War II. [4]

The world is starting to reap the consequences of past neglect of

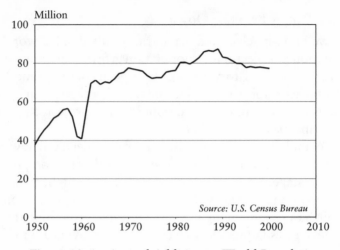

Figure 10–1. *Annual Addition to World Population*

the population issue. The two regions where death rates either are already rising or are likely to do so are sub-Saharan Africa and the Indian subcontinent, which together contain 1.9 billion people—nearly one third of humanity. Without clearly defined government strategies in countries with rapid population growth to lower birth rates quickly and a commitment by the international community to support them, one third of humanity could slide into a demographic black hole.

After nearly half a century of continuous population growth, the demand in many countries for food, water, and forest products is simply outrunning the capacity of local life-support systems. In addition, the ever growing number of young people who need health care and education is exceeding the availability of these services. If birth rates do not come down soon, these natural systems and social services are likely to deteriorate to the point where death rates will rise.

But what will cause death rates to go up in individual countries? Will it be starvation? An outbreak of disease? War? Social disintegration? At some point as population pressures build, governments are simply overwhelmed and are not able to respond to new threats. There are now three clearly identifiable threats that either are already pushing death rates up or have the potential to do so—the HIV epidemic, aquifer depletion, and land hunger.

Of these three, the HIV epidemic is the first to spiral out of control in developing countries. The epidemic should be seen for what it is: an international emergency of epic proportions, one that could claim more lives in the early part of this century than World War II did in the last one. In sub-Saharan Africa, HIV infection rates are soaring, already affecting one fifth to one third or more of adults in Botswana, Namibia, South Africa, Zambia, and Zimbabwe.[5]

Barring a medical miracle, many African countries will lose a fifth or more of their adult populations to AIDS by the end of this decade. To find a precedent for such a potentially devastating loss of life from an infectious disease, we have to go back to the decimation of New World Indian communities by the introduction of smallpox in the sixteenth century or to the Bubonic plague that claimed roughly a third of Europe's population during the fourteenth century.[6]

Ominously, the virus has also established a foothold in the Indian subcontinent. With 3.7 million adults now HIV-positive, India is home to more infected individuals than any other nation except South Africa. And with the infection rate among India's adults at roughly 1 percent—a critical threshold for potentially rapid spread—the epidemic threatens to engulf the country if the government does not move quickly to check it. The virus is also spreading rapidly in Myanmar, Cambodia, and China.[7]

One consequence of continuing population growth is potentially life-threatening water shortages. If rapid population growth continues indefinitely, the demand for water eventually exceeds the sustainable yield of aquifers. The result is excessive water withdrawals and falling water tables. (See Chapter 2.) Since 40 percent of the world's food comes from irrigated land, water shortages can quickly translate into food shortages.[8]

Dozens of developing countries face acute water shortages, but none illustrate the threat better than India, whose population—expanding by 18 million a year—has already surpassed 1 billion. New estimates for India indicate that in some areas water withdrawals are now double the rate of aquifer recharge. As a result, water tables are falling by 1 meter or more per year over parts of the country. Overpumping today means water supply cutbacks tomorrow, a serious matter where half of the harvest comes from irrigated land.[9]

The International Water Management Institute estimates that

aquifer depletion and the resulting cutbacks in irrigation water could override technology gains, reducing the grain harvest in water-short regions of India. In a country where 53 percent of all children are already malnourished and underweight, a shrinking harvest could increase hunger-related deaths, adding to the 6 million worldwide who die each year from hunger and malnutrition. In contrast to AIDS, which takes a heavy toll among young adults, hunger claims mostly infants and children.[10]

The third threat hanging over the future of countries with rapid population growth is land hunger. Once cropland per person shrinks to a certain point, people can no longer feed themselves and they either turn to imported food or go hungry. The risk is that countries will not be able to afford the imported food or that food simply will not be available if world import needs exceed exportable supplies.

Among the larger countries where shrinking cropland per person threatens future food security are Ethiopia, Nigeria, and Pakistan, all countries with weak family planning programs. As Nigeria's population goes from 114 million today to a projected 278 million in 2050, its grainland per person will shrink from 0.16 hectares to 0.06 hectares. Pakistan's projected growth from 141 million today to 344 million by 2050 will reduce its grainland per person from 0.09 hectares at present to 0.04 hectares—scarcely the size of a tennis court. Countries where this number has shrunk to 0.03 hectares, such as Japan, South Korea, and Taiwan, import 70 percent or more of their grain.[11]

The threats from HIV, aquifer depletion, and shrinking cropland are not new or unexpected. We have known for more than a decade that AIDS could decimate human populations if it were not controlled. In each of the last 18 years, the number of new HIV infections has risen. Of the 58 million infected by the year 2000, 22 million people have died. In the absence of a low-cost cure, nearly all the remaining 36 million will die by 2010. It is hard to believe, given our advanced medical knowledge, that a controllable disease could devastate human populations in so many countries.[12]

Similarly, it is hard to imagine that falling water tables, which may prove an even greater threat to future economic progress and political stability, could be so widely ignored. The arithmetic of emerging water shortages is not difficult. A growing population with a water supply that is essentially fixed by nature means that the water per person will diminish over time, eventually dropping below the level needed to meet basic needs for drinking water, food production, and sanitation.

The same holds true for cropland per person. The mystery is not in the arithmetic. That is straightforward. The mystery is in our failure to respond to the threats associated with continuing population growth.

Africa Breaking Down

A generation ago, virtually the entire world appeared to be progressing economically and socially. A better future was in prospect for all. Now that has changed as the HIV epidemic ravages Africa. It is not only causing millions of deaths, it is undermining the continent's economic future. If issues rooted in population growth, such as land hunger and water shortages, are not addressed, they could be equally disastrous. By analyzing what happened in Africa, perhaps we can avoid a social catastrophe of similar dimensions elsewhere.

History offers few examples of leadership failure comparable to that of Africa's in response to the HIV crisis. The HIV epidemic that is raging across Africa is now taking some 6,030 lives each day, the equivalent of 15 fully loaded jumbo jets crashing daily—with no survivors. This number, climbing higher each year, is expected to double during this decade.[13]

Public attention has initially focused on the dramatic rise in adult mortality and the precipitous drop in life expectancy. But we need now to look at the longer-term economic consequences—falling food production, deteriorating health care, and disintegrating educational systems. Effectively dealing with this epidemic and the heavy loss of adults will make the rebuilding of Europe after World War II seem like child's play by comparison.

While industrial countries have held the HIV infection rate among adults to less than 1 percent, in 16 African countries the figure is over 10 percent. In South Africa, it is 20 percent. In Zimbabwe and Swaziland, 25 percent. And in Botswana, which has the highest infection rate, 36 percent of adults are HIV-positive. These countries are expected to lose one fifth to one third of their adults by the end of this decade.[14]

Attention is focusing on the high cost of treating those already ill, but the virus is continuing to spread. As deaths multiply, life expectancy—the sentinel indicator of economic development—is falling. Without AIDS, countries with high infection rates, like Botswana, South Africa, and Zimbabwe, would have a life expectancy of some 65 years or more. With the virus continuing to spread, life expectancy could drop to 35 years—a medieval life span.[15]

Whereas infectious diseases typically take their heaviest toll among the eldest and the very young who have weaker immune systems, AIDS claims mostly young adults, depriving countries of their most productive workers. In the epidemic's early stages, the virus typically spreads most rapidly among the better educated, more socially mobile segment of society. It claims the agronomists, engineers, and teachers needed for economic development.

The HIV epidemic is affecting every segment of society, every sector of the economy, and every facet of life. For example, close to half of Zimbabwe's health care budget is used to treat AIDS patients. In some hospitals in Burundi and South Africa, AIDS patients occupy 60 percent of the beds. Health care workers labor until the point of exhaustion. This epidemic could easily produce 40 million orphans by 2010, a number that will overwhelm the resources of extended families.[16]

Education is also suffering. In Zambia, the number of teachers dying with AIDS each year approaches the number of new teachers being trained. In the Central African Republic, the reduction of the teaching force by AIDS closed 107 primary schools, leaving only 66 open. At the college level, the damage is equally devastating. At the University of Durban-Westville in South Africa, 25 percent of the student body is HIV-positive.[17]

In addition to the continuing handicaps of a lack of infrastructure and trained personnel, Africa must now contend with the adverse economic effects of the epidemic. AIDS dramatically increases the dependency ratio—the number of young and elderly who depend on productive adults. This in turn makes it much more difficult for a society to save. Reduced savings means reduced investment and slower economic growth or even decline.

At the corporate level, firms in countries with high infection rates are seeing their employee health care insurance costs double, triple, or even quadruple. Companies that were until recently comfortably in the black now find themselves in the red. Under these circumstances, investment inflows from abroad are dwindling and could dry up entirely.[18]

Even as disease consumes Africa, food security is deteriorating. Land hunger, water scarcity, and nutrient depletion are reducing the grain produced per person. In East, Central, and Southern Africa, the undernourished share of the population has increased over the last two decades.[19]

Making matters worse, food security is declining as the epidemic progresses. At the family level, food supplies drop precipitously when the first adult develops full-blown AIDS. This deprives the family not only of a worker in the fields, but also of the work time of the adult caring for the AIDS sufferer. A survey in Tanzania found that a woman whose husband had AIDS spent 60 percent less time tending the crops. Declines in food production from the epidemic have been reported in Burkina Faso, Côte d'Ivoire, and Zimbabwe. In pastoral economies, such as Namibia, the loss of the male head of household is often followed by the loss of cattle, the family's livelihood.[20]

Sub-Saharan Africa, a region of 600 million people, is moving into uncharted territory. There are historical precedents for epidemics on this scale, but not for such a concentrated loss of adults. The good news is that some countries are halting the spread of the virus. The key is strong leadership from the top. In Uganda, where the epidemic first took root, the active personal leadership of President Yoweri Museveni over the last dozen years has reduced the share of adults infected with the virus from a peak of 14 percent down to 8 percent. In effect, the number of new infections has dropped well below the number of deaths from AIDS. Senegal also responded early to the threat from the virus. As a result, it prevented AIDS from gaining momentum and held the infection rate to 2 percent of its adults, a number only slightly higher than in industrial countries.[21]

Saving Africa depends on a Marshall Plan–scale effort on two fronts: one to curb the spread of HIV and the other to restore economic progress. Winning the former depends directly on Africa's national political leaders. Unless they personally lead, the effort will almost certainly fail. Once a leader outlines the behavioral changes needed to contain the virus—such as delaying first intercourse, reducing the number of sexual partners, and using condoms—then others can contribute. This includes the medical establishment within the country, religious leaders, nongovernmental groups, and international health and family planning agencies.

To compensate for the "missing generation," countries will need assistance across the board in education. This is an area where the U.S. Peace Corps and its equivalents in other countries can play a central role, particularly in supplying the teachers needed to keep schools open. Social workers are needed to work with orphans. A program of financial assistance is necessary for the extended families trying to absorb the projected millions of orphans.

Given the high cost of doing business in an AIDS-ridden society, special incentives in the form of tax relief are needed to attract corporate investors, incentives that could be underwritten by international development agencies. And debt relief is essential to the rebuilding of sub-Saharan Africa.

The bottom line is that there is no precedent in international development for the challenge the world now faces in Africa. The question is not whether we can respond to this challenge. We can. We have the resources to do so. If we fail to respond to Africa's pain, we may not only witness the economic decline of an entire continent, but in the process we will forfeit the right to call ourselves a civilized society.

Filling the Family Planning Gap

Given the immediate need to slow world population growth, it would be easy to assume that couples everywhere by now have access to family planning services. Unfortunately, despite the pivotal influence of family planning services on the global future, there is still a huge gap between people who want to plan their families and their access to family planning services.

The first step in stabilizing population is to remove the physical and social barriers that prevent women from using family planning services. John Bongaarts of the Population Council reports that 42 percent of all pregnancies in the developing world are unintended. Of these, 23 percent end in abortion. This leads Bongaarts to conclude that one third of projected world population growth will be due to unintended pregnancies. Of all the unmet social needs in the world today, none is more likely to adversely affect the human prospect more than the unmet need for family planning.[22]

There are several reasons why couples are not planning their families despite their desire for fewer children. In many countries, such as Saudi Arabia and Argentina, government policies restrict access to contraceptives. Geographic accessibility also affects use; in some rural areas of sub-Saharan Africa, it can take two hours or more to reach the nearest contraceptive provider. For those with low incomes, family planning services can be expensive. Even where family planning clinics are accessible, they are often underfunded, leaving them short of supplies and understaffed.[23]

Women who want fewer children may also be constrained from using family planning by a lack of knowledge, prevailing cultural and religious values, or the disapproval of family members. Studies have shown that a husband's opposition to family planning constrains the efforts to limit family size in numerous countries, including Egypt, Guatemala, India, Nepal, and Pakistan. Moreover, some 14 countries require a woman to obtain her husband's consent before she can receive any contraceptive services, while 60 require spousal authorization for permanent birth control methods. Although it has been argued that these practices lessen conflicts between spouses and health care personnel, they are serious impediments to a woman's ability to control her fertility.[24]

One way of reducing the unplanned pregnancies that account for a large share of world population growth is through medical abortions. A prescription drug used for many years in France to induce abortion, RU 486 (also known as mifepristone), is now available in several other European countries, the United States, China, India, Pakistan, and several smaller countries in Asia. Another drug, methotrexate, used worldwide in cancer therapy, works well as a "morning after" pill when used in combination with misoprostol. This procedure, prescribed by many U.S. doctors before RU 486 was approved in 2000, typically induces abortion within 72 hours. Although medical abortions are widely used in industrial countries, such as France and the United States, they are of even greater value in developing countries, where many people do not have access to family planning services and, even if they do, where supplies of contraceptives sometimes run out.[25]

Information about contraceptives and family planning for young men and women facilitates the use of birth control. In Thailand, people of all ages have been educated on the importance of family planning. Mechai Viravidaiya, the charismatic founder of the Thai Population and Community Development Association (PCDA), encouraged familiarity with contraceptives through demonstrations, ads, and witty songs. Math teachers even use population-related examples in their classes. As a result of the efforts of Mechai, the PCDA, and the government, the growth of Thailand's population has slowed from more than 3 percent in 1960 to approximately 1 percent in 2000—the same as that of the United States.[26]

More recently, Iran has emerged as a leader in population policy. After the Islamic revolution in 1979, when Ayatollah Khomeini came to power, the family planning programs put in place by the Shah were dismantled. Khomeini exhorted women to have more babies to create "soldiers for Islam," pushing annual population growth rates to over 4 percent—some of the highest ever recorded. By the late 1980s, the social and environmental costs of such growth rates were becoming apparent. As a result, policy shifted. Religious leaders argued that having fewer children was a social responsibility. Eighty percent of family planning costs were covered in the budget. Some 15,000 "health houses" were established to provide family planning and health services to Iran's rural population. As literacy levels among rural women climbed from 17 percent in 1976 to nearly 90 percent, fertility dropped to an average of 2.6 children per woman. Within 15 years, Iran's population growth rate has fallen from over 4 percent a year to scarcely 1 percent, making it a model for other developing countries.[27]

A comparison of population trends in Bangladesh and Pakistan illustrates the importance of acting now. When Bangladesh was created in a split with Pakistan in 1971, the former had 66 million people and the latter 62 million, roughly the same population sizes. Then their demographic trends diverged. Bangladesh's political leaders made a strong commitment to reduce fertility rates, while the leaders in Islamabad wavered over the need to do so. As a result, the average number of children per family in Bangladesh today is 3.3, compared with 5.6 in Pakistan. Each year the gap in the population trajectories of the two countries widens. By putting family planning programs in place sooner rather than later, Bangladesh— the poorer country—is projected to have 79 million fewer people than Pakistan in 2050. (See Figure 10–2.)[28]

The world now faces a similar choice. The United Nations projects that the number of people on the earth could reach anywhere from 7.9 billion to 10.9 billion by 2050. According to its latest medium-level projections, population in the developing world is projected to rise from 4.9 billion in 2000 to 8.1 billion in 2050. Such an increase would likely lead to organizational overload and

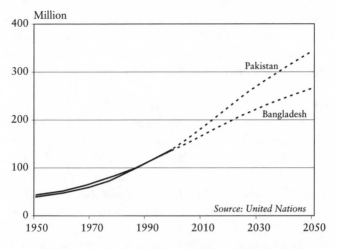

Figure 10–2. *Populations of Bangladesh and Pakistan, 1950–2000, with Projections to 2050*

ecosystem collapse in dozens of countries.

Heading off such a prospect depends on filling the family planning gap by ensuring that women everywhere have access to a full complement of family planning services, including the "morning after" pill. The second front in this worldwide effort to stabilize population is to help create the social conditions that will lead to smaller families, specifically by improving the status of women. George Moffett, author of *Critical Masses*, observes quite rightly that "There's a critical connection between a woman's productive role—the improved legal, educational, and economic opportunities that are the source of empowerment—and a woman's reproductive role."[29]

In some developing countries, having many children is seen as a matter of survival: children are a vital part of the family economy and a source of security in old age. Institutions such as the Grameen Bank in Bangladesh, which specializes in microenterprise loans, are attempting to change this situation by providing credit to well over a million villagers—mostly impoverished women. These loans are empowering women, helping to end the cycle of poverty, and thus reducing the need for large families.[30]

Rapid economic growth is not always a prerequisite for reduced fertility rates. Bangladesh has reduced fertility rates from nearly 7 children per woman in the early 1970s to 3.3 children today despite incomes averaging only $200 a year, among the lowest in the world. In the struggle to slow population growth, government leadership, access to family planning services, and improvement in social conditions are proving to be more important than the growth of a nation's economy.[31]

Slowly, governments are realizing the value of investing in population stabilization. One study found that the government of Bangladesh spends $62 to prevent a birth, but saves $615 on social services expenditures for each birth averted—a 10-fold difference in cost. Based on the study's estimate, the program prevents 890,000 births annually. The net savings to the government total $547 million each year, leaving more to invest in education and health care.[32]

At the 1994 International Conference on Population and Development in Cairo, the governments of the world agreed to a 20-year population and reproductive health program. The United Nations estimated that $17 billion a year would be needed for this effort by 2000 and $22 billion by 2015. (By comparison, $22 billion is less than is spent every 10 days on military expenditures.) Developing countries and countries in transition agreed to cover two thirds of the price tag, while donor countries promised to pay the rest—$5.7 billion a year by 2000 and $7.2 billion by 2015.[33]

Unfortunately, while developing countries are largely on track with their part of the expenditures, having covered about two thirds of their allotted payments, donor countries have fallen far behind—honoring only one third of their commitment. As a result of shortfalls following the Cairo conference, the United Nations estimated that there were an additional 122 million unintended pregnancies by 2000. An estimated one third of these were aborted. Moreover, an estimated 65,000 women who did not wish to be pregnant died in childbirth and 844,000 suffered chronic or permanent injury from their pregnancies.[34]

Slowing population growth depends on simultaneously creating the social conditions for fertility decline and filling the family planning gap. "Global population problems cannot be put on hold while countries reform their health care, rebuild their inner cities, and reduce budget deficit[s]. Avoiding another world population doubling...requires rapid action," notes Sharon Camp, former vice president of Population Action International. The difference between acting today and putting it off until tomorrow is the difference between population stabilizing at a level the earth can support and population expanding until environmental deterioration disrupts economic progress.[35]

The Role of Female Education

Over the last two decades, scores of studies have analyzed the relationship between female education and fertility and have concluded that the more education women have, the fewer children they bear. A 1999 survey of research by the U.S. National Academy of Sciences (NAS) analyzes studies that compare countries with varying levels of female education and studies that examine changing levels of female education in individual countries over time. Both groups of studies support this basic hypothesis.[36]

The NAS study contrasts Sri Lanka and Pakistan, for example. Sri Lanka, which has a female literacy level of 87 percent for women over age 15, has a total fertility rate of just over two children per woman. In Pakistan, where only 24 percent of adult women can read and write, the fertility rate is 5.6 children. Pakistan is typical of most countries, but there are occasional exceptions. For example, in Jordan 86 percent of the women are literate, but the fertility rate is the same as in Pakistan. Bangladesh is also something of an anomaly, because although only 26 percent of its women are literate, its fertility rate has dropped by half over the last generation.[37]

As the NAS survey notes, the relationship between educational level and fertility is not always a simple one. For example, while rising female educational levels lead to smaller family size, so does the desire to educate children. Once couples decide that they want to educate their children, including girls, they are faced with the cost of education. This in itself is apparently reducing family size.[38]

In Bangladesh, as noted earlier, the fertility rate was almost cut in half within 16 years. One factor apparently affecting family size was spreading land poverty as land was divided and subdivided from one generation to the next. Among families with relatively small plots of land to begin with, fragmentation leads to basic changes in thinking. At one time, economic security came from owning land. It was always a source of employment and food. But as the land per family shrinks, this security diminishes, leading many couples to define economic security for their children, and thus indirectly for themselves, in the form of a wage-paying job. Getting such a job requires education. This is costly, leading to a conscious reduction in family size that is not necessarily dependent on any gains in income or female literacy.[39]

Research in Bangladesh shows that thinking about family size is not occurring in a vacuum. As people are exposed to higher living standards elsewhere in the world, they begin to think about how to achieve the same thing for their children. Again, they come back to education. Investment in education is the key both to a better life for their children and to their old age security. Large families, which were an asset when there was more land to farm, have now become a liability.

While sociologists have looked at the relation between education and family size, economists have looked at the economics of this relationship. Lawrence Summers, while Director of Research at the World Bank, pointed out that at prevailing levels of education, each additional year of female education reduces fertility by roughly 10 percent. Using this information to analyze the economics of educating girls, he noted that raising female enrollment in primary school to the same level as that of males in developing countries would mean adding some 25 million girls to the current primary school enrollment. This, he estimated, would cost $938 million per year. Gender balancing in secondary schools would mean adding 21 million girls to current enrollment at a cost of roughly $1.4 billion per year.[40]

Summers then went on to estimate that this investment of $2.3 billion would yield a return of 20 percent annually. He noted that it was the most effective way of breaking the cycle of poverty. As female education levels rise, women have healthier, better-educated children, a gain that is typically passed from one generation to the next. The difficult part is the initial break out of poverty.[41]

This 20-percent annual return dwarfs that of almost any other investment in development. For example, the roughly $1 trillion that developing countries were planning to spend on new power generating facilities over the next decade would yield an annual return of at most 6 percent, and sometimes substantially less. Diverting a small amount of investment from power generation to the education of girls and young women could both raise families out of poverty and accelerate development.[42]

Using Soap Operas and Sitcoms

While the attention of researchers has focused on the role of formal education in reducing fertility, soap operas on radio and television can even more quickly change people's attitudes about reproductive health, gender equity, family size, and environmental protection. A well-written soap opera can have a profound short-term effect on population growth. It costs little and can proceed even while formal educational systems are being expanded.

This approach was pioneered by Miguel Sabido, a vice president of Televisa, Mexico's national television network. The power of this medium was first illustrated by Sabido when he did a series of soap opera segments on illiteracy. The day after one of the characters in his soap opera visited a literacy office wanting to learn how to read and write, a quarter-million people showed up at these offices in Mexico City. Eventually 840,000 Mexicans enrolled in literacy courses after watching the series.[43]

Sabido dealt with contraception in a soap opera entitled *Acompaneme*, which translates as *Come With Me*. According to one observer, "This serial, which ran over two years, featured a fairly typical, poor young family. The mother, a sympathetic but ignorant character, was desperate to stop at the three children she already had but didn't know how. Her husband, macho and lusty, resented her efforts to try the rhythm method. Over a period of time, and many melodramatic arguments and tears, the woman decided to seek the advice of another woman she knew who had 'miraculously' restricted her family size. Eventually she learned about birth control. By the time she and her smiling husband walked out of the gynecologist's office with a prescription in hand, values had changed—in this family and among viewers—about ideal family size, about not having more children than one can afford and about the woman's role in her family."[44]

As these family planning soap operas continued over the next decade, the birth rate fell by 34 percent. In 1986, Mexico was awarded the United Nations Population Prize for its outstanding achievement in slowing population growth. David Poindexter, founder of Population Communications International (PCI) in 1985, used his new organization to promote Sabido's model as a prototype for other countries. Today PCI is operating in 6 of the 10 most populous countries—China, India, Brazil, Pakistan, Nigeria, and Mexico.[45]

In Kenya, PCI has developed a similarly oriented soap opera that has aired on the radio, the medium of choice for 96 percent of the country's people. After the highly popular early evening news, people stay tuned for a radio serial entitled *Ushikwapo Shikamana* (which means *If Assisted, Assist Yourself*). With close to half the country's people following the twice weekly program, this has provided an ideal vehicle for communicating information on a range of topics from reproductive health and family planning to environment, gender equality, and protection from AIDS. These examples are but two of many that illustrate the success of radio and television in raising public understanding and in changing attitudes.[46]

Stopping at Two

You do not need to be a mathematician to understand that there is no long-term alternative to having only two children per couple, the number needed for replacement. Joel Cohen, population analyst at Rockefeller University, makes this point rather effectively. He notes that if the 1990 population growth rates in various regions had continued until 2150, there would be 694 billion people in the world. This compares with 6.1 billion people today. "No way," says Cohen. "Not enough water falls from the sky to satisfy the needs of such a vast human population."[47]

The basic arithmetic is not new. We have always known that a seemingly innocuous growth of 3 percent a year, a rate that has been common in many developing countries, would lead to a 20-fold increase in one century and a 400-fold increase in two centuries. Saudi Arabia today has 20 million people and a population that is expanding at this rate. If this were to continue throughout this century, it would have 440 million people in 2100—more than the current population of North America.

Or look at Nigeria, also growing at roughly 3 percent a year. A century from now, Nigeria's 114 million people would total 2.46 billion. Considering that all of Africa is supporting 800 million today, it is impossible to visualize 2.46 billion people in Nigeria alone. It is hard to argue with Cohen's basic point that the only viable long-term option is two children per couple. A population that is growing, however slowly, will eventually overwhelm its life-support systems. Conversely, a population that is declining, however slowly, will eventually disappear.

The growth in world population over the last half-century is sufficiently recent that we are still struggling to understand what it means. We may intuitively understand that a 20-fold increase in a century is not possible, but we have yet to come to terms with the reasons why. For some threats to our future we have designed response systems. For example, an outbreak of a deadly infectious disease such as the Ebola virus sets off programmed responses to contain and eradicate it. This response involves the World Health Organization, the U.S. Centers for Disease Control and Prevention, and the appropriate agencies in the government of the county affected. And if the currency of a country like Indonesia or Russia collapses, the international monetary system is programmed to respond to that threat. Such is not the case when population growth crosses key support system thresholds.

When the water use of a growing population surpasses the sustainable yield of an aquifer and the water table starts to fall, there is no alarm system that triggers a response in the councils of government. As a result, the gap between the demand for water and the sustainable yield of the aquifer widens. Each year, the drop in the aquifer is greater than the year before, setting the stage for an eventual dramatic reduction in the water supply as an aquifer is depleted and the amount pumped out is reduced to the recharge level. If overpumping is extensive, the drop in water supply could be traumatic, disrupting food production.

Unfortunately, no one regularly measures the water table level under the North China Plain, the Punjab in India, or the southern Great Plains of the United States, announcing when overpumping begins, how much water is left, and when the aquifer will be depleted. As a result, instead of societies planning for a soft landing by bringing the demand for water into balance with sustainable yield, they keep going until the inevitable crash occurs.

Societies with water demands surpassing the sustainable yield of the aquifers and desiring more water per person in the future will have to consider the possibility of reducing population size, a trend already under way in some European countries. This means shifting not to a two-child family, but to a one-child family.

In countries where rural populations continue to grow and holdings are divided among the children in each generation, the land per family eventually shrinks to the point where survival is threatened. Halting the fragmentation that is creating a nightmarish situation in many rural communities in Africa and Asia depends either on moving quickly to replacement-level fertility or accepting massive rural-urban migration.

Although population projections for the world have been available since the 1950s, remarkably little has been done to analyze the relationship between the size of current and future populations and the earth's capacity to satisfy people's needs for basic resources, such as water and cropland. Demographers who do the projections have long since abandoned this area as a field of research. In his 1996 book *How Many People Can the Earth Support?*, Joel Cohen analyzed the 1992 and 1993 annual meetings of the Population Association of America, where there were some 200 symposia. Not one of these panels attempted to analyze the relationship between projected population growth and the earth's natural resource base.[48]

The good news is that the world is making progress in achieving replacement-level fertility. Fifty-four countries have now reduced average family size to two children or less. (See Table 10–1.) Together these countries contain 2.5 billion people. Family size in China, at 1.8 children per couple, is now below the level in the United States (2.1). Even so, the large number of young people reaching reproductive age in China means that the population is still expected to reach 1.49 billion by 2038, before its numbers begin to decline, dropping to 1.46 billion in 2050. Some countries have seen fertility drop well below replacement level. For example, Russia's fertility rate is 1.2 children. As a result of this decline, and a rise in mortality over the last decade, Russia's population of 144 million is now declining by 900,000 per year. Other countries where population is beginning to decline include Bulgaria, the Czech Republic, Italy, and the Ukraine.[49]

Despite these trends, the threat of continuing population growth in more than a hundred developing countries is all too real. Perhaps the most dangerous educational gap is the lack of understanding of the relationship between family size, the longer-term population trajectory, and the future availability of resources per person. Filling this gap requires projections that link a range of family sizes—say, two, four, or six children—to the future availability of land, water, and other basic resources. Without this information, individuals may simply not understand the urgency of shifting to smaller families. And of even more concern, political leaders will not be able to make responsible decisions on population and related poli-

Table 10–1. *Fertility Levels in Selected Countries in 2001*

Country	Average Number of Children Per Woman[1]	Population, Mid-2001
	(number)	(million)
Countries with Fertility at or Below Replacement Level[2]		
Russia	1.2	144
Italy	1.2	58
Japan	1.3	127
Germany	1.3	82
Poland	1.4	39
Australia	1.7	19
United Kingdom	1.7	60
China	1.8	1,273
France	1.8	59
United States	2.1	285
Countries with Fertility Above Replacement Level[2]		
Brazil	2.4	172
Indonesia	2.7	206
India	3.2	1,033
Pakistan	5.6	145
Tanzania	5.6	36
Saudi Arabia	5.7	21
Nigeria	5.8	127
Ethiopia	5.9	65
Dem. Rep. of Congo	7.0	54
Yemen	7.2	18

[1]The average number of children born to a woman in her lifetime is also known as the Total Fertility Rate.   [2]Replacement-level fertility is an average of 2.1 children per woman.

Source: Population Reference Bureau, *2001 World Population Data Sheet*, wall chart (Washington, DC: 2001).

cies, such as investment in family planning services.

Discussions of future population growth in this chapter use the U.N. medium projections, those that have world population going from 6.1 billion at present to 9.3 billion by 2050. There is also a high projection, which has human numbers approaching 11 bil-

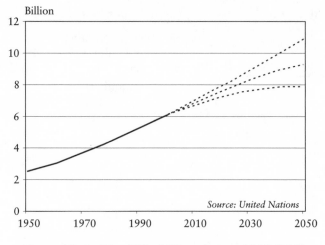

Figure 10–3. *Total World Population, 1950–2050,*
Under Three Assumptions of Growth

lion by 2050, and a low projection, which has population peaking
at 7.9 billion in 2046 and then declining. (See Figure 10–3.)[50]

This low number assumes that the entire world will quickly
move below replacement-level fertility to 1.7 children per couple.
This is not only achievable, it is the only humane population option. Otherwise the land and water scarcity that is already increasing hunger and deaths in some countries could spread to many
more.

Achieving this lower figure is the responsibility of national political leaders, but unless world leaders—the Secretary-General of
the United Nations, the President of the World Bank, and the President of the United States—urge governments and couples everywhere to adopt a goal of two surviving children per couple, resource constraints will likely lead to economic decline. The issue
today is not whether individual couples can afford more than two
children, but whether the earth can afford for couples to have more
than two children.

11

Tools for Restructuring the Economy

In Chapter 1, I cited Øystein Dahle's warning that the failure of prices to tell the ecological truth could undermine capitalism, just as the failure of prices to tell the economic truth undermined socialism. The Chinese recognized this risk of prices not telling the ecological truth when they banned tree cutting in the Yangtze river basin following the near-record flooding in 1998. They said that a tree standing was worth three times as much as a tree cut. If they had included not only the flood control value of trees but also the value in recycling rainfall to the country's interior, a tree standing might easily be worth six times as much as a tree cut.[1]

The use of a highly valued resource such as a tree for a lowly valued purpose such as lumber imposes an economic cost on society. Similarly, since the price of a gallon of gasoline does not include the cost of climate change, it too imposes a cost on society. If losses such as these, now occurring on an ever larger scale, keep accumulating, the resulting economic stresses could bankrupt some countries.

The key to sustaining economic progress is getting prices to tell the ecological truth. Ecologists and economists—working together—can calculate the ecological costs of various economic activities. These costs can then be incorporated into the market price of a product or service in the form of a tax. Additional taxes on goods and services can be offset by a reduction in income taxes. The issue in "tax shifting," as the Europeans call it, is not the level of taxes but what they tax.

There are several policy instruments that can be used to restructure the economy, including fiscal policy, government regulation, eco-labeling, and tradable permits. But restructuring the tax system is the key to eliminating the crippling economic distortions. Tax policy is particularly effective because it is systemic in nature. If taxes raise the price of fossil fuels to reflect the full cost of their use, this will permeate the economy, affecting all energy-related economic decisions.

Today's fiscal systems, a combination of subsidies and taxes, reflect the goals of another era—a time when it was in the interest of countries to exploit their natural resources as rapidly and competitively as possible. That age has ended. Now natural capital is the scarce resource. The goal is to restructure the fiscal system so that the prices reflect the truth, protecting the economy's natural supports.

It is not easy to grasp the scale and urgency of the needed restructuring. Reestablishing a stable, sustainable relationship between the global economy and the earth's ecosystem depends on restructuring the economy at a pace that historically has occurred only in wartime. When national security is threatened, governments take extreme measures, such as drafting able-bodied men into the armed forces, commandeering natural resources, and sometimes even taking over strategic industries. Although it may not yet be obvious to everyone, we may well be facing a threat that is comparable in scale and urgency to a world war.

The Fiscal Steering Wheel

Fiscal policy is an ideal policy instrument for building an eco-economy because both taxes and subsides are widely used and work through the market. By relying primarily on these two tools to build an eco-economy, we capitalize on the market's strengths, including its inherent efficiency in allocating resources. The challenge is to use taxes and subsidies to help the market reflect not only the direct costs and benefits of economic activities but the indirect ones as well. If we use fiscal policy to encourage environmentally constructive activities and to discourage destructive ones, we can steer the economy in a sustainable direction.

Some environmental goals—such as limiting the catch in a fishery or properly disposing of nuclear waste—can be achieved only by government regulation. Edwin Clark, former senior economist with the White House Council on Environmental Quality, observes that some of the other tools discussed here, such as tradable permits, "require establishing complex regulatory frameworks, defining the permits, establishing the rules for trades, and preventing people from acting without permits." In some cases, it is simply more efficient to ban environmentally destructive activities than to try to tax them out of existence. While the advantage has shifted toward the use of tax policy in achieving environmental goals, there is still a role for regulation to play.[2]

A major weakness of the market is that while nature's goods—lumber, fish, or grain—move through the market, many of nature's services do not. Since there is no bill rendered for pollinating crops, controlling floods, or protecting soil from erosion, these services are often thought of as free. And because they have no apparent market value, they are often not protected. Fiscal policy can be used to compensate for this shortfall as well.

A market that tells the ecological truth will incorporate the value of ecosystem services. For example, if we buy furniture from a forest products corporation that engages in clearcutting, we pay the costs of logging and converting the logs into furniture, but not the costs of the flooding downstream. If we restructure the tax system and raise taxes on clearcutting timber so that its price reflects the cost to society of the resultant flooding, this method of harvesting timber likely would be eliminated.

Taxes designed to incorporate in their prices the environmental costs of producing goods or providing services enable the market to send the right signal. They discourage such activities as coal burning, the use of throwaway beverage containers, or cyanide gold mining. Subsidies can be used to encourage such activities as planting trees, using water more efficiently, and harnessing wind energy. Environmental taxes and subsidies also can be used to represent the interests of future generations in situations where traditional economics simply discounts the future.

The advantage of using fiscal policy to incorporate the indirect environmental cost is that economic decisions at all levels—from those made by political leaders and corporate planners to those made by individual consumers—are guided by the market. It has a pervasive influence. If it tells the ecological truth, it minimizes the information that individual decisionmakers need to make an environmentally responsible decision.

Tax Shifting

Tax shifting involves changing the composition of taxes but not the level. It means reducing income taxes and offsetting them with taxes on environmentally destructive activities such as carbon emissions, the generation of toxic waste, the use of virgin raw materials, the use of nonrefillable beverage containers, mercury emissions, the generation of garbage, the use of pesticides, and the use of throwaway products. This is by no means a comprehensive list, but it does include the more important activities that should be discouraged by taxing. There is wide agreement among environmental scientists on the kinds of activities that need to be taxed more. The question now is how to generate public support for the wholesale tax shifting that is needed.

In this area, Europe is well ahead of the United States, largely because of the pioneering efforts of Ernst von Weizsäcker, formerly head of the Wuppertal Institute and now a member of the German Bundestag. He not only pioneered this concept, but has provided ongoing intellectual leadership on the issue.[3]

The way tax shifting works can be seen in the table compiled by Worldwatch researcher David Roodman. (See Table 11–1.) It looks at Europe, where most of the shifting has occurred, and gives a sense of how nine countries have reduced taxes on personal income or wages while increasing them on environmentally destructive activities. Sweden was the first country to begin this process, with a program to lower taxes on personal income while raising them on carbon and sulfur emissions to discourage the burning of fossil fuels, particularly those with high sulfur content. For several years, only the smaller countries of Europe, such as Denmark, the Netherlands, and Sweden, followed this path. But during the late 1990s, France, Germany, Italy, and the United Kingdom joined in.

Tax shifting has appeal in Europe in part because it creates jobs, an issue of concern in a region plagued with high unemployment.

Table 11–1. *Shifting Taxes from Income to Environmentally Destructive Activities*

Country, First Year in Effect	Taxes Cut on	Taxes Raised on	Revenue Shifted[1]
			(percent)
Sweden, 1991	personal income	carbon and sulfur emissions	1.9
Denmark, 1994	personal income	motor fuel, coal, electricity, and water sales; waste incineration and landfilling; motor vehicle ownership	2.5
Spain, 1995	wages	motor fuel sales	0.2
Denmark, 1996	wages, agricultural property	carbon emissions from industry; pesticide, chlorinated solvent, and battery sales	0.5
Netherlands, 1996	personal income and wages	natural gas and electricity sales	0.8
United Kingdom, 1996	wages	landfilling	0.1
Finland, 1996	personal income and wages	energy sales, landfilling	0.5
Germany, 1999	wages	energy sales	2.1
Italy, 1999	wages	fossil fuel sales	0.2
Netherlands, 1999	personal income	energy sales, landfilling, household water sales	0.9
France, 2000	wages	solid waste; air and water pollution	0.1

[1]Expressed relative to tax revenue raised by all levels of government.
Source: Adapted from David Malin Roodman, "Environmental Tax Shifts Multiplying," in Lester R. Brown et al., *Vital Signs 2000* (New York: W.W. Norton & Company, 2000), pp. 138–39.

Shifting from the use of virgin raw materials to recycled materials, for example, not only reduces environmental disruption, it also increases employment since recycling is more labor-intensive. This was one of the reasons Germany adopted a four-year plan of gradually reducing taxes on incomes while increasing those on energy use in 1999. When completed, this will shift 2.1 percent of total revenue generated; with an annual revenue budget of nearly $1 trillion, it would shift $20 billion a year. Denmark leads the way in the amount of taxes being shifted, with a total of 3 percent moved thus far by measures adopted in 1994 and 1996. The Danish government taxes the use of motor fuels, the burning of coal, the use of electricity, landfilling, and ownership of motor vehicles. The tax on the purchase of a new car in Denmark is typically higher than the price of the vehicle itself.[4]

The Netherlands, a country with an advanced industrial economy concentrated in a small land area, uses taxes to curb the release of heavy metals, including cadmium, copper, lead, mercury, and zinc. Between 1976 and the mid-1990s, the industrial discharge of these various elements fell 86–97 percent each. The Dutch firms that developed the pollution control equipment used to achieve these reductions gained an edge on firms in other countries, greatly expanding their export sales and earnings.[5]

The environmentally destructive activities now taxed in Europe include carbon emissions, sulfur emissions, coal mining, landfilling, electricity sales, and vehicle ownership. Countries elsewhere might tax other activities to reflect their particular circumstances. Among these might be taxes on excessive water use, the conversion of cropland to nonfarm uses, tree cutting, pesticide use, and the use of cyanide in gold mining. Over time, taxes on environmentally destructive activities could increase substantially, perhaps one day accounting for the lion's share of tax collection.

Governments typically take care to ensure that environmental taxes are not socially regressive. David Roodman describes how Portugal has avoided this with its tax on water, an increasingly scarce resource in this semiarid country. The town of Setúbal provides households with 25 cubic meters of water per month that is tax-free. It then "terraces" additional water taxes, raising the tax through three successively higher levels of consumption.[6]

The concept of taxing environmentally destructive activities received a major boost in the United States in November 1998 when the U.S. tobacco industry agreed to reimburse state governments $251 billion for past Medicare costs of treating smoking-related illnesses. This was, in effect, a retroactive tax on the billions of packs of cigarettes sold in the United States during the preceding decades. It was a staggering sum of money—nearly $1,000 for every American. This was a tax on cigarette smoke, a pollutant that is so destructive to human health that it may cause more damage than all other pollutants combined.[7]

This "tax" that the industry is paying on past damage associated with smoking will be funded by raising the price of cigarettes. Between January 1998 and April 2001, the average U.S. wholesale price of cigarettes climbed from $1.33 per pack to $2.21, a 66-percent increase in two years. It is expected to climb further, helping to discourage cigarette smoking.[8]

Another value of environmental taxes is that they communicate information. When a government taxes a product because it is environmentally destructive, it tells the consumer that it is concerned about this. And restructuring the tax system has a systemic effect, steering millions of consumer decisions in an environmentally sustainable direction every day—ranging from how to get to work to what to order for lunch.

Tax shifting to achieve environmental goals has broad support. Polls taken in the late 1990s in both the United States and Europe show overwhelming support for the concept once it is explained. On both sides of the Atlantic, support of the electorate is 70 percent or greater. Tax shifting is also an attractive economic tool because it can be used to achieve so many environmental goals. Once it is used in one context, it can easily be applied in others.[9]

If the world is to restructure the economy before environmental destruction leads to economic decline, tax restructuring almost certainly will be at the center of the effort. No other set of policies can bring about the systemic changes needed quickly enough. In an article in *Fortune* magazine that argued for a 10-percent reduction in U.S. income taxes and a 50¢-per-gallon hike in the tax on gasoline, Harvard economist N. Gregory Mankiw summarized his thinking as follows: "Cutting income taxes while increasing gasoline taxes would lead to more rapid economic growth, less traffic congestion, safer roads, and reduced risk of global warming—all without jeopardizing long-term fiscal solvency. This may be the closest thing to a free lunch that economics has to offer."[10]

Subsidy Shifting

In 1997, the Earth Council published a study entitled *Subsidizing Unsustainable Development*. Its purpose was to identify and tabulate environmentally destructive governmental subsidies. It found an astonishing number of examples—at least $700 billion worth per year. The authors noted, "There is something unbelievable about the world spending hundreds of billions of dollars annually to subsidize its own destruction."[11]

In effect, governments were spending $700 billion of taxpayers' money a year to encourage the use of water, the burning of fossil fuels, the use of pesticides, fishing, and driving. The report documented countless examples of taxpayers subsidizing the use of water in countries where water tables are falling. Governments are spending billions of dollars each year to encourage the use of fossil fuels at a time when both atmospheric carbon dioxide levels and public concern about climate change are rising. Additional billions are being spent to expand the world fishing fleet when its capacity is already nearly double the sustainable catch.[12]

Just as we use taxes to discourage destructive activities, we can use subsidies to encourage environmentally constructive activities, financing them by shifting funds from environmentally destructive subsidies. If these subsidies of $700 billion per year were shifted into funding environmentally *con*structive activities, such as investing in renewable energy, tree planting, family planning, and the education of young women in developing countries, our future could be far brighter.[13]

In his seminal work on fiscal restructuring for environmental purposes, *The Natural Wealth of Nations,* David Roodman observes: "Few public policies are as unpopular in theory and popular in practice as subsidies. The very word can make economists shudder and taxpayers fume, turn the poor into cynics, and enrage environmentalists." Despite this common response, some of our greatest achievements—from ending the Dust Bowl to developing the Internet—were based on government subsidies.[14]

The principal activities worldwide that are subsidized are food production, automobile driving, and fossil fuel use. Within agriculture, governments subsidize the use of irrigation water, crop production, the use of fertilizers and pesticides, and the consumption of food itself. Almost all governments subsidize irrigation water, keeping the food produced with it artificially low in price. The

Punjab, India's breadbasket state, went a step further when the chief minister gave farmers free electricity in return for their political support. In a state where irrigation pumps are powered by electricity, this dramatically lowered the price of water, encouraging its use at a time when overpumping was already lowering the water table. By accelerating aquifer depletion, the time in which to adjust to the eventual decline in the groundwater supply is reduced. Expanding food production by overpumping creates a false sense of food security. In contrast to India, China's recent decision to phase in a water price increase in steps over the next five years is a giant step toward reducing the subsidization of water use.[15]

Some countries subsidize food consumption. Iran subsidizes bread consumption to the tune of $4 billion a year, or $63 per person. The government buys wheat from farmers at roughly 70¢ per kilogram, makes it into flour, and then sells it to bakeries at 2¢ per kilogram. This across-the-board subsidy, which encourages consumption by the affluent as well as the poor, is also an indirect subsidy to the use of irrigation water, one of the country's scarcest resources.[16]

Another subsector of the world food economy that is heavily subsidized is oceanic fishing. Originally, coastal countries subsidized fishing to develop this basic industry and take advantage of a locally available supply of animal protein. More recently, subsidies have been designed to ensure that each country maximized its share of the oceanic fish catch. Over the last two decades, this practice has spread, until today the capacity of the world fishing fleet is roughly double the sustainable yield of oceanic fisheries. This leads to overfishing and the destruction of the fisheries themselves, an excellent example of the law of unintended consequences.[17]

Extraction industries, particularly in mining and forestry, are another major recipient of subsidies. Coal mining, for example, is now heavily supported in some countries because the cost of extracting coal from an ever greater depth in old mines has increased. But coal mining is declining sharply in a number of countries, including the United Kingdom, where the Industrial Revolution began, and China, the world's largest user of coal. Belgium has phased out coal mining entirely.[18]

Germany, however, continues to subsidize coal mining. German subsidies, designed to protect the jobs of miners, have reached levels that defy belief. From 1983 to 1991, subsidies climbed per miner from "a generous $21,700 to a lavish $85,800," as Roodman put it. He notes that it would be cheaper for Germany simply to close the mines and pay the miners not to work.[19]

This contrasts sharply with the situation in China, which abruptly cut its coal subsidies from $750 million in 1993 to $240 million in 1995. In addition, China has introduced a tax on high sulfur coals. China's largest cities—with some of the worst air pollution in the world, largely due to burning coal—are even banning coal use. Beijing, Shanghai, Lanzhou, Xi'an, and Shenyan are planning to phase out coal use entirely. The combination of bold subsidy reductions and the new tax on high sulfur coal cut China's coal use by an estimated 14 percent between 1996 and 2000. (See Figure 11–1.) This provides an excellent example of the effective use of fiscal policy to reach the environmental goals of reducing local air pollution and global carbon emissions. In addition, China is subsidizing an ambitious plan to develop its wind resources, generating electricity to reduce further its reliance on coal. In effect, it is shifting subsidies from coal to wind.[20]

Tree cutting is also subsidized by governments for various reasons. For example, the government of the Australian state of Victoria pays logging companies $170 million more each year to get timber out than the wood is worth. A similar situation used to exist in the United States, where for decades U.S. taxpayers financed the construction of roads into national forests to facilitate clearcutting by

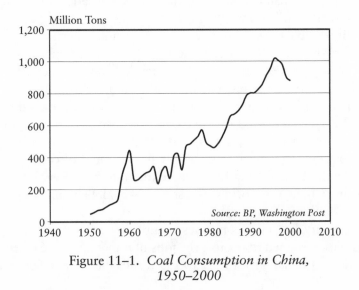

Figure 11–1. *Coal Consumption in China,*
1950–2000

timber companies. In 1999, the U.S. Forest Service, the government agency responsible for the management of national forests, announced a moratorium on the construction of new roads in national forests.[21]

A study by the World Resources Institute indicates that U.S. government subsidies of automobile use, including construction and maintenance of highways, highway patrols, and other supports to motorists, exceed the taxes paid on motor fuel, vehicle purchases, and license plates by $111 billion per year. This means that automobile driving is being heavily subsidized by those who do not even own a car.[22]

The Earth Council's 1997 report observes, "The car has liberated individuals just as surely as it has enslaved societies. Every day vast reaches of prime agricultural land are paved and offered up as sacrifices. Every month the population equivalence of entire towns perish from road accidents and automobile pollution."[23]

These destructive subsidies are but a few of those that need to be eliminated. The challenge now is to shift subsidies from environmentally destructive activities to ones that will help build an eco-economy.

The use of subsidies for environmentally constructive purposes is not new. For example, in 1934 the U.S. Congress created the Soil Conservation Service, a nationwide agency with employees in every state whose responsibility was to protect the agricultural resource base for future generations. Farmers were paid to plant windbreaks, to strip-crop, and to adopt other cropping practices that would protect their soils from wind erosion. This reduced soil erosion, helping to bring the disastrous Dust Bowl era to an end.[24]

A more recent example of subsidies playing a strategic environmental role is tax credits for investment in wind electricity generation two decades ago. On the heels of the energy crisis of the 1970s, the U.S. government provided tax incentives for those investing in renewable sources of energy, such as wind. At the same time, California adopted a strong tax incentive for wind power. Together these led to a large investment in wind in California and the creation of a new industry, one that used advanced technologies to convert wind energy into electricity.[25]

When these two tax incentives were discontinued, progress on wind power in the United States came to a near standstill. Meanwhile, the large but short-lived U.S. market led Europeans to start investing in wind energy, including in a wind turbine manufacturing industry. The Danes, who had also introduced wind energy subsidies, continued to develop the technology and to expand their capacity. Ironically, the principal beneficiary of the California tax incentive was Denmark, which now leads the world in wind energy generation per person and in manufacturing wind turbines. It is an excellent example of how a modest subsidy can launch a new industry.[26]

In recent years, a new U.S. wind production tax credit has encouraged heavy investment in wind farms in Colorado, Iowa, Kansas, Minnesota, Oregon, Pennsylvania, Texas, Washington, Wyoming, and other states. Strong fiscal incentives to invest in wind energy encouraged the private development of more-efficient wind turbines. The resulting precipitous drop in costs of wind electric generation explains the 24-percent annual worldwide growth in wind electric generation from 1990 to 2000 and the projected 60-percent growth in the United States in 2001. As the industry has evolved and grown, it has reached the point where some investments in wind power are now being made without subsidies.[27]

Tax credits were also used to subsidize investments in energy efficiency beginning in the late 1970s. This, too, paid large dividends, but as a policy instrument it was neglected after oil prices dropped from their highs of the late 1970s and early 1980s. With the rise in oil prices during the last half of 2000, public attention is again shifting to efficiency and renewables.

The potential for building an environmentally sustainable economy by restructuring subsidies is enormous. The economics of shifting from destructive subsidies to constructive ones is as attractive as the logic is compelling. Today we should be subsidizing not mining but recycling, not fossil fuels but climate-benign energy sources, and not urban automobile dependency but state-of-the-art urban rail systems.

Ecolabeling: Voting with Our Wallets

Labeling products that are produced with environmentally sound practices lets consumers vote with their wallets. Ecolabeling is now used in many sectors of the economy, including to identify energy-efficient household appliances, forest products from sustainably managed forests, fishery products from sustainably managed fisheries, and "green" electricity from environmentally friendly renewable sources.

Among the youngest of the ecolabels is that awarded by the Marine Stewardship Council (MSC) for seafood. In March 2000, the MSC launched its fisheries certification program when it approved the Western Australia Rock Lobster. Also earning approval that day was the West Thames Herring Fishery. Among the key players in the seafood processing and retail sectors supporting the MSC initiative were Unilever, Youngs-Bluecrest, and Sainsbury's.[28]

In September 2000, the Alaska salmon fishery received its certification, the first American fishery to do so. Brendan May, chief executive of the MSC, in referring to the Alaska salmon fishery, said, "With its high profile and international market penetration, it is the perfect product to carry our ecolabel, telling consumers that it is the best environmental choice in seafood. This is a triple victory for Alaska, for the marine environment, and for seafood consumers everywhere."[29]

To be certified, a fishery must demonstrate that it is being managed sustainably. Specifically, according to the MSC: "First, the fishery must be conducted in a way that does not take more fish than can be replenished naturally or kills other species through harmful fishing practices. Secondly, the fishery must operate in a manner that ensures the health and diversity of the marine ecosystem on which it depends. Finally, the fishery must respect local, national, and international laws and regulations for responsible and sustainable fishing."[30]

The MSC's counterpart for forest products is the Forest Stewardship Council (FSC), which was founded in 1993 by the World Wide Fund for Nature (WWF) and other groups. Its role is to provide information on forest management practices within the forest products industry. Some of the world's forests are managed to sustain a steady harvest in perpetuity; others are clearcut, decimated overnight in the quest for quick profits. The FSC distinguishes between these two forms of management in its labels for forest products, whether it be lumber sold at a hardware store, furniture in a furniture store, or paper in a stationery store.[31]

Headquartered in Oaxaca, Mexico, the FSC in effect accredits national organizations that verify that forests are being sustainably managed. In addition to this on-the-ground monitoring, the accredited organizations must also be able to trace the raw product through the various stages of processing to the consumer. The FSC sets the standards and provides the FSC label, the stamp of approval, but the actual work is done by national organizations.[32]

The FSC has established nine principles that must be satisfied if forests are to qualify for its label. Those managing the forests must have a written plan that describes the objectives and the means of achieving them. The management plan must respect the rights of indigenous peoples who live in the forests or have the responsibility for the forested land. There are numerous other principles, but the central one is that the forest is managed in a way that ensures that its yield can be sustained indefinitely. This means careful selective cutting, in effect mimicking nature's management of a forest by removing the more mature, older trees over time. Simply stated, the management preserves the capacity of the forest to provide both products and services.[33]

WWF describes the certification system as a way of "identifying wood and wood products that come from well managed sources anywhere in the world backed up by a label that would be clear, unambiguous, and easily recognized." This provides consumers with the information they need to support good forestry through their purchases of forest products. By identifying timber companies and retailers that are participating in the certification program, socially minded investors also have the information they need for responsible investing.[34]

In March 1996, the first certified wood products were introduced into the United Kingdom. Since then, the certification process has grown worldwide. As of June 2001, some 24 million hectares of forests had been certified under the auspices of the FSC. This area included more than 300 forests in 45 countries.[35]

To support this certification program, forest and trade networks have been set up in Austria, Brazil, Canada, France, Germany, the Nordic countries, Russia, Spain, Switzerland, the United Kingdom, and the United States. These networks, whose combined corporate membership may reach 1,000 by the end of 2001, are part of the vast support group of companies that adhere to the FSC standards in their marketing. Among the world's five largest wood buyers, the top three—Home Base, Home Depot, and Ikea—buy only FSC-certified wood.[36]

In June 2001, the Natural Resources Ministry in Moscow announced that it was introducing national mandatory certification of wood. Although a small portion of its timber harvest is already certified, buyers' discrimination against the rest of the harvest costs Russia $1 billion in export revenues. The ministry estimates that its uncertified wood sells for 20–30 percent less than certified wood from competing countries.[37]

Another commodity that is getting an environmental label is electricity. In the United States, many state utility commissions are requiring utilities to offer consumers a green power option. This is defined as power from renewable sources other than hydroelectric, and it includes wind power, solar cells, solar thermal energy, geothermal energy, and biomass. Utilities simply enclose a return card with the monthly bill, giving consumers the option of checking a box if they would prefer to get green power. The offer specifies the additional cost of the green power, which typically is from 3 to 15 percent.[38]

Utility officials are often surprised by how many consumers sign up for green power. Many people are apparently prepared to pay more for their electricity in order to help ensure a stable climate for future generations. Local governments, including, for example, those in Santa Monica and Oakland in California, have signed up to use green power exclusively. This includes the power they use for municipal buildings as well as that required to operate various municipal services, such as street lights and traffic signals.[39]

Many corporations are signing up as well. Toyota's North American marketing headquarters in California, with some 7,000 employees, has opted for green power. Literally scores of companies in California—some larger, like Kinko's and Patagonia, and many smaller ones—are subscribing. Even colleges and universities are getting in on the act. In April 2000, as an Earth Day project, students at the University of Colorado sponsored a referendum that committed themselves to an increase in student fees of $1 per semester in exchange for the university's purchase of green power. The measure was approved by an overwhelming 85 percent of the voters. In the San Francisco Bay area, some 30 churches are also subscribing to green power. Within the Episcopal church, a group called Episcopal Power and Light has launched a nationwide effort to get not only churches to buy green power, but their members as well.[40]

The net effect of these growing numbers of green power proponents is a tidal wave of demand that is forcing many utilities to scramble in their search for an adequate supply of green electricity.

One reason wind farms are springing up in so many states is that this is one of the fastest ways of bringing new green power online. While green power marketing appears to be more advanced in the United States, it will likely spread to other countries soon.

Other types of ecolabeling include the efficiency labels put on household appliances that achieve a certain standard in the use of electricity or other forms of energy. These have been in effect in many countries since the energy crisis of the late 1970s. There are also green labels provided by environmental or governmental groups at the national level. Among the better known environmental seal of approval programs are Germany's Blue Angel, Canada's Environmental Choice, and the U.S. Environmental Protection Agency's Energy Star.[41]

Tradable Permits

Environmental taxes and tradable permits are both economic instruments that can be used to reach environmental goals. The principal difference between the two is that with permits, governments set the amount of a given activity that is allowed, such as the harvest from a fishery, and let the market set the price of the permits as they are auctioned off. With environmental taxes, in contrast, the price of the environmentally destructive activity is set by government in the tax rate, and the market determines the amount of the activity that will occur at that price. Both economic instruments can be used to discourage environmentally irresponsible behavior.[42]

The decision of when to use taxes as opposed to permits is not always a clearcut one. When it is desirable to keep an environmentally destructive activity below a certain level, permits are more precise than taxes, which have a less certain effect. Once permits are set at the desirable level, the market decides what they are worth. When taxes are fixed at a certain level, the market decides how best to minimize their effect by reducing the undesirable environmental activity. Governments have much more experience with environmental taxes. It is also clear that environmental taxes work under a wide range of conditions. Still, permits have been used successfully in two widely differing situations: restricting the catch in an Australian fishery and reducing sulfur emissions in the United States.

Concerned about the threat of overfishing to its lobster fishery, the government of Australia estimated the sustainable yield of the fishery and then issued permits totaling that amount. Fishers could then bid for these permits. In effect, the government decided how many lobsters could be taken each year and let the market decide how much the permits were worth. Since the permit trading system was adopted in 1986, the fisheries have stabilized and appear to be operating on a sustainable basis.[43]

Perhaps the most ambitious effort to date to use tradable permits was the U.S. effort to reduce sulfur emissions by half from 1990 to 2000. Permits were assigned to some 263 of the more sulfur-dioxide-intensive electrical generating units operated by 61 electric utilities. These were mostly coal-fired power plants east of the Mississippi River. The result was that sulfur emissions were cut in half between 1990 and 1995, well ahead of schedule. Although this approach has occasional hitches, the sulfur reduction effort is widely seen as successful, an approach that minimized the costs of achieving an environmental goal.[44]

Trading permits had been proposed by the U.S. government as a way to reach the carbon reduction goals of the Kyoto Protocol. Permits are desirable when there is a specific goal, but if the purpose is to stimulate a long-term trend, then graduated taxes over time may be preferable. If the goal is to reduce carbon emissions worldwide, with higher goals for industrial countries who burn disproportionately large amounts of fossil fuels, then governments can set taxes at a level appropriate to each country's situation.[45]

Support for Fiscal Restructuring

Taxes and subsidies designed specifically to reach environmental goals are not yet widespread. As noted earlier, there has been some tax shifting in Europe, but it is still in the early stages, not exceeding more than 3 percent of the official revenue of any country. Governments have used environmental taxes to reduce the discharge of heavy metals into the environment in the Netherlands or the use of leaded gasoline in countries such as Malaysia, Thailand, and Turkey. But they have not yet been used effectively on big-ticket items. For example, no government has seriously discussed adopting a carbon tax that would phase out fossil fuel use.

As mentioned, in both Europe and North America polls show that 70 percent of voters on both sides of the Atlantic think it is a good idea. The challenge is to translate this approval into support. There has been little political leadership on the issue, especially from the United States, the country the world looks to for leadership on major issues. The focus in the United States is almost exclusively on whether taxes are being raised or lowered, not on restructuring the system.[46]

With subsidies, there is little public knowledge of the scale of subsidies. Many are hidden, some carefully disguised to reduce their public visibility. As the Earth Council report concluded, many governments of industrial countries have no way of knowing how much they subsidize fossil fuel use with various direct and indirect subsidies. For example, the U.S. oil depletion allowance, though it is not highly visible or regularly debated in Congress, is a powerful subsidy for oil use.[47]

David Roodman notes in *The Natural Wealth of Nations* that there is little organized support within the environmental community for tax shifting. Among the major environmental membership organizations in the United States, not one has a full-time staff person working on these issues. There are now two small U.S. groups working on fiscal shifting. The first is Taxpayers for Common Sense, a group established in 1995 that has 1,000 members. The second is Green Scissors, a group that works specifically to eliminate environmentally destructive subsidies from the federal government's annual budget.[48]

Among economists, there is strong support for tax restructuring. This was evident in 1997 when some 2,500 leading economists worldwide, including eight Nobel laureates, endorsed the idea of a carbon tax. The actions of this group made it clear that it is not the wisdom of restructuring our fiscal system that is the question, but whether we can overcome political inertia and the obstacles posed by the interests vested in the status quo.[49]

MIT economist Paul Krugman writes in the *New York Times* about the distortions in our economy that result from the failure of the market to reflect the full costs of many products and services. He observes, "you don't have to be an elitist to think that the nation has lately been making some bad choices about energy use, and about lifestyles more generally. Why? Because the choices we make don't reflect the true costs of our actions." Starting with the estimated annual $2.6 billion cost of traffic congestion in Atlanta in 1999, Krugman calculates that the decision by one person to commute by car in Atlanta now imposes on others an additional congestion cost of $3,500 per year—or $14 per workday. This is each driver's part of the indirect or social costs per person of traffic congestion in Atlanta. As Krugman and other prominent economists focus on these issues, it will help to raise public understanding of the need to incorporate indirect costs in the market prices that shape our decisions.[50]

Some key organizations are beginning to support the idea. A report on the environmental outlook in the 30 members of the Organisation for Economic Co-operation and Development (OECD) recommended a broad-based tax restructuring to deal with environmental threats. Since the OECD represents nearly all the leading industrial countries, its recommendations are certain to garner public attention.[51]

During 2001, *The Economist*—traditionally not a leader on environmental issues—has become an outspoken advocate of fiscal restructuring. The editors recommend that governments not attempt to pick "the winners" among new energy technologies but instead "they would do better to provide a level playing field by scrapping the huge and usually hidden subsidies for fossil fuels, and by introducing measures such as carbon taxes so that the price of fossil fuels reflects the costs they impose on the environment and human health."[52]

The potential benefits of fiscal restructuring are obvious. Fiscal policy, including the shifting of both taxes and subsidies, is the key to our success in building an eco-economy because it is systemic. Reducing mining subsidies not only makes metals produced from virgin ore more costly, for example, but it also indirectly encourages the recycling of metals. Similarly, raising the price of gasoline with a carbon tax that reflects the full cost to society of burning this fuel will permeate the entire economy, sending signals through the market that will lead to more environmentally responsible behavior.

12

Accelerating the Transition

At a 1999 conference of corporate leaders and bankers, Robert Nef, the head of a Swiss research institute, shared with me a thoughtful definition of technology. "Technology," he said, "is nature's experiment with man." At issue for us today is how this experiment will turn out.[1]

Earlier chapters described the dimensions of the restructuring needed to build an eco-economy. The scale of the change needed is matched only by its urgency. Time is running out. The central question facing our generation is whether we can reverse environmental deterioration before it spirals out of control, leading to global economic decline.

We would like to think that such a tragedy cannot happen in the modern age, but we need only look at Africa to see what happens when governments delay in responding to a threat—in this case, the spread of HIV. Nearly 40 million Africans have now been infected with the virus that causes AIDS. Several countries, including Botswana, Zimbabwe, and South Africa, could lose one fifth to one third of their adult populations by 2010. Africa's AIDS fatalities during this decade may eclipse all fatalities during World War II.[2]

Just as the governments of Africa let the AIDS virus spread, so the governments of India and China are letting water tables fall.

Since the ability to pump water from underground faster than nature replenishes it has evolved only during the last century, the world has little experience in dealing with aquifer depletion. We do know that failing to address the issue early on risks an even more catastrophic result when the aquifer is depleted and the rate of pumping is reduced to the rate of recharge.

Even while African governments let HIV spread and Asian governments let water tables fall, the United States is letting atmospheric carbon dioxide (CO_2) levels rise. The one country that is capable of single-handedly disrupting the earth's climate is doing so. The United States could reduce its carbon emissions by the modest amount called for in the Kyoto Protocol by 2010 and make a profit doing so, but it chooses not to.

Other governments are watching as populations grow, doing little to facilitate family planning and the shift to smaller families. After nearly half a century of rapid population growth, farms already divided once are now being divided again as another generation comes of age. Shrinking plots of land are driving hundreds of millions of people either into nearby cities or across national borders in search of a job.

As water scarcity and land hunger spread, people become desperate. It is this quiet desperation of trying to survive that drives them across national borders. In some cases, it drives them to their deaths, as tragically seen in the bodies of Mexicans who regularly perish trying to enter the United States by crossing the Arizona desert, and in the bodies of Africans washing ashore in Spain when their fragile watercraft come apart as they try to cross the Mediterranean. The combination of land hunger, water scarcity, soil erosion, desertification, and rising sea level all coming at once is a recipe for human migration on a scale that has no precedent.

Unless we can build an eco-economy, the world that we leave our children will be a troubled one indeed. Restructuring the economy depends on restructuring taxes. (See Chapter 11.) If we fail to restructure the tax system, we will almost certainly fail to reverse the trends that are undermining our future. If this effort is not actively supported by all segments of society—not only governments, but also the communications media, corporations, nongovernmental organizations (NGOs), and individuals, we will fail. Building an eco-economy is not a spectator sport. Everyone has a role to play.

United Nations Leadership

In an age when so many environmental issues are binational, multinational, or global in scale, countries often look to the United Nations for leadership. The first international environmental treaty completed after the founding of this world body was the International Convention for the Regulation of Whales. Negotiated by delegates from 57 countries, it was signed in Washington, D.C., in 1946. During the half-century since then, the United Nations has played a key role in negotiating 240 international environmental treaties ranging from the preservation of migratory birds to the protection of the stratospheric ozone layer.[3]

Over the decades, the United Nations has dealt with numerous threats to the earth's health. In May 1985, scientists reported a "hole" in the stratospheric ozone layer over Antarctica. This alarmed the international scientific community because the stratospheric ozone layer protects life on earth from harmful ultraviolet radiation. Two years later, the U.N. Environment Programme (UNEP) assembled delegates from 150 countries in Montreal to negotiate the Protocol on Substances That Deplete the Ozone Layer. This international agreement set the stage for phasing out the widespread use of chlorofluorocarbons (CFCs), the family of chemicals primarily responsible for ozone layer depletion, reducing their use by more than 90 percent over the next 13 years. The negotiation of the Montreal Protocol and its implementation represent one of the finest hours of the United Nations.[4]

Another landmark treaty, the Convention on International Trade on Endangered Species of Wild Fauna and Flora (CITES), was negotiated in 1973. This set the stage for active U.N. intercession in protecting endangered species. In 2001 this entailed trying to save Caspian Sea sturgeon. The catch of this fish, the source of world-renowned caviar, had fallen precipitously as illegal harvesting spread out of control. The United Nations convened a meeting of the countries involved—Russia, Kazakhstan, Azerbaijan, and Turkmenistan. Iran, which was managing the sturgeon on its coastal waters responsibly, was not called to the conference. Using its enforcement authority, CITES threatened to impose an embargo on trade in caviar if the countries did not work together to protect the sturgeon from extinction. In an early indication of the influence CITES now has, Russia announced in July 2001 that it was suspending commercial fishing for sturgeon.[5]

Another of the many environmental contributions by the United Nations is the Law of the Sea Treaty, which established off-shore limits of up to 200 miles. Individual countries were given the responsibility for managing their own fisheries. This treaty gives national governments the authority they need to protect their coastal fisheries and to manage them for maximum sustainable yield.

The United Nations also plays a prominent role on the climate front. It has mobilized 2,600 of the world's leading scientists to work in the Intergovernmental Panel on Climate Change (IPCC). This group, which contains numerous working groups, publishes a report every few years that provides the latest findings on climate change. The IPCC research and projections underpin international negotiations on climate stabilization.[6]

Despite the 240 international environmental treaties negotiated over the last half-century, degradation of the global environment continues. Although the United Nations has recorded numerous successes on the environmental front, the gap between what needs to be done and what is being done to ensure a sustainable future is widening. In the end, the United Nations cannot move any faster than its member governments will permit.

When the United Nations convened the first conference on the environment in Stockholm in 1972, it gave the fledgling international environmental movement a legitimacy it had lacked. When it convened the Earth Summit in Rio de Janeiro in 1992, its principal product was Agenda 21, a voluminous work on sustainable development. Although this consisted of bits and pieces of a sustainable future, it did not deal with the systemic economic change needed to create a sustainable future.

In September 2002, the United Nations will convene the World Summit on Sustainable Development in Johannesburg, South Africa. In many ways, this conference will be a test of whether the international community is ready to take the steps needed to reverse the earth's environmental deterioration before time runs out. Recognizing this, U.N. Secretary General Kofi Annan said in a 2001 commencement address at Tufts University, "We must stop being so economically defensive and start being more politically courageous."[7]

New Responsibility of Governments

Building an eco-economy depends on a shared global vision and a broad understanding of the fiscal restructuring needed to realize the vision. It is up to governments to foster the national vision of an eco-economy and to adopt the ecologically defined economic policies needed to build it. This will require a systematic effort to incorporate input from ecologists in economic policy formulation, especially in restructuring taxes and subsidies to help the market reflect the ecological truth.

Building public support for change of this scale will not be easy because it involves challenging vested economic interests. A sustainable economy will not emerge by accident, but only as a result of concerted, intelligent effort by an informed citizenry supporting strong political leaders. There is no substitute for political leadership in building an eco-economy.

It is up to national governments to develop long-term plans of where we want to go and how we plan to get there. The basic components of this plan are rather straightforward. They include reestablishing a balance between carbon emissions and carbon fixation, between aquifer withdrawals and aquifer recharge, between trees cut and trees planted, between soil loss and soil regeneration, and between human births and deaths.

The issue is not whether these balances will eventually be established. The only question is how. If societies do not achieve a balance between births and deaths by reducing births, nature eventually will do so by raising deaths. With aquifers, the choice is whether to balance pumping and recharge soon—while there is time to adjust—or to delay until the aquifer is depleted and the resulting fall in food production leads to potentially catastrophic food shortages.

Formidable though the effort to build a sustainable economy appears to be, almost all the component goals have been achieved by at least one country. China, for example, has reduced its fertility rate to below two children per woman and is thus headed for population stability within a few decades. Denmark has banned the construction of coal-fired power plants. Israel has pioneered new technologies to raise water productivity. South Korea has covered its hills and mountains with trees. Costa Rica has a national energy plan to shift entirely to renewable sources to meet its future energy needs. Germany is leading the way in a major tax-shifting exercise to reduce income taxes and to offset this with an increase in energy taxes. Iceland is planning the world's first hydrogen-based economy. The United States has cut soil erosion by nearly 40 percent since 1982. The Dutch are showing the world how to build urban transport systems that give the bicycle a central role in increasing urban mobility and improving the quality of urban life. And Finland has banned the use of nonrefillable beverage containers. The challenge now is for each country to put all the pieces of an eco-economy together.[8]

Conveying the information needed to help people understand the imperative for change means collecting and disseminating information on key environmental indicators on a regular basis. For example, governments publish economic data on such trends as new housing starts, employment levels, labor productivity, and international trade balances each month. There is now a need for governments to systematically gather and publish the environmental data on such trends as carbon emissions, tree planting, water productivity, recycling rates, ice melting, and wind turbine installations, so we can measure progress on the environmental front.

An ideal way to transmit this information is through regular governmental press briefings that would relate these trends to the evolution of an eco-economy. Doing so could raise public understanding to where people will not only accept change, but actively work for it. This could include, for example, a press conference on melting glaciers and ice caps and the consequences for the country of resulting rises in sea level. In countries where population continues to grow, regularly assessing the future effect on the water supply and cropland availability per person could help build public support for stabilizing population.

Making the shift from a carbon-based to a hydrogen-based energy economy will require a major government effort to lead and inform. While many environmentalists and professionals in the energy industry understand the need for this, few understand the technologies that will be involved or the incentives needed to ensure that this fundamental shift proceeds on schedule. There is also a need for national annual reports on progress toward an eco-economy. The role of government, always important, is now even more so.

New Role for the Media

Building an eco-economy quickly depends on a broad change in our public priorities and our private behavior, not only as consumers but, more important, as eco-economy activists. People change their behavior because of new information or new experiences. Our goal is to realize the needed changes in the economy through providing new information, for if this fails, the inevitable adjustment could be painful.

When thinking of the scale of the educational challenge, it is tempting to rely too heavily on the formal education system. But the generational time lags from teacher to student to eventual decisionmakers mean this approach is too slow on its own to facilitate a massive economic restructuring in time. Given this constraint of time, the world is necessarily dependent on the communications media to raise public awareness. Only the media have the capacity to disseminate the needed information in the time available.

The communications media have an extraordinary ability to raise public understanding of issues if they wish to—witness their role in raising awareness of smoking and health issues in recent decades. A global environmental educational effort would rely heavily on the world's major news organizations, including such wire services as Associated Press and Reuters in English, Deutsche Press Agency in German, Agence France Presse in French, Kyodo News Service in Japanese, the Press Trust of India in English and local languages, Tass in Russian, EFE in Spanish, and Xinhua in Chinese. The global electronic news organizations, such as the British Broadcasting Corporation, Voice of America, and Cable News Network (CNN), also have a pivotal role to play. At the national level, television networks, news magazines, and newspapers are key players.

One media shortcoming is the failure to convey the big picture. A newspaper might report that ice is melting in Alaska or on Mount Kilimanjaro, but fail to observe that ice is melting almost everywhere. A research report of a particular glacier or ice cap melting is news, to be sure, but the bigger story is not being well covered.

The same can be said about fish farming. There are occasionally stories of salmon farming in Norway, catfish farming in the southern United States, or fish farming in China. But the typical reader would have no way of knowing from newspaper coverage that fish farming expanded by 11 percent a year during the 1990s and is on track to overtake world beef production by the end of this decade. That is the story. It is not being told.[9]

One reason for this information gap is that news media are not organized to deal with global issues and trends. A major news organization typically has a national desk and a foreign desk. The latter includes reporters based abroad, operating at the country or regional level. But a foreign desk is not a global desk, regularly assigning global stories. These often go uncovered, falling through the cracks in an outmoded organizational structure. In the past, when virtually all news was local, when there were no perceptible climate changes, ozone layer depletion, or collapsing oceanic fisheries, there was no need for global coverage. Today the key stories are global in scope, but there is no global desk to deal with them systematically.

Despite occasional weaknesses, some news organizations have provided exemplary coverage of environmental issues. In the United States, *Time* magazine stands out. It moved to the forefront a decade ago when, instead of selecting a "man of the year" as it usually does in the first issue of each year, it surprised readers by selecting Earth as "planet of the year," devoting the issue to an analysis of the environmental issues facing humanity.[10]

Then in the fall of 1997, under the leadership of Charles Alexander, *Time* produced a special issue of its international edition entitled "Our Precious Planet: Why Saving the Environment Will be the Next Century's Biggest Challenge." The issue recognized, in a way that few major news organizations have, the extraordinary dimensions of the challenge facing humanity as we try to sustain economic progress in the face of continuing environmental deterioration.[11]

After President Bush shocked the world by abandoning the Kyoto Protocol, *Time* devoted an issue to the President's decision and its consequences, with 16 pages of discussion of the basic science and evidence of climate change. This issue also included the results of a CNN/*Time* poll showing that the majority of Americans are concerned about global warming, and a statement by 10 eminent global citizens, including Jimmy Carter and Mikhail Gorbachev, calling for the President to support the Kyoto Protocol.[12]

Also at the front of the media pack is *Nihon Kezai Shimbun*,

Japan's premier business newspaper, which has a larger circulation than the *Wall Street Journal*. Under the leadership of editorial page director Tadahiro Mitsuhashi, this business newspaper has published numerous cutting-edge articles and editorials on environmental issues, including support of zero emissions as a goal for industry.[13]

At the international level, CNN under Ted Turner's leadership has been a consistent leader in covering environmental issues. In addition to regular weekly programs, CNN has carried numerous specials on the environment.

One of the strengths of large news organizations is that they can draw global attention to local environmental issues, often before they escalate into global issues. Media coverage of the ozone hole discovered over Antarctica in 1985 played a key role in mobilizing worldwide public support for phasing out CFCs. The media can also share with the world successful local responses to environmental issues, which would help in replicating them elsewhere.[14]

The bottom line is that disseminating information on the scale needed to build an eco-economy in the time available is not likely to succeed unless the communications media can raise public understanding to the point where people will support these changes. This is not a responsibility that editors and reporters have asked for or, indeed, that most would want to assume. But there is no alternative. We are facing a situation so totally different from any that our modern civilization has faced before that entirely new initiatives are required.

The Corporate Interest

Like the rest of society, corporations have a stake in building an eco-economy. Profits do not fare well when an economy is declining or threatening to collapse. The stakes are particularly high in the energy sector, which is affected much more than, for example, the food sector. To become sustainable, the latter needs to be modified, but the former needs to be fundamentally restructured.

There are essentially two approaches that fossil fuel firms can take. They can try to defend the status quo or they can see climate stabilization as the greatest investment opportunity in history. In the United States, the Global Climate Coalition (GCC)—an industry group—was formed by those who wanted to resist the restructuring of the global energy economy. In opposition to the Kyoto agreement, the GCC engaged in a massive disinformation campaign, one designed to confuse the American public about the urgent problem of climate change.[15]

The first break in the united front presented by the fossil fuel industry came in a speech by John Browne, the head of BP, at Stanford University in May 1997. (See Chapter 5.) He acknowledged that climate change was a potentially serious threat and announced that BP was no longer an oil company, but an energy company. Browne's talk sent shock waves of distress through the oil community and ripples of excitement through the environmental community. A major oil company had broken ranks.[16]

Browne's speech set the stage for change. He announced that BP was withdrawing from the Global Climate Coalition. Dupont had already left. The following year, Royal Dutch Shell announced that it, too, was leaving. Its corporate goals, like those of BP and Dupont, no longer meshed with those of the GCC. Like BP, it no longer viewed itself as an oil company, but as an energy company.[17]

In 1999, the Ford Motor Company withdrew from the GCC. In rapid succession in the early months of 2000, DaimlerChrysler, Texaco, and General Motors (GM) announced that they too were leaving the coalition. With the departure of GM, the world's largest automobile company, the die was cast. A spokesman for the Sierra Club quipped, "Maybe it is time to ask the last one out to turn out the lights."[18]

Some major corporations are not only visualizing an eco-economy, but are starting to build it. As described in Chapter 5, Royal Dutch Shell and DaimlerChrysler are leading a consortium of corporations that is working with the Icelandic government to make that country the world's first hydrogen-powered economy. And in June 2000, ABB, the Swiss-based giant in the global power industry, with an annual turnover of $24 billion, announced a major restructuring. It indicated that henceforth it would be emphasizing alternative energy sources, such as wind. It announced that its engineers had designed a new wind turbine called the Wind Former, a machine that reduces generating costs by 20 percent below the most efficient turbines now in use.[19]

ABB is abandoning its traditionally dominant role in the construction of large-scale thermal power plants, including those powered by coal, oil, gas, and nuclear energy. In 1999, ABB sold off its large-scale power generating business, with the principal units going to Alston, of France, and to British Nuclear Fuels. It was thus repositioning itself for a major push in the development of small-scale, renewable energy generation. A company with a vision of the new energy economy, ABB is planning to concentrate on developing wind and small-scale combined-cycle heat and power, as well as fuel cells. It plans to use information technology to integrate these distributed sources into a single grid.[20]

Looking to the future, ABB sees 755 million households in the world without electricity. The overwhelming majority of these households do not even have access to an electricity grid. For them, ABB believes it will be cheaper to install small-scale power than to invest in large thermal power plants and building a grid, both of which are costly. In its vision of the new energy economy, ABB suggests, for example, that "a small town might be supplied by a mix of combined heat and power, generating facilities, wind power, fuel cells, and photovoltaic energy with output from individual sources being adjusted via a micro-grid to compensate for seasonal variations in wind speeds and sunshine."[21]

Many companies have set their own goals for reducing carbon emissions—and they substantially exceed the goals of the Kyoto Protocol. For example, Dupont, measuring its goals in terms of CO_2 equivalent emissions, plans to reduce greenhouse gas emissions 65 percent from 1990 levels.[22]

Firms in some other industries are going even further in setting environmental goals. Among these are Interface, a manufacturer of industrial carpet based in Atlanta, Georgia, and STMicroelectronics, an Italian-based semiconductor manufacturer. Ray Anderson, the CEO of Interface, became an avid environmentalist in 1994 after reading *The Ecology of Commerce* by Paul Hawkins. Since his conversion, he has become an enthusiastic advocate of building an eco-economy. In *Fortune* magazine, he described plans for his firm: "Interface of Atlanta, my company, is changing course to become sustainable—to grow without damaging the earth and to manufacture without pollution, waste, or fossil fuels. If we get it right, our company and our supply chain will never have to take another drop of oil."[23]

The Interface plan is to generate no waste and no carbon emissions—to be totally sustainable. Instead of selling carpet to companies, Anderson wants to sell carpeting services, an arrangement whereby Interface agrees to maintain a certain style and level of carpeting in a company's offices for, say, 10 years. Worn carpet will be returned to the factory, melted down, and respun into new fiber. This new carpet then goes on the floor. "Our goal," Anderson says, "is not to lose a single molecule of carpeting material." This system, which requires no raw materials and sends nothing to the landfill, closes the loop.[24]

Interface's zero carbon emissions goal is being achieved by turning to solar cells and wind energy to power its plants. For energy uses that cannot be covered by these renewable sources, the company plans to offset carbon emissions by planting trees.[25]

STMicroelectronics, one of the world's largest manufacturer of semiconductors, is also committed to an environmentally sustainable operation. Pasquale Pistorio, president and CEO, matches the fervor of Ray Anderson. After being ranked first in eco-efficiency among 14 semiconductor companies worldwide, Pistorio said that "none of ST's environmental initiatives have taken more than three years to pay back, while our reputation as the semiconductor industry's 'green leader' helps us to attract the young, talented engineers that are essential to sustain our growth and keep us at the leading edge of the industry that is transforming the world."[26]

Like Anderson, Pistorio also wants to build an environmentally neutral corporation, and to do it by 2010. The company plans to reduce carbon emissions by shifting to an energy mix for 2010 that relies on cogeneration for 65 percent of its energy, conventional sources for 30 percent, and renewables for 5 percent. This will still leave it with a net contribution of CO_2 into the atmosphere, which it plans to offset by planting enough trees to sequester roughly 1 million tons of carbon emissions per year. The company's net revenues in 1999 exceeded $5 billion, with net earnings of $547 million; in 2000, net revenues were estimated at $6.7 billion, with earnings of $1.3 billion.[27]

Pistorio dates his environmental conversion to reading *State of the World 1994* from the Worldwatch Institute. Since then, he not only has begun to reshape his company, but each year he distributes English, Italian, and French editions of *State of the World* to his senior staff and to European political and business leaders.[28]

These two firms are models of future corporations, the companies that will make up the eco-economy. Both CEOs support a restructuring of the tax system, one that reduces income taxes and increases taxes on environmentally destructive activities, including the carbon emissions that are disrupting the earth's climate. These two firms, in different industries and from different cultures, have identical goals. Each wants to build a corporation that meets human needs, provides generous profits to stockholders, and does it in a way that is environmentally neutral. Their CEOs have reached this point for the same reasons. They understand that the economy depends entirely on the earth's natural support systems. If these deteriorate, the deterioration of the economy cannot be far behind. In the end, their interest is not altruism, it is self-interest.

Both emphasize that being "green" pays. This is perhaps not surprising, since more-enlightened managers are more aware of environmental issues. Those clinging to the past, always trying to defend the status quo, are by definition not likely to be the more talented managers. As Ray Anderson has "greened" his firm since 1994, sales have surged 77 percent, profits are up 81 percent, and the stock price is up 70 percent. Amory Lovins, a longtime energy efficiency advocate who has served as a consultant to Anderson, notes that the sales representatives adopt the CEO's vision and become eco-crusaders as they pitch their carpeting with renewed fervor. Lovins observes, "This happens a lot in green companies. Freeing up the contradictions between making a living and doing it in a way that your kids can be proud of you causes an implosion of energy."[29]

NGOs and Individuals

Few areas of human activity have been so dominated by NGOs as the environmental movement. Broadly speaking, NGOs evolve to fill gaps left by government and the business sector. Literally thousands of such groups have been formed in both industrial and developing societies. Most NGOs are public interest groups as opposed to special interest groups.

Environmental groups are sometimes local, single-issue organizations with a handful of members. Others are full-spectrum groups that are global in their membership and orientation. Membership may vary from a handful of people to several million. The World Wide Fund for Nature (WWF), for example, with a worldwide membership that climbed from 570,000 in 1985 to 5.2 million in 1995, has an influence on environmental policy that exceeds that of many governments. Environmental groups play a major educational role through their press releases, magazines, newsletters, Web sites, and electronic mailing lists. When coalitions mobilize to focus on a single issue, they can become a formidable political force.[30]

Using the Internet to mobilize political support for environmental actions is a valuable new asset in the effort to build an eco-economy. Thousands of environmental NGOs have Web sites and electronic mailing lists that provide information on key issues. Concerned individuals can develop their own electronic mailing lists, distributing environmental information to hundreds, if not thousands, of friends and associates.

Research by environmental groups provides information to guide environmental activists. The Worldwatch Institute, founded in 1974 in Washington, D.C., was the first such global environmental research group, followed by the World Resources Institute (WRI) in 1982, also in Washington, and the Wuppertal Institute in Germany. Research by these and other groups underpinned much of the discussion at the Earth Summit in Rio de Janeiro in 1992.

The annual *State of the World* report launched by Worldwatch in 1984 was designed to fill the gap in the series of U.N. annual reports. For example, the World Health Organization produces *The State of the World's Health*, the U.N. Food and Agriculture Organization publishes *The State of Food and Agriculture*, and the U.N. Population Fund, *The State of the World's Population*. But until UNEP launched a comprehensive *Global Environmental Outlook* report, the United Nations had failed to produce a regular state of the environment report. As evidence of the hunger for environmental information, Worldwatch Institute's annual *State of the World* report has been translated into more than 30 languages.

The World Resources Institute is anchoring a worldwide collaborative effort on a "Millennium Ecosystem Assessment." This project, in which WRI has involved the World Bank, UNEP, and the U.N. Development Programme, is by far the most ambitious, detailed assessment of global ecosystems ever undertaken. Involving major scientific bodies and hundreds of scientists, this project is designed to provide information on the present and likely future condition of the world's ecosystems to guide future ecosystem management.[31]

At the other end of the environmental spectrum is Greenpeace, an activist organization. It shares the same goals as the research institutes, but whereas they rely on analysis and information to bring about change, Greenpeace relies primarily on political confrontation and media events that can rally public opinion. Even the threat of a boycott of a company product can induce changes in corporate policy. This was perhaps most dramatically displayed in 1996, when Shell was planning to dispose of a wornout oil rig, the Brent Spar, by simply dumping it in the North Sea. Greenpeace's attack on Shell over this plan took the form of a boycott of service stations in Germany. In the face of declining gasoline sales, Shell acquiesced and developed another means of disposal.[32]

NGOs have greatly strengthened their role at the international level as a result of advances in communication, including the fax machine, e-mail, and the cell phone. In 1998, for example, governments of 29 of the more affluent countries entered into closed-door negotiations on a multilateral agreement on investment. NGOs mounted a worldwide challenge to this secretive process and aroused so much public concern that they were able to bring it to a halt. The groups that objected to these negotiations were concerned that this agreement on investment would lead to a downward spiral in both environmental standards and wages—in the words of one analyst, "a race to the cellar."[33]

In late 1999, the World Trade Organization (WTO), which was founded in 1995 as the successor to the General Agreement on Tariffs and Trade, convened a meeting in Seattle to develop the agenda for a new round of trade talks—the Millennium Round. Although only a few years old, the WTO had gained a reputation for recognizing only bottom-line economic issues. It seemed more or less oblivious to environmental and social issues affected by trade policy decisions. In virtually every case involving conflicts between trade expansion and environmental protection, the WTO had ruled in favor of trade expansion.[34]

The WTO had set off alarm bells for those in environmental groups, in organized labor, and in developing countries, which often came out on the wrong end of trade liberalization negotiations. The Seattle meeting was attended by some 5,000 delegates and political leaders, including environment and trade ministers, from more than 150 countries. But there were also 50,000 protesters who used civil disobedience to disrupt transportation and the convening and progress of the talks. The U.S. National Guard intervened, using tear gas and arresting hundreds of protesters in a response reminiscent of anti-war demonstrations of the early 1970s. A dusk-to-dawn curfew was imposed. Fifty square blocks in downtown Seattle were set aside as a "no protest zone."[35]

In the end, the talks collapsed largely because of public criticism of the failure to consider environment and poverty adequately. WTO officials were in a state of shock and may never be the same again. Nor should they be. If they were not aware of environmental and social issues before the protests in Seattle, they are now. Most U.N. agencies, the World Bank, and national governments now recognize that NGOs are stakeholders, that they often represent societal interests even more effectively than do elected politicians, who are sometimes corrupted by the political process. NGOs have acquired experience, expertise, and skill in analyzing issues and in confronting governments that they believe are behaving irresponsibly. They are now treated less as mere critics on the sidelines and more as partners in negotiations and in developing agendas for international conferences.

From time to time, a government or group of governments sides with NGOs on an issue. In 1997, for example, Taiwan announced a plan to dispose of nuclear waste in North Korea. Unwilling or unable to dispose of it within its boundaries, the government was taking advantage of the abysmal poverty in North Korea to buy a place to dump the waste from nuclear power plants. The government of South Korea and the powerful Korean Federation of Environmental Movement combined forces in opposition to this plan. In the end, they succeeded.[36]

In 1997, a loose array of some 400 NGOs and the Canadian government launched an effort to ban the use of landmines. Although the United States was opposed to the effort, the NGOs mobilized enough public opinion to get the signatures of 122 governments on the landmine-banning treaty. By now, 117 countries have ratified the accord, which went into force on 1 March 1999. New communications technologies played a central role in mobilizing worldwide political support in support of the ban.[37]

Individuals also play an important role in the global environmental movement. Indeed, Rachel Carson, who wrote *Silent Spring*, is widely credited with being the founder of the modern environmental movement. Her book, which dealt with the use of pesticides, such as DDT, that were threatening bird populations, filled a gap because the U.S. government was not responding to this threat.

Ted Turner, founder of CNN, set the standard for individual philanthropy when in 1997 he announced his gift of $1 billion to the United Nations to support work on population stabilization, environmental protection, and the provision of health care. He created the UN Foundation to serve as a vehicle through which the resources could be transferred. Turner could have waited, leaving a bequest to set up the foundation after his death. But given the urgency of the situation, he argued that billionaires needed to respond now to the world's most pressing problems before they spin out of control, becoming unmanageable. It is quite likely that Turner's initiative affected Bill Gates of Microsoft and other newly minted billionaires. Gates himself has now set up the world's largest foundation and is allocating sums of money that dwarf the resources of many governments in an effort to improve health and stabilize population in developing countries.[38]

At the grassroots level, Wangari Maathai, who has organized women in Kenya to plant trees, serves as a model for environmentalists everywhere. She wants to reforest Kenya and restore its environmental health. Because she often challenges corrupt political leaders, she has been beaten and threatened numerous times. Similarly, Chico Mendes organized rubber tappers in the Amazon who depend on the trees for their livelihoods. They opposed the large ranchers who wanted to convert these forested regions to rangeland. Although Mendes paid the ultimate price when he was gunned down by killers hired by the ranchers, the movement he started continues.[39]

NGOs and individuals have been instrumental in bringing about many basic changes, playing a leading role in bringing the growth of nuclear power to a halt, in raising public awareness of climate change, and in putting water scarcity on the global agenda. The challenge to environmental groups now is to broaden their agendas so they can promote a shared vision of an eco-economy and can work together to make it a reality.

Crossing the Threshold

Students of social change often think in terms of thresholds of change. A threshold, a concept widely used in ecology in reference to the sustainable yield of natural systems, is a point that when crossed can bring rapid and sometimes unpredictable change in a trend. In the social world, the thresholds of sudden change are no less real, though they may be more difficult to identify and anticipate. Among the more dramatic recent threshold crossings is the one that led to the political revolution in Eastern Europe in 1989 and 1990, the year the Berlin Wall came down, as well as the one that led to the dramatic decline in cigarette smoking in the United States.

The political change in Eastern Europe came with no apparent warning. It almost seems as if one morning people woke up and realized that the great socialist experiment, with its one-party political system and centrally planned economy, was over. Even those in power realized this, which was why it was essentially a bloodless political revolution. Interestingly, no articles in political science journals during the 1980s forecast this fundamental change in governance. Although we do not understand the process well, we do know that at some point in Eastern Europe a critical mass had been reached—that a time came when so many people were convinced of the need for change that the process achieved an irresistible momentum.

A similar scenario unfolded with smoking in the United States. In the early 1960s, smoking was increasingly popular among Americans—a habit that was aggressively promoted by the cigarette manufacturers. Then in 1964 the U.S. Surgeon General released a report on the relationship between smoking and health, the first in a series that has appeared almost every year since then. These reports, and media coverage of the thousands of research projects the reports spawned, fundamentally altered the way people think not only about their own smoking but also about secondhand smoke from the cigarettes of others.

So strong was this shift in thinking that in November 1998 the tobacco industry, after arguing under oath for decades that there was no proof of a link between smoking and health, agreed to reimburse state governments for the past Medicare costs of treating smoking-related illness. This settlement with 46 state governments, plus separate agreements reached earlier with the other four states, totaled $251 billion. (See also Chapter 11.) If anyone had forecast in, say, 1995 that the tobacco industry would cave in and agree to this massive reimbursement, it would have been hard to believe. At that time the tobacco industry was still hiring "medical experts" to testify before congressional committees that there was no proof of a link between smoking and health.[40]

This revolution in attitudes has reversed the trend in cigarette smoking in the United States, dropping it from a high of 2,810 cigarettes per person in 1980 to 1,633 in 1999—a decline of 42 percent. It has also spread to other countries, leading to a worldwide decline in cigarettes smoked per person of 11 percent from the historical peak reached in 1990. The number of cigarettes smoked per person has dropped 19 percent in France since peaking in 1985, 8 percent in China since 1990, and 4 percent in Japan since 1992.[41]

Emboldened by this effort and the realization that an estimated 4 million people die prematurely each year from smoking cigarettes, the World Health Organization under the leadership of Gro Harlem Brundtland, former Prime Minister of Norway, is now putting together a worldwide campaign to eradicate cigarette smoking. The global effort to reverse the worldwide smoking trend began with a research and information dissemination initiative by a national government. The information in the countless reports on smoking and health over the decades was regularly disseminated by news organizations and used by NGOs to mobilize support for restrictions on smoking.[42]

An earlier, much more abrupt shift in thinking in the United States may be even more relevant to the economic restructuring needed today. In 1940 and 1941, there was a vigorous debate in the United States about whether the country should become involved in the war in Europe. Although most Americans were strongly opposed to U.S. entrance into the war, President Franklin Roosevelt felt that U.S. involvement was inevitable. But the majority of the American people did not want to be pulled into Europe's internal conflicts again, arguing that 160,000 young American men had died in World War I without being able to establish a lasting peace.

Then came the Japanese attack on Pearl Harbor on December 7, 1941, which crippled the U.S. Pacific fleet. The debate was over. The United States declared war and began to mobilize. Things changed rapidly. One day men were working in factories and offices. The next they were in military training camps. Women who had been working at home suddenly found themselves on assembly lines. One day Chrysler was making cars. The next it was making tanks. Consumption of gasoline, rubber, and sugar was rationed. The entire U.S. economy was restructured almost overnight in what was referred to as the "war effort." The attack on Pearl Harbor had lifted the United States past a threshold.

Now as we face the need for a wholesale restructuring of the global economy, for a Copernican-scale shift in economic thinking, we need to be lifted past a similar threshold. The ecological trends of recent years are driving a paradigm shift toward an eco-economy. For years, these trends were marginalized by policymakers as "special interest" topics, but as developments have come to impinge more and more directly on people's lives, this has begun to change.

We see these changes occurring with energy, for example. Most leaders in the energy economy now realize that shifting from a carbon-based to a hydrogen-based energy economy is almost inevitable. Attitudes toward various energy sources are changing. Coal, which fueled the early Industrial Revolution, is now seen as a villain among fuels. Natural gas is the fossil fuel of choice.

And attitudes toward nuclear power have changed. The destructive explosion at the Chernobyl nuclear reactor in the Soviet Ukraine in early April 1986 did what hundreds of studies assessing the risks of nuclear power could never have done: it made the dangers real. Fresh vegetables were declared unfit for human consumption in northern Italy. Polish authorities launched an emergency effort to administer iodine tablets to children. The livelihood of the Lapps in northern Scandinavia was threatened when reindeer became too radioactive to bring to market. In the Soviet Union itself, 100,000 people in the vicinity of the reactor were forced to abandon their homes.[43]

More fundamentally, nuclear power is no longer an economically viable energy source. Wherever markets for electricity have been opened to competition, as in the United States, no one is investing in nuclear reactors. When the costs of decommissioning nuclear power plants, which may rival those of construction, and the costs of disposing of nuclear waste are incorporated into cost calculations, it seems clear that nuclear power has no economic future.

Meanwhile, in sharp contrast, wind power is gaining rapidly in public favor. In the United States, where the modern wind energy industry was born in the early 1980s, four trends are converging to create a potentially explosive growth in wind energy use. One, the cost of generating electricity from wind is falling fast. (See Chapter 5.) Two, there is a growing realization of the worldwide abundance of wind energy. Three, as farmers and ranchers realize that they own most of the wind rights in the country, a new agricultural lobby is emerging in support of wind power, joining the environmental lobby that has been supporting it for years.

The fourth trend that is spurring the growth in wind power is the requirement by more and more state utility commissions that utilities offer their customers a "green power" option. (See Chapter 11.) This is enabling individuals, companies, and local governments to vote with their pocketbooks. And they are doing so in growing numbers. The convergence of these four trends is creating a situation where wind electric generation is likely to soon become a major U.S. energy source.

Changes are also under way in other sectors, such as the forest products industry. The United States appears to be crossing the threshold for responsible forest management as the principles of ecology replace basic economics in shaping the management of national forests. After several decades of building roads with taxpayers' money to help logging companies clearcut publicly owned forests, the Forest Service announced in early 1999 that it was imposing a moratorium on road building. For decades the goal of the forest management system, which had built some 600,000 kilometers (400,000 miles) of roads to facilitate clearcutting, had been to maximize the timber harvest in the short run.[44]

But in 1998, Forest Service chief Michael Dombeck, responding to a major shift in public opinion, introduced a new management system—one designed to maintain the integrity of the ecosystem and to be governed by ecology, by a complete cost accounting that includes both the goods and the services that forests provide. Henceforth, the 78 million hectares of national forests—more than the area planted to grain in the United States—will be managed with several goals in mind. For example, the system will recognize the need to manage the forest so as to eliminate the excessive flooding, soil erosion, silting of rivers, and destruction of fisheries associated with the now-banned practice of clearcutting. Under the new policy, the timber harvest from national forests, which reached an all-time high of 12 billion board feet per year during the 1980s, has been reduced to 3 billion board feet.[45]

The United States is not the only country to institute a radical change in forest management. In mid-August 1998, after several weeks of near-record flooding in the Yangtze river basin, Beijing acknowledged for the first time that the flooding was not merely an act of nature but was exacerbated by the deforestation of the upper reaches of the watershed. Premier Zhu Rongji, recognizing the water storage and flood control capacity of forests, personally ordered not only a halt to the tree cutting in that area, but also the conversion of some state timbering firms into tree-planting firms. (See Chapter 3.) Another key threshold was crossed.[46]

A chastened tobacco industry, oil companies investing in hydrogen, reformed forest management in the United States and China—these are just some of the signs that the world may be approaching a paradigm shift on the scale described in Chapter 1. Across a spectrum of activities, places, and institutions, attitudes toward the environment have changed markedly in just the last few years. Among giant corporations that could once be counted on to mount a monolithic opposition to serious environmental reform, a growing number of high-profile CEOs have begun to sound more like environmentalists than representatives of the bastions of global capitalism.

If the evidence of a global environmental awakening were limited to only government initiatives or a few corporate initiatives, it might be dubious. But with the evidence of growing momentum now coming on both fronts, the prospect that we are approaching the threshold of a major transformation becomes more convincing. The question is, Will it happen soon enough? Will it happen before the deterioration of natural support systems leads to economic decline?

Is There Enough Time?

Can we do what needs to be done fast enough? We know that social change often takes time. In Eastern Europe, it was fully four decades from the imposition of socialism until its demise. Thirty-four years passed between the first U.S. Surgeon General's report on smoking and health and the landmark agreement between the tobacco industry and state governments. Thirty-eight years have passed since biologist Rachel Carson published *Silent Spring*, the wakeup call that gave rise to the modern environmental movement.

Sometimes things move much faster, especially when the magnitude of the threat is understood and the nature of the response is obvious, such as the U.S. response to the attack on Pearl Harbor. Within one year, the U.S. economy had largely been restructured. In less than four years, the war was over.

Accelerating the transition to a sustainable future means overcoming the inertia of both individuals and institutions. In some ways, inertia is our worst enemy. As individuals we often resist change. When we are grouped into large organizations, we resist it even more.

At the institutional level, we are looking for massive changes in industry, especially in energy. We are looking for changes in the material economy, shifting from a throwaway mentality to a closed loop/recycle mindset. If future food needs are to be satisfied adequately, we need a worldwide effort to reforest the land, conserve soil, and raise water productivity. Stabilizing population means quite literally a revolution in human reproductive behavior, one that recognizes that a sustainable future is possible only if we average two children per couple. This is not a debatable point. It is a mathematical reality.

The big remaining challenge is on the educational front: how can we help literally billions of people in the world understand not only the need for change, but how that change can bring a life far better than they have today?

I am frequently asked if it is too late. My response is, Too late for what? Is it too late to save the Aral Sea? Yes, the Aral Sea is dead. Its fish have died; its fisheries have collapsed. Is it too late to save the glaciers in Glacier National Park in the United States? Most likely. They are already half gone and it would be virtually impossible now to reverse the rise in temperature in time to save them. Is it too late to avoid a rise in temperature from the buildup in greenhouse gases? Yes. A greenhouse gas–induced rise in temperature is apparently already under way. But is it too late to avoid runaway climate change? Perhaps not, if we quickly restructure the energy economy.

For many specifics, the answer is, Yes, it is too late. But there is a broader, more fundamental question: Is it too late to reverse the trends that will eventually lead to economic decline? Here I think the answer is no, not if we move quickly.

Perhaps the biggest single challenge we face is shifting from a carbon-based to a hydrogen-based energy economy, basically moving from fossil fuels to renewable sources of energy, such as solar, wind, and geothermal. How fast can we make this change? Can it be done before we trigger irreversible damage, such as a disastrous rise in sea level? We know from the U.S. response to the attack on

Pearl Harbor that economic restructuring can occur at an incredible pace if a society is convinced of the need for it.

We study the archeological sites of civilizations that moved onto economic paths that were environmentally destructive and could not make the needed course corrections in time. We face the same risk.

There is no middle path. Do we join together to build an economy that is sustainable? Or do we stay with our environmentally unsustainable economy until it declines? It is not a goal that can be compromised. One way or another, the choice will be made by our generation. But it will affect life on earth for all generations to come.

Notes

Chapter 1. The Economy and the Earth

1. Nicolaus Copernicus, *De Revolutionibus Orbium Coelestium, Libri VI (Six Books on the Revolutions of the Celestial Spheres)* (1543).

2. Growth in global economy from historical series compiled by Worldwatch Institute from Angus Maddison, *Monitoring the World Economy 1820–1992* (Paris: Organisation for Economic Co-operation and Development, 1995), using deflators and recent growth rates from International Monetary Fund (IMF), *World Economic Outlook* (Washington, DC: October 2000).

3. Grain prices from IMF, *International Financial Statistics* (Washington, DC: various years); share of global population fed by grain produced by overpumping aquifers calculated using grain consumption from U.S. Department of Agriculture (USDA), *Production, Supply, and Distribution*, electronic database, Washington, DC, updated May 2001, and annual water deficit of 160 billion cubic meters in Sandra Postel, *Pillar of Sand* (New York: W.W. Norton & Company, 1999), p. 255.

4. Thomas Kuhn, *The Structure of Scientific Revolutions* (Chicago: University of Chicago Press, November 1996).

5. The International Society for Ecological Economics, <www.ecologicaleconomics.org>, viewed 31 July 2001; Redefining Progress, "2,500 Economists Agree That Combating Global Warming Need Not Necessarily Harm the U.S. Economy Nor Living Standards," press release (Oakland, CA: 29 March 2001).

6. Economic expansion from Worldwatch Institute, op. cit. note 2; Dow Jones Index available from <www.djindexes.com/jsp/index.jsp>.

7. Loss of topsoil calculated from Mohan K. Wali et al., "Assessing Terrestrial Ecosystem Sustainability," *Nature & Resources*, October-December 1999, pp. 21–33, and from World Resources Institute (WRI), *World Resources 2000–01* (Washington, DC: September 2000); grassland deterioration from Robin P. White et al., *Pilot Analysis of Global Ecosystems: Grassland Eco-*

systems (Washington, DC: WRI, 2000), p. 3; shrinking of forests from U.N. Food and Agriculture Organization (FAO), *Forest Resources Assessment (FRA) 2000*, <www.fao.org/forestry/fo/fra/index.jsp>, updated 10 April 2001; overfishing from FAO, *The State of World Fisheries and Aquaculture 2000* (Rome: 2000), p. 10; overpumping from Postel, op. cit. note 3, p. 6.

8. USDA, Farm Service Agency Online, "History of the CRP," *The Conservation Reserve Program*, <www.fsa.usda.gov/dafp/cepd/12logocv.htm>, viewed 5 July 2001.

9. Loss of productive land in Nigeria from Samuel Ajetunmobi, "Alarm Over Rate of Desertification," *This Day* (Lagos, Nigeria), 23 January 2001; Kazakhstan from FAO, *The State of Food and Agriculture 1995* (Rome: 1995), pp. 174–95; grain production from USDA, op. cit. note 3, and from Sharon S. Sheffield and Christian J. Foster, *Agricultural Statistics of the Former USSR Republics and the Baltic States* (Washington, DC: Economic Research Service, USDA, September 1993), p. 147; grain prices from IMF, op. cit. note 3.

10. Livestock herd size from FAO, *FAOSTAT Statistics Database*, <apps.fao.org>, updated 2 May 2001; cost of lost livestock production from H. Dregne et al., "A New Assessment of the World Status of Desertification," *Desertification Control Bulletin*, no. 20, 1991, cited in Lester R. Brown and Hal Kane, *Full House* (New York: W.W. Norton & Company, 1994), p. 95; country gross domestic products from IMF, *World Economic Outlook (WEO) Database*, <www.imf.org/external/pubs/ft/weo/2000/02/data/index.htm>, September 2000.

11. Expansion of Chinese economy calculated from IMF, op. cit. note 10; plowing of China from Hong Yang and Xiubin Li, "Cultivated Land and Food Supply in China," *Land Use Policy*, vol. 17, no. 2 (2000); Hou Dongmin, Duan Chengrong, and Zhang Dandan, "Grassland Ecology and Population Growth: Striking a Balance," *China Population Today*, June 2000, pp. 27–28.

12. FAO, op. cit. note 10.

13. Dong Zhibao, Wang Xunming, and Liu Lianyou, "Wind Erosion in Arid and Semiarid China: An Overview," *Journal of Soil and Water Conservation*, vol. 55, no. 4 (2000), pp. 439–44; Erik Eckholm, "Chinese Farmers See a New Desert Erode Their Way of Life," *New York Times*, 30 July 2000.

14. Water tables in key food-producing areas from Postel, op. cit. note 3; share of China's grain harvest from the North China Plain based on Hong Yang and Alexander Zehnder, "China's Regional Water Scarcity and Implications for Grain Supply and Trade," *Environment and Planning A*, vol. 33, January 2001, pp. 79–95, and on USDA, op. cit. note 3; water tables falling in China from James Kynge, "China Approves Controversial Plan to Shift Water to Drought-Hit Beijing," *Financial Times*, 7 January 2000; water tables in China and India from International Water Management Institute, "Groundwater Depletion: The Hidden Threat to Food Security," Brief 2, <www.cgiar.org/iwmi/intro/brief2.htm>, 2001; Bonnie L. Terrell and Phillip N. Johnson, "Economic Impact of the Depletion of the Ogallala Aquifer: A Case Study of the Southern High Plains of Texas," paper presented at the

American Agricultural Economics Association annual meeting in Nashville, TN, 8–11 August 1999.

15. Jim Carrier, "The Colorado: A River Drained Dry," *National Geographic*, June 1991, pp. 4–32; loss of Aral Sea in Postel, op. cit note 3, pp. 93–95, and in Philip P. Mickin, "Desiccation of the Aral Sea: A Water Management Disaster in the Soviet Union," *Science*, 2 September 1988; Aral Sea fishery from Lester R. Brown, "The Aral Sea: Going, Going...," *World Watch*, January/February 1991, pp. 20–27; Eric Zusman, "A River Without Water: Examining the Shortages in the Yellow River Basin," *LBJ Journal of Public Affairs*, spring 1998, pp. 31–41.

16. FAO, *Forest Resources Assessment (FRA) 2000*, op. cit. note 7.

17. Cindy Shiner, "Thousands of Fires Ravage Drought-Stricken Borneo," *Washington Post*, 24 April 1998; World Wide Fund for Nature, *The Year the World Caught on Fire*, WWF International Discussion Paper (Gland: Switzerland: December 1997).

18. "Flood Impact on Economy Limited," *China Daily*, 1 September 1998; Doug Rekenthaler, "China Survives Fourth Yangtze Flood Crest as Fifth Begins its Journey," *Disaster Relief*, 11 August 1998; removal of tree cover from Carmen Revenga et al., *Watersheds of the World* (Washington, DC: WRI and Worldwatch Institute, 1998).

19. Eneas Salati and Peter B. Vose, "Amazon Basin: A System in Equilibrium," *Science*, 13 July 1984, pp. 129–38.

20. Overfishing from FAO, *The State of World Fisheries and Aquaculture 2000*, op. cit. note 7; Mark Clayton, "Hunt for Jobs Intensifies as Fishing Industry Implodes," *Christian Science Monitor*, 25 August 1993; Clyde H. Farnsworth, "Cod are Almost Gone and a Culture Could Follow," *New York Times*, 28 May 1994.

21. Chesapeake Bay from Anita Huslin, "In Bay Water Off Virginia, Seeds of Hope for Oyster," *Washington Post*, 5 June 2001; "Regional Crisis Adds to Danger of Overfishing in Gulf of Thailand," *Agence France Presse*, 22 July 1998; "Bans on Fishing Gear Widens," *Bangkok Post*, 14 February 2001.

22. Species Survival Commission, *2000 IUCN Red List of Threatened Species* (Gland, Switzerland, and Cambridge, UK: World Conservation Union–IUCN, 2000).

23. Robert James Lee Hawke, "Launch of Statement on the Environment," speech by the Prime Minister, Wentworth, NSW, 20 July 1989; John Tuxill and Chris Bright, "Losing Strands in the Web of Life," in Lester R. Brown et al., *State of the World 1998* (New York: W.W. Norton & Company, 1998), p. 53.

24. J. Hansen, "Global Temperature Anomalies in .01 C," <www.giss.nasa.gov/data/update/gistemp>, viewed 8 June 2001.

25. Munich Re, *Topics 2000: Natural Catastrophes—The Current Position* (Munich: Münchener Ruckversicherungs-Gesellschaft, December 1999), and MRNatCatSERVICE, *Significant Natural Disasters in 1999* (Munich: REF/Geo, January 2000); United Nations, *World Population Prospects: The 2000 Revision* (New York: February 2001).

26. Janet N. Abramovitz, "Averting Unnatural Disasters," in Lester R. Brown et al., *State of the World 2001* (New York: W.W. Norton & Company, 2001), pp. 123–24.

27. Ibid.; gross domestic product from IMF, op. cit. note 10.

28. Munich Re, op. cit. note 25, p. 43.

29. Andrew Dlugolecki, "Climate Change and the Financial Services Industry," speech delivered at the opening of the UNEP Financial Services Roundtable, Frankfurt, Germany, 16 November 2000.

30. Ibid.; "Climate Change Could Bankrupt Us by 2065," *Environment News Service*, 24 November 2000.

31. Lars H. Smedsrud and Tore Furevik, "Towards an Ice-Free Arctic?" *Cicerone*, 2/2000; John Noble Wilford, "Ages-Old Icecap at North Pole Is Now Liquid, Scientists Find," *New York Times*, 19 August 2000.

32. Dorthe Dahl-Jensen, "The Greenland Ice Sheet Reacts," *Science*, 21 July 2000; Bangladesh inundation estimate from World Bank, *World Development Report 1999/2000* (New York: Oxford University Press, September 1999).

33. Joseph Tainter, *The Collapse of Complex Civilizations* (Cambridge: Cambridge University Press, 1988), p. 1.

34. Ibid.

35. Postel, op. cit note 3, pp. 13–21.

36. Ibid.

37. Ibid.

38. "Maya," *Encyclopaedia Britannica*, online encyclopedia, viewed 7 August 2000.

39. Ibid.

40. Jared Diamond, "Easter's End," *Discover*, August 1995, pp. 63–69.

41. Ibid.

42. Population addition from United Nations, op. cit. note 25.

43. Ibid.; expanding economy from IMF, op. cit. note 10.

44. FAO, op. cit. note 10; population for per capita calculation from United Nations, op. cit. note 25; conversion ratio of grain to beef from Allen Baker, Feed Situation and Outlook staff, Economic Research Service, USDA, Washington, DC, discussion with author, 27 April 1992.

45. Seafood consumption from FAO, *Yearbook of Fishery Statistics: Capture Production* (Rome: various years); population from United Nations, op. cit. note 25.

46. Joseph Kahn, "China's Next Great Leap: The Family Car," *Wall Street Journal*, 24 June 1994; oil production and consumption levels from BP, *BP Statistical Review of World Energy 2001* (London: Group Media Publications, June 2001), p. 7; for more information on the calculations of paved area, see Lester R. Brown, "Paving the Planet: Cars and Rice Competing for Crop Land," *Earth Policy Alert 12* (Washington, DC: Earth Policy Institute, 14 February 2001); rice harvest from USDA, op. cit. note 3.

47. Calculated from FAO, op. cit. note 10, forest data updated 7 February 2001, and from United Nations, op. cit. note 25.

48. World oil availability from James J. MacKenzie, "Oil as a Finite Resource: When is Global Production Likely to Peak?" WRI, <www.wri.org/climate/jm_oil_000.html>, updated 20 March 2000; Richard A. Kerr, "USGS Optimistic on World Oil Prospects, *Science*, 14 July 2000, p. 237.

49. United Nations, op. cit. note 25.

50. Ding Guangwei and Li Shishun, "Analysis of Impetuses to Change of Agricultural Land Resources in China," *Bulletin of the Chinese Academy of Sciences*, vol. 13, no. 1 (1999).

51. Bill Joy, "Why the Future Doesn't Need Us," *Wired*, April 2000.

52. United Nations, op. cit. note 25; IMF, op. cit. note 10.

53. USDA, op. cit. note 3.

54. IMF, op. cit. note 10.

55. Ibid.

56. Joint United Nations Programme on HIV/AIDS, *Report on the Global HIV/AIDS Epidemic* (Geneva: June 2000), p. 6; The U.K. Creutzfeldt-Jakob Disease Surveillance Unit, "CJD Statistics," <www.cjd.ed.ac.uk>, updated 7 July 2001; CJD Support Network, "Variant CJD," Information Sheet 4, Alzheimer's Society, April 2001.

57. H.G. Wells, *The Outline of History* (London: The Macmillan Company, 1921).

58. Population from United Nations, op. cit. note 25.

59. Herman E. Daly, "From Empty-World Economics to Full-World Economics: A Historical Turning Point in Economic Development," in Kilaparti Ramakrishna and George M. Woodwell, eds., *The Future of World Forests: Their Use and Conservation* (New Haven, CT: Yale University Press, 1993), p. 79.

60. Discussion with author at Worldwatch Briefing, Aspen, CO, 22 July 2001.

Chapter 2. Signs of Stress: Climate and Water

1. John Noble Wilford, "Ages-Old Icecap at North Pole Is Now Liquid, Scientists Find," *New York Times*, 19 August 2000.

2. J. Hansen, "Global Temperature Anomalies in .01 C," <www.giss.nasa.gov/data/update/gistemp>, viewed 8 June 2001.

3. Sandra Postel, *Last Oasis*, rev. ed. (New York: W.W. Norton & Company, 1997).

4. Population estimate for 2050 is medium-variant estimate from United Nations, *World Population Prospects: The 2000 Revision* (New York: February 2001); share of food from irrigated cropland from World Resources Institute (WRI), *World Resources 2000–2001* (Washington, DC: 2001), p. 64.

5. Fossil fuel-related carbon emissions figure from Seth Dunn, "Carbon Emis-

sions Continue Decline," in Worldwatch Institute, *Vital Signs 2001* (New York: W.W. Norton & Company, 2001), p. 53; WRI estimates emissions of 1.6 billion tons carbon per year from land use change, most of which is related to deforestation, in WRI, op. cit. note 4, p. 101.

6. Figure 2–1 from Dunn, op. cit. note 5.

7. Carbon and fossil fuels information from Energy Information Administration, *Annual Energy Outlook 2001, with Projections to 2020* (Washington, DC: U.S. Department of Energy, 2000), p. 48; Michael Renner, "Vehicle Production Sets New Record," in Worldwatch Institute, op. cit. note 5, p. 68.

8. Changing forest cover from U.N. Food and Agriculture Organization (FAO), *Forest Resources Assessment (FRA) 2000*, <www.fao.org/forestry/fo/fra/index.jsp>, updated 10 April 2001, but see note in Chapter 8 on variations among estimates; forests store 20 to 100 times more carbon than cleared land, according to Mohan Wali et al., "Assessing Terrestrial Ecosystem Sustainability: Usefulness of Regional Carbon and Nitrogen Models," *Nature & Resources*, October-December 1999, p. 27.

9. Figure 2–2 from Dunn, op. cit. note 5, pp. 52–53.

10. Hansen, op. cit. note 2; Seth Dunn, "Global Temperature Steady," in Worldwatch Institute, op. cit. note 5, pp. 50–51.

11. Intergovernmental Panel on Climate Change (IPCC), "Climate Change 2001: Impacts, Adaptation, and Vulnerability (Summary for Policy Makers)" (draft Feb 2001), <www.ipcc.ch/pub/wg2SPMfinal.pdf>; Figure 2–3 based on Hansen, op. cit. note 2.

12. Cindy Schreuder and Sharman Stein, "Heat's Toll Worse Than Believed, Study Says at Least 200 More Died," *Chicago Tribune*, 21 September 1995; corn harvest data from U.S. Department of Agriculture (USDA), *Production, Supply, and Distribution*, electronic database, Washington, DC, updated May 2001.

13. John Noble Wilford, "Move Over, Iceman! New Star From the Andes," *New York Times*, 25 October 1995; James Brooke, "Remains of Ancient Man Discovered in Melting Canadian Glacier," *New York Times*, 25 August 1999.

14. Lisa Mastny, "Melting of Earth's Ice Cover Reaches New High," *Worldwatch News Brief* (Washington, DC: 6 March 2000); Wilford, op. cit. note 1; 50-year projection in Lars H. Smedsrud and Tore Furevik, "Towards an Ice-Free Arctic?" *Cicerone*, no. 2, 2000.

15. W. Krabill et al., "Greenland Ice Sheet: High Elevation Balance and Peripheral Thinning," *Science*, 21 July 2000, p. 428; usable flow of the Nile River is 74 billion cubic meters, according to Sandra Postel, *Pillar of Sand* (New York: W.W. Norton & Company, 1999), pp. 71, 146.

16. "Melting of Antarctic Ice Shelves Accelerates," *Environmental News Network*, 9 April 1999.

17. Ibid.

18. Mastny, op. cit. note 14.

19. Ibid.

20. Lonnie G. Thompson, "Disappearing Glaciers Evidence of a Rapidly Changing Earth," American Association for the Advancement of Science annual meeting proceedings, San Francisco, CA February 2001; response by Zakia Meghji in "Newswire," *New Scientist*, 26 May 2001.

21. Christopher B. Field et al., *Confronting Climate Change in California: Ecological Impacts on the Golden State* (Cambridge, MA: Union of Concerned Scientists, 1999), pp. 2–3, 10.

22. Robert Marquand, "Glaciers in the Himalayas Melting at Rapid Rate," *Christian Science Monitor*, 5 November 1999.

23. Stuart R. Gaffin, *High Water Blues: Impacts of Sea Level Rise on Selected Coasts and Islands* (Washington, DC: Environmental Defense Fund, 1997), p. 6.

24. Ibid.; IPCC, "Summary for Policy Makers: A Report of Working Group I of the Intergovernmental Panel on Climate Change" (February 2001), viewed at <www.ipcc.ch/pub/spm22-01.pdf>, pp. 2, 10.

25. Saltwater intrusion information from James E. Neumann et al., "Increases in Global Temperature Could Accelerate Historical Rate of Sea-Level Rise" (Washington, DC: Pew Center on Global Climate Change, 29 February 2000).

26. Boesch cited in Bette Hileman, "Consequences of Climate Change," *Chemical & Engineering News*, 27 March 2000, pp. 18–19.

27. Figure 2–4 from World Bank, *World Development Report 1999/2000* (New York: Oxford University Press, 2000), p. 100; $3.2 billion figure estimated from USDA, op. cit. note 12, and from U.N. Food and Agriculture Organization, *Rice Market Monitor*, March 2001, p. 13.

28. James E. Neumann et al., *Sea-level Rise & Global Climate Change: A Review of Impacts to U.S. Coasts* (Arlington, VA: Pew Center on Global Climate Change, 2000), p. 30; Japan from Center for Global Environmental Research, *Data Book on Sea-Level Rise* (Tokyo: Environment Agency of Japan, 1996), pp. 67–68.

29. Neumann et al., op. cit. note 28, p. 31.

30. "China Says Huge Dam Project is Going Smoothly," *New York Times*, 26 October 2000.

31. Mastny, op. cit. note 14; Dorthe Dahl-Jensen, "The Greenland Ice Sheet Reacts," *Science*, 21 July 2000, p. 404–05.

32. A correlation is made between increased sea surface temperatures and increased storm activity in Steven J. Lambert, "Intense Extratropical Northern Hemisphere Winter Cyclone Events: 1899–1991," *Journal of Geophysical Research*, 27 September 1996, pp. 21, 319–21, 325.

33. Munich Re, *Topics 2000: Natural Catastrophes—The Current Position* (Munich: Münchener Ruckversicherungs-Gesellschaft, December 1999), p. 43, and MRNatCatSERVICE, *Significant Natural Disasters in 1999* (Munich: REF/Geo, January 2000).

34. Ed Rappaport, "Preliminary Report: Hurricane Andrew 16–28 August, 1992" (Miami, FL: National Oceanic and Atmospheric Administration, National

Hurricane Center, 10 December 1993); damage report estimates range from $25 billion in ibid. to $33 billion in William K. Stevens, "Storm Warning: Bigger Hurricanes and More of Them," *New York Times*, 3 June 1997.

35. Hurricane Georges in Munich Re, "Munich Re's Review of Natural Catastrophes in 1998," press release (Munich: 29 December 1998); December 1999 storm in Munich Re, op. cit. note 33.

36. Munich Re, op. cit. note 33, p. 15.

37. Lambert, op. cit. note 32; European storm information from Munich Re, op. cit. note 33, p. 48.

38. Robert Engelman et al., *People in the Balance: Population and Natural Resources at the Turn of the Millennium* (Washington, D.C.: Population Action International, 2000), pp. 8–9.

39. Postel, op. cit. note 15, p. 71.

40. Lester R. Brown, "The Aral Sea: Going, Going...," *World Watch*, January/February 1991, pp. 20–27.

41. Ibid.

42. Ibid., p. 20.

43. Postel, op. cit. note 15, pp. 261–62.

44. Lester R. Brown and Brian Halweil, "China's Water Shortages Could Shake World Food Security," *World Watch*, July/August 1998, pp. 11–12.

45. Ibid.

46. Ibid., p. 15.

47. Ibid.

48. Postel, op. cit. note 15, pp. 141–49.

49. Egypt imported 10.5 million tons of the total 26.7 tons of grain consumed in 2000, according to USDA, op. cit. note 12; populations from United Nations, op. cit. note 4.

50. Fertility rate from Population Reference Bureau, *2001 World Population Data Sheet*, wall chart (Washington, DC: Population Reference Bureau, 2001); population projections from United Nations, op. cit. note 4; dams from Tom Gardner-Outlaw and Robert Engelman, *Sustaining Water, Easing Scarcity* (Washington, DC: Population Action International, 1997), p. 12.

51. World Bank, *World Development Indicators Database*, April 2001.

52. Harvey Morris and Gareth Smyth, "Israel Talks of 'Water War' with Lebanon," *Financial Times*, 16 March 2001; Friends of the Earth–Middle East, *Let the Dead Sea Live* (Amman, Jordan: 2000), p. 11.

53. Postel, op. cit. note 15, pp. 155–57; Milton Osborne, "The Strategic Significance of the Mekong," *Contemporary Southeast Asia*, December 2000, pp. 429–44.

54. Share of China's grain harvest from the North China Plain based on Hong Yang and Alexander Zehnder, "China's Regional Water Scarcity and Implications for Grain Supply and Trade," *Environment and Planning A*, vol. 33 (2001), and on USDA, op. cit. note 12; India in Postel, op. cit. note 3, p.

170; United States from Postel, op. cit. note 15, pp. 56-57, 252.

55. Brown and Halweil, op. cit. note 44; water resource distribution in China also discussed in Fred W. Crook and Xinshen Diao, "Water Pressure in China: Growth Strains Resources," *Agricultural Outlook* (USDA, Economic Research Service), January/February 2000, pp. 25–29.

56. James Kynge, "China Approves Controversial Plan to Shift Water to Drought-Hit Beijing," *Financial Times*, 7 January 2000; World Bank, *China: Agenda for Water Sector Strategy for North China* (Washington, DC: April 2001), pp. vii, xi.

57. Hong and Zehnder, op. cit. note 54, p. 85.

58. Kynge, op. cit. note 56; Dennis Engi, *China Infrastructure Initiative*, Sandia National Laboratory, <www.cmc.sandia.gov/iGAIA/china/ciihome.html>.

59. Engi, op. cit. note 58; World Bank, op. cit. note 56.

60. Population projection from United Nations, op. cit. note 4; Albert Nyberg and Scott Rozelle, *Accelerating China's Rural Transformation* (Washington, DC: World Bank, 1999).

61. Postel, op. cit. note 15, p. 73.

62. Ibid., p. 77.

63. Bonnie Terrell and Phillip N. Johnson, "Economic Impact of the Depletion of the Ogallala Aquifer: A Case Study of the Southern High Plains of Texas," presented at the American Agricultural Economics Association annual meeting in Nashville, TN, 8–11 August 1999.

64. David Hurlbut, "The Good, the Bad, and the Arid," *Forum* (Tennessee Valley Authority and Energy Environment and Resources Center, University of Tennessee), spring 2001, p. 11.

65. Postel, op. cit. note 15, p. 255; rule of thumb from FAO, *Yield Response to Water* (Rome: 1979); USDA, op. cit. note 12.

66. USDA, op. cit. note 12.

67. Irrigation water information from WRI, op. cit. note 4, p. 64; calculation based on 1,000 tons of water for 1 ton of grain from FAO, op. cit. note 65, on global wheat prices from International Monetary Fund, *International Financial Statistics* (Washington, DC: various years), and on industrial water intensity in Mark W. Rosegrant, Claudia Ringler, and Roberta V. Gerpacio, "Water and Land Resources and Global Food Supply," paper prepared for the 23rd International Conference of Agricultural Economists on Food Security, Diversification, and Resource Management: Refocusing the Role of Agriculture?, Sacramento, CA, August 10–16, 1997.

68. Average grain consumption per person derived from USDA, op. cit. note 12, and from United Nations, op. cit. note 4.

69. WRI, op. cit. note 4, p. 274.

70. USDA, op. cit. note 12.

71. Ibid.; this shows grain imports alone into the region of over 63 million tons, equivalent to 63 billion tons (63 billion cubic meters) of water, nearly the 74 billion cubic meters of usable flow of the Nile River reported in Postel, op.

cit. note 15, p. 146.

72. Morris and Smyth, op. cit. note 52.

73. World Bank, op. cit. note 51; Chinese soy import history from USDA, Foreign Agricultural Service, *Oilseeds: World Markets and Trade*, July 2001, p. 22.

74. Liang Chao, "Officials: Water Price to Increase," *China Daily*, 21 February 2001.

75. While officially adhering to a grain self-sufficiency policy, China has redefined "self-sufficiency" as importing up to 20 percent of its grain supplies, in National Conditions and Analysis Research Group, *Agriculture and Development—A Study of China's Grain and Agricultural Development Strategy in the 21st Century*, National Conditions Report No. 5 (Beijing: Chinese Academy of Sciences, March 1997); water preference to industry in Crook and Xinshen, op. cit. note 55.

76. China's trade surplus from Geoff Hiscock, "Weighing Up the Impact of Sino-U.S. Trade Sanctions," *Cable News Network*, 16 April 2001.

Chapter 3. Signs of Stress: The Biological Base

1. "China Dust Storm Strikes USA," *NOAA News* (National Oceanic and Atmospheric Administration), 18 April 2001; Ann Schrader, "Latest Import From China: Haze," *Denver Post*, 18 April 2001.

2. Dust storms in China from National Center for Atmospheric Research (NCAR), "Scientists, Ships, Aircraft to Profile Asian Pollution and Dust." press release (Boulder, CO: 20 March 2001); U.S. Dust Bowl from William K. Stevens, "Great Plains or Great Desert? The Sea of Dunes Lies in Wait," *New York Times*, 28 May 1996.

3. Livestock data from U.N. Food and Agriculture Organization (FAO), *FAOSTAT Statistics Database*, <apps.fao.org>, updated 2 May 2001.

4. Shrinkage of forests from FAO, *Forest Resources Assessment (FRA) 2000*, <www.fao.org/forestry/fo/fra/index.jsp>, updated 10 April 2001, but see note in Chapter 8 on variations in estimates; information on forest fires from Emily Matthews et al., *Pilot Analysis of Global Ecosystems: Forest Ecosystems* (Washington, DC: World Resources Institute (WRI), 2000), pp. 24–26.

5. Loss of topsoil calculated from Mohan K. Wali et al., "Assessing Terrestrial Ecosystem Sustainability," *Nature & Resources*, October-December 1999, pp. 21–33, and from WRI, *World Resources 2000–01* (Washington, DC: 2000); yield from U.S. Department of Agriculture (USDA), *Production, Supply, and Distribution*, electronic database, Washington, DC, updated May 2001; jobs from WRI, op. cit. this note, p. 4.

6. FAO, *Yearbook of Fishery Statistics: Capture Production* (Rome: various years); United Nations, *World Population Prospects: The 2000 Revision* (New York: February 2001).

7. FAO, *The State of Food and Agriculture 1993* (Rome: 1993); Mark Clayton, "Hunt for Jobs Intensifies as Fishing Industry Implodes," *Christian Science Monitor*, 25 August 1993; Clyde H. Farnsworth, "Cod are Almost Gone and

a Culture Could Follow," *New York Times*, 28 May 1994.

8. "Salmon Fishing Banned Along Washington Coast," *Washington Post*, 10 April 1994.

9. Based on "Bluefin Tuna Reported on Brink of Extinction," *Journal of Commerce*, 10 November 1993, and on Ted Williams, "The Last Bluefin Hunt," in Valerie Harms et al., *The National Audubon Society Almanac of the Environment: The Ecology of Everyday Life* (New York: Grosset/Putnam, 1994), p. 185.

10. Lester R. Brown, "The Aral Sea: Going, Going...," *World Watch*, January/February 1991, pp. 20–27.

11. Paul Goble, "Another Dying Sea," *Radio Free Europe/Radio Liberty*, 20 June 2001.

12. Dead lakes in Canada from "Planet in Peril," *New Internationalist*, May 1987; mercury contaminated fish from Patricia Glick, *The Toll From Coal* (Washington, DC: National Wildlife Federation, April 2000), p. 10.

13. Lauretta Burke et al., *Pilot Analysis of Global Ecosystems: Coastal Ecosystems* (Washington, DC: WRI, 2000), pp. 19, 51; coastal wetland loss in Italy from Lester R. Brown and Hal Kane, *Full House* (New York: W.W. Norton & Company, 1994), p. 82.

14. Clive Wilkinson, *Status of Coral Reefs of the World: 2000* (Townsville, Australia: Global Coral Reef Monitoring Network, 2000), p. 1.

15. Brown and Kane, op. cit. note 13, pp. 83–84.

16. Organisation for Economic Cooperation and Development, *OECD Environmental Outlook* (Paris: 2001), pp. 109–20.

17. J.A. Gulland, ed., *Fish Resources of the Ocean* (Surrey: U.K.: Fishing News Ltd., 1971), an FAO-sponsored publication that estimated that oceanic fisheries would not be able to sustain an annual yield of more than 100 million tons.

18. Caroline Southey, "EU Puts New Curbs on Fishing," *Financial Times*, 16 April 1997.

19. Dan Bilefsky, "North Sea's Cod Grounds to be Closed for 12 Weeks," *Financial Times*, 25 January 2001; Paul Brown and Andrew Osborn, "Ban on North Sea Cod Fishing," *Guardian*, 25 January 2001; Alex Kirby, "UK Cod Fishing 'Could be Halted,'" *BBC News*, 6 November 2000.

20. Diadie Ba, "Senegal, EU Prepare for Fisheries Deal Tussle," *Reuters*, 28 May 2001.

21. Frederick Noronha, "Overfishing Along India's West Coast Threatens to Wipe Out Fish," *Environment News Service*, 16 October 2000.

22. FAO, op. cit. note 6; United Nations, op. cit. note 6.

23. World forested area from Matthews et al., op. cit. note 4, pp. 3, 16; world cropland from FAO, op. cit. note 3.

24. FAO, *Agriculture: Towards 2015/30, Technical Interim Report* (Geneva: Economic and Social Department, April 2000).

25. Forest Frontiers Initiative, *The Last Frontier Forests: Ecosystems and Econo-*

mies on the Edge (Washington, DC: WRI, 1997).

26. FAO, op. cit. note 3.

27. Alain Marcoux, "Population and Deforestation," in *Population and the Environment* (Rome: FAO, June 2000).

28. Nigel Sizer and Dominiek Plouvier, *Increased Investment and Trade by Transnational Logging Companies in Africa, the Caribbean, and the Pacific* (Belgium: World Wide Fund for Nature and WRI Forest Frontiers Initiative, 2000), pp. 21–35.

29. Deforestation in Brazil from Geoff Dyer, "Brazilian Forest Logging Escalates," *Financial Times*, 13 April 2000; Brazilian Embassy, Environment Section, response to William F. Laurance et al., "The Future of the Brazilian Amazon," *Science*, 19 January 2001, from discussion with author, 22 January 2001, with data from the Brazilian National Institute for Space Research (INPE), <www.grid.inpe.br>; Indonesia in Diarmid O'Sullivan, "Indonesia Faces Fires Disaster," *Financial Times*, 9 March 2000; "Indonesia Warns Planters to End Fires or Face Jail," *Reuters*, 15 March 2000.

30. Lester R. Brown, "Nature's Limits," in Lester R. Brown et al., *State of the World 1995* (New York: W.W. Norton & Company: 1995), p. 9.

31. Yangtze flooding from "Flood Impact on Economy Limited," *China Daily*, 1 September 1998; Doug Rekenthaler, "China Survives Fourth Yangtze Flood Crest as Fifth Begins its Journey," *Disaster Relief*, 11 August 1998; Mozambique flooding from "Aid Agencies Gear Up in Mozambique Flood Rescue Effort," *CNN*, 1 March 2000; loss of forest cover from Carmen Revenga et al., *Watersheds of the World* (Washington, DC: WRI and Worldwatch Institute, 1998).

32. Eneas Salati and Peter B. Vose, "Amazon Basin: A System in Equilibrium," *Science*, 13 July 1984, pp. 129–38.

33. Ibid.

34. Ibid.

35. Deforestation in Africa from WRI, op. cit. note 5, pp. 90–95; Wang Hongchang, "Deforestation and Desiccation in China: A Preliminary Study," study for the Beijing Center for Environment and Development, Chinese Academy of Social Sciences, 1999.

36. Bans on logging from "Over 11 Million Hectares of Forest Cover are Lost Throughout the World Each Year," *Environmental News Network*, March 1999; U.N. Environment Programme, *Global Environment Outlook 2000* (London: Earthscan, 1999), pp. 78–80; protected forest area estimate from FAO, op. cit. note 24.

37. Land area estimate from Stanley Wood, Kate Sebastian, and Sara J. Scherr, *Pilot Analysis of Global Ecosystems: Agroecosystems* (Washington, DC: International Food Policy Research Institute and WRI, 2000), p. 3; livestock counts from FAO, op. cit. note 3.

38. Number of pastoralists from "Investing in Pastoralism," *Agriculture Technology Notes* (Rural Development Department, World Bank), March 1998, p. 1; FAO, op. cit. note 3.

39. FAO, op. cit. note 3; United Nations, op. cit. note 6.

40. Per capita beef consumption from USDA, Foreign Agricultural Service (FAS), *Livestock and Poultry: World Markets and Trade* (Washington, DC: March 2001); mutton consumption from USDA, FAS, *Livestock and Poultry: World Markets and Trade* (Washington, DC: March 2000); population from United Nations, op. cit. note 6.

41. Global estimates from Robin P. White, Siobhan Murray, and Mark Rohweder, *Pilot Analysis of Global Ecosystems: Grassland Ecosystems* (Washington, DC: WRI, 2000), p. 3; U.S. data from U.S. Department of the Interior, Bureau of Land Management, *National Rangeland Inventory, Monitoring and Evaluation Report, Fiscal Year 2000* (Washington, DC: 2000).

42. FAO, op. cit. note 3; United Nations, op. cit. note 6.

43. Africa's 3 million buffalo are included in the estimate for cattle, found in FAO, op. cit. note 3; Southern African Development Coordination Conference, *SADCC Agriculture: Toward 2000* (Rome: FAO, 1984).

44. FAO, op. cit. note 3; United Nations, op. cit. note 6.

45. Erik Eckholm, "Chinese Farmers See a New Desert Erode Their Way of Life," *New York Times*, 30 July 2000.

46. Edward C. Wolf, "Managing Rangelands," in Lester Brown et al., *State of the World 1986* (New York, W.W. Norton & Company, 1986); Government of India, "Strategies, Structures, Policies: National Wastelands Development Board," New Delhi, mimeographed, 6 February 1986.

47. Figure 3–1 from FAO, op. cit. note 3; Worldwatch Institute, *Vital Signs 2000*, electronic database, Washington, DC, 2000; United Nations, op. cit. note 6; mutton production for 2000 is an Earth Policy Institute estimate.

48. Table 3–2 from H. Dregne et al., "A New Assessment of the World Status of Desertification," *Desertification Control Bulletin*, no. 20, 1991, cited in Brown and Kane, op. cit. note 13, p. 95.

49. Ibid.; economic information available from International Monetary Fund (IMF), *World Economic Outlook (WEO) Database*, <www.imf.org/exter nal/pubs/ft/weo/2000/02/data/index.htm>, September 2000.

50. Wali et al., op. cit. note 5; WRI, op. cit. note 5.

51. Robert Henson, Steve Horstmeyer, and Eric Pinder, "The 20th Century's Top Ten U.S. Weather and Climate Events," *Weatherwise*, November/December 1999, pp. 14–19.

52. Grain prices from IMF, *International Financial Statistics* (Washington, DC: various years); topsoil loss from USDA, Economic Research Service, *Agri-Environmental Policy at the Crossroads: Guideposts on a Changing Landscape*, Agricultural Economic Report No. 794 (Washington, DC: January 2001), p. 16.

53. Loss of topsoil from water erosion from USDA, *Summary Report: 1997 Natural Resources Inventory* (Washington, DC: December 1999, rev. December 2000), pp. 46–51; effect of topsoil loss on yields in Leon Lyles, "Possible Effects of Wind Erosion on Soil Productivity," *Journal of Soil and Water Conservation*, November/December 1975, discussed in Lester R. Brown,

"Conserving Soils," in Lester R. Brown et al., *State of the World 1984* (New York: W.W. Norton & Company, 1984), pp. 62–65.

54. USDA, op. cit. note 52.

55. Ibid.

56. FAO, *The State of Food and Agriculture 1995* (Rome: 1995), pp. 174–95; USDA, op. cit. note 5.

57. Figure 3–2 and Institute of Soil Management from FAO, op. cit. note 56; USDA, op. cit. note 5.

58. USDA, op. cit. note 5.

59. United Nations, op. cit. note 6; IMF, op. cit. note 49; USDA, op. cit. note 5.

60. Hong Yang and Xiubin Li, "Cultivated Land and Food Supply in China," *Land Use Policy*, vol. 17, no. 2 (2000).

61. "Combating Desertification," *China Daily*, 25 May 2000.

62. NCAR, op. cit. note 2; "Drought Promotes Sandstorms in North China," *People's Daily*, 10 March 2001; "Sandstorms to Increase in China," *Xinhua*, 10 April 2000; Gareth Cook, "Massive Dust Cloud to Travel Over N.E.," *Boston Globe*, 20 April 2001; Philip P. Pan, "In Inner Mongolia, Nature Lets Loose a Blizzard of Calamity," *Washington Post*, 21 January 2001; Dong Zhibao, Wang Xunming, and Liu Lianyou, "Wind Erosion in Arid and Semiarid China: An Overview," *Journal of Soil and Water Conservation*, vol. 55, no. 4 (2000).

63. Rattan Lal, "Erosion-Crop Productivity Relationships for Soils of Africa," *Soil Science Society of America Journal*, May-June 1995.

64. Ibid.; Samuel Ajetunmobi, "Alarm Over Rate of Desertification," *This Day* (Lagos, Nigeria), 23 January 2001.

65. "Algeria to Convert Large Cereal Land to Tree-Planting," *Reuters*, 8 December 2000.

66. United Nations, op. cit. note 6; Mark Turner, "You Can't Blame it All on the Weather," *Financial Times*, 14 October 2000.

67. United Nations, op. cit. note 6.

68. Michelle Leighton Schwartz and Jessica Notini, *Desertification and Migration: Mexico and the United States*, U.S. Commission on Immigration Reform Research Paper (San Francisco: fall 1994).

69. World Bank, *World Development Report 1992* (New York: Oxford University Press, 1992), p. 56; soil erosion in Ethiopia from personal observation; grain area in the former Soviet Union from USDA, op. cit. note 5.

70. M. Kassas, "Desertification: A General Review," *Journal of Arid Environments*, vol. 30 (1995), p. 118.

71. David Quammen, "Planet of Weeds," *Harper's Magazine*, October 1998.

72. Species Survival Commission, *2000 IUCN Red List of Threatened Species* (Gland, Switzerland, and Cambridge, UK: World Conservation Union–IUCN, 2000).

73. Ibid., p. 8.

74. IUCN, "Confirming the Global Extinction Crisis," press release (Gland, Switzerland: 28 September 2000).

75. Species Survival Commission, op. cit. note 72; Cat Lazaroff, "New Primates Discovered in Madagascar and Brazil," *Environment News Service*, 26 January 2001; TRAFFIC, *Food for Thought: The Utilization of Wild Meat in Eastern and Southern Africa* (Cambridge, UK: 2000).

76. Danna Harman, "Bonobos' Threat to Hungry Humans," *Christian Science Monitor*, 7 June 2001.

77. Species Survival Commission, op. cit. note 72, p. 8; Ashley T. Mattoon, "Bird Species Threatened," in Worldwatch Institute, *Vital Signs 2001* (New York: W.W. Norton & Company, 2001), pp. 98–99; "Great Indian Bustard Facing Extinction," *India Abroad Daily*, 12 February 2001; Carol Kaesuk Yoon, "Penguins in Trouble Worldwide," *New York Times*, 26 June 2001.

78. Janet N. Abramovitz, *Imperiled Waters, Impoverished Future: The Decline of Freshwater Ecosystems*, Worldwatch Paper 128 (Washington, DC: Worldwatch Institute, March 1996), p. 159.

79. Cat Lazaroff, "Caviar Export Ban Could Save Caspian Sea Sturgeon," *Environment News Service*, 13 June 2001.

80. Ashley Mattoon, "Deciphering Amphibian Declines," in Lester R. Brown et al., *State of the World 2001* (New York: W.W. Norton & Company, 2001), pp. 63–82.

81. James R. Spotila et al., "Pacific Leatherback Turtles Face Extinction," *Nature*, 1 June 2000; "Leatherback Turtles Threatened," *Washington Post*, 5 June 2000.

82. Species Survival Commission, op. cit. note 72, p. 28.

83. Ibid., p. 1.

84. Chris Bright, "The Nemesis Effect," *World Watch*, May/June 1999, pp. 12–23.

85. D.A. Rothrock, Y. Yu, and G.A. Maykut, "Thinning of Arctic Sea-Ice Cover," *Geophysical Research Letters*, 1 December 1999, pp. 3469–72; W. Krabill et al., "Greenland Ice Sheet: High-Elevation Balance and Peripheral Thinning," *Science*, 21 July 2000.

86. Burning of forests from Matthews et al., op. cit. note 4, pp. 24–26.

87. John Noble Wilford, "Ages-Old Icecap at North Pole Is Now Liquid, Scientists Find," *New York Times*, 19 August 2000; coral reefs from Lisa Mastny, "World's Coral Reefs Dying Off," in Worldwatch Institute, op. cit. note 77, pp. 92–93.

88. Chris Bright, "Anticipating Environmental 'Surprise,'" in Lester R. Brown et al., *State of the World 2000* (New York: W.W. Norton & Company, 2000), p. 37.

Chapter 4. The Shape of the Eco-Economy

1. World Commission on Environment and Development, *Our Common Future* (Oxford: Oxford University Press, 1987).

2. Gary Gardner, "Fish Harvest Down," in Lester R. Brown et al., *Vital Signs 2000* (New York: W.W. Norton & Company, 2000), p. 41; paper demand in Janet N. Abramovitz and Ashley T. Mattoon, *Paper Cuts: Recovering the Paper Landscape*, Worldwatch Paper 149 (Washington, DC: Worldwatch Institute, December 1999), p. 10; animals in U.N. Food and Agriculture Organization (FAO), *FAOSTAT Statistics Database*, <apps.fao.org>, updated 2 May 2001.

3. U.S. Forest Service and effects of logging in David Malin Roodman, *Paying the Piper: Subsidies, Politics, and the Environment*, Worldwatch Paper 133 (Washington, DC: Worldwatch Institute, December 1996), p. 19; Janet N. Abramovitz, "Averting Unnatural Disasters," in Lester R. Brown et al., *State of the World 2001* (New York: W.W. Norton & Company, 2001), p. 128; logging's relation to northwest Pacific fisheries in T.W. Chamberlin, R.D. Harr, and F.H. Everest, "Timber Harvesting, Silviculture, and Watershed Processes," in W.R. Meehan, ed., *Influences of Forest and Rangeland Management on Salmonoid Fishes and Their Habitats* (Bethesda, MD: American Fisheries Society, 1991).

4. Hong Yang and Alexander Zehnder, "China's Regional Water Scarcity and Implications for Grain Supply and Trade," *Environment and Planning A*, vol. 33 (2001), p. 85.

5. Lester R. Brown, "World Economy Expands," in Worldwatch Institute, *Vital Signs 2001* (New York: W.W. Norton & Company, 2001), pp. 56–57.

6. Population stabilization from Population Reference Bureau, *2001 World Population Data Sheet*, wall chart (Washington, DC: 2001).

7. Denmark population from ibid.; coal-plant ban in International Energy Agency, *Energy Policies of IEA Countries: Denmark 1998 Review* (London: October 1998); beverage containers in Brenda Platt and Neil Seldman, *Wasting and Recycling in the United States 2000* (Athens, GA: GrassRoots Recycling Network, 2000); wind energy from Christopher Flavin, Worldwatch Institute, *Vital Signs 2001* press briefing, Washington, DC, 24 May 2001; bicycles in Molly O'Meara Sheehan, *City Limits: Putting the Brakes on Sprawl*, Worldwatch Paper 156 (Washington, DC: Worldwatch Institute, June 2001), p. 11.

8. South Korea is author's personal observation while in the country, November 2000; Costa Rica from United Nations Development Programme, Sustainable Development Networking Programme, Capacity 21 Programme, *Costa Rice Country Report 1998*, <www.sdnp.undp.org/c21>, viewed 7 August 2001; Iceland from Seth Dunn, "The Hydrogen Experiment," *World Watch*, November/December 2000, pp. 14–25.

9. Mark Schrope, "A Change of Climate for Big Oil," *Nature*, 31 May 2001, pp. 516–18.

10. Rosamond L. Naylor et al., "Nature's Subsidies to Shrimp and Salmon Farming," *Science*, 30 October 1998.

11. A. Banerjee, "Dairying Systems in India," *World Animal Review*, vol. 79/2 (Rome: FAO, 1994); Gao Tengyun, "Treatment and Utilization of Crop Straw and Stover in China," *Livestock Research for Rural Development*, February

2000.

12. Coal consumption from BP, *BP Statistical Review of World Energy* (London: Group Media & Publications, June 2001), p. 33.

13. Anne Platt McGinn, "Aquaculture Growing Rapidly," in Lester R. Brown et al., *Vital Signs 1998* (New York: W.W. Norton & Company, 1998), pp. 36–37.

14. FAO, *Yearbook of Fisheries Statistics: Capture Production* and *Aquaculture Production* (Rome: various years); K.J. Rana, "FAO Fisheries Department Review of the State of World Aquaculture: China," <www.fao.org/fi/publ/circular/c886.1/china3.asp>; beef production from FAO, op. cit. note 2.

15. Michael Renner, "Vehicle Production Sets New Record," and Gary Gardner, "Bicycle Production Recovers," both in Worldwatch Institute, op. cit. note 5, pp. 68–71.

16. Figure of 60 percent based on consumption and production figures from Institute of Scrap Recycling Industries, Washington, DC, and on Bill Heenan of Steel Recycling Institute, Pittsburgh, PA; electric arc furnace in Gary Gardner, "Steel Recycling Rising," in Lester R. Brown et al., *Vital Signs 1995* (New York: W.W. Norton & Company, 1995), p. 128.

17. Total land area is 14.8 billion hectares, according to Charles R. Coble et al., *Earth Science* (Englewood Cliffs, NJ: Prentice-Hall, 1987), p. 102; arable land is 1.4 billion hectares according to FAO, op. cit. note 2.

18. World oil consumption and price per barrel for 2000 from U.S. Department of Energy (DOE), Energy Information Administration, <www.eia.doe.gov >.

19. Based on $1 million/megawatt installed cost of wind turbines and 40-percent capacity factor, and on 12.8 trillion kilowatt-hours world electricity consumption from DOE, op. cit. note 18.

20. FAO, op. cit. note 14.

21. FAO, *Forest Resources Assessment (FRA) 2000*, <www.fao.org/forestry/fo/fra/index.jsp>, updated 10 April 2001.

Chapter 5. Building the Solar/Hydrogen Economy

1. National Energy Policy Development Group, *National Energy Policy* (Washington, DC: U.S. Government Printing Office, May 2001).

2. Coal consumption from John Pomfret, "Research Casts Doubt on China's Pollution Claim," *Washington Post*, 15 August 2001.

3. National Energy Policy Development Group, op. cit. note 1, p. 1-10; Christopher Flavin, "Wind Energy Growth Continues," in Worldwatch Institute, *Vital Signs 2001* (New York: W.W. Norton & Company, 2001), pp. 44–45; American Wind Energy Association (AWEA), "President's Energy Plan is Useful First Step, Wind Energy Association Says," press release (Washington, DC: 17 May 2001).

4. Seth Dunn, "Fossil Fuel Use Falls Again," in Worldwatch Institute, op. cit. note 3, pp. 40–41.

5. Ibid.; Walter Youngquist, "Shale Oil: The Elusive Energy," in *Hubbert Cen-*

ter Newsletter (M. King Hubbert Center, Golden, CO), no. 4, 1998, p. 2.

6. Colin Campbell predicts that oil production will peak by 2010, in Colin J. Campbell and Jean H. Laherrere, "The End of Cheap Oil," *Scientific American*, March 1998, pp. 78–83; natural gas figures from Dunn, op. cit. note 4.

7. John Browne, Chief Executive, British Petroleum, speech delivered at Stanford University, Stanford, CA, 19 May 1997; Michael Bowlin, speech to Cambridge Energy Research Associates, 18th annual meeting, 9 February 1999.

8. Seth Dunn, "The Hydrogen Experiment," *World Watch*, November/December 2000, pp. 14–25.

9. John Noble Wilford, "Ages-Old Icecap at North Pole Is Now Liquid, Scientists Find," *New York Times*, 19 August 2000.

10. Bill Prindle, "How Energy Efficiency Can Turn 1300 New Power Plants Into 170" (Washington, DC: Alliance to Save Energy, 2 May 2001).

11. Ibid.

12. Ibid.; 30 percent return in Poornima Gupta, "US, Industry Energy Efficiency Program Saves 75 Bln KW Power," *Reuters*, 22 March 2001.

13. Peter Coy, "Electricity: Reforms That Will Save Money," *Business Week*, 11 June 2001, p. 140.

14. Janet Ginsburg, "Amory Lovins: 'Efficiency Goes Straight to the Bottom Line,' Asserts the Alternate-Energy Guru in an Interview," *Business Week*, 7 April 2001, p. 198.

15. Burton Richter, "Energy, The Key: Reduce Demand," *Los Angeles Times*, 20 May 2001.

16. "Britain Gives Tax Relief for Energy-Saving Investments," SolarAccess.com, 1 August 2001.

17. Erik Eckholm, "China Said to Sharply Reduce Carbon Dioxide Emissions," *New York Times*, 15 June 2001; Susan M. Booker, "Chinese Fridges Keep Food and the Planet Cool," *Environmental Health Perspectives*, 4 April 2000, p. A164.

18. Alliance to Save Energy, "Enlightening Comparisons," <www.ase.org/powersmart/fbulbs.htm>, viewed 1 August 2001; U.S. Department of Energy (DOE), Energy Information Administration (EIA), *Residential Lighting Use and Potential Savings* (Washington, DC: September 1996).

19. Keith Bradsher, "Fuel Economy for New Cars Is at Lowest Level Since '80," *New York Times*, 18 May 2001; likely congressional action from Senator John Kerry and others, discussion with author, Washington, DC, 17 July 2001.

20. "Honda Insight Tops EPA Fuel Economy List for 2001," *Reuters*, 3 October 2000; "Honda Has New Fuel-Cell Car, Toyota Expands Hybrids," *Reuters*, 29 September 2000.

21. In letter from Donella Meadows to Linda Harrar, independent documentary producer, Boston, MA, undated.

22. Colin Woodard, "Wind Power Pays Well for Denmark," *San Francisco Chronicle*, 23 April 2001; Peter Asmus, *Reaping the Wind* (Washington,

DC: Island Press, 2000).

23. Figure 5–1 from Flavin, op. cit. note 3; AWEA, op. cit. note 3.

24. Denmark from Christopher Flavin, Worldwatch Institute, *Vital Signs 2001* press briefing, Washington, DC, 24 May 2001; Germany from AWEA, *Wind Energy Press Background Information* (Washington, DC: February 2001), and from Christian Hinsch, "Wind Power Flying Even Higher," *New Energy*, February 2001, pp. 14–20; information on Navarra from Felix Avia Aranda and Ignacio Cruz Cruz, "Breezing Ahead: The Spanish Wind Energy Market," *Renewable Energy World*, May-June 2000; Table 5–1 from AWEA, *Global Wind Energy Market Report 2000*, <www.awea.org/faq/global2000.html>, viewed 25 June 2001.

25. Cost reduction history from Glenn Hasek, "Powering the Future," *Industry Week*, 1 May 2000; Figure 5–2 from Flavin, op. cit. note 3.

26. According to AWEA, Texas, North Dakota, and Kansas would be able to produce 3,470 billion kilowatt-hours (kWh), exceeding the 3,087 billion kWh used by the United States in 2000, as reported by DOE, EIA; AWEA, *AWEA Wind Energy Projects Database*, <www.awea.org/projects/index.html> and EIA Country Analysis Brief, DOE, <www.eia.doe.gov/emeu/cabs/usa.html>. According to Debra Lew and Jeffrey Logan, "Energizing China's Wind Power Sector," Pacific Northwest Laboratory, 2001, <www.pnl.gov/china/ChinaWnd.htm>, China has at least 250 gigawatts of exploitable wind potential, roughly equal to the current installed electrical capacity in China as reported by EIA.

27. Dominique Magada, "France Sets Ambitious Target for Renewable Power," *Reuters*, 10 December 2000; Argentina from "Under Spanish Proposal, 15 Percent of Total Would be Eolic Energy," *Agencia EFE*, 7 February 2001; "UK Makes Leap into Offshore Wind Big Time," *Renewable Energy Report* (*Financial Times*), May 2001; "China Sets Wind Power Development," *Asia Pulse*, 19 October 2000.

28. European Wind Energy Association, "Wind Energy in Europe," <www.ewea.org/src/europe.htm>.

29. AWEA, "US Installed Capacity (MW) 1981–2001," <www.awea.org/faq/instcap.html>, viewed 25 June 2001; families powered per megawatt based on Louise Guey-Lee, "Forces Behind Wind Power," in DOE, EIA, *Renewable Energy 2000: Issues and Trends* (Washington, DC: February 2001), and on Don Hopey, "Wind Turbines to be Installed Near Pennsylvania Turnpike," *Pittsburgh Post-Gazette*, 24 April 2001; "World's Largest Wind Plant to Energize the West," PacifiCorp and FPL Energy, press release (Salt Lake City, UT, and Juno Beach, FL: 10 January 2001).

30. George Darr, "Astonishing Number of Wind Proposals Blows into BPA," Bonneville Power Administration, press release (Portland, OR: 26 April 2001).

31. Jim Dehlsen, Clipper Wind, discussion with author, 30 May 2001.

32. Lester R. Brown, "U.S. Farmers Double-Cropping Corn and Wind Energy," *Earth Policy Alert* (Washington, DC: Earth Policy Institute, 7 June 2001).

33. "DaimlerChrysler Unveils Fuel Cell Vehicle," *Environmental News Network*, 18 March 1999; "Honda Has New Fuel-Cell Car," op. cit. note 20.

34. "Corn Growers' Association Launches Education Program on Wind Power," *Wind Energy Weekly* (AWEA), 25 May 2001, p. 4.

35. "BTM Predicts Continued Growth for Wind Industry," *Renewable Energy Report (Financial Times)*, May 2001, p. 8; figure of 60 percent is based on listed market shares of top wind turbine suppliers; Tom Gray, "Wind is Getting Stronger and is On Course for the Next Decade," *Renewable Energy World*, May 1999.

36. Christopher Flavin and Nicholas Lenssen, *Power Surge* (New York: W.W. Norton & Company, 1994), pp. 154–55.

37. Estimate by Paul Maycock, PV Energy Systems, discussion with Shane Ratterman, Earth Policy Institute, 15 July 2001.

38. "Power to the Poor," *The Economist*, 10 February 2001, pp. 21–23.

39. International Energy Agency, "Japan: Overview of Renewable Energy Policy," <www.iea.org/pubs/studies/files/renenp2/ren/25-ren.htm>.

40. According to North Carolina Solar Center's Database of State Incentives for Renewable Energy, 37 states now have some form of net metering; see <www.dcs.ncsu.edu/solar/dsire/dsire.cfm>; Germany and Japan from Paul Maycock and Steven J. Strong, in seminar at American Solar Energy Society Annual Conference, May 2000, Madison, WI.

41. Figure 5–3 from Paul Maycock, *PV Energy Systems,* discussion with Shane Ratterman, Earth Policy Institute, 28 May 2001.

42. Christopher Flavin, "Solar Power Market Jumps," in Lester R. Brown et al., *Vital Signs 2000* (New York: W.W. Norton & Company, 2000), p. 58.

43. Maycock, op. cit. note 41.

44. Siemens Solar, "New German Government Announces 100,000 Rooftop Photovoltaic Program," press release, <www.siemenssolar.com/german_rooftop_program.html>, viewed 25 June 2001; Million Solar Roofs program from DOE, <www.eren.doe.gov/millionroofs/>; Italian program in Molly O'Meara, "Solar Cells Continue Double-Digit Growth," in Lester R. Brown et al., *Vital Signs 1999* (New York: W.W. Norton & Company, 1999), pp. 54–55; German program in Christopher Flavin, "Solar Power Market Surges," in Worldwatch Institute, op. cit. note 3, p. 46.

45. R. Hill, N.M. Pearsall, and P. Claiden, *The Potential Generating Capacity of PV-Clad Buildings in the UK*, Vol. 1 (London: Department of Trade and Industry, 1992).

46. O'Meara, op. cit. note 44; prices for photovoltaic modules held steady at $3.50/watt for 2000–01, according to Christopher Flavin, "Solar Power Market Surges," in Worldwatch Institute, op. cit. note 3, pp. 46–47.

47. International Geothermal Association, *World Interactive Map Project*, <www.demon.co.uk/geosci/world.html>.

48. From International Geothermal Association, <www.demon.co.uk/geosci/igahome.html>.

49. Figure 5–4 based on Seth Dunn, "Geothermal Power Rises," in Lester R. Brown et al., *Vital Signs 1997* (New York: W.W. Norton & Company, 1997), pp. 50–51, with figure for 1998 from International Geothermal Association,

<www.demon.co.uk/geosci/wrtab.html>.

50. Ibid.

51. Hal Kane, "Geothermal Power Gains," in Lester R. Brown et al., *Vital Signs 1993* (New York: W.W. Norton & Company, 1993), p. 54.

52. DOE, "GeoPowering the West" Program, <www.eren.doe.gov/geopoweringthewest/geopowering.html>.

53. Figure 5–5 from Dunn, op. cit. note 4.

54. Gregg Marland, "Carbon Dioxide Emissions Rates for Conventional and Synthetic Fuels," *Energy*, vol. 8, no. 12 (1983); DOE, EIA, *Impacts of the Kyoto Protocol on US Energy Markets and Economic Activity* (Washington, DC: October 1998), p. 95.

55. EIA, "Country Analysis Brief: China" (Washington, DC: DOE, April 2001), <www.eia.doe.gov/emeu/cabs/china.html>.

56. Lester R. Brown and Christopher Flavin, "A New Economy for a New Century," in Lester R. Brown et al., *State of the World 1999* (New York: W.W. Norton & Company, 1999), p. 17.

57. Enron purchases of solar companies (Zond in the United States and Tacke in Germany) from AWEA and from Enron Wind, "Enron Forms Enron Renewable Energy Corp.," press release (Houston, TX: 6 January 1997).

58. Dunn, op. cit. note 4; Flavin, op. cit. note 3; Flavin, op. cit. note 42; Nicholas Lenssen, "Nuclear Power Inches Up," in Worldwatch Institute, op. cit. note 3, pp. 42–43; and graphs compiled by Worldwatch Institute, 2001.

59. Decline in coal use based on BP, *BP Statistical Review of World Energy* (London: Group Media & Publications, June 2001), p. 33. According to EIA, coal subsidies have been halved in China since 1984; EIA, "China: Environmental Issues" (Washington, DC: DOE, April 2001), p. 4.

60. Lenssen, op. cit. note 58.

61. Ibid.; France, China, and Japan news from Nicholas Lenssen, "Nuclear Power Rises Slightly," in Brown et al., op. cit. note 42, p. 54.

62. Price history of wind from AWEA, <www.awea.org>; Flavin, op. cit. note 3; Lenssen, op. cit. note 58.

63. Ford cited in David Bjerklie et al., "Look Who's Trying to Turn Green," *Time*, 9 November 1998.

64. Seth Dunn, *Micropower: The Next Electrical Era*, Worldwatch Paper 151 (Washington, DC: Worldwatch Institute, July 2000).

65. Payal Sampat, "Internet Use Accelerates," in Brown et al., op. cit. note 42, p. 95.

66. World wind electric generation in 1998 and 2000 from Flavin, op. cit. note 3; U.S. example based on 1999 U.S. electricity consumption of 3 trillion kilowatt-hours, from DOE, op. cit. note 26, and output from projected wind capacity of 2.2 trillion kWh, taking into account a 40-percent capacity factor.

67. Gross world product of $40 trillion from International Monetary Fund, *World Economic Outlook* (Washington, DC: October 2000); David Malin Roodman,

Paying the Piper: Subsidies, Politics, and the Environment, Worldwatch Paper 133 (Washington, DC: Worldwatch Institute, December 1996), p. 6.

68. Expansion during last decade from Flavin, op. cit. note 3.

69. Seth Dunn, *Hydrogen Futures: Toward a Sustainable Energy System*, Worldwatch Paper 157 (Washington, DC: Worldwatch Institute, August 2001), p. 75.

70. "Beyond Carbon," *The Economist*, 10 February 2001, p. 24; Organisation for Economic Co-operation and Development, *OECD Environmental Outlook* (Paris: 2001), p. 163.

Chapter 6. Designing a New Materials Economy

1. Eric Lipton, "The Long and Winding Road Now Followed by New York City's Trash," *New York Times*, 24 March 2001.

2. Paper from U.S. Environmental Protection Agency, "Municipal Solid Waste Generation, Disposal and Recycling in the United States, Facts and Figures for 1998," source data and fact sheet (Washington, DC: April 2000).

3. Lipton, op. cit. note 1.

4. U.S. Department of the Interior, U.S. Geological Survey (USGS), *Mineral Commodity Summaries 2001* (Washington, DC: 2001); stone, sand and gravel, and clays from John E. Young, *Mining the Earth*, Worldwatch Paper 109 (Washington, DC: Worldwatch Institute, July 1992); fossil fuels in oil equivalent, from BP, *BP Statistical Review of World Energy 2001* (London: Group Media & Publications, June 2001); wood figures from Emily Matthews et al., *Pilot Analysis of Global Ecosystems: Forest Ecosystems* (Washington, DC: World Resources Institute, 2000), pp. 27, 39.

5. Steel and iron ore production from USGS, op. cit. note 4; United Nations, *World Population Prospects: The 2000 Revision* (New York: February 2001).

6. John E. Young, "For the Love of Gold," *World Watch*, May/June 1993, pp. 19–26.

7. International Iron and Steel Institute (IISI), "The Major Steel Producing Countries," <www.worldsteel.org>, viewed 21 May 2001; United Nations, op. cit. note 5.

8. Hal Kane, "Steel Production Falls," in Lester R. Brown et al., *Vital Signs 1993* (New York: W.W. Norton & Company, 1993), p. 76.

9. William McDonough and Michael Braungart, "The NEXT Industrial Revolution," *The Atlantic Monthly*, October 1998, p. 88.

10. Silicon Valley Toxics Coalition, *Poison PCs and Toxic TVs* (San Jose, CA: 2001); refrigerators from 77-percent appliance recycling rate in the United States, in Jim Woods, "Steel Recycling Rates Resume Upward Trend," press release (Pittsburgh, PA: Steel Recycling Institute, 7 April 2000).

11. Silicon Valley Toxics Coalition, op. cit. note 10.

12. Table 6–2 from USGS, op. cit. note 4, with stone, sand and gravel, and clays from Young, op. cit. note 4.

13. Young, op. cit. note 4, p. 9.

14. Ibid.

15. Soviet Union, United States, and China in IISI, op. cit. note 7; Figure 6–1 compiled from IISI; metals production from USGS, op. cit. note 4.

16. Historical steel production to 1995 from Hal Kane, "Steel Production Rebounds Slightly," in Lester R. Brown et al., *Vital Signs 1996* (New York: W.W. Norton & Company, 1996), p. 79; current steel production of 833 million tons from USGS, op. cit. note 4; population from United Nations, op. cit. note 5.

17. USGS, op. cit. note 4.

18. John E. Young, "Aluminum Production Keeps Growing," in Worldwatch Institute, *Vital Signs 2001* (New York: W.W. Norton & Company, 2001), p. 64; Australia and other countries from John E. Young, "Aluminum's Real Tab," *World Watch*, March/April 1992, p. 27.

19. The Aluminum Association, Inc., "Aluminum Facts at a Glance," fact sheet (Washington, DC: June 2000).

20. Lisa Mastny, "World Air Traffic Soaring," in Lester R. Brown et al., *Vital Signs 1999* (New York: W.W. Norton & Company, 1999), pp. 86–87.

21. The Aluminum Association, Inc., "Aluminum: An American Industry in Profile" (Washington, DC: 2000), p. 2; Carole Vaporean, "Aluminum Moves to Third Place in Car Content," *Reuters*, 16 February 2001.

22. Young, "Aluminum's Real Tab," op. cit. note 18.

23. Electricity use by aluminum industry from Young, "Aluminum Production Keeps Growing," op. cit. note 18; African electricity use in 1999 from U.S. Department of Energy, Energy Information Agency, "World Total Net Electricity Consumption, 1990–1999," <www.eia.doe.gov/emeu/iea/table62.html>; Young, op. cit. note 4, p. 26.

24. Payal Sampat, "Gold Loses Its Luster," in Lester R. Brown et al., *Vital Signs 2000* (New York: W.W. Norton & Company, 2000), pp. 80–81; 85 percent of gold in jewelry from "Don't Mine Gold for Jewels," *Reuters*, 10 December 2000.

25. Sampat, op. cit. note 24; "Central-Bank Gold: Melting Away," *The Economist*, 4 April 1992.

26. Young, op. cit. note 6, pp. 22–23.

27. "Hungary Seeks Millions in Damages for Cyanide Spill," *Associated Press*, 11 July 2000; worst since Chernobyl from "International Mining Groups Call for Worldwide Mining Law Reforms," press release (Washington, DC: Friends of the Earth, Mineral Policy Center, and Mineral Policy Institute, 15 December 2000).

28. Timothy Egan, "The Death of a River Looms Over Choice for Interior Post," *New York Times*, 7 January 2001; "Cyanide-Spill Suit Is Settled in Colorado," *New York Times*, 24 December 2000.

29. Young, op. cit. note 6, p. 25; Minamata Bay update in Peter Hadfield, "Court Win Follows 40 Years of Suffering," *South China Morning Post*, 2 May 2001.

30. John E. Young, "Gold Production at Record High," in Lester R. Brown et

al., *Vital Signs 1994* (New York: W.W. Norton & Company, 1994), pp. 82–83; Patricia Glick, *The Toll From Coal* (Washington, DC: National Wildlife Federation, April 2000), p. 9.

31. Roger Moody, "The Lure of Gold: How Golden Is the Future?" Panos Media Briefing No. 9 (London: Panos Institute, 1996).

32. Anne Platt McGinn, *Why Poison Ourselves? A Precautionary Approach to Synthetic Chemicals*, Worldwatch Paper 153 (Washington, DC: Worldwatch Institute, November 2000), p. 7; 200 chemicals in the body from Pete Myers, plenary discussion on Emerging Environmental Issues, at U.S. Agency for International Development Environmental Officers Training Workshop, "Meeting the Environmental Challenges of the 21st Century," Airlie Center, Warrenton, VA, 26 July 1999.

33. Alister Doyle, "Bears Take Brunt of Toxic Chemicals as Ban Looms," *Reuters*, 22 May 2001.

34. U.S. Environmental Protection Agency (EPA), *Toxic Release Inventory 1999* (Washington, DC: 2001).

35. Ibid.

36. Mercury in the Amazon in "Mercury Poisoning Disease Hits Amazon Villages," *Reuters*, 4 February 1999; mercury emissions from U.S. coal plants in EPA, Office of Air Quality Planning and Standards and Office of Research and Development, *Mercury Study Report to Congress Volume II* (Washington, DC: December 1997), p. ES-4; mercury in rivers and lakes in Glick, op. cit. note 30; "EPA Decides Mercury Emissions from Power Plants Must Be Reduced," press release (Washington, DC: 15 December 2000); New England in Robert Braile, "Mercury Danger Rising, Group Says," *Boston Globe*, 19 September 2000; newborns in National Academy of Sciences, *Toxicological Effects of Methylmercury* (Washington, DC: National Academy Press, 2000).

37. "EPA Issues New Toxics Report, Improves Means of Reporting," press release (Washington, DC: 11 April 2001); TRI available on Internet at <www.epa.gov/tri>.

38. McGinn, op. cit. note 32, pp. 6–12.

39. European forest damage in U.N. Economic Commission for Europe and European Commission, *Forest Condition in Europe 2000* (Hamburg, Germany: 2000); Norilsk from Koko Warner, *An Emissions Tax in Siberia: Economic Theory, Firm Response and Noncompliance in Imperfect Markets* (Laxenburg, Austria: International Institute for Applied Systems Analysis, 7 July 1997), pp. 1, 32, 37.

40. Sharon LaFraniere, "Mother Russia's Poisoned Land," *Washington Post*, 22 June 1999.

41. Payal Sampat, "Groundwater Shock," *World Watch*, January/February 2000, pp. 10–22.

42. Ibid.

43. "Japan Emits Most Dioxin Among 15 Nations: Study," *Japan Times*, 22 June 1999.

44. "Governments Agree to Ban or Limit 'Dirty Dozen' POPs," *Bridges Weekly Trade News Digest* (International Centre for Trade and Sustainable Development, Geneva), 12 December 2000; Persson quoted in "Toxic Chemicals Outlawed," *Cable News Network*, 22 May 2001.

45. Denmark and Finland in Brenda Platt and Neil Seldman, *Wasting and Recycling in the United States 2000* (Athens, GA: GrassRoots Recycling Network, 2000).

46. Steel production from USGS, op. cit. note 4; automobile recycling rate from Woods, op. cit. note 10.

47. Woods, op. cit. note 10.

48. Figure 6–2 from Bill Heenan, Steel Recycling Institute, Pittsburgh, PA, e-mail to Earth Policy Institute, spring 2001; 33 percent from Gary Gardner, "Steel Recycling Rising," in Lester R. Brown et al., *Vital Signs 1995* (New York: W.W. Norton & Company, 1995), pp. 128–29; Italy and Spain from Hal Kane, "Steel Recycling Rising Slowly," in Lester R. Brown et al., *Vital Signs 1992* (New York: W.W. Norton & Company, 1992), p. 98.

49. Minimills in Kane, op. cit. note 16, pp. 78–79; "Government, Steel Maker Reach $98 Million Environmental Settlement," *Cable News Network*, 20 December 2000.

50. Can recycling in the United States from The Aluminum Association, Inc., "Aluminum Can Reclamation," fact sheet (Washington, DC: 2000); Fumiko Fujisaki, "Japan Aluminum Can Recycling Ratio up to 78.5 pct," *Reuters*, 14 July 2000; "Brazil's Poor Hunt Aluminum Cans as Swap for Food," *Reuters*, 17 October 2000.

51. "Brazil's Poor Hunt Aluminum Cans," op. cit. note 50.

52. The Aluminum Association, op. cit. note 19.

53. Brenda Platt and David Morris, *The Economic Benefits of Recycling* (Washington, DC: Institute for Local Self-Reliance, January 1993).

54. Tim Burt, "VW is Set for $500m Recycling Provision," *Financial Times*, 12 February 2001; Mark Magnier, "Disassembly Lines Hum in Japan's New Industry," *Los Angeles Times*, 13 May 2001.

55. Platt and Seldman, op. cit. note 45.

56. Based on John E. Young, "Refillable Bottles: Return of a Good Thing," *World Watch*, March/April 1991, p. 35.

57. Dupont will cut all material waste and emission of toxic substances to the environment, according to its "Safety, Health, and Environmental Commitment," as reported 15 April 1998 by University of California at Berkeley "People Product Strategy" program, at <best.me.berkeley.edu/~pps/pps/dupont_dfe.html>.

58. NEC Corporation, *Annual Environmental Report 2000: Ecology and Technology* (Tokyo: July 2000), pp. 24–27.

59. John E. Young, "The Sudden New Strength of Recycling," *World Watch*, July/August 1995, p. 24.

60. John Young, "The New Materialism: A Matter of Policy," *World Watch*, September/October 1994, p. 37.

61. Molly O. Sheehan, "Telephone Network Diversifies," in Brown et al., op. cit. note 24, p. 93; 1999 data from International Telecommunication Union, *World Telecommunication Indicators 2000/2001* (Geneva, Switzerland: March 2001), pp. 11, 35.

62. "China is No. 1 in Asian Cell Phone Market," *International Herald Tribune*, 17 August 2000.

63. Friedrich Schmidt-Bleek et al., *Factor 10: Making Sustainability Accountable, Putting Resource Productivity into Praxis* (Carnoules, France: Factor 10 Club, 1998), p. 5.

64. Share of gold to jewelry and Lempke from "Don't Mine Gold...," op. cit. note 24.

65. Young, op. cit. note 4.

66. Catherine Ferrier, *Bottled Water: Understanding a Social Phenomenon* (Surrey, U.K.: World Wide Fund for Nature, April 2001).

67. Ibid.

68. Ibid.

69. Young, "Aluminum's Real Tab," op. cit. note 18, pp. 26–33.

70. Weizsäcker quoted in Young, op. cit. note 60, p. 34.

Chapter 7. Feeding Everyone Well

1. U.S. Department of Agriculture (USDA), *Production, Supply, and Distribution*, electronic database, Washington, DC, updated May 2001.

2. Medium population projection from United Nations, *World Population Prospects: The 2000 Revision* (New York: February 2001).

3. Grain production from USDA, op. cit. note 1.

4. Figure of 1.1 billion hungry is a Worldwatch Institute estimate from United Nations Administrative Committee on Coordination, Sub-Committee on Nutrition (UN ACC/SCN) in collaboration with International Food Policy Research Institute (IFPRI), *Fourth Report on the World Nutrition Situation* (Geneva: January 2000), and from Rafael Flores, Research Fellow, IFPRI, Washington, DC, e-mail to Brian Halweil, Worldwatch Institute, 5 November 1999, and discussion with Gary Gardner, Worldwatch Institute, 3 February 2000, found in Gary Gardner and Brian Halweil, *Underfed and Overfed: The Global Epidemic of Malnutrition,* Worldwatch Paper 150 (Washington, DC: Worldwatch Institute, March 2000); U.N. Food and Agriculture Organization (FAO), *The State of Food Insecurity in the World* (Rome: 1999), p. 6.

5. UN ACC/SCN, op. cit. note 4; 1.3 billion in poverty from World Bank, *Rural Development: From Vision to Action*, Environmentally and Socially Sustainable Development Studies and Monographs Series No. 12 (Washington, DC: 1997), p. 1.

6. World Bank, op. cit. note 5, p. 1.

7. United Nations, op. cit. note 2.

8. R.K. Pachauri and P.V. Sridharan, eds., *Looking Back to Think Ahead (abridged version)*, GREEN India 2047 Project (New Delhi: Tata Energy Research Institute, 1998), p. 7.

9. Michael Morris, Nuimuddin Chowdhury, and Craig Meisner, *Wheat Production in Bangladesh: Technological, Economic, and Policy Issues* (Washington, DC: IFPRI, 1997), p. 10.

10. Population data from United Nations, op. cit. note 2; grain harvested area from USDA, op. cit. note 1.

11. Population data from United Nations, op. cit. note 2; Sandra Postel, *Pillar of Sand* (New York: W.W. Norton & Company, 1999), pp. 73–74.

12. Table 7–1 from USDA, op. cit. note 1; population data from United Nations, op. cit. note 2; economic information available from International Monetary Fund (IMF), *World Economic Outlook (WEO) Database*, <www.imf.org/external/pubs/ft/weo/2000/02/data/index.htm>, September 2000.

13. USDA, op. cit. note 1.

14. FAO, *1948–1985 World Crop and Livestock Statistics* (Rome: 1987); FAO, *FAOSTAT Statistics Database*, <apps.fao.org>, updated 2 May 2001.

15. Conversion ratio for grain to beef based on Allen Baker, Feed Situation and Outlook staff, Economic Research Service (ERS), USDA, Washington, DC, discussion with author, 27 April 1992.

16. Fish catch data for 1989 to 1998 from FAO, *Yearbook of Fishery Statistics: Capture Production* (Rome: various years); grain equivalent of farmed fish from USDA, ERS, "China's Aquatic Products Economy: Production, Marketing, Consumption, and Foreign Trade," *International Agriculture and Trade Reports: China* (Washington, DC: July 1998), p. 45.

17. Percent photosynthate to seed from L.T. Evans, *Crop Evolution, Adaptation and Yield* (Cambridge: Cambridge University Press, 1993), pp. 242–44; theoretical upper limit from Thomas R. Sinclair, "Options for Sustaining and Increasing the Limiting Yield-Plateaus of Grain Crops," paper prepared for the 1998 Symposium on World Food Security, Kyoto, Japan (Washington, DC: USDA Agricultural Research Service, September 1998), p. 14.

18. Fertilizer usage numbers based on series from FAO, *Fertilizer Yearbook* (Rome: various years), and on Kim Gay Soh and Michel Prud'homme, *Fertilizer Consumption Report: World and Regional Overview and Country Reports* (Paris: International Fertilizer Industry Association (IFA), December 2000).

19. Tom Horton and Heather Dewar, "Feeding the World, Poisoning the Planet," *Baltimore Sun*, 24 September 2000.

20. European Union from M. Prud'homme and K.G. Soh, *Short Term Prospects for World Agriculture and Fertilizer Use* (Paris: IFA, November 2000), p. 9; International Institute for Sustainable Development, "Iowa's 1987 Groundwater Protection Act," <iisd1.iisd.ca/greenbud/iowa.htm>, viewed 1 August 2001.

21. Sandra Postel, "Redesigning Irrigated Agriculture," in Lester Brown et al.,

State of the World 2000 (New York: W.W. Norton & Company, 2000), p. 40.

22. USDA, op. cit. note 1.

23. Yields and Figure 7–1 from ibid.

24. Ibid.

25. "The 1896 Olympics: Ancient Greece," <www.olympicwebsite.com/ancientgames.htm>, viewed 1 August 2001; Gerald Holland, "Roger Bannister: Sportsman of the Year," *Sports Illustrated*, 3 January 1955.

26. Double-cropping information for China from W. Hunter Colby, Frederick W. Crook, and Shwu-Eng H. Webb, *Agricultural Statistics of the People's Republic of China, 1949–90* (Washington, DC: USDA, ERS National Agricultural Statistics Service (ERS-NASS), December 1992), p. 48; Praduman Kumar et al., "Sustainability of Rice-Wheat Based Cropping Systems in India: Socio-Economic and Policy Issues," *Economic and Political Weekly*, 26 September 1998, p. A-152–58; Argentina information from USDA, ERS, "Commodity Spotlight," *Agricultural Outlook*, September 2000, p. 6.

27. Conservation Technology Information Center (CTIC), "Conservation Tillage Survey Data: Crop Residue Management 1998," CTIC Core 4 Conservation Web site, <www.ctic.purdue.edu/Core4/CT/CT.html>, updated 19 May 2000.

28. Figure 7–2 is an Earth Policy Institute estimate based on FAO, *FAOSTAT*, op. cit. note 14, and on USDA, *Agricultural Resources and Environmental Indicators* (Washington, DC: 1996–97).

29. Gershon Feder and Andrew Keck, *Increasing Competition for Land and Water Resources: A Global Perspective* (Washington, DC: World Bank, March 1995), pp. 28–29.

30. Estimates of water prices and priorities based on ratio of 1,000 tons of water for 1 ton of grain from FAO, *Yield Response to Water* (Rome: 1979), on global wheat prices from IMF, *International Financial Statistics* (Washington, DC: various years), and on industrial water intensity in Mark W. Rosegrant, Claudia Ringler, and Roberta V. Gerpacio, "Water and Land Resources and Global Food Supply," paper prepared for the 23rd International Conference of Agricultural Economists on Food Security, Diversification, and Resource Management: Refocusing the Role of Agriculture?, Sacramento, CA, 10–16 August 1997.

31. Postel, op. cit. note 11, pp. 56–57, 252.

32. Sandra Postel, *Last Oasis*, rev. ed. (New York: W.W. Norton & Company, 1997), p. 170.

33. Figure of 70 percent calculated from I.A. Shiklomanov, "World Fresh Water Resources," in Peter H. Gleick, ed., *Water in Crisis: A Guide to the World's Fresh Water Resources* (New York: Oxford University Press, 1993).

34. Postel, op. cit. note 11.

35. Postel, op. cit. note 32, p. 102.

36. Sandra Postel et al., "Drip Irrigation for Small Farmers: A New Initiative to Alleviate Hunger and Poverty," *Water International*, March 2001, pp. 3–

13.

37. Ibid.

38. Water efficiency of wheat and rice production from Postel, op. cit. note 32, p. 71.

39. Figure 7–3 from FAO, *FAOSTAT*, op. cit. note 14.

40. Conversion ratio for grain to beef based on Baker, op. cit. note 15; pork conversion data from Leland Southard, Livestock and Poultry Situation and Outlook Staff, ERS, USDA, Washington, DC, discussion with author, 27 April 1992; feed-to-poultry conversion ratio derived from data in Robert V. Bishop et al., *The World Poultry Market—Government Intervention and Multilateral Policy Reform* (Washington, DC: USDA, 1990); conversion ratio for fish from USDA, op. cit. note 16.

41. FAO, *Yearbook of Fishery Statistics: Capture Production* and *Aquaculture Production* (Rome: various years); FAO, *FAOSTAT*, op. cit. note 14.

42. Oceanic fish catch growth rate from FAO, op. cit. note 16; for aquacultural output data, see FAO, *Yearbook of Fishery Statistics: Aquaculture Production 1998*, vol. 86/2 (Rome: 2000).

43. FAO, op. cit. note 42.

44. K.J. Rana, "China," in *Review of the State of World Aquaculture*, FAO Fisheries Circular No. 886 (Rome: 1997), <www.fao.org/fi/publ/circular/c886.1/c886-1.asp>; information on rice and fish polyculture from Li Kangmin, "Rice Aquaculture Systems in China: A Case of Rice-Fish Farming from Protein Crops to Cash Crops," *Proceedings of the Internet Conference on Integrated Biosystems 1998* <www.ias.unu.edu/proceedings/icibs/li/paper.htm>, viewed 5 July 2000.

45. Information on China's carp polyculture from Rosamond L. Naylor et al., "Effect of Aquaculture on World Fish Supplies," *Nature*, 29 June 2000, p. 1022; polyculture in India from W.C. Nandeesha et al., "Breeding of Carp with Oviprim," in Indian Branch, Asian Fisheries Society, India, Special Publication No. 4 (Mangalore, India: 1990), p. 1.

46. Krishen Rana, "Changing Scenarios in Aquaculture Development in China," *FAO Aquaculture Newsletter*, August 1999, p. 18.

47. Catfish feed requirements from Naylor et al., op. cit. note 45, p. 1019; U.S. catfish production data from USDA, ERS-NASS, *Catfish Production* (Washington, DC: July 2000), p. 3.

48. FAO, op. cit. note 42.

49. For information on the role of ruminants in agriculture, see Council for Agricultural Science and Technology, "Animal Production Systems and Resource Use," *Animal Agriculture and Global Food Supply* (Ames, IA: July 1999), pp. 25–54, and H.A. Fitzhugh et al., *The Role of Ruminants in Support of Man* (Morrilton, AR: Winrock International Livestock Research and Training Center, April 1978), p. 5.

50. Roughage conversion from A. Banerjee, "Dairying Systems in India," *World Animal Review*, vol. 79/2 (Rome: FAO, 1994), and from S.C. Dhall and Meena Dhall, "Dairy Industry—India's Strength Is in Its Livestock," *Busi-*

ness Line, Internet Edition of *Financial Daily* from *The Hindu* group of publications, <www.indiaserver.com/businessline/1997/11/07/stories/ 03070311.htm>, 7 November 1997; Figure 7–4 from FAO, *Food Outlook,* no. 5, November 2000; FAO, *FAOSTAT,* op. cit. note 14.

51. Calculation based on data from FAO, op. cit. note 50.

52. Banerjee, op. cit. note 50.

53. China's crop residue production and use from Gao Tengyun, "Treatment and Utilization of Crop Straw and Stover in China," *Livestock Research for Rural Development,* February 2000.

54. Ibid.; China's "Beef Belt" from USDA, ERS, "China's Beef Economy: Production, Marketing, Consumption, and Foreign Trade," *International Agriculture and Trade Reports: China* (Washington, DC: July 1998), p. 28.

55. United Nations, op. cit. note 2.

56. USDA, op. cit. note 1.

57. Roger Classen et al., "Success of Agri-Environmental Protection," in *Agri-Environmental Policy at the Crossroads: Guideposts on a Changing Landscape,* Agricultural Economic Report No. 794 (Washington, DC: ERS, USDA, January 2001), p. 3.

58. World Bank, op. cit. note 5, p. 1.

59. Farm size in India from Pachauri and Sridharan, op. cit. note 8; information on China's economy from U.S. State Department, Bureau of Economic Policy and Trade Practices, *1999 Country Reports on Economic Policy and Trade Practices: People's Republic of China* (Washington, DC: March 2000).

60. Consumption levels from USDA, op. cit. note 1.

61. Inundation in Asia from World Bank, *World Development Report 1999/ 2000* (New York: Oxford University Press, 1999), p. 100; upper estimate of sea level rise from Tom M.L. Wigley, *The Science of Climate Change: Global and U.S. Perspectives* (Arlington, VA: Pew Center on Global Climate Change, June 1999).

62. USDA, *Grain: World Markets and Trade* (Washington, DC: September 2000), p. 19.

63. Ibid.

64. Grain production and consumption data from USDA, op. cit. note 1.

65. India's expenditures estimated from Christopher Hellman, *Military Budget Fact Sheet,* Center for Defense Information, <www.cdi.org/issues/wme/ spendersFY01.html>, and from World Bank, *World Development Indicators 2000* (Washington, DC: March 2000).

Chapter 8. Protecting Forest Products and Services

1. "Flood Impact on Economy Limited," *China Daily,* 1 September 1998; Doug Rekenthaler, "China Survives Fourth Yangtze Flood Crest as Fifth Begins its Journey," *Disaster Relief,* 11 August 1998; economic losses and deaths from Munich Re, "Munich Re's Review of Natural Catastrophes in 1998," press release (Munich: 19 December 1998); removal of tree cover from Carmen

Revenga et al., *Watersheds of the World* (Washington, DC: World Resources Institute (WRI) and Worldwatch Institute, 1998).

2. "Forestry Cuts Down on Logging," *China Daily*, 26 May 1998; Erik Eckholm, "Chinese Leaders Vow to Mend Ecological Ways," *New York Times*, 30 August 1998; Erik Eckholm, "China Admits Ecological Sins Played Role in Flood Disaster," *New York Times*, 26 August 1998; Erik Eckholm, "Stunned by Floods, China Hastens Logging Curbs," *New York Times*, 27 February 1998.

3. WRI, *World Resources 2000–01* (Washington, DC: 2000), p. 93.

4. Emily Matthews et al., *Pilot Analysis of Global Ecosystems: Forest Ecosystems* (Washington, DC: WRI, 2000), p. 16.

5. U.N. Food and Agriculture Organization (FAO), *Forest Resources Assessment (FRA) 2000*, <www.fao.org/forestry/fo/fra/index.jsp>, updated 10 April 2001; developing versus industrial nations from ibid., p. 3.

6. FAO, *Agriculture: Towards 2015/30, Technical Interim Report* (Geneva: Economic and Social Department, April 2000), pp. 156–57.

7. FAO, op. cit. note 5; Emily Matthews, *Understanding the FRA 2000*, Forest Briefing No. 1 (Washington, DC: WRI, March 2001); University of Maryland, NASA Goddard Space Flight Center, "UM Research Points the Way to Better Monitoring of National and Global Deforestation," press release (College Park, MD: 30 May 2001).

8. FAO, op. cit. note 6, p. 159; Emin Zeki Baskent and Haci Achmet Yolasigmaz, "Forest Management Revisited," *Environmental Management*, vol. 24, no. 4 (1999), pp. 437–48.

9. Wood harvest and proportion used as fuel from FAO, *FAOSTAT Statistics Database*, <apps.fao.org>, forest data updated 7 February 2001, but regional studies, as noted in Matthews et al., op. cit. note 4, p. 41, have indicated that nonforest collection is likely to supply two thirds of fuelwood; number of fuelwood consumers from WRI, op. cit. note 3.

10. Energy usage from Matthews et al., op. cit. note 4, p. 39, and from FAO, op. cit. note 6, p. 165; data on forest products from FAO, op. cit. note 9.

11. FAO, op. cit. note 6; United Nations, *World Population Prospects: The 2000 Revision* (New York: February 2001).

12. Janet N. Abramovitz and Ashley T. Mattoon, *Paper Cuts: Recovering the Paper Landscape*, Worldwatch Paper 149 (Washington, DC: Worldwatch Institute, December 1999), p. 12.

13. FAO, op. cit. note 6, pp. 166–67.

14. Table 8–2 from Robert Costanza et al., "The Value of the World's Ecosystem Services and Natural Capital," *Nature*, 15 May 1997, pp. 253–59; value of corn per hectare calculated assuming corn prices of $2.25 per bushel and yields of 345 bushels per hectare.

15. Floods in China from Rekenthaler, op. cit. note 1; Thailand from "Score One for the Trees," *The Economist*, 14 January 1989; Mozambique from "Aid Agencies Gear Up in Mozambique Flood Rescue Effort," *CNN*, 1 March 2000.

16. Walter V. Reid, "Ecosystem Data to Guide Hard Choices," *Issues in Science and Technology*, spring 2000, pp. 37–44.

17. Panos Institute, *Economics Forever: Building Sustainability into Economic Policy*, Panos Briefing No. 38 (London: March 2000); population from United Nations, *World Urbanization Prospects: The 1999 Revision* (New York: 2000).

18. Wang Hongchang, "Deforestation and Desiccation in China: A Preliminary Study," study for the Beijing Center for Environment and Development, Chinese Academy of Social Sciences, 1999; FAO, *The State of Food and Agriculture 1995* (Rome: 1995), pp. 174–95.

19. "Algeria to Convert Large Cereal Land to Tree-Planting," *Reuters*, 8 December 2000; Samuel Ajetunmobi, "Alarm Over Rate of Desertification," *This Day* (Lagos, Nigeria), 23 January 2001.

20. Michael T. Coe and Jonathan A. Foley, "Human Impacts on the Water Resources of Lake Chad," *Journal of Geophysical Research-Atmospheres*, 27 February 2001, pp. 3349–56.

21. WRI, op. cit. note 3, pp. 99–100.

22. T.W. Chamberlin, R.D. Harr, and F.H. Everest, "Timber Harvesting, Silviculture, and Watershed Processes," in W.R. Meehan, ed., *Influences of Forest and Rangeland Management on Salmonoid Fishes and Their Habitats* (Bethesda, MD: American Fisheries Society, 1991).

23. Hal Kane, "Hydroelectric Power Growth Steady," in Lester R. Brown et al., *Vital Signs 1993* (New York: W.W. Norton & Company, 1993), pp. 58–59.

24. Table 8–3 from FAO, op. cit. note 6. The total forested area of 3.2 billion hectares differs from the figure of 3.9 billion hectares cited throughout the chapter because it is from an older FAO assessment that uses a more narrow definition of forest cover.

25. Ibid.

26. Johanna Son, "Philippines: Row Rages Over Lifting of Ban on Lumber Exports," *InterPress Service*, 17 April 1998.

27. World Bank, *Forests and Forestry Sector*, <www.worldbank.org>, viewed 26 July 2001.

28. World Wide Fund for Nature, *The Forest Industry in the 21st Century* (Surrey, UK: 2001); Forest Stewardship Council, *Forests Certified by FSC-Accredited Bodies*, <www.fscoax.org>, updated 30 June 2001.

29. Steven Schwartzman and Molly Kingston, *Global Deforestation, Timber, and the Struggle for Sustainability: Making the Label Stick* (Washington, DC: Environmental Defense, 1997), p. 51; FAO, "Brazil," in FAO Advisory Committee on Paper and Wood Products, *The State of the Industry*, Forty-first Session, Rotura, New Zealand, 2–3 May 2000.

30. Forest loss from FAO, op. cit. note 6, p. 156.

31. Janet N. Abramovitz, "Paper Recycling Remains Strong," in Lester R. Brown et al., *Vital Signs 2000* (New York: W.W. Norton & Company, 2000), pp. 132–33; John Young, "The Sudden New Strength of Recycling," *World Watch*, July/August 1995, p. 24.

32. Abramovitz, op. cit. note 31, p. 132.

33. Japan and China from Philip P. Pan, "China's Chopsticks Crusade," *Washington Post*, 6 February 2001.

34. On-line addresses: *International Herald Tribune*, <www.iht.com>; *USA Today*, <www.usatoday.com>.

35. Fuelwood as a proportion of total harvested wood from FAO, op. cit. note 9; Daniel M. Kammen, "From Energy Efficiency to Social Utility: Lessons from Cookstove Design, Dissemination, and Use," in José Goldemberg and Thomas B. Johansson, *Energy as an Instrument for Socio-Economic Development* (New York: United Nations Development Programme, 1995).

36. Plantation area from FAO, op. cit. note 5; grain area from U.S. Department of Agriculture (USDA), *Production, Supply, and Distribution*, electronic database, Washington, DC, updated May 2001.

37. FAO, op. cit. note 6, p. 167.

38. Ibid., p. 160; FAO, op. cit. note 9.

39. Table 8–5 adapted from FAO, op. cit. note 6, p. 161, updated with FAO, op. cit. note 5.

40. FAO, op. cit. note 6, p. 161.

41. Ashley T. Mattoon, "Paper Forests," *World Watch*, March/April 1998, p. 20.

42. Ibid.; corn yields from USDA, op. cit. note 36.

43. Mattoon, op. cit. note 41, p. 24.

44. Ibid., p. 23.

45. FAO, op. cit. note 5; FAO, op. cit. note 6, pp. 160–61.

46. M. Davis et al., "New England-Acadian Forests," in Taylor H. Ricketts et al., eds., *Terrestrial Ecoregions of North American: A Conservation Assessment* (Washington, DC: Island Press, 1999); David R. Foster, "Harvard Forest: Addressing Major Issues in Policy Debates and in the Understanding of Ecosystem Process and Pattern," *LTER Network News: The Newsletter of the Long-term Ecological Network*, spring/summer 1996.

47. C. Csaki, "Agricultural Reforms in Central and Eastern Europe and the Former Soviet Union: Status and Perspectives," *Agricultural Economics*, vol. 22 (2000), pp. 37–54; Igor Shvytov, *Agriculturally Induced Environmental Problems in Russia*, Discussion Paper No. 17 (Halle, Germany: Institute of Agricultural Development in Central and Eastern Europe, 1998), p. 13.

48. The Turkish Foundation for Combating Soil Erosion, <www.tema.org.tr/english>, viewed 26 July 2001.

49. "China's Great Green Wall," *BBC*, 3 March 2001; Ron Gluckman, "Beijing's Desert Storm," *Asiaweek*, October 2000.

50. "China Chokes on Desert Sands," *MSNBC*, 20 January 2001.

51. "China Unveils First 'Green' Plan," *Reuters*, 5 March 2001.

52. Hongchang, op. cit. note 18.

Chapter 9. Redesigning Cities for People

1. Urban population in 1900 cited in Mario Polèse, "Urbanization and Development, *Development Express*, no. 4, 1997; United Nations, *World Urbanization Prospects: The 1999 Revision* (New York: 2000).

2. Molly O'Meara Sheehan, *Reinventing Cities for People and the Planet*, Worldwatch Paper 147 (Washington, DC: Worldwatch Institute, June 1999), pp. 14–15; United Nations, op. cit. note 1; United Nations, *World Population Prospects: The 2000 Revision* (New York: February 2001).

3. Sheehan, op. cit. note 2, p. 7.

4. United Nations, op. cit. note 1.

5. Los Angeles from Sandra Postel, *Last Oasis*, rev. ed. (New York: W.W. Norton & Company, 1997), p. 20; Mexico City from Joel Simon, *Endangered Mexico* (San Francisco, CA: Sierra Club Books, 1997); Beijing from "State to Minimize Adverse Effects of Water Diversion," *China Daily*, 8 March 2001, and from "Water More Precious than Ever," *China Daily*, 14 March 2001.

6. U.S. Department of Agriculture (USDA), Foreign Agricultural Service, *Grain: World Markets and Trade*, and *Oilseeds: World Markets and Trade* (Washington, DC: various issues).

7. Figure of 70 percent from I.A. Shiklomanov, "World Fresh Water Resources," in Peter H. Gleick, ed., *Water in Crisis: A Guide to the World's Fresh Water Resources* (New York: Oxford University Press, 1993).

8. Donald D.T. Chen, "The Science of Smart Growth," *Scientific American*, December 2000, pp. 84–91.

9. Ibid.

10. Richard Moe, President of the National Trust for Historic Preservation, speech on sprawl, 1999 Red Hills Spring Event Dinner, Tall Timbers Research Station, Tallahassee, FL, 24 March 1999.

11. Chen, op. cit. note 8.

12. Ibid.

13. Ibid.

14. David Schrank and Tim Lomax, *The 2001 Urban Mobility Report* (Texas Transportation Institute and The Texas A&M University System, May 2001).

15. Ibid.

16. Moe, op. cit. note 10.

17. Average travel speeds from Peter Newman and Jeffrey Kenworthy, *Sustainability and Cities: Overcoming Automobile Dependence* (Washington, DC: Island Press, 1999), pp. 82–83.

18. Chen, op. cit. note 8, p. 84.

19. Moe, op. cit. note 10.

20. Table 9–3 from Arthur C. Nelson, "Regulations to Improve Development Patterns," in Lincoln Institute of Land Policy, *Metropolitan Development Patterns: Annual Roundtable 2000* (Cambridge, MA: 2000), p. 78, discussed in Molly O'Meara Sheehan, *City Limits: Putting the Breaks on Sprawl*,

Worldwatch Paper 156 (Washington, DC: Worldwatch Institute, June 2001), pp. 31–32.

21. USDA, *Production, Supply, and Distribution*, electronic database, Washington, DC, updated May 2001.

22. Barry M. Popkin, "Urbanization and the Nutrition Transition," *Achieving Urban Food and Nutrition Security in the Developing World, A 2020 Vision for Food, Agriculture, and the Environment*, Focus 3, Brief 7 (Washington, DC: International Food Policy Research Institute (IFPRI), August 2000).

23. William H. Dietz, "Battling Obesity: Notes from the Front," National Center for Chronic Disease Prevention and Health Promotion, *Chronic Disease Notes & Reports*, winter 2000, p. 2; Ali H. Mokdad et al., "The Continuing Epidemic of Obesity in the United States," *Journal of the American Medical Association*, 4 October 2000, p. 1650.

24. J.M. Friedman, "Obesity in the New Millennium," *Nature*, 6 April 2000, pp. 632–34.

25. National Center for Health Statistics, Centers for Disease Control and Prevention (CDC), "Prevalence of Overweight and Obesity Among Adults," <www.cdc.gov/nchs/products/pubs/pubd/hestats/obese/obse99.htm>, 11 December 2000; Gary Gardner and Brian Halweil, *Underfed and Overfed: The Global Epidemic of Malnutrition*, Worldwatch Paper 150 (Washington, DC: Worldwatch Institute, March 2000), p. 11; Peter G. Kopelman, "Obesity as a Medical Problem," *Nature*, 6 April 2000, p. 636; Barry M. Popkin and Colleen M. Doak, "The Obesity Epidemic is a Worldwide Phenomenon," *Nutrition Reviews*, April 1998, pp. 106–14.

26. Kopelman, op. cit. note 25; World Health Organization, *Obesity: Preventing and Managing the Global Epidemic, Report of a WHO Consultation on Obesity* (Geneva: 1997).

27. National Center for Chronic Disease Prevention and Health Promotion, "Preventing Obesity Among Children," *Chronic Disease Notes & Reports*, winter 2000, p. 1.

28. Gardner and Halweil, op. cit. note 25, p. 11; Kopelman, op. cit. note 25, p. 635.

29. Kopelman, op. cit. note 25, pp. 635–43; Ron Winslow, "Why Fitness Matters," *Wall Street Journal*, 1 May 2000.

30. Kopelman, op. cit. note 25, p. 635.

31. Deaths from smoking from CDC, *Targeting Tobacco Use: The Nations' Leading Cause of Death* (Washington, DC: 2000); cigarette consumption from USDA, Foreign Agricultural Service, *World Cigarette Electronic Database*, December 1999, and from USDA, Economic Research Service, *Tobacco: Situation and Outlook Report* (Washington, DC: April 2001).

32. Winslow, op. cit. note 29; Judy Putnam and Shirley Gerrior, "Trends in the U.S. Food Supply, 1970–97," in Elizabet Frazao, ed., *America's Eating Habits: Changes and Consequences* (Washington, DC: USDA, Economic Research Service, May 1999), p. 152.

33. Winslow, op. cit. note 29.

34. Kopelman, op. cit. note 25, p. 638.

35. Ibid.

36. Denise Grady, "Doctor's Review of Five Deaths Raises Concern About the Safety of Liposuction," *New York Times*, 13 May 1999.

37. Sheehan, op. cit. note 2, p. 45.

38. Ibid., p. 44.

39. China's bicycle production compiled from United Nations, *The Growth of World Industry: 1969 Edition*, vol. 1 (New York: 1970), *Yearbook of Industrial Statistics*, various years, and *Industrial Commodity Statistics Yearbook* (New York: various years); "World Market Report," *Interbike Directory* (Laguna Beach, CA: Miller-Freeman, various years); Edward A. Gragan, "Booming China Has Fewer Bikes on Road Ahead," *Seattle Times*, 4 October 2000.

40. Number of police forces in Matthew Hickman and Brian A. Reaves, *Local Police Departments 1999* (Washington, DC: U.S. Department of Justice, Bureau of Justice Statistics, May 2001); arrest rate from a conversation with a member of the Washington, DC, police force.

41. Glenn Collins, "Old Form of Delivery Thrives in New World of E-Commerce," *New York Times*, 24 December 1999.

42. Sheehan, op. cit. note 2, pp. 47–48.

43. Ibid.

44. Ibid.; Japan from personal observation.

45. Jonathan Theobald, "The Lanes in Spain Run Mainly on the Plain," *Environmental News Network*, 6 November 2000.

46. E.O. Wilson, *Biophilia* (Cambridge, MA: Harvard University Press, 1984); S.R. Kellert and E.O. Wilson, eds., *The Biophilia Hypothesis* (Washington, DC: Island Press, 1993).

47. Theodore Roszak, Mary Gomes, and Allen Kanner, eds., *Restoring the Earth, Healing the Mind* (San Francisco: Sierra Club Books, 1995).

48. Lyndsey Layton, "Mass Transit Popularity Surges in U.S.," *Washington Post*, 30 April 2000.

49. Ding Guangwei and Li Shishun, "Analysis of Impetuses to Change of Agricultural Land Resources in China," *Bulletin of the Chinese Academy of Sciences*, vol. 13, no. 1, 1999.

50. Sheehan, op. cit. note 2, p. 47.

51. Table 9–4 from Sheehan, op. cit. note 20, p. 11, from United Nations, op. cit. note 1, from Habitat, Global Urban Indicators Database, <www.urbanobservatory.org/indicators/database>, updated 25 February 1999, from Dita Smith, "Taming Urban Sprawl," *Washington Post*, July 2001, and from Shrank and Lomax, op. cit. note 14.

52. Number of vehicles in operation from Ward's Communications, *Ward's World Motor Vehicle Data 2000* (Southfield, MI: 2000).

53. Sheehan, op. cit. note 2, p. 49.

54. Ibid.; Donald C. Shoup, "Congress Okays Cash Out," *Access*, fall 1998, pp. 2-8.

55. Molly O'Meara Sheehan, "Making Better Transportation Choices," in Lester R. Brown et al., *State of the World 2001* (New York: W.W. Norton & Company), p. 116.

56. Mark Vernon, "Road Pricing," *Financial Times*, 6 June 2001.

57. J.H. Crawford, "Existing Carfree Places," <www.carfree.com>; see also J.H. Crawford, *Carfree Cities* (Utrecht, The Netherlands: International Books, July 2000); "Ban on Cars Along the Seine Proposed," *Chicago Tribune*, 21 May 2001.

58. Gary Gardner, "Why Share?" *World Watch*, July/August 1999, pp. 12–15.

59. Ibid.

60. Layton, op. cit. note 48; Bruce Younkin, Manager of Fleet Operations at Penn State University, State College, PA, discussion with Janet Larsen, Earth Policy Institute, 4 December 2000.

61. Sheehan, op. cit. note 2, p. 51.

62. Ibid., p. 63.

63. Ibid., p. 47.

Chapter 10. Stabilizing Population by Reducing Fertility

1. All population data in this chapter, including per capita calculations and future projections, are from the United Nations, *World Population Prospects: The 2000 Revision* (New York: February 2001) unless otherwise noted.

2. United Nations, *Long-range World Population Projections: Based on the 1998 Revision* (New York: 1999).

3. Lester R. Brown, Gary Gardner, and Brian Halweil, *Beyond Malthus* (New York: W.W. Norton & Company, 1999), pp. 112–13.

4. Figure 10–1 from U.S. Bureau of the Census, *International Data Base*, electronic database, Suitland, MD, updated 10 May 2000.

5. Joint United Nations Programme on HIV/AIDS (UNAIDS), *Report on the Global HIV/AIDS Epidemic* (Geneva: June 2000).

6. William H. McNeill, *Plagues and Peoples* (New York: Anchor Press/ Doubleday, 1976).

7. UNAIDS, op. cit. note 5.

8. Sandra Postel, *Pillar of Sand* (New York: W.W. Norton & Company, 1999), p. 5.

9. David Seckler, David Molden, and Randolph Barker, *Water Scarcity in the 21st Century*, IWMI Water Brief 1 (Colombo, Sri Lanka: International Water Management Institute (IWMI), July 1998).

10. Irrigation cutbacks from ibid., and from Randolph Barker and Barbara van Koppen, *Water Scarcity and Poverty*, IWMI Water Brief 3 (Colombo, Sri Lanka: IWMI, 1999), p. 3; estimates of child malnutrition and underweight in United Nations Administrative Committee on Coordination, Sub-Com-

mittee on Nutrition (UN ACC/SCN) in collaboration with International Food Policy Research Institute, *Fourth Report on the World Nutrition Situation* (Geneva: January 2000), pp. 94–96; annual deaths worldwide from Brown, Gardner, and Halweil, op. cit. note 3.

11. Cropland from U.S. Department of Agriculture (USDA), *Production, Supply, and Distribution*, electronic database, Washington, DC, updated May 2001.

12. UNAIDS, *AIDS Epidemic Update* (Geneva: UNAIDS/WHO, December 2000), p. 3.

13. UNAIDS, op. cit. note 5.

14. Ibid.

15. Ibid.

16. Ibid.; "AIDS, Diseases to Leave 44 Million Orphans by 2010," *Reuters*, 13 July 2000.

17. UNAIDS, op. cit. note 5, p. 29; university study from Prega Govender, "Shock AIDS Test Result at Varsity," (Johannesburg) *Sunday Times*, 25 April 1999; "South Africa: University Finds 25 Percent of Students Infected," *Kaiser Daily HIV/AIDS Report*, 27 April 1999.

18. UNAIDS, op. cit. note 5.

19. Grain production from USDA, op. cit. note 11; information on malnutrition from U.N. Food and Agriculture Organization (FAO), *The State of Food Insecurity in the World 2000* (Rome: 2000), pp. 27–28.

20. UNAIDS, op. cit. note 5, pp. 32–33.

21. Ibid.

22. John Bongaarts and Charles F. Westoff, *The Potential Role of Contraception in Reducing Abortion*, Working Paper No. 134 (New York: Population Council, 2000).

23. Nada Chaya, *Contraceptive Choice: Worldwide Access to Family Planning*, wall chart (Washington, DC: Population Action International, 1997); Macro International, *Contraceptive Knowledge, Use, and Sources: Comparative Studies Number 19* (Calverton, MD: 1996).

24. John B. Casterline, Zeba A Sathar, and Minhaj ul Haque, *Obstacles to Contraceptive Use in Pakistan: A Study in Punjab*, Working Paper No. 145 (New York: Population Council, 2001); John A. Ross, W. Parker Mauldin, and Vincent C. Miller, *Family Planning and Population: A Compendium of International Statistics* (New York: Population Council, 1993).

25. Mark Kaufman, "Abortion Pill Deliveries Begin Soon," *Washington Post*, 16 November 2000; Susan Okie, "RU-486 Joining Methotrexate in Reshaping Abortion," *Washington Post*, 13 October 2000; Craig S. Smith, "Chinese Factory to Soon Begin Exporting Recently Approved Abortion Pills to U.S.," *New York Times*, 13 October 2000; Susan Toner, "U.S. Approves Abortion Pill; Drug Offers More Privacy and Could Reshape Debate," *New York Times*, 29 September 2000.

26. G. Tyler Miller, "Copps and Rubbers Day in Thailand," in *Living in the Environment*, 8th ed. (Belmont, CA: Wadsworth Publishing Company, 1994).

27. Farzaneh Roudi, "Iran's Revolutionary Approach to Family Planning," *Population Today*, July/August 1999; Abubakar Dungus, "Iran's Other Revolution," *Populi*, September 2000; Akbar Aghajanian and Amir H. Mehryar, "Fertility Transition in the Islamic Republic of Iran: 1976–1996," *Asia-Pacific Population Journal*, vol. 14, no. 1 (1999), pp. 21–42; total fertility rate (the average number of children born to a woman) from Population Reference Bureau (PRB), *2001 World Population Data Sheet*, wall chart (Washington, DC: 2001).

28. Figure 10–2 from United Nations, op. cit. note 1; total fertility rate from PRB, op. cit. note 27.

29. George D. Moffett, *Critical Masses* (New York: Penguin Books, 1994), cited in Laurent Belsie, "How Many People Does it Take to Change the World?" *Christian Science Monitor*, 22 June 2000.

30. Gary Gardner, "Microcredit Expanding Rapidly," in Worldwatch Institute, *Vital Signs 2001* (New York: W.W. Norton & Company, 2001), pp. 110–11.

31. Bruce Caldwell and Barkat-e-Khuda, "The First Generation to Control Family Size: A Microstudy of the Causes of Fertility Decline in a Rural Area of Bangladesh," *Studies in Family Planning*, September 2000, pp. 239–51.

32. "Bangladesh: National Family Planning Program," *Family Planning Programs: Diverse Solutions for a Global Challenge* (Washington, DC: PRB, February 1994).

33. U.N. Population Fund (UNFPA), "Meeting the Goals of the ICPD: Consequences of Resource Shortfalls up to the Year 2000," paper presented to the Executive Board of the U.N. Development Programme and the UNFPA, New York, 12–23 May 1997; military expenditures calculated from U.S. Department of State, Bureau of Verification and Compliance, *World Military Expenditures and Arms Transfers 1998* (Washington, DC: U.S. Government Printing Office, April 2000), p. 61.

34. UNFPA, op. cit. note 33; UNFPA, *Population Issues Briefing Kit* (New York: Prographics, Inc., 2001), p. 23.

35. Sharon L. Camp, "Population: The Critical Decade," *Foreign Policy*, spring 1993.

36. Caroline H. Bledsoe et al., eds., *Critical Perspectives on Schooling and Fertility in the Developing World* (Washington, DC: National Academy Press, 1999).

37. Ibid., p. 3.

38. Ibid.

39. Caldwell and Barkat-e-Khuda, op. cit. note 31.

40. Lawrence Summers, "The Most Influential Investment," reprinted in *People and the Planet*, vol. 2, no. 1 (1993), p. 10.

41. Ibid.

42. Ibid.

43. Pamela Polston, "Lowering the Boom: Population Activist Bill Ryerson is Saving the World—One 'Soap' at a Time," *Seven Days*, available at <www.populationmedia.org/popnews/popnews.html>, viewed 6 December

2000.

44. Ibid.

45. Ibid.; Kathy Henderson, "Telling Stories, Saving Lives: Hope from Soaps," *Ford Foundation Report*, fall 2000.

46. Henderson, op. cit. note 45.

47. Joel E. Cohen, *How Many People Can the Earth Support?* (New York: W.W. Norton & Company, 1996).

48. Ibid.

49. PRB, op. cit. note 27.

50. Figure 10–3 from United Nations, op. cit. note 1.

Chapter 11. Tools for Restructuring the Economy

1. Parallel of ecological and economic truths from Øystein Dahle, discussion with author at Worldwatch Briefing, Aspen, CO, 22 July 2001; Erik Eckholm, "Chinese Leaders Vow to Mend Ecological Ways," *New York Times*, 30 August 1998; Erik Eckholm, "China Admits Ecological Sins Played Role in Flood Disaster," *New York Times*, 26 August 1998; Erik Eckholm, "Stunned by Floods, China Hastens Logging Curbs," *New York Times*, 27 February 1998.

2. Edwin Clark, letter to author, 25 July 2001.

3. Ernst U. von Weizsäcker and Jochen Jesinghaus, *Ecological Tax Reform* (London: Zed Books, 1992).

4. David Malin Roodman, "Environmental Tax Shifts Multiplying," in Lester R. Brown et al., *Vital Signs 2000* (New York: W.W. Norton & Company, 2000), pp. 138–39; German annual budget from U.S. Central Intelligence Agency, *World Fact Book*, <www.cia.gov/cia/publications/factbook>, viewed 1 August 2001; vehicle tax in Denmark is 180 percent, as reported by Marjorie Miller, "British Car Buyers Taken for a Ride," *Los Angeles Times*, 23 July 1999.

5. David Malin Roodman, *Getting the Signals Right: Tax Reform to Protect the Environment and the Economy*, Worldwatch Paper 134 (Washington, DC: Worldwatch Institute, May 1997), p. 11.

6. David Malin Roodman, *The Natural Wealth of Nations* (New York: W.W. Norton & Company, 1998), p. 189.

7. U.S. Department of Agriculture (USDA), Economic Research Service (ERS), "Cigarette Price Increase Follows Tobacco Pact," *Agricultural Outlook*, January-February 1999.

8. USDA, ERS, *Tobacco Situation and Outlook*, September 2000, p. 8; USDA, ERS, *Tobacco Situation and Outlook*, April 2001, p. 5.

9. Roodman, op. cit. note 6, p. 243.

10. N. Gregory Mankiw, "Gas Tax Now!" *Fortune*, 24 May 1999, pp. 60–64.

11. André de Moor and Peter Calamai, *Subsidizing Unsustainable Development* (San Jose, Costa Rica: Earth Council, 1997); authors quoted in Barbara

Crossette, "Subsidies Hurt Environment, Critics Say Before Talks," *New York Times*, 23 June 1997.

12. De Moor and Calamai, op. cit. note 11.

13. Ibid., p. 1.

14. Roodman, op. cit. note 6, p. 31.

15. David Malin Roodman, "Reforming Subsidies," in Lester R. Brown et al., *State of the World 1997* (New York: W.W. Norton & Company, 1997), p. 132; Roodman, op. cit. note 6, pp. 42, 81; David Gardner, "Farm Subsidies Under Attack 'for Causing Hunger'," *Financial Times*, 28 February 2001; "China to Reform Water Pricing System to Enhance Conservation—Vice Minister," *Xinhua*, 21 June 2001.

16. "Minister Says Iranian Bakery Must Be Revised to Improve its Nutrition Value," *Islamic Republic News Agency*, 31 May 2001; exchange rate of 1750 Iranian rials per U.S. dollar from *Financial Times*, 31 July 2001; per capita number based on United Nations, *World Population Prospects: The 2000 Revision* (New York: February 2001).

17. Anne Platt McGinn, *Rocking the Boat: Conserving Fisheries and Protecting Jobs*, Worldwatch Paper 142 (Washington, DC: Worldwatch Institute, June 1998), p. 7.

18. Seth Dunn, "King Coal's Weakening Grip on Power," *World Watch*, September/October 1999, pp. 10-19.

19. Roodman, op. cit. note 6, p. 73.

20. Subsidy cut figures in ibid., p. 109; U.S. Department of Energy, Energy Information Administration, *China: Environmental Issues* (Washington, DC: April 2001); Figure 11–1 based on BP, *BP Statistical Review of World Energy* (London: Group Media & Publications, June 2001), and on historical data from BP Amoco, e-mail to Janet Larsen, Earth Policy Institute, June 2001; 1996–2001 data based on John Pomfret, "Research Casts Doubt on China's Pollution Claim," *Washington Post*, 15 August 2001.

21. Victoria logging in "Worldwatch Proposes $2000 Tax Cut Per Family to Save the Planet," press release (Washington, DC: Worldwatch Institute, 12 September 1998); USDA, Forest Service, "Forest Service Limits New Road Construction in Most National Forests," press release (Washington, DC: 11 February 1999).

22. Study cited in David Malin Roodman, *Paying the Piper: Subsidies, Politics, and the Environment*, Worldwatch Paper 133 (Washington, DC: Worldwatch Institute, December 1996), p. 9.

23. De Moor and Calamai, op. cit. note 11, p. 39.

24. Douglas Helms, *History of the Natural Resources Conservation Service* (Washington, DC: Natural Resources Conservation Service, 31 May 2001).

25. History of wind power in California from Colin Woodard, "Wind Power Pays Well for Denmark," *San Francisco Chronicle*, 23 April 2001.

26. Ibid.

27. Christopher Flavin, "Wind Energy Growth Continues," in Worldwatch Institute, *Vital Signs 2001* (New York: W.W. Norton & Company, 2001), pp.

44–45; 60-percent projection in American Wind Energy Association, "President's Energy Plan is Useful First Step, Wind Energy Association Says," press release (Washington, DC: 17 May 2001).

28. Marine Stewardship Council, "World's First Sustainable Seafood Products Launched," press release (London: 3 March 2000).

29. "Marine Stewardship Council Awards Sustainability Label to Alaska Salmon," press release (London: 5 September 2000).

30. Ibid.

31. World Wide Fund for Nature (WWF), *The Forest Industry in the 21st Century* (Surrey, U.K.: 2001).

32. Ibid.

33. Ibid.

34. WWF, *Certification: A Future for the World's Forests* (Surrey, U.K.: WWF Forests for Life Campaign, May 2000), p. 4.

35. Ibid.; Forest Stewardship Council, *Forests Certified by FSC-Accredited Bodies*, <www.fscoax.org>, updated 30 June 2001.

36. WWF, op. cit. note 31.

37. "Russia Set to Begin Certification of Forests," and "Russia Works Out System for Mandatory Wood Certification," *Interfax*, 5 June 2001.

38. National Renewable Energy Laboratory, *Summary of Green Pricing Programs* (Golden, CO: updated 12 July 2001).

39. Global Green USA, "Santa Monica Unanimously Approves RFP Process to Switch All City Facilities to Green Power," press release (Los Angeles: 14 October 1998); Oakland from Peter Asmus, *Reaping the Wind* (Washington, DC: Island Press, 2000).

40. Green Power Network, "Toyota Motor Sales USA Becomes Firest Green-e Certified Company," press release (San Francisco: 8 May 1998); CU Environmental Center, "University of Colorado Students Vote 'Yes' for Wind Power!" press release (Boulder, CO: 17 April 2000); Center for Resource Solutions, "Episcopal Church Puts Faith into Environmental Action With Switch to Green Power," press release (San Francisco: 11 June 1999).

41. Consumers Union, "In Time for Earth Day, Consumers Union Launches <www.eco-labels.org>," press release (Yonkers, NY: 10 April 2001); Federal Environmental Agency (Germany), "Information Sheet for Submission of New Proposals for the 'Blue Angel' Environmental Label" (Berlin: Federal Environmental Agency, March 2001), <www.blauer-engel.de>; Canada Environmental Choice from <www.environmentalchoice.com>; U.S. Energy Star program information from <www.energystar.gov>.

42. Roodman, op. cit. note 6, pp. 15–27.

43. Australia in John Tierney, "A Tale of Two Fisheries," *New York Times Magazine*, 27 August 2000.

44. Richard Schmalensee et al., "An Interim Evaluation of Sulfur Dioxide Emissions Trading," in Robert N. Stavins, ed., *Economics of the Environment* (New York: W.W. Norton & Company, 2000), pp. 455–71; actual reduction

from ibid., p. 460.

45. "Bush Charts Global Warming Course," *Associated Press*, 6 June 2001.

46. Polls from Roodman, op. cit. note 6, p. 243.

47. De Moor and Calamai, op. cit. note 11, p. 32.

48. Ibid., p. 243; information on both Taxpayers for Common Sense (TCS) and Green Scissors at Taxpayers for Common Sense, <www.taxpayer.net>, viewed 25 July 2001; membership numbers from TCS, discussion with Shane Ratterman, Earth Policy Institute, 25 July 2001.

49. Redefining Progress, "2,500 Economists Agree That Combating Global Warming Need Not Necessarily Harm the U.S. Economy Nor Living Standards," press release (Oakland, CA: 29 March 2001).

50. Paul Krugman, "Nation in a Jam," *New York Times*, 13 May 2001.

51. Organisation for Economic Co-operation and Development, *OECD Environmental Outlook* (Paris: 2001).

52. "A Brighter Future," *The Economist*, 10 February 2001, p. 6.

Chapter 12: Accelerating the Transition

1. Robert Nef, Tiroler Wirtschaftsforum, Innsbruck, Austria, discussion with author, 6 October 1999.

2. Number of HIV-positive Africans based on Anne Hwang, "AIDS Erodes Decades of Progress," in Worldwatch Institute, *Vital Signs 2001* (New York: W.W. Norton & Company, 2001), pp. 78–79; specific countries in Population Reference Bureau (PRB), *2001 World Population Data Sheet*, wall chart (Washington, DC: 2001).

3. International Convention for the Regulation of Whales, signed 2 December 1946, Washington, DC, entered into force 10 November 1948, from Harvard University, International Environmental Policy Reference Guide, <environment.harvard.edu/esppa/home.html>, viewed 18 July 2001; Hilary French, "Environmental Treaties Gain Ground," in Lester R. Brown et al., *Vital Signs 2000* (New York: W.W. Norton & Company, 1990), p. 134.

4. Discovery of ozone hole first reported in J.C. Farman, B.G. Gardiner, and J.D., Shanklin, "Large Losses of Total Ozone in Antarctica Reveal Seasonal ClO_x/NO_x Interaction," *Nature*, 16 May 1985, pp. 207–10; Montreal Protocol signed 16 September 1987, entered into force 1 January 1989, from Harvard University, op. cit. note 3; 90 percent reduction in French, op. cit. note 3, p. 135.

5. Convention on International Trade in Endangered Species of Wild Fauna and Flora (CITES), signed 3 March 1973, Washington, DC, and entered into force 1 July 1975, from Harvard University, op. cit. note 3; Greg Frost, "Caviar Clampdown Eyed to Help Sturgeon Burgeon," *Reuters*, 20 June 2001; "World Briefing—Russia: Saving the Caspian Sturgeon," *New York Times*, 17 July 2001.

6. U.N. role in Intergovernmental Panel on Climate Change in Vanessa Houlder, "Keeping a Cool Head in the Global Warming Hothouse," *Financial Times*,

13 March 2001; Randall Mikkelsen, "US Abandons Kyoto Climate Pact—A Blow to Europe," *Reuters*, 29 March 2001.

7. U.N. Commission on Sustainable Development, "Rio + 10: Time to Get Started," *CSD Update Special Issue*, August 2000, <www.johannes burgsummit.org>; Kofi Annan, Keynote Address, Tufts University Fletcher School of Law and Diplomacy, 20 May 2001.

8. China fertility rate in PRB, op. cit. note 2; International Energy Agency, *Energy Policies of IEA Countries: Denmark 1998 Review* (London: October 1998); Israel in Sandra Postel, *Last Oasis*, rev. ed. (New York: W.W. Norton & Company, 1997), pp. 58, 118–19, 128–30, 148, 189; South Korea from author's observations, November 2000; Costa Rica in U.S. Department of State, "Background Note: Costa Rica," April 2001, <www.state.gov/www/background_notes/costa_rica_0600_bgn.html>; Germany from David Malin Roodman, "Environmental Tax Shifts Multiplying," in Brown et al., op. cit. note 3, pp. 138–39; Iceland from Seth Dunn, "The Hydrogen Experiment," *World Watch*, November/December 2000, pp. 14–25; U.S. soil erosion in *Agriculture Economic Report Number 794* (Washington, DC: U.S. Department of Agriculture (USDA), January 2001), p. 3; Netherlands in "White Bikes Return to Amsterdam," *Bicycle Retailer and Industry News*, 1 November 1999; Finland in Brenda Platt and Neil Seldman, *Wasting and Recycling in the United States 2000* (Athens, GA: GrassRoots Recycling Network, 2000).

9. Anne Platt McGinn, "Aquaculture Growing Rapidly," in Lester R. Brown et al., *Vital Signs 1998* (New York: W.W. Norton & Company, 1998), pp. 36–37.

10. Eugene Linden, "Planet of the Year: Endangered Earth," *Time*, 2 January 1989.

11. "Our Precious Planet," *Time* Special Issue, November 1997.

12. *Time*, 9 April 2001.

13. Tadahiro Mitsuhashi, *Nihon Kezai Shimbun*, Tokyo, discussion with author, 11 November 2000.

14. Farman, Gardiner, and Shanklin, op. cit. note 4.

15. William Drozdiak, "U.S. Firms Become 'Green' Advocates," *Washington Post*, 24 November 2000.

16. John Browne, Chief Executive, BP, speech delivered at Stanford University, Stanford, CA, 19 May 1997; Michael Bowlin, speech to Cambridge Energy Research Associates, 18th annual meeting, 9 February 1999.

17. Browne, op. cit. note 16; Martha M. Hamilton, "Shell Leaves Coalition That Opposes Global Warming Treaty," *Washington Post*, 22 April 1998.

18. Keith Bradsher, "Ford Announces Its Withdrawal From Global Climate Coalition," *New York Times*, 7 December 1999; David Goodman, "GM Joins DaimlerChrysler, Ford, Quits Global Warming Lobby Group," *Associated Press*, 14 March 2000; "Texaco Leaving Anti-Global Warming Treaty Group," *Reuters*, 29 February 2000; Sierra Club quoted in Lester R. Brown, "The Rise and Fall of the Global Climate Coalition," *Earth Policy Alert* (Washington, DC: Earth Policy Institute, 25 July 2000).

19. Hydrogen consortium in Dunn, op. cit. note 8; "ABB Puts Alternative Energy in the Mainstream," *Environmental Data Services (ENDS) Report 305*, June 2000, pp. 3–4.

20. "ABB Puts Alternative Energy in the Mainstream," op. cit. note 19.

21. Ibid.

22. Dupont will cut emissions by 65 percent by 2010, according to their position statement, "Global Climate Change" (Wilmington, DE: 5 June 2001).

23. Eileen P. Gunn, "The Green CEO," *Fortune*, 24 May 1999, pp. 190–200.

24. Ibid.

25. Ibid.

26. "STMicroelectronics Ranked First By Innovest Strategic Value Advisors as World's Only 'AAA' Eco-Efficient Semiconductor Company," press release (Geneva: STMicroelectronics (STM), 31 October 2000).

27. Ibid.; carbon emissions and energy mix in STM, *STMicroelectronics Corporate Environmental Report 1999* (Agrate Brianza, Italy: 1999), p. 17; Pasquale Pistorio, discussion with author, Tokyo, 9 November 2000.

28. Pistorio, op. cit. note 27.

29. Interface and Amory Lovins quoted in Gunn, op. cit. note 23.

30. WWF membership growth from Curtis Runyan, "Action on the Front Lines," *World Watch*, November/December 1999, p. 14.

31. World Resources Institute, *World Resources 2000–2001* (Washington, DC: 2001).

32. Greenpeace and Brent Spar in P.J. Simmons, "Learning to Live with NGOs," *Foreign Policy*, fall 1998, p. 90.

33. Runyan, op. cit. note 30.

34. "A WTO Primer," *Time*, 5 December 2000.

35. Richard Lacayo, "Rage Against the Machine," *Time*, 13 December 1999.

36. Choi Yul, Director General of Korean Federation of Environmental Movement, discussion with author, 3 June 1997.

37. From International Campaign to Ban Landmines, <www.icbl.org>, updated as of 17 July 2001.

38. David Rhode, "Ted Turner Plans a $1 Billion Gift for U.N. Agencies," *New York Times*, 19 September 1997; John Donnelly, "Bill Gates, Caregiver: The Microsoft Founder is Spending Billions to Provide Health Services to the World's Poor," *Boston Globe*, 24 December 2000.

39. Elissa Sonnenberg, "Environmental Hero: Wangari Maathai," *Environmental News Network*, 25 September 2000; Andrew Revkin, *The Burning Season: The Murder of Chico Mendes and the Fight for the Amazon Rain Forest* (New York: Plume, 1994).

40. USDA, Economic Research Service, "Cigarette Price Increase Follows Tobacco Pact," *Agricultural Outlook*, January-February 1999.

41. USDA, Foreign Agricultural Service, *World Cigarette Electronic Database*, December 1999; USDA, *Special Report: World Cigarette Situation*, August

1999; U.S. Bureau of the Census, *International Data Base*, electronic database, Suitland, MD, updated 10 May 2000.

42. Jacqui Thornton, "WHO Looks to Ban Tobacco Advertising Worldwide," *Associated Press*, 30 January 1999.

43. Christopher Flavin, *Reassessing Nuclear Power: The Fallout From Chernobyl*, Worldwatch Paper 75 (Washington, DC: Worldwatch Institute, March 1987).

44. USDA, Forest Service, "Forest Service Limits New Road Construction in Most National Forests," press release (Washington, DC: 11 February 1999).

45. USDA, Forest Service, "New Forest Service Chief Outlines Plan To Move Into 21st Century," press release (Washington, DC: 6 January 1997); board-feet statistics in USDA, Forest Service, *1998 Report of the Forest Service* (Washington, DC: April 1999).

46. "Forestry Cuts Down on Logging," *China Daily*, 26 May 1998.

INDEX

ABOUT THE AUTHOR

Lester R. Brown has been described as "one of the world's most influential thinkers" by the *Washington Post*. He is President of Earth Policy Institute, a nonprofit, interdisciplinary research organization based in Washington, D.C., which he founded in May 2001. The purpose of the Earth Policy Institute is to provide a vision of an environmentally sustainable economy, an eco-economy, along with a roadmap of how to get from here to there and an ongoing assessment of where we are moving ahead and where we are not.

Twenty-five years ago, he helped pioneer the concept of environmentally sustainable development, a concept he uses in his design of an eco-economy. He is widely known as the Founder and former President of the Worldwatch Institute, whose Board he now chairs. He launched the influential *State of the World* report, which is now published in over 30 languages.

During a career that started with tomato farming, Brown has been awarded some 22 honorary degrees and has authored or coauthored 47 books, 19 monographs, and countless articles. He is also a MacArthur Fellow and the recipient of many prizes and awards, including the 1987 United Nations Environment Prize, the 1989 World Wide Fund for Nature Gold Medal, and the 1994 Blue Planet Prize for his "exceptional contributions to solving global environmental problems." In 1995, Marquis *Who's Who*, on the occasion of its fiftieth edition, selected Lester Brown as one of 50 Great Americans. He lives in Washington, D.C.